The Architecture of Paul Rudolph

The Architecture of Paul Rudolph

Timothy M. Rohan

Yale University Press

New Haven and London

Publication of this book is supported by grants from the Architectural History Foundation and the University of Massachusetts, Amherst.

yalebooks.com/art

Discussions in this book appeared in earlier forms in these articles by Timothy M. Rohan:

"Challenging the Curtain Wall: Paul Rudolph's Blue Cross and Blue Shield Building," *Journal of the Society of Architectural Historians* 66 (March 2007): 84–109.

"The Dangers of Eclecticism: Paul Rudolph's Jewett Arts Center," in *Anxious Modernisms: Experimentation in Postwar Architectural Culture,* edited by Sarah Williams Goldhagen and Réjean Legault (Montreal: Canadian Centre for Architecture and the MIT Press, 2000), 191–214.

"Rendering the Surface: Paul Rudolph's Art & Architecture Building at Yale," *Grey Room* 1 (Fall 2000): 84–107.

"Public and Private Spectacles: Paul Rudolph's Manhattan Penthouse, 1977–1997," *Casabella* 673/674 (December 1999): 138–49.

Designed by Thumb/Luke Bulman
Set in Atlas Grotesk
Printed in China by Regent Publishing Services Limited

Library of Congress Cataloging-in-Publication Data
Rohan, Timothy M.
    The architecture of Paul Rudolph / Timothy M. Rohan.
      pages cm
    Includes biographical references and index.
    ISBN 978-0-300-14939-5 (cloth : alk. paper) 1. Rudolph, Paul, 1918–1997—Criticism and interpretation. I. Title.
    NA737.R8R64 2014
    720.92—dc23   2013029234

A catalogue record for this book is available from the British Library.

This paper meets the requirements of ANSI/NISO Z 39.48-1992 (Permanence of Paper).

10 9 8 7 6 5 4 3 2 1

Jacket illustration: Paul Rudolph, Temple Street Parking Garage (detail of figure 3.7)

This book is dedicated with much love to my
mother and father, Mary and Martin Rohan

Contents

Acknowledgments

I wish to thank all those who helped me write this book. It was a remarkable and rewarding experience to work closely with the Library of Congress to transform Rudolph's uncatalogued papers into a well-organized archive, made accessible to all by this great public institution.

Many teachers, friends, and colleagues helped in shaping the research and ideas for this manuscript. The patience and support of Michelle Komie at Yale University Press was greatly appreciated. My thanks to Heidi Downey and Elma Sanders for preparing the manuscript and Luke Bulman for designing it. Anonymous readers provided many helpful, substantive comments that improved the scope and organization of the book. Andrea Monfried's skilled editing gave the manuscript its final form and came at a crucial moment. At Harvard, Neil Levine encouraged me to pursue Rudolph's architecture as a research topic. He shaped my thinking about Rudolph and architecture in general. Sarah Goldhagen and Yve-Alain Bois also helped develop the dissertation at Harvard. At the Library of Congress, Ford Peatross, Helena Zinkham, and Gregory Marcangelo in particular made Rudolph's archive accessible to me. Robert A. M. Stern provided many insights and enlisted me to curate an exhibition about Rudolph and organize a symposium about him at Yale in 2008 and 2009 that also shaped this book. Robert Bruegmann offered many astute suggestions over the years. Carl Fiocchi helped in understanding the construction of Rudolph's buildings. Martie Lieberman provided a key document, William Rupp's unpublished paper "Paul Rudolph: The Florida Years" (1978). Grattan Gill shared fascinating insights into working with Rudolph on the Southeastern Massachusetts Technical Institute. Joseph King provided knowledge and camaraderie while visiting Rudolph's Florida projects, as did Christopher Domin. John Damico related interesting reminiscences about working with Rudolph. Cheah Kok Ming was an invaluable guide in Singapore. David Sagita devoted days to showing me Rudolph's Indonesian projects. Brian Shelburne at the University of Massachusetts, Amherst, spent hours preparing images for publication. Dean Lee Edwards, Dean Joel Martin, Dean Julie Hayes, and William T. Oedel from the University of Massachusetts provided financial support for research and the publication. Many more people were involved than I can list here, but I thank all those I interviewed who are footnoted in the text.

Financial support for research, images, and publication was provided by:
> A Research and Development Grant and a Production and Presentation Grant from the Graham Foundation for Advanced Studies in the Fine Arts
> Foundation for Advanced Studies in the Fine Arts
> Canadian Centre for Architecture
> Whiting Foundation Fellowship
> United States Indonesia Society Travel Award
> Architectural History Foundation Publication Grant

Additional research and publication support came from the College of Humanities and Fine Arts (CHFA), University of Massachusetts, Amherst (UMass):
> CHFA UMass Associate Professor Research Renewal Pilot Program
> MSP Research Support Fund
> Art History Program of the Department of Art, Architecture and Art History
> Subvention Grant, Office of Research Affairs, UMass

Family provided the greatest support of all. My thanks for the love and support of my partner Richard S. Kaplan and all the Rohans, Sullivans, and Kaplans.

I. Rudolph (c. 1963) with a fragment of bush-hammered, corrugated concrete in the drafting room of the Yale Art & Architecture Building (New Haven, Connecticut, 1958–63).

Introduction
Rudolph's Search for Expression

In the firmament of post–World War II American architecture, few stars shone brighter than Paul Rudolph's. A "star architect" long before the term was coined, Rudolph (1918–1997) was profiled in a 1960 *Time* article that captured the admiration for his design and teaching skills in the early days of the Space Age: "Most bright new comets in the architectural sky soon settle into orbit around such suns as the late Frank Lloyd Wright, Chicago's Mies van der Rohe or France's Le Corbusier. It is a rare one that grows to be a force in his own right. For architectural stargazers, the most exciting new arrival is crew-cut Paul Rudolph, 41, who two years ago was appointed chairman of Yale's department of architecture, and is already beginning to collect a few satellites of his own."[1] Quiet, determined, and ambitious, known for his short hair and forthright manner, Rudolph would complete his masterwork, the Yale Art & Architecture Building (New Haven, Connecticut, 1958–63), known as the A & A, just three years later.

Through talent, hard work, and the fostering of useful relationships, Rudolph had risen steadily from humble origins. After briefly studying with Walter Gropius at Harvard and working in the Brooklyn Navy Yards during World War II, he attained international recognition for his widely published Sarasota, Florida, houses of the late 1940s and early 1950s. Embodying the optimism and energy of the postwar era, Rudolph made swooping, vaulted roofs for his houses out of wartime materials, including plastics and plywoods, that captivated the architectural world. In the early 1960s, Rudolph's large-scale concrete "brutalist" buildings, with their signature, widely emulated, bush-hammered corrugated concrete surfaces, exemplified by the A & A Building, were celebrated by critics as a breakthrough for modernism (figure I). Reflecting this dynamic attitude in his writings and pedagogy, Rudolph advocated a heroic approach to modernism that extolled individuality, aesthetics, and creativity. He cultivated the image of a maverick who would save architecture from the monotony of the dominant International Style by reintroducing subjects that he said had been "brushed aside," namely: monumentality, decoration, symbolism, and urbanism.

Rudolph made Yale one of the most important places to study architecture in the world. His students became the leaders of the next generation. Among them were Norman Foster, Richard Rogers, Charles Gwathmey, and Robert A. M. Stern. By the mid-1960s, it was nearly impossible to open the pages of an architectural journal or even a popular publication without glimpsing a photo of Rudolph, seeing one of his many new academic or civic buildings, or reading his pronouncements about architecture.

But then Rudolph's star fell with astonishing rapidity. Young people radicalized by the Vietnam War–era political and social protest movements considered Rudolph a member of the Establishment and rejected his monumentality as egotistical and authoritarian. His epic downfall came complete with a calamitous, mysterious fire that in 1969 gutted the A & A Building and reduced him to traumatized silence. It was widely rumored that students had set the fire as a protest against Rudolph's type of architecture and the Establishment values it represented. Though he had left Yale before the conflagration to pursue his own practice, notoriety from the incident clung to him afterward just as the odor of smoke would permeate the building for decades to come.

At a time when modernism was being widely questioned, Rudolph became more symbolic of its failures than any other architect of his generation. His practice declined in the 1970s and 1980s, along with his reputation, and he virtually disappeared from discussions about architecture. Retreating to the periphery of the profession, he spent his last three decades quietly working on apartments, residences, and a series of high-rise buildings in Southeast Asia. He died in 1997. Interest in Rudolph revived in the twenty-first century as postwar modernism was reappraised, but why he sought to create such complex, dramatic buildings is largely forgotten.

In this book, the first comprehensive monograph on Rudolph, I describe his architecture, career, and changing reputation and discuss how his standpoint on modernism related to architectural discourse in the second half of the twentieth century and earlier. Rudolph is notable as the foremost postwar advocate in the United States of a subjective approach to modernism emphasizing dramatic expression, a position formulated as an alternative to the objectivity of functionalism and the International Style dominant in the 1940s and 1950s.

I explicate key projects to explain Rudolph's "search for expression" during a six-decade career and examine the critical reception to the architect and his works. His career parallels and therefore illuminates the rise and fall of postwar modernism and the subsequent rise of postmodernism. The later, lesser-known residential projects of the 1970s and the tall buildings he built in Asia during the 1980s reiterated his primary concerns and anticipated new ones for architecture, such as the twenty-first century's interest in sustainability and iconic form.

A Point of View

Though often dismissed as idiosyncratic or anomalous, Rudolph's position on modernism related closely to the architectural and cultural ethos of his times. Rudolph's projects therefore provide means for exploring subjects such as expression, representation, monumentality, symbolism, decoration, and urbanism, subjects that preoccupied him and postwar architecture consistently and that continue to interest scholars and architects.

This study joins the growing body of scholarship on postwar architecture that has examined individual architects as well as subjects like urbanism and has thus helped explain the architecture culture of that era.[2] Like Louis Kahn and Eero Saarinen, Rudolph was a leading member of the second generation of modernists, those who came after the recognized primary figures of the first generation: Wright, Le Corbusier, Mies, and Gropius. Reconciling their legacies was difficult for Rudolph and his contemporaries. Though he ultimately found Wright's architecture, romanticism, and individualism more significant, Rudolph hoped to combine the best of Le Corbusier and Wright, who for him represented the contrasting strains of European and American modernism.

Like other members of the second generation, including Edward Durell Stone, Josep Lluís Sert, Philip Johnson, Saarinen, and Kahn, Rudolph was a member of the elite, architectural world of the U.S. Northeast that centered around the architecture schools at Harvard and Yale and the Museum of Modern Art in New York. His omnipresence in this milieu from the late 1940s through the late 1960s made his virtual disappearance from it in the 1970s all the more surprising.

What distinguished Rudolph from his contemporaries was his heroic attitude about architecture. Often dismissed as merely self-aggrandizing, the ideas that informed what Rudolph called his "search for expression" have not been adequately explained. Those who knew Rudolph well noted that he was searching for "personal answers" to contemporary architectural problems in ways that reflected the American character. Yale architectural historian Vincent Scully said of him, "Rudolph probably best represents that side of the American consciousness which is always trying to find and identify the self."[3] It would be easy to reduce Rudolph to the megalomaniacal caricature of the architect embodied by Howard Roark in Ayn Rand's popular novel *The Fountainhead* (1943). Shades of Roark can be found in Rudolph (though he was no follower of Rand), but he complicates the stereotype of the genius architect.[4]

Rudolph's emphasis on the self and creativity is informed by the nature of the postwar United States and the concerns of mid-twentieth-century modernism, including the belief that forceful, heroic action had to be taken to preserve individuality from the conformity caused by increasing emphasis on organization in corporate life, the sciences, and mass culture. Some of the best-sellers of the 1950s, such as William H. Whyte's *Organization Man* (1956), Alan Valentine's *Age of Conformity* (1954), and Sloan Wilson's *Man in the Gray Flannel Suit* (1955), took on these topics. Postwar U.S. culture acclaimed heroes from Superman to Jonas Salk and Jackson Pollock for saving and transforming the world. Joseph Campbell's popular *Hero with a Thousand Faces* (1949) explained that heroes performed their tasks to restore the social order, not just to bolster their egos.

Architectural discourse—that is, the ongoing discussions between the architects, historians, and critics most involved in shaping the discipline—was also preoccupied with the effects of conformity on modernism. From Rudolph's formative years during the Great Depression and well into his maturity, observers had seen modernism as being in a state of perpetual crisis, in danger of becoming dull because of the repetitive vocabulary of European functionalism, or equally in danger of splintering because of the type of mid-1950s experimentation that in fact characterized Rudolph's Florida houses and first large-scale projects.

Rudolph hoped to improve modernism by "humanizing" it, as many others had proposed from the 1930s onward. In his case, this meant taking into account the scale of the human body and psychological reactions to form and space. In doing so, he reacted against the objectivity of Gropius's functionalist-based teaching and of the International Style, instead adopting a subjective approach that reflected his own viewpoint and was intended to affect the user physically and emotionally. Many modernists believed in transforming society through architecture, but they saw this as a collaborative rather than an individual effort. Gropius advocated teamwork and rejected the notion of the solitary architect developing a unique form of self-expression. But Rudolph rejected his teacher's approach, as well as corporate models for practice, and believed that the architect should work alone. He disdained partnerships, preferring to run his practice like a small, informal studio or atelier.

Rudolph hoped to combat conformity via "expression," a word much used at the time, applying a vocabulary of his own consisting of bold, often symbolic forms and sculpted surfaces. What was referred to as expression in the 1950s differed from the German expressionism of the early twentieth century about which Rudolph knew little. The expressive qualities of American modernism in the 1950s emerged from experiments with structure and form, as demonstrated by the different roofs Rudolph employed in his early Florida houses and in the parabola-derived shapes of the TWA Terminal (John F. Kennedy Airport, New York, 1956–62) by Saarinen and the North Carolina Livestock Judging Pavilion (Raleigh, 1948–54) by Matthew Nowicki (an architect whose ideas were important for Rudolph). Emphasizing action and working intuitively, American expression in architecture had much in common with action painting or abstract expressionism. In 1959, the architect Gerhard Kallmann proposed calling it "Action Architecture."[5]

Rudolph's buildings were meant to affect the beholders' minds and bodies. The rise of the psychological in postwar architecture has been addressed in depth by only a few studies; these have mostly concentrated on the analytic methods of psychoanalysis rather than on more loosely structured, empathy-based approaches.[6] Rudolph wanted to foster emotion using intuitive, design-based approaches informed by his own perception. He prized the immediate impression and showed little interest in recording his reactions. Unlike many architects, he never kept travel sketchbooks, though he loved to draw, and he never photographed buildings he saw during his travels. He believed that the experience of the encounter was more significant than any reproduction. Rudolph's intuitive practice contrasted with the science-based, corporate-influenced methodologies of his contemporaries. Rudolph's model for how empathy could stimulate human beings was Geoffrey Scott's *Architecture of Humanism* (1914), a well-known early twentieth-century critique of conventional explanations of renaissance and baroque architecture.[7] Scott maintained that the great buildings of those eras were the individual efforts of genius architect-artists, such as Michelangelo and Bernini, who drew upon and expressed the zeitgeist.

To achieve what he called psychological effects, Rudolph marshaled symbols, bold gestural forms, and highly worked surfaces into dramatic spaces, both inside and outside of his buildings, that would stimulate users. Rudolph believed that every cantilevered beam, every twist of a passageway, and every bright orange carpet could awaken the creativity and individuality of a building's inhabitants and thus combat the monotony and conformity of postwar life. In developing his vocabulary of symbols, forms, and surfaces, Rudolph engaged with subjects that he and others believed modernism had not adequately addressed, chief among them being monumentality, urbanism, symbolism, and decoration.

Monumentality, a subject with which modernism had long struggled, was explored by Rudolph and his colleagues during the 1950s and early 1960s. Big, bold, and dynamic, the A & A Building ushered in the concrete monumentality that became known as brutalism. Many others achieved a similar type of concrete expression in the 1960s, such as Rudolph's Harvard classmates and colleagues Ulrich Franzen and John Johansen, and most notably Kallmann, McKinnell, and Knowles in their Boston City Hall (1961–69), but few were as consistent as Rudolph in their approach to it.

Rudolph believed that archetypal symbolic forms, like the pinwheel and the gateway, could, in addition to stimulating emotional reactions, reestablish historical connections to the past. Modernism had long had difficulty confronting history, but during the 1950s and 1960s architecture reengaged with it and other previously forbidden subjects in complicated and sometimes unadmitted ways. Rudolph experimented with decoration as well; though virtually prohibited by modernism, it was of great interest to him as early as his undergraduate days at the Alabama Polytechnic Institute. Rudolph believed that coming to terms with monumentality, symbolism, and decoration contributed to better urbanism, as did relating buildings to their contexts. Few others thought about context as consistently as Rudolph did in the postwar era. Monumentality, symbolism, decoration, and urbanism were the primary themes that he pursued in nearly every one of his projects.

Rudolph was inspired by heterogeneous sources in his exploration of these themes, accounting for the diversity of expression that some saw as eclectic. He was also attuned to new tendencies from abroad. Similarities between Rudolph's buildings and those of his international colleagues can be found in designs by architects ranging from the Italian neoliberty to the Japanese of the postwar period, such as Kenzo Tange and Fumihiko Maki. Rudolph was also open to ideas sponsored by those with views different from his own, such as Sert and the Congrès Internationaux d'Architecture Moderne (CIAM), or Alison and Peter Smithson, the originators of the brutalist style of architecture, whom he invited to Yale in the early 1960s. Rudolph's involvement with these figures clarifies some of the fissures in postwar architecture, especially the differences between European and American approaches.

Rudolph has been considered prescient for calling for improved architectural theory, long before others did, in his first speech as chairman of the architecture department at Yale in 1958. Yet his call for theory was paradoxical. In part because his intuitive approach defied easy definition, Rudolph never developed a coherent theory for his own architecture. He did, however, often refer to the ideas of some of the most important theorists and historians of his day, such as Sigfried Giedion, the Swiss theorist and historian who had close ties to Harvard when Rudolph studied there, and, of course, Scully at Yale. Evidence of Rudolph's familiarity with the discourse of the day (and previous days) can be culled from many sources. Philip Johnson provided an insightful running commentary on Rudolph's work from the 1950s to the 1980s; his lectures and articles illuminate its relationship to the architectural tendencies of the times.[8] Rudolph's long friendship with this mandarin of modern architecture itself helps in understanding the discipline's complicated network of affiliations in the mid- and late twentieth century.

Though an architect of the postwar era, Rudolph plays a role in the longer continuum of architecture as well. He touched on and creatively violated principles and ideas about architecture important from the eighteenth century on, including Marc-Antoine Laugier's structural rationalism, John Ruskin's truth to materials, and Augustus Pugin's decoration of construction. At times, he seemed to look directly to nineteenth-century theorists such as Eugène Viollet-le-Duc, though he was most drawn to the theorists and architects of the late nineteenth and early twentieth centuries, such as Scott, Camillo Sitte, and Louis Sullivan. Rudolph's search for expression may be considered the postwar installment of architecture's much longer engagement with problems of structure, expression, representation, and decoration. In raising these subjects, Rudolph also anticipated their pursuit by postmodernism and its successors.[9]

Approaches

For all Rudolph's contributions to modernism and theory, his architecture has drawbacks as well. By the early 1960s he had foregrounded his point of view above all others, with the result that spaces that he designed to be complex and compelling were often claustrophobic, confusing, and dangerous for those who used them. His craggy, corrugated concrete often scraped passersby. As he drew on mannerist and baroque forms, Rudolph's monumental architecture became increasingly grandiose in character and scale—"overwrought," as Robert A. M. Stern described his Boston Government Service Center in 1969, a time when such monumentality was falling out of favor.[10]

Nevertheless, this overwrought quality is among the most interesting aspects of Rudolph's work. His search for expression is materially manifested in the elaborate and often labyrinthine movements through space that he choreographed in such structures as the Jewett Arts Center at Wellesley College (1955–58) and the A & A Building. Unable to limit himself to just one idea, Rudolph attempted to investigate all the subjects that concerned him in almost all of his projects. Though it requires lengthy explication, it is valuable to reconstruct Rudolph's formalist viewpoint. He had a tendency, shared by many in his circle, to see buildings as "forms" related to other, often disparate forms from architecture and other disciplines.

Characterizing Rudolph has been difficult since he was exceptionally private and introverted, but doing so is important because he claimed that his architecture manifested his individuality. Though he could be charming, witty, and talkative, Rudolph was more often shy and reserved—paradoxical for someone whose architecture was intended to be expressive, emotional, stimulating, and dramatic. He was often brusque, though this may have been another aspect of his shyness. Rudolph sometimes fell mute when he was most under attack and seemed strangely absent from the maelstroms that engulfed him in the late 1960s. He said little about his personal life even to those who knew him for years. Many of Rudolph's longtime friends and acquaintances had little knowledge about his parents or lovers and heard little about his professional difficulties. He had a powerful impact upon those around him, and some of those closest to him chose not to speak about Rudolph for this study. There were many reasons for his reticence. Enormously ambitious from an early age, Rudolph focused on his career almost to the exclusion of everything else, living almost entirely at the drawing board. Profiles in architectural journals of the 1950s and 1960s said he was too busy for relationships. Russell Bourne wrote in *Architectural Forum* in 1958, "Neither his temperament nor his schedule allow much relaxation. Rudolph remains a bachelor today."[11] He did, however, have lovers and companions, who today might be called partners in the romantic rather than the professional sense. Rudolph, a homosexual, came of age in a time when homosexuality was considered an aberrance and was never discussed, especially if an individual wanted to have a career in the public eye. To some degree, Rudolph's homosexuality conforms to the pattern of closeting described by Eve Kosofsky Sedgwick.[12] Though he never talked about his sexuality, Rudolph did not attempt to pass as heterosexual either, never marrying or dating women in order to conceal his orientation.

Finding a Place for Rudolph

Because of the varied character of Rudolph's architecture, historians of his era and after have found categorizing his work challenging; as a result, it has been ignored or depicted as idiosyncratic. Rudolph's absence from the existing literature, including textbooks, is part of a larger lacuna of information about postwar modernism that has been remedied in part by scholarship of roughly the last decade.[13]

This study had its origins in my doctoral dissertation on Rudolph's academic buildings of the 1950s and 1960s, completed at Harvard University in 2001 under the supervision of Neil Levine.[14] I began by interviewing Rudolph and examined papers in his archive both before and after his death in 1997. I assisted the Rudolph Archive at the Library of Congress in moving his papers from his New York apartment to Washington and helped organize the archive there. The librarians' efforts to make accessible this trove of fifty years of architectural practice have been herculean. Other projects that contributed to this book include the exhibition and symposium that I organized in conjunction with the renovation and rededication of the Yale A & A Building as Rudolph Hall in 2008.

To a certain extent I have drawn on previous publications on Rudolph, though few are critical in tone or explain the motivations that informed his architecture, and almost none examine his entire oeuvre. Two of the most useful are catalogue-style studies by Rudolph from the early 1970s; these demonstrate how Rudolph conceived of his architecture as an alternative to the status quo in postwar modernism. *The Architecture of Paul Rudolph* (1970) has self-critical comments by him about his work and an excellent introduction by his friend Sibyl Moholy-Nagy, the historian and critic. The second book, *Paul Rudolph: Architectural Drawings* (1972), showcased the superlative drawing style for which he was famed.

Although there is much material for study concerning Rudolph and his architecture, it requires a great deal of interpretation. The Rudolph Archive consists primarily of drawings; few documents explain the development of projects or the intentions behind them. Rudolph left little correspondence. Extensive interviews with those who worked with Rudolph—and were willing to speak about him—have greatly contributed to understanding his projects.

Published sources—Rudolph's own articles and interviews—have often provided better explanations of his work than the primary source material. Rudolph was one of the most published architects of the 1950s and 1960s, and articles from the journals of the day have yielded much information. In some cases, Rudolph's clients have preserved documentation. Wellesley College, for example, has extensive correspondence about Rudolph's Jewett Art Center. On the other hand, Yale has surprisingly little documentation about the A & A Building or Rudolph's other projects for the university. Nor is there a great deal of material at Yale from Rudolph's tenure as chairman of its architecture department.

Much visual documentation exists in addition to Rudolph's own drawings. His work was photographed by some of the best postwar American photographers, including Ezra Stoller, with whom he had a long professional relationship. Commissioned by journals for publication, these images show Rudolph's buildings in their original pristine state and will be revelatory for those who have only experienced Rudolph's buildings in their latter-day states of disrepair.

For someone with a relatively small staff, Rudolph was a prolific architect who completed a little more than 150 buildings and designed an almost equal number of unrealized projects.[15] His works are concentrated in Florida and the American Northeast; a few are in other places in the United States, including Texas. He designed many buildings for locations in Asia at the end of his career, but just a few were built. Having pared down the body of works to the buildings included here, I especially regret not being able to include his masterful chapel for Tuskegee University (Tuskegee, Alabama, 1960–69) and the Cannon Chapel for Emory University (Atlanta, 1975–81). Rudolph's religious buildings deserve their own treatment, as do the architect's later residential works.

With this account of Rudolph, his architecture and his times, I hope to deepen knowledge about the subjects that concerned modern architecture during the second half of the twentieth century. Though it has drawbacks as obvious as its strengths, Rudolph's championing of expression represents a standpoint about architecture. This standpoint is important for understanding how modernism developed during the mid- and late twentieth century and is likewise relevant to the early decades of the new millennium, which again favor dramatic, iconic buildings. Rudolph remains admirable for his commitment to architecture and the passion with which he pursued every project. His remarkable buildings are adaptable for the present and future and constitute an important part of the world's architectural heritage.

One
Origins

Paul Rudolph first achieved international renown after World War II for his vacation houses on the sunny beaches and shady bayous of Sarasota, Florida. Designed in partnership with Ralph Twitchell, these houses literally stretched the dimensions of modern architecture in exciting new directions. Rudolph was acclaimed for using new materials, like the plywood and plastics he encountered while supervising wartime ship construction in the Brooklyn Navy Yard, to build vaulted and catenary roofs that somersaulted across space in nearly acrobatic ways.

Architectural historian Robin Middleton later rhapsodized about the appeal of these houses for the war-weary world of the late 1940s and early 1950s: "As delicate shelter succeeded delicate shelter, it seemed that his blithe inventiveness on the theme of elegant living in Florida would never be exhausted. . . . Rudolph's architecture had a very bright-young-boyish charm."[1] The houses with roofs of plywood and plastic attracted the most attention, but there was remarkable diversity among the fifty or so built and unbuilt projects Rudolph designed with Twitchell and independently by 1954—from sturdy post and beam structures with heavy wood ceiling beams to delicate, white plywood pavilions on the beach that looked as if the first seasonal hurricane might blow them away. Each seemed to indicate a different direction for Rudolph's development; together they constitute a series of related experiments with structure and materials in which Rudolph mastered the ideas and vocabulary of modern architecture and its pioneers from Frank Lloyd Wright to Le Corbusier. An examination of these early years promotes an understanding of the formation of the powerful personality and strongly held predilections that drove these investigations, all of which were way stations in his search for expression.

Formation

Born in 1918 in Elkton, Kentucky, and raised amid the austerities of Prohibition and the Great Depression, Paul Marvin Rudolph was the child of a Methodist minister and educator, the Reverend Dr. Keener L. Rudolph (1886–1980), and an amateur artist, Eurie Stone Rudolph (1890–1981). He had three sisters and was the only son. From the pulpit and in the home, Rudolph's father successfully instilled in the boy the need for discipline, forbearance, and an unswerving commitment to one's deeply held values, a position leavened by a tolerance for others' beliefs.

The Rudolphs lived a peculiarly isolated and unsettled existence during their son's early years because the Methodist hierarchy limited ministers to presiding over congregations for only short periods of time. Rudolph's mother estimated that they moved fourteen times among small towns in Kentucky, Tennessee, Oklahoma, and Alabama during Rudolph's childhood. Frequent moves made it

difficult for Rudolph and his sisters to establish long-lasting friendships. As the minister's children, they were expected to behave as models for others, which won them few playmates. Given to solitude, Rudolph played apart even from his sisters.[2]

Despite having a temperament and outlook similar to his father's, Rudolph was closer to his mother, who fostered her son's artistic and musical skills. She was his greatest supporter, and he faithfully sent her his every press clipping. Rudolph established the disciplined habits of a lifetime during childhood, practicing piano diligently, painting, and drawing. Making art and making music were nearly interchangeable for him. Determined to be the very best at whatever he did, Rudolph abandoned his ambitions to become a concert pianist when he came in second place in a national competition in Chicago at the age of fourteen. Though he continued to play the piano for his own pleasure, an interest in architecture was sparked as he helped repair the family's run-down parsonages and took an interest in plans for a new church commissioned by his father. He built a large model of a house that traveled with the family; it was regularly given pride of place on the dining room table, making the surface impossible to use for meals.[3]

The Rudolphs received a respite from their travels in 1931 when the Reverend Rudolph left the ministry to teach theology at Athens College, a small Methodist school in Athens, Alabama. They first inhabited an apartment on the upper floors of Founders' Hall (Hiram Higgins, 1843–45), an imposing building with a two-story colonnade typical of the nineteenth-century Greek revival style and a balcony redolent of the relaxed ways of the Old South (figure 1.1). Rudolph later claimed that local exemplars of the Greek revival style and their monumental qualities, humble vernacular cottages of the community, one of which the family soon occupied, and buildings clustered around the town's square and courthouse were his first introductions to architecture and urbanism.[4]

In high school, Rudolph took after-school classes in painting and sculpture that introduced him to modern art; the instructor was Ida O'Keeffe, a teacher at the college and sister of the artist Georgia O'Keeffe. Though quiet, he won friends in the class with his wry sense of humor.[5] In 1935, Rudolph enrolled at Athens College, planning to save his money and then transfer to a school where he could study architecture. The *Crow's Nest,* the Athens College campus newspaper, profiled Rudolph at eighteen in May 1936 because he looked "like a great artist," chiefly due to his bushy shock of hair. Taciturn, Rudolph told the interviewer little about himself except that, "Moving around and being a preacher's son has been hard."[6] He said his ambition was to study architecture and design movie sets. Though the Reverend Rudolph disapproved of movies, Rudolph was a devoted if indiscriminate filmgoer all his life, often plunging into darkened cinemas when he was frustrated or upset. A refuge from the everyday, movies gave Rudolph some of his first glimpses of the buildings that would inspire him for life, everything from ancient Rome to the skyscrapers of New York.

More than Rudolph's hair impressed the *Crow's Nest.* He was shy, of medium height, slight of build, and he stuttered, but he had a remarkable air of self-possession and confidence that convinced nearly everyone who encountered him that he was destined to be a "great artist." No one was more sure of this than he. The campus paper profile captured his extraordinary, if reserved, intensity and passion for music and art. The *Crow's Nest* reported that the strains of Rudolph furiously playing Franz Liszt's "Liebesträume" (Dreams of Love, 1850), often drifted out of the campus music building. One of romanticism's most famous compositions, the tempestuous masterwork about the search for different kinds of love was Rudolph's favorite; its many dramatic shifts of mood can be considered the musical score for his own search for expression.[7]

After a year at Athens College, Rudolph transferred to the Alabama Polytechnic Institute (API) in Auburn, Alabama, now Auburn University, to study architecture. Despite his shyness, he quickly became the "big man" on campus in the arts. He was president of the Glee Club and the favorite student of the architecture faculty, recognized for his skill in drawing and sculpting. At a time when jackets and ties were typical for male students, he affected an artistic air with loose cardigan sweaters and bushy long hair. The institute provided Rudolph with standard instruction in Beaux-Arts methods, the system of architectural education based on traditional prototypes that had been the primary way of training architects for over a hundred years. Rudolph believed it left little impact on him, though he would later speak favorably of its approaches to urbanism.[8] The API program also encouraged the study of modern architecture. Professor Walter Burkhardt lectured about modernism

1.1 Hiram Higgins, Founders' Hall, Athens College (Athens, Alabama, 1843–45).

1.2 Frank Lloyd Wright, Rosenbaum House (Florence, Alabama, 1939).

and at the same time kindled Rudolph's interest in the local vernacular (his area of expertise) in his classes about architectural history. Reworkings of traditional southern elements such as the dogtrot, a covered open-air hall or space between rooms that admitted breezes and light into the center of houses; screened porches; and light-controlling shutters would all appear in Rudolph's early Florida works.[9]

A visit to Frank Lloyd Wright's Rosenbaum House in Florence, Alabama (1939), made an indelible impression on Rudolph in his final years at API. It was one of the economical Usonian houses developed by Wright to suit Depression-era budgets (figure 1.2). Rudolph was captivated by the Rosenbaum House's cantilevered carport, the piano hinges used on doors, and the interior spaces. Wright designed all details to form a cohesive environment, including built-in furniture, such as a dining table supported on one end by a wall. He juxtaposed large and small areas and darkness and light in complex ways intended to affect the resident or visitor and draw them from one area to another.[10]

The most popular modernist architect of the time in the United States, Wright would become the architect who most influenced Rudolph. Wright was a model for more than his architecture. Wright, too, was the son of a minister, was raised in rural surroundings, and had aspired to become an architect from an early age. He also was a pianist who saw similarities between architecture and music. In a way that would have encouraged Rudolph's already strong sense of individuality, Wright espoused self-expression in architecture in keeping with the American tradition of self-reliance described by Ralph Waldo Emerson. Wright, however, was not universally admired. Critic and architectural historian Henry-Russell Hitchcock, in his defining book for American modernism, *The International Style* of 1932, said that Wright practiced "romantic individualism." It was not meant as a compliment.[11]

An independent, questioning attitude and other lifelong predilections were already evident in the culminating experiences of Rudolph's undergraduate years, the simultaneous writing of a senior thesis and construction of a house of his own design in 1940. In his senior thesis for API, *Glass in Architecture and Decoration,* he discussed how the substance had been employed since antiquity, and he summarized new developments. Magazine photos illustrated ornamental mosaics and chandeliers as well as examples of recent applications by important modernists: Wright's Fallingwater (Mill Run, Pennsylvania, 1934–37) and Walter Gropius's Bauhaus (Dessau, Germany, 1925–26). To a remarkable degree Rudolph's thesis investigated subjects that he would consistently return to in his maturity, including new glass-like materials, such as the transparent plastics Lucite and Plexiglas, and decoration, a fascinating if problematic issue for him and for modernism.

With coauthor Philip Johnson, Hitchcock had famously recommended avoiding applied decoration, in *The International Style*. The writers found contemporary attempts to imitate the ornament of the past inadequate.[12] Most modernists found decoration too traditional. Clearly aware of these caveats, though he did not cite the book, Rudolph said that glass and plastic, if thoughtfully used, could help modernism overcome its "disfavor" with decoration. Engagement with this topic showed a contrarian

1.3 Rudolph, Atkinson House (Auburn, Alabama, 1940).

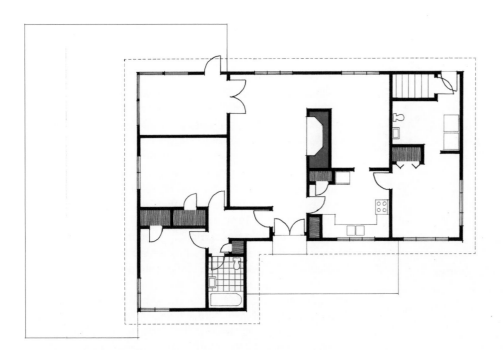

1.4 Plan, Atkinson House.

streak in Rudolph's thinking. His openness about pursuing decoration would vary, but he repeatedly attempted to recover it for modernism over the next few decades. Demonstrating that he was already beginning to think about architecture as a search for expression, Rudolph ended his thesis on a wistful note: "Perhaps I am young, and some day will come to a true understanding; perhaps I will always search and never find a base upon which to build. Changes must be motivated by intellect."[13]

Atkinson House

Rudolph's ambitious nature and his interest in decoration and materials were apparent in his first built work, a 1,364-square-foot brick house in Auburn for T. P. Atkinson (1940), a professor of languages at API, and his family (figure 1.3). Costing $5,500, the small residence was set apart from other local homes with details that recalled Wright's houses, including a hip roof with overhanging eaves and a built-in dining table (figure 1.4).

Giving shape to the ideas outlined in his thesis, Rudolph demonstrated how new materials could be used to create modern decoration by designing and carving from Homasote panels a large-scale mural above the fireplace depicting heroic, nude men struggling with fishing nets amid great waves (figure 1.5). Never intended for artistic or decorative purposes, Homasote was a soft fiberboard made of paper, similar to papier-mâché, developed to insulate railroad cars in the early 1900s. This was the first of many innovative experiments with new materials, the hallmark of Rudolph's early work.

The mural form was itself unusual for a small house, and it suggests many things about Rudolph. Large-scale murals featuring stylized depictions of mythical, heroic subject matter or exotic, primitive scenes were typical of art deco, the mainstream, popular modernist architectural style of the 1930s. It is unlikely that Rudolph created the depiction of struggling men, a subject in keeping with his liking for romantic and heroic themes, himself. He preferred appropriating images from published sources and probably found the original source in a magazine while researching his thesis. He carved its outlines into the soft boards so that the incised lines cast shadows, dramatically amplifying the expressive depiction of this confrontation between men and nature. Such evocative plays of lightness and dark were typical of 1920s and 1930s aesthetics in general, for example in the woodcut prints of the German expressionists.[14] Rudolph's decision to carve the images into the Homasote panels reflects his liking for sculpture. He consistently chose materials with plastic properties, probably because they had three-dimensional qualities akin to those of architecture. His surfaces and walls were often highly modeled or worked in some fashion.

The mural may have had a personal meaning for Rudolph. The rounded forms of the splay-legged figures have a sensual quality; whether they were homoerotic or simply typical of art deco imagery is open to question. Later work by Rudolph suggests that this was indeed the beginning of a sexual undercurrent in his architecture. In the 1960s, Rudolph executed murals with a more pronounced homoerotic character for himself and a Manhattan client.

It is important to consider Rudolph's homosexuality if only because he maintained that self-expression was intrinsic to his architecture. For men of Rudolph's generation living in a homophobic society, exposure as a homosexual could be professionally and personally disastrous.[15] Discreet about his sexual preferences, Rudolph never dated women or married. For much of his career, there were many ways to account for his solitary status and eruptions of the sensual in his work. He appeared too busy and too serious for relationships, and suggestions of sexuality fell under the loose category of artistry. Though Rudolph did in fact have

1.5 Mural, Atkinson House.

1.6 Frank Lloyd Wright, Ann Pfeiffer Chapel (1940), Florida Southern College (Lakeland, Florida, 1938–59).

male partners in adulthood, and his orientation was known to many of his colleagues, the subject was simply never raised publicly.

In 1940, the year of its completion, the mural could easily be seen as an ambitious experiment by a young man; yet it can also be interpreted as a possible unconscious slippage, a representation of the repressed by a young man only beginning to understand and express himself. Though highly self-aware and self-critical, Rudolph had several psychological or cognitive blind spots, such as believing that his homosexuality was not apparent to others. Like his solitary hours at the piano, the mural was perhaps an introspective, self-involved aesthetic exercise, suggestive of his lifelong naïveté about what subject matter like the male nude might reveal depending on its context and who was executing it.

Much about the Atkinson House mural, which is still almost perfectly preserved in Auburn, remains unknown, such as the client's feelings about it. What is certain is that, though somewhat awkward, house and mural demonstrated Rudolph's precocity and ambition. Bolstering his confidence at the time was the prize he won in the Rorimer Competition from the American Institute of Decorators. No trace of the project, a basement recreation room, remains, but it initiated his interest in interior design. From this time on, Rudolph would follow closely new developments in the use of color, texture, and materials for interiors. Architects often handed over the design of interiors to specialists, but Rudolph preferred to design them himself, remaining supremely confident that this too was something at which he excelled.

Recognizing Rudolph's talents, Walter Burkhardt encouraged him to apply to the most important graduate programs in the United States. Rudolph ruled out Wright's Taliesin Fellowship or Ludwig Mies van der Rohe's Illinois Institute of Technology because he believed that neither program had produced students whose work was distinguished from that of their world-famous masters. Of the several schools that accepted him, Harvard proved most attractive. Gropius, at the university's Graduate School of Design (GSD), was recognized as a great teacher who could develop a student's best qualities.[16] And a scholarship made enrollment financially feasible.

Florida Interlude

Rudolph graduated from API in the spring of 1940 and took a year off before matriculating at Harvard. For the first six months, he worked for a large Birmingham architecture firm, E. B. Van Koeren, where his assigned task was to translate architect's sketches into working drawings, the documents used at building sites to guide construction. Translating concepts into buildings was often a stumbling block for Rudolph, and he said the experience shocked him into silence for his entire time at the firm. Shutting down verbally and emotionally was, in fact, Rudolph's consistent response when faced with stressful situations.[17] In the spring of 1941, Rudolph found work in Florida with architect Ralph Twitchell, who was building modernist-inspired houses in the resort town of Sarasota. Modernist residences were uncommon in the United States, especially in the South before World War II, so Rudolph seized this opportunity to assist in their design.

The Florida sojourn was a seminal period that introduced Rudolph to a place that helped define him and his architecture. One attraction for Rudolph was Wright's extension to the campus of Florida Southern College in Lakeland (1938–59, figure 1.6), probably familiar to him as well because it was a Methodist institution. Rudolph would recall its singular features many times in his own work. Wright aligned Florida Southern's buildings along a mall crisscrossed by covered walkways, or esplanades. He constructed the buildings from decoratively patterned concrete blocks made on site from local Ocala sand.

The beautiful Gulf Coast resort community of Sarasota was a seasonal home for well-to-do, often artistic vacationers from the Midwest and Northeast, including the Ringling family of circus fame. The Ringlings developed the town and burnished its reputation as an oasis of high and low cultural delights.

A Beaux-Arts trained architect from the Northeast born in 1890 who supervised the construction of the

1.7 Rudolph and Ralph Twitchell, Twitchell House (Siesta Key, Florida, 1941).

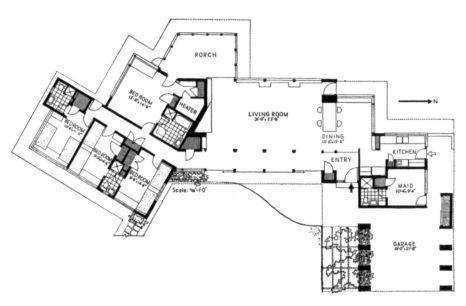

1.8 Plan, Twitchell House.

Mediterranean-style Ringling mansion in the 1920s, Twitchell had stayed on in Sarasota with his family. In the late 1930s, as the economy recovered from the Great Depression, he departed from the red-tile-roofed, Mediterranean houses popular during the 1920s boom years and began building modern ones on the long narrow islands called keys that were lined with palm trees, pines, and scenic bayous overlooking Sarasota harbor and the Gulf of Mexico. The cultured wintertime residents were open to architectural experimentation for their second homes. Twitchell took Rudolph into his small office and treated him like a member of his family. For the young, abstemious son of a minister, Sarasota's cocktail parties must have been eye-opening, like something out of a Hollywood movie. In the spring and summer of 1941, Rudolph assisted Twitchell with several new houses; the most significant was a home for Twitchell and his family overlooking the Gulf of Mexico on Siesta Key. Many of Rudolph and Twitchell's

important early houses were in this island district adjacent to Sarasota. Twitchell probably developed the basic scheme for the low, one-story residence, but Rudolph brought to it his familiarity with the Rosenbaum House, resulting in what was practically a Usonian house on the beach. The rambling Twitchell House paralleled the flat sands and horizon line of the gulf, recalling how Wright's houses often emulated the qualities of their sites (figure 1.7). Walls of concrete block resembled Wright's at Florida Southern, but were simpler and unornamented. An expansive combined living and dining room overlooked the beach, and the bedroom wing was skewed at an angle to take advantage of the views and breezes (figure 1.8). The earth-toned hues of the Ocala sand block (sometimes called lime block) and heavy, cypress post and beam construction imbued the Twitchell residence with a rustic, regional, and relaxed character that reflected Sarasota's informality. Rudolph intended to design a decorative mural for the overmantel, like the one in his Atkinson

13

House, but left Florida for Harvard before the house was completed.[18] The house became the prototype for the post and beam dwellings that Rudolph developed in partnership with Twitchell after World War II.

Harvard

Rudolph appeared confident in a photo accompanying a May 1941 newspaper article announcing that he was leaving his parent's home to study architecture at Harvard (figure 1.9).[19] In Cambridge, however, Rudolph quickly realized that he was facing more formidable competition than anything he had encountered previously. His contemporaries at the Graduate School of Design in the 1940s included students who became the foremost architects of the post–World War II United States: Edward Larrabee Barnes, I. M. Pei, John Johansen, Ulrich Franzen, John Harkness, Victor Lundy, and Philip Johnson, among others. Nevertheless, Rudolph immediately stood out among his classmates, and his studies there, though brief, defined his architecture greatly. Surprisingly for one who was often identified as a product of the GSD, Rudolph studied there for only two semesters: fall 1941 and fall 1946, his education interrupted by World War II and service in the navy.[20] Gropius acknowledged Rudolph's talent as soon as he arrived by granting him one of the coveted spots in the studio he taught himself.[21]

None of Rudolph's studio projects from his first semester have survived, but the concerns that informed them can be outlined. As Rudolph later recounted, Gropius introduced him to the "new space concept," an allusion to the 1941 book *Space, Time and Architecture* by Sigfried Giedion, the Swiss theorist, historian, and leader of the Congrès Internationaux d'Architecture Moderne (CIAM), the important European modernist group. Rudolph later called Giedion's work, considered a bible for architecture students well into the 1980s, "the single most influential book in my professional life."[22] Rudolph had studied architectural history at API but never took a class in history or theory of architecture at Harvard. Gropius believed that coursework in those subjects should conclude an architect's education, but Rudolph's studies were interrupted by the war, and when he returned he was exempted from many requirements, such as history, so that he could quickly receive his degree. Giedion's polemically driven account was therefore one of his only sources for architectural history. Rudolph would display a keen interest in historical buildings and styles but had little knowledge about or interest in what social, political, and economic forces shaped them. Giedion selected examples from the history of architecture, emphasizing the baroque and the role of technology and engineering to explain the development of modern architecture. He said one of modernism's primary achievements was "space-time," an elusive concept about architecture's ability to achieve the simultaneity of cubist painting through transparency and movement.

In the studio, Gropius introduced Rudolph to functionalism, in which the most functional or pragmatic approach was thought to be the most efficient and therefore beautiful solution. Modernist functionalism had been significant in Europe after World War I. As practiced at the GSD and other American architecture schools beginning in the late 1930s, functionalism usually eschewed the more expressive, aesthetic aspects of design, including decoration, as well as approaches that drew attention to the designer's individuality. Gropius instead advocated teamwork, with architects collaborating in groups like scientists, and the objective forms typical of the machine-inspired aesthetic of the 1920s and 1930s.

What was encouraged at Harvard was in-depth research about climate, structure, technology, materials, and prefabrication, the last being a subject of growing interest in 1941. In keeping with the school's preference for science-based methods, GSD students often produced detailed studies for their buildings that measured environmental factors, such as diagrams charting the movement of the sun, and these methods probably enhanced Rudolph's understanding of climate and site, an awareness already enhanced by his Florida experiences.

He encountered prefabrication in Gropius's fall 1941 studio where the problem was a "demountable" school of prefabricated parts that could be disassembled and rebuilt multiple times in different places. Believing that it would be the ideal way to quickly build structures for the military, Gropius researched prefabrication with the assistance of another German émigré, Konrad Wachsmann, with whom he later formed the General Panel Corporation.[23] Wachsmann's space frames, expandable structures of prefabricated trusses, fascinated Rudolph and his classmates.[24]

Modernism as it was practiced at the GSD had a lasting if complicated impact on Rudolph. The space-time concept, functionalism, the legacy of European modernism Gropius represented, and prefabrication all engaged him deeply, but the subjects that he had explored at Alabama Polytechnic— decoration, art deco, and Wright's architecture—were not current in the discourse at the GSD. The school considered Wright too individualistic.[25] For Rudolph, on the other hand, reconciling Wright's and the GSD's contrasting approaches to modernism became a marked source of creative tension for him over the next decade and beyond.

1.9 Paul Rudolph (1941).

1.10 Rudolph and Twitchell, rendering, Denman House (Siesta Key, Florida, 1946–47).

War

Rudolph's first period of study with Gropius ended soon after the United States entered World War II in December 1941. Rudolph immediately enlisted, as did most of his GSD classmates. He joined the navy, took maritime architecture courses at MIT in the spring of 1942, and became a lieutenant in charge of ship repair at the Brooklyn Navy Yard, where he continued for the duration of the war. Working there gave Rudolph practical building experience, teaching him about how lightweight framing techniques used in maritime construction could be used in architecture.[26] The Navy Yards introduced Rudolph, already interested in innovative materials, to other new ones, such as plastics and plywood. Rudolph also began devising signature drawing methods characterized by strong graphic qualities that would convey the expressive qualities of his architecture and his "personal vision."[27]

New York's size, diversity, and anonymity gave many young people, especially young homosexual men from small towns, opportunities to remake themselves.[28] Little is known about Rudolph's daily life, but it may have been then that he became an ascetic and a sensualist, alternating between intense periods of hard work and an equally intense enjoyment of pleasure. Developing a pattern of behavior he followed throughout his life, Rudolph compartmentalized his different sides: he remained a dutiful son and brother, but he no longer regularly attended church or abstained from alcoholic beverages.[29] Military service also transformed the appearance of the young man from rural Alabama. Rudolph's shock of bushy hair was shorn away; the resulting crew cut became his trademark for life. He retained the masculine aura of the navy, perhaps as a way of deflecting any suggestions of effeminacy, which was often associated with homosexuality at the time. Though he was soft-spoken and in private maintained the courtly manners and sometimes the speech of his Southern upbringing, Rudolph would later teach studios and manage his office with the curt, impatient manner of a naval officer.[30]

Exposure to new art and architecture completed Rudolph's education. In the 1940s, New York became the capital of the art world, and it was just as important for architecture. At the Museum of Modern Art (MoMA), exhibitions such as *Built in USA, 1932–1944* presented an overview of recent modern architecture in the United States. The show was organized in part by Rudolph's GSD classmate Philip Johnson, who had been a founder of the museum's department of architecture and design. Though they had met in Cambridge in the fall of 1941, their friendship only developed in New York in the mid- and late 1940s, and it opened doors for Rudolph to the circles of journalists, architects, and artists that intersected at MoMA. Johnson was also a central figure for the city's artistic, cultured homosexual men. During the war years and immediately afterward, Rudolph made friends who moved freely among these circles, such as Peter Blake and Arthur Drexler, who had both been journalists and curators at the museum. Each would write about Rudolph's architecture over the next several decades, beginning with his first postwar Florida works.[31]

Return to Florida

Like many, Rudolph was eager to return to the pursuits interrupted by the war when it ended in 1945. He needed to complete his degree in architecture at Harvard, but at the same time he wanted to design and build. He could easily have found work in New York, where he preferred living, but he thought working for a big firm would be detrimental to his development as a designer. Instead he returned to Sarasota, which, in part due to Twitchell's pioneering efforts of the late 1930s, had become an enclave for modern architecture comparable to Southern California; Lincoln, Massachusetts; and New Canaan, Connecticut.

Rudolph became Twitchell's associate in 1948 and partner in 1950, after he received his architectural accreditation in Florida and New York. Though they built no large-scale developments, the two architects benefitted from Florida's postwar real estate boom. The abstract expressionist painter Syd Solomon, the mystery writer John D. MacDonald, and the film director Elia Kazan vacationed for extended periods in Sarasota after the war, bringing it new energy and wider fame. These and other newcomers to Sarasota were even more open to architectural experimentation than their predecessors. The Ringling mansion became a public art museum during this period. Its first director, A. Everett "Chick" Austin, the former head of Hartford's Wadsworth Atheneum and Johnson's close friend, organized events that brought members of the northeastern architectural community to Sarasota, including Henry-Russell Hitchcock and MoMA curator John McAndrew, who both saw and wrote favorably about Rudolph's early work.[32]

Altogether, Twitchell and Rudolph collaborated for about six years and completed about twenty-four houses of a varied and experimental character.[33] The work was often exciting and innovative. With few zoning or code requirements, problems could be creatively solved on site. Twitchell supervised construction, took care of the firm's business matters, and secured commissions from Sarasota's wealthy winter-time residents. Rudolph was free to concentrate on design, especially experimental ideas. Twitchell, almost thirty years older than Rudolph, connected socially and experienced in construction, maintained the upper hand in the partnership. As the firm grew, and because Rudolph

was frequently away, Twitchell hired other young architects to assist in preparing working drawings, supervising construction, and executing other tasks, including Jack West and Mark Hampton. Pinpointing each architect's specific contributions to the firm's projects is difficult; the process was by necessity collaborative.

The firm's houses of the late 1940s refined the Usonian details and post and beam construction of the Twitchell House. Praised as examples of warm weather regionalism, these works were immediately published in the architectural journals because of Rudolph's connections with New York editors. In the late 1930s and 1940s, regionalism was seen as an important counterbalance to the universalizing tendencies of functionalism and the International Style. It was usually achieved by employing local forms and materials, such as the pecky cypress and Ocala block favored by Rudolph and Twitchell, to temper or humanize the machine-inspired ones usually associated with modernism.

Denman House

The Denman House of 1946–47 on Siesta Key was typical of the firm's immediate postwar work. Louise Denman was a well-to-do, midwestern widow who entertained her seven vacationing grown children and their large families in relays in the one-story, four-bedroom beachfront house overlooking the Gulf of Mexico. According to an article in *Progressive Architecture*, she wanted an "environment for informal living, relaxation (sun bathing, reading, writing etc.) and group activities, such as dancing" (figure 1.10).[34] Three wings enclosed a central courtyard, which itself seemed like an outdoor room (figure 1.11). Exemplifying Rudolph and Twitchell's sensitivity to landscape and topography, the floor plane of the residence was flush with the ground

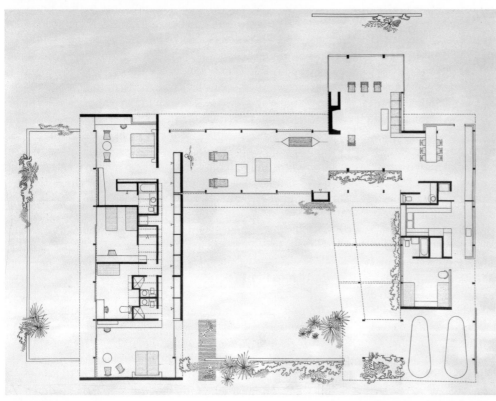

1.11 Plan, Denman House.

1.12 Living room and screened passage, Denman House.

1.13 Rudolph, Weekend House for an Architect (Siesta Key, Florida, project, 1946–47).

so that house, beach, lawn, and courtyard melded almost seamlessly, as in a Usonian House.

Rudolph imbued the house with a regional quality using the vernacular forms he had learned about from Burkhardt at API. He joined the Denman House's living room and bedroom wings with an unglazed, screened passageway for relaxing and dancing that was loosely inspired by the open halls found in traditional southern houses (figure 1.12). Other elements inspired by the vernacular, such as porches, shutters, and vents, helped cool the Denman House naturally. These traditional forms gave this and similar houses by the firm greater historical and regional resonance than other modernist houses of the time. In the transcript of the critique that accompanied the *Progressive Architecture* article, Edward Larrabee Barnes approved of the Denman House, concluding, "It has an informality of appearance which is disarming. . . . It has a certain regional character and seems to belong to Florida."[35]

Taking a break from the intense work in Sarasota, Rudolph returned to Harvard in the fall of 1946 and completed his master's degree in only one semester with two studios overseen by Gropius. Rudolph's virtuosity was apparent in a studio project for a weekend house for an architect (project, 1946–47). He chose a familiar setting, Siesta Key, and developed a design that, not surprisingly, resembled the post and beam houses he had already built there, though it was markedly lighter in structure, reflecting the aesthetics of the GSD's functionalism (figure 1.13). After the war ended, universities generally accommodated returning veterans eager to finish their degrees and resume their lives; the GSD granted Rudolph his degree in early 1947, without requiring him to submit a thesis project.[36] He was also awarded the prestigious Wheelwright Traveling Fellowship.

Europe

The Wheelwright Fellowship gave Rudolph the opportunity to visit Europe between mid-1948 and mid-1949. While traveling, he continued working with Twitchell, refining designs through correspondence. Rudolph never spoke of the wartime damage he must have seen, though it was typical of many of the World War II generation to overlook, forget, or repress such things. Rudolph was committed to modernism, but what made the greatest impression on him and his fellow American architects were Europe's historic buildings and cities, its English castles, French cathedrals, and particularly the piazzas, palazzos, and campaniles of Italian cities; these were considered lessons in urbanism, a subject whose importance had been emphasized at the GSD. Impressions mattered more to him than sketching or photographing these places. He analyzed what he saw and memorized details.[37]

In his continuing work with Twitchell, Rudolph frequently mailed to Sarasota sketches and letters with detailed instructions for new residences; Twitchell and his assistants modified them as needed and developed working drawings and specifications. Rudolph worked even when he was supposed to be studying historic architecture. At the American Academy in Rome, a Harvard contemporary was surprised to find him assiduously drawing a house for Sarasota when he could have been touring the city.[38] This ability to design by correspondence would stand Rudolph in good stead when he started his own practice.

The postwar buildings of Le Corbusier in France were just as revelatory for Rudolph as anything he found in Italy. Rudolph had met Le Corbusier in New York in 1948 when Le Corbusier was preparing designs for the United Nations. In France, Rudolph visited Le Corbusier's Parisian office and the Unité d'Habitation (1946–52), his apartment building then under construction in Marseilles.[39] Its monumentality, sculptural qualities, and rough concrete surfaces signaled a new, more expressive direction in Le Corbusier's architecture—a departure from the objective rationalism of his machine-inspired work of the 1920s—and greatly inspired Rudolph and his contemporaries (figure 1.14).

As he had in New York, Rudolph formed relationships with journalists in Europe who were interested in his work and in what was happening in the United States, recognizing that it was emerging as a center for postwar modernism. The editors of the most important French architectural journal, *L'Architecture d'aujourd'hui,* in addition to publishing many of Rudolph and Twitchell's houses, asked Rudolph to edit an issue devoted to Gropius and his American students.[40] Published in February of 1950, the special issue was the most complete catalogue of the work designed by GSD students in the 1940s. It also surveyed the work of the Institute of Design in Chicago, another school modeled on the Bauhaus, which was presided over by Serge Chermayeff; Rudolph and Chermayeff would develop a complicated friendship over the next decades. Giedion contributed an account of Gropius's career, which he expanded into a book that became the standard text about the Bauhaus founder for many years.[41] In his brief preface

1.14 Le Corbusier, Unité d'Habitation (Marseilles, France, 1946–52).

to the journal, Rudolph said that the most notable quality of Gropius's teaching was "his ability to incorporate diverse ideas and yet still give a sense of direction."[42]

Diversity might have been Rudolph's tactful way of accounting for the considerable differences evident in the work of Gropius's students. The publication in fact illustrated the developing split between those students who faithfully practiced Gropius's philosophy of functionalism and teamwork (members of The Architects' Collaborative, for instance) and those who were already departing from his precepts (Rudolph, Victor Lundy, John Johansen, Ulrich Franzen, and others). The latter group found Gropius's approach to functionalism too restrictive.[43] Dean Joseph Hudnut of the GSD had worried that functionalism as it was being taught in the 1940s limited individuality and creativity in architecture and urban design.[44] Similar discontent with functionalism was increasingly heard across America and Europe. In 1950, the Danish architect Kay Fisker complained that functionalism had ossified to the point of making architecture "skeletal, sterile, and antiseptic. At times the whole movement seemed inhuman."[45] In Europe, some of the younger members of CIAM, led by Peter and Alison Smithson, would question the emphasis on functionalism and break away to form the group Team 10. Though Rudolph and the Smithsons would later have their differences, at that time, they all appeared to be headed in a similar direction.[46]

Healy "Cocoon" House

One of the houses Rudolph designed, at least in part, by correspondence was the Healy "Cocoon" House (Siesta Key, Florida, 1948–50). Internationally acclaimed for its plastic, catenary roof, it was more about experimentation than functionalism or practicality. Located on an Edenic Siesta Key site, the Cocoon House sat on a raised wood platform that hovered over the edge of a bayou. Rudolph packed a

living room and dining area, two bedrooms, a bathroom, and a galley kitchen into its twenty-two-foot width (figure 1.15). The clients for the unusual guesthouse were the parents of Twitchell's fiancée, Roberta Healy Finney. (He and his first wife had divorced in the late 1940s.)

Twitchell's construction expertise got the house built, but it was clearly a product of Rudolph's experiences and ideas. "Cocoon" was a plastic, spray-on foam developed by the U.S. government and manufactured by the Hollingshead Corporation; Rudolph had seen it used to mothball unused ship components in the Brooklyn Navy Yard.[47] He thought Cocoon could form a roof flexible enough to move with hurricane winds, like tent canvas. Unlike the firm's earlier and heavier wood post and beam structures, the house was comparatively lightweight, recalling the qualities of the maritime construction Rudolph had supervised during the war, as well as the GSD preference for lightness. The Healy House was a distinct object in the landscape rather than one that melded with its surroundings like the Denman Residence.

To form the remarkable roof, workmen strung flat steel straps between two conventionally framed wood stud walls, laid insulating panels across them, and sprayed them with Cocoon—a process the public was invited to see in order to attract publicity for the project (figure 1.16). The steel straps drooped in the middle, forming a suspended structural configuration known as a "catenary," familiar as the form of a suspension bridge or a rope hammock (figure 1.17). External steel diagonal staves braced the walls and roof, shoring up the building against hurricane winds and preventing the tightly compressed structure from collapsing or flying apart. Adjustable, louvered jalousies clad the side walls, admitting light and air, making the house feel like a large porch.

Rudolph's published drawings showed that every element appeared to be necessary and convinced many that he pursued architecture in a wholly rational way (figure 1.18).[48] Rudolph later admitted that using the catenary

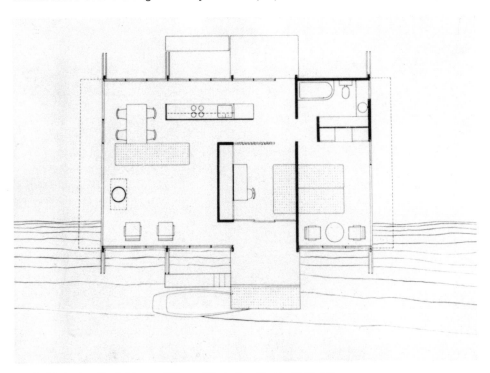

1.15 Rudolph, plan, Healy "Cocoon" House (Siesta Key, Florida, 1948–50).

1.16 Spraying Cocoon, Healy House.

1.17 Healy House.

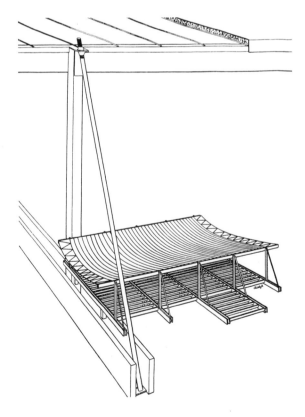

1.18 Framework analysis, Healy House.

1.19 Living room, Healy House.

to span the twenty-two feet between the walls was pure "structural exhibitionism" rather than the rational expression of structure that it appeared to be.[49] Rudolph's attention to design did not extend to the construction of his own buildings, which often had practical flaws. The Cocoon-covered roof leaked; conventional roofing materials soon replaced it.[50]

Though celebrated by the architectural press for its use of Cocoon, the catenary roof of the Healy House for Rudolph evoked things of greater significance. He ambitiously emulated the catenary roof that Le Corbusier and Pierre Jeanneret had designed for their Pavilion des Temps Nouveaux (Paris, 1937), a temporary exhibition pavilion. The Healy House roof also resembled a canvas tent, which recalled both the revival tents of Rudolph's childhood and the enormous tents pitched by the Ringling Brothers Circus in Sarasota.

The house in its primeval setting also recalled the "primitive hut." That mythic building from the origins of architecture was a simple post and beam structure; the architectural theoreticians of the eighteenth and nineteenth centuries, such as the Abbé Laugier and Viollet-le-Duc, had used it to explain the principle of structural rationalism, in which every structural element had a reason for being. The concept was foundational for modern architecture.[51] Rudolph had little formal instruction in architectural history or theory, but such concepts informed the experimental architecture of the day. Historian Peter Collins wrote that it "would be unwise to underrate the very profound influence which the taste for Structural Rationalism . . . has had on contemporary architectural speculation."[52] Seen in light of these influences, the Cocoon House can be considered the postwar embodiment of the primitive hut and structural rationalism and Rudolph's first groping steps toward finding theories that would inform his architecture.

While the primitive had informed the rationalism of the eighteenth century, in the postwar era it was often used to suggest the exact opposite, an irrational undercurrent. Rudolph and his contemporaries liked to evoke the powerful emotions of the primitive with archetypal forms like the flaming hearth, and in a drawing of the living room of the Cocoon House he placed a hearth made from a large, ancient-looking iron pot beneath a tempered glass chimney (figure 1.19). The assembly was more appealing as an idea than as a reality: the pot was never made into a hearth, and the chimney that was built smoked in the house.[53] Primitivism pervaded the art and architecture of the late 1930s and 1940s, becoming a powerful source of inspiration for the surrealist and abstract expressionist painters and persisting in Rudolph's work well into his maturity.[54]

Rudolph's dramatic drawing of the flaming hearth exemplified his still developing but already distinctive drawing style. He favored more subjective depictions than the objective diagrams preferred at the GSD, employing deep perspectival views from novel angles and emphasizing differences between darkness and light to convey emotion. In addition to pen and ink, he made use of new plastic materials, such as Zip-a-Tone, a plastic tape with a patterned texture. Rudolph believed that he had to develop compelling images of his projects if he was to win attention for them. He always supervised closely the making of drawings in his office, especially presentation drawings for publication.

Rudolph also recognized the importance of photography for getting his houses published. He developed an important partnership with Ezra Stoller, one of the most skilled postwar American architectural photographers. Stoller crafted dramatic depictions of Rudolph's houses that emphasized the play of light and shadow in sunny Florida. Together, they "styled" interiors in order to photograph them to their best advantage, often borrowing appropriate

1.20 Bayou side, Healy House.

modernist furniture. Stoller's images captured the houses' appeal as ideal visions of postwar leisure (figure 1.20).[55]

Independent Practice

The Rudolph and Twitchell partnership became strained—each felt the other took too much credit for projects—and ended in the spring of 1952. Additionally, the thirty-four-year-old Rudolph wanted commissions outside of Florida to advance his career and believed that achieving independence as a designer was vital if he was to maintain his integrity and find his own means of expression.[56] Contact ceased forever in 1952 after Rudolph lost a climactic phone argument about dividing the firm's few earnings. The fuming Rudolph retreated to a Sarasota cinema for the rest of the day. Afterward he effectively erased traces of his collaboration with Twitchell by insisting to his admirers that he was the mastermind behind every house.[57]

Rudolph opened a small office on Main Street in downtown Sarasota and concentrated on completing his share of the commissions. While finding new work was difficult at first without Twitchell's social contacts, Rudolph soon attracted clients who appreciated his experimental emphasis and growing fame. Rudolph rarely employed more than two architects at any time in Sarasota, but bright young graduates of architecture schools who had admired his houses in journals—Bert Brosmith, Joseph Farrell, William Rupp, Wilder Green, Gene Leedy, and others—were eager to work for him. Rudolph explained to them that though he was increasingly successful, he was not running a conventional business; his practice was experimental and always would be. Income from the firm barely covered the two or so staff members' salaries; Rupp was paid $50 a week in 1953, a sum he considered low, though it was probably not unusually so at the time.[58]

Rudolph's personal income came largely from teaching in architecture schools and lecturing about his work, which he had been doing even before ending his partnership with Twitchell. Rudolph taught studios at schools across the nation during the 1950s, including the University of California at Los Angeles, Tulane, Cornell, the University of Pennsylvania, Harvard, MIT, and Yale. Students found his strong presence unforgettable and admired his total commitment to architecture.[59] These teaching stints introduced Rudolph to new developments in architectural thinking about form, space, and urbanism; he tested many of these in his Florida houses.

By 1952, Rudolph spent only summers in Sarasota. Brosmith ran the Sarasota office for most of the 1950s, relying on detailed correspondence with sketches to implement Rudolph's ideas. Rudolph specified every detail and asked Brosmith to follow up with clients about their needs or to research new products he read about in journals or encountered in his travels. The engaged but distant way of working, developed earlier with Twitchell, still suited Rudolph well. Few letters survive, making individual contributions to the design process hard to determine; in any case, Rudolph, who was still bitter about sharing credit with Twitchell, made it clear to all that his would be the sole name on all projects.[60]

Rudolph's Sarasota office, cramped and intense, consisted of one room of only twelve by twenty-four feet. Seeing the office as an opportunity to design an interior entirely his own, Rudolph covered the ceiling with leaves of gold Japanese tea paper and hung a shimmering curtain of metal disks beneath a skylight. During brief visits and summer stays Rudolph often slept on his office sofa or rented houses he had designed, like the Cocoon House. In Sarasota, he permitted himself only one indulgence, a used British-made Riley sports car.[61] Though he was a poor driver and admittedly mechanically inept in almost every way, Rudolph was fascinated with the rounded, sculptural bodies of automobiles. By the mid-1950s, he often spoke of how architects and city planners needed to accommodate the automobile's growing presence.

In addition to building houses and teaching, Rudolph designed exhibitions for MoMA. His installations for *Good Design* (1952) and *Family of Man* (1954) were opportunities to experiment with materials, space, lighting, and new and historically inspired forms to create purely interior spaces free of the constraints of site and conventional construction (figure 1.21). For *Good Design*, an annual exhibition of low-priced, well-designed household goods curated by Edgar Kaufmann, Jr., Rudolph made transparent walls out of Cocoon and Lucite. The curtain of metal disks in his Sarasota office came from this exhibition. In another demonstration of his virtuosity, Rudolph designed different versions of the exhibition installation when it was mounted in New York and in Chicago.

Finding the "Form Sense"

Shortly after establishing his practice, Rudolph talked about his development for the first issue of the Yale architecture department's student-run journal, *Perspecta*, published in the summer of 1952. The student editors' selection of Rudolph indicated his growing popularity among architects, and his account was the beginning of his long association with the important journal and the university, where he soon became a visiting studio critic. Rudolph was eager to dispel the persistent notion that he was simply a builder of regionally sensitive houses in a southern-inspired vein. He wrote in *Perspecta*, "My work in Florida has centered on developing some of its regional characteristics; however, the work actually executed seldom represents my true intentions. So far it has been limited to free-standing residences, an interesting but limited field. Use of locally available materials, such as lime block and cypress, have produced an effect which some might term regional; true regionalism, however, comes principally through form."[62]

Rudolph had started distancing himself from the material-based approach typical of regionalism from the late 1930s to the early 1950s; instead he favored an approach determined by "form," a concept of increasing significance for architectural discourse at the time. Rudolph discovered what he called the "form sense" during his European travels of 1948 and 1949. He explained in *Perspecta*, "I returned to this country with the reinforced conviction of the necessity of regaining the 'form sense' which helped to shape Western man's building until the nineteenth century."[63] By "form" Rudolph meant a three-dimensional, geometric form

1.21 Rudolph, *Good Design*, installation at Merchandise Mart, Chicago, 1952.

such as an arch or vault. He envisioned making arches and vaults out of new materials while still retaining their archetypal resonance.

In general, such forms had not been part of modern architecture's vocabulary during the 1920s and 1930s because they were associated with traditional architecture. In the late 1940s and early 1950s, however, modernist architects returned to these historically inspired forms as they cast about for alternatives to the limited vocabulary of functionalism. In this way, history again became a consideration for modernism. The word "form" became ubiquitous in discussions about architecture.[64] In his 1948 book *Search for Form,* Eliel Saarinen explained architectural form in sweeping terms as something inspired by the complex historical, cultural, and psychological motivations of both societies and individuals. For Louis Kahn, form led to greater order in architecture and was therefore rational. Others, like Rudolph, associated it with emotion. In the early 1950s, the literary critic Susanne K. Langer wrote about how age-old forms could stimulate feelings in the onlooker.[65]

What Rudolph called the "form sense" was close to what Langer described. Quite different from the objectivity of functionalism or the International Style, it was subjective, was arrived at intuitively, and could stimulate the emotions of others, like a Jungian archetype.[66] Historians critical of functionalism and the ahistorical, science-based methods of the 1940s took up the cause of form, seeing it as a way to reintroduce history, emotion, and humanism to modernism. A reader of Langer, the Yale architectural historian Vincent Scully said in 1954 that the reappearance of vaults, arches,

and domes in the work of Johnson, Rudolph, and Kahn "reveals the yearnings of a complex age for direct and simple experience, deeply felt and presented as general truth, without rhetoric."[67]

Hook House

The significance of form for Rudolph was apparent in one of the first projects he completed after splitting with Twitchell, the Hook House (Siesta Key, Florida, 1952–53) (figure 1.22). Mary Hook, a wealthy architect from Missouri, commissioned the house as part of a Gulf-front artists' colony she was building; it eventually included houses by Sarasota's other modernist architects, such as Frank Folsom Smith and Rudolph's GSD classmate Victor Lundy.[68] Attracted to the region by Twitchell's and Rudolph's efforts, these architects later became known as the "Sarasota School." It is important to note that Rudolph had little contact with Lundy or these newcomers beyond the occasional lunch with them at Sarasota's Plaza Hotel.[69]

Like the Healy House, the Hook House was compact and experimental. Rudolph raised the one-bedroom structure high on a platform overlooking a lagoon and topped it with three barrel vaults that exemplified "form." The area beneath the platform was screened, making an additional living area. Inspiration for the vaults came from the roughly textured concrete and plywood vaults of Le Corbusier's primitivist-inspired houses in France of the late 1930s and early 1950s, the Maison du Weekend (La Celle St. Cloud, 1935) and Maisons Jaoul (Neuilly, 1952–54).[70] Rudolph had

25

1.22 Rudolph, Hook House (Siesta Key, Florida, 1952–53).

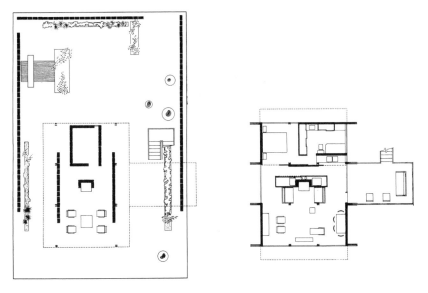

1.23 Ground floor and main living floor plans, Hook House.

1.24 Living room, Hook House.

considered making the vaults for the Hook House from Cocoon, but it proved too complicated and expensive, so he turned to plywood, another manufactured building material, which appealed to him almost as much because of its malleable, sculptural qualities. Rudolph claimed it was the first application of the material in this unique way.[71] Rudolph had employed plywood in the Navy Yard, and in the postwar era it was increasingly used for residential construction.

The vaults for the Hook House consisted of two quarter-inch sheets of 4-foot by 8-foot plywood, glued and nailed together, and then bent into shape by hand. Bending the plywood vaults proved difficult on site.[72] Gene Leedy, one of the architects employed by Rudolph, remembered the vaults breaking loose from their moorings and flying across the lagoon before workmen could bolt them into place. Rudolph and his architects solved the problem by nailing the plywood sheets to a temporary construction brace and then bending, gluing, and bolting the wood into place.[73]

Without the assistance of Twitchell, Rudolph found building his experiments more difficult than he had imagined. The pursuit of form led at times to "formalism" in Rudolph's work, or the foregrounding of the conceptual, often largely aesthetic, over the functional. Despite problems, Rudolph persevered with the plywood vaults, successfully employing shallower ones for the Sanderling Beach Club (Siesta Key, 1952–53).

Rudolph's desire to conjure up the subjective, expressive qualities of the "form sense" was evident inside the Hook House (figure 1.23). The three vaults shaped the interior, forming a balanced symmetrical space more like a traditional room than the "open plan" typical of modernism. The architectural historian Colin Rowe noted at this time that modern houses were increasingly focused on central spaces that imparted a sense of balance and symmetry like that found in the classical structures of the past (figure 1.24).[74] Clearly exemplifying this development, Rudolph centered the living room of the Hook House on a hearth flanked by two identical suspended sofas. The vault above the hearth curved upward to a plastic skylight enclosing the chimney, forming an expanding, light-filled space above the inhabitant's head that was emotionally uplifting; the effect was the inverse of that of the concave roof of the Healy House, which Rudolph later admitted was "psychologically, spatially uncomfortable" because it drooped oppressively in the middle of the room.[75]

Walker Guest House

Rudolph's experiments of the early 1950s culminated in the Walker Guest House (1952–53) on Sanibel Island, an affluent seasonal resort island community 110 miles south of Sarasota (figure 1.25). Widely acclaimed at the time, the residence was named one of the most important houses of the twentieth century in a 1957 survey of *Architectural Record*'s readers, along with Mies's Farnsworth House and Johnson's Glass House, two projects to which it was clearly related.[76] The delicate wood structure was a beachside retreat overlooking the Gulf of Mexico for Dr. Walter Walker, a Minneapolis physician whose family founded that city's Walker Art Center. In 1951, while still in partnership with Twitchell, Rudolph had designed a larger rectangular house

1.25 Rudolph, Walker Guest House (Sanibel Island, Florida, 1952–53).

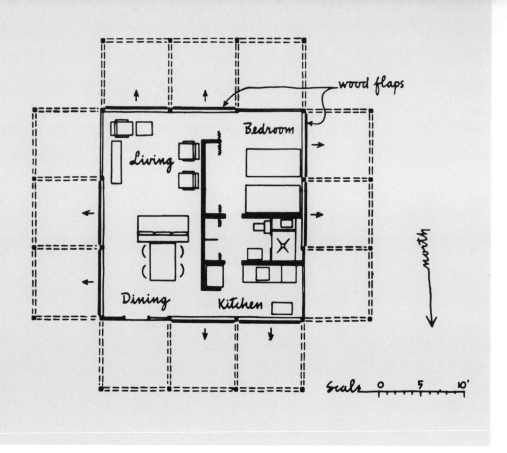

1.26 Plan, Walker Guest House.

for this site. The next year, Walker instead asked Rudolph to design a small guesthouse that his family could use until he decided to move forward with the main house.[77]

Seeing this as an opportunity to test an idea he had probably had in mind for some time, Rudolph returned to Walker in just two weeks with a plan for a guesthouse that was entirely different from the original, main house. As Rudolph explained later, the Walker Guest House was a breakthrough for him. He realized that he could design buildings and interiors that could stimulate the emotions and bodies of the user, while still reflecting his own strongly held and increasingly critical views about modern architecture.[78]

Small and experimental like both the Healy House and the Hook House, the Walker Guest House was a white wood-framed pavilion containing two bedrooms, a galley kitchen, a bath, and a living room. Object-like yet intimately tied to its locale, the house, surrounded by scrub pines, sat on a platform raised above a Gulf-front beach. It was memorable for the giant shutters that enclosed it; supported by an external wood framework, they could be manipulated by a system of rigging and cannonball-like weights painted red. The arrangement was perhaps inspired by the weights used to adjust hurricane shutters or the rigging of a sail-boat. A sense of motion, like that of a toy, imparted a joyful quality.

The square block of the house and the frame around it together formed a plan that resembled a Greek cross, exemplifying Rudolph's already evident and growing appreciation for the idealized geometric forms that had inspired classical architecture over the centuries, as seen for example in the centralized churches of the renaissance. The discussion and diagrams of such buildings in Rudolf Wittkower's 1949 book *Architectural Principles in the Age*

of Humanism influenced many British and American architects at the time by showing how the past could reinvigorate the present (figure 1.26). However, the great centralized churches of the renaissance were an unlikely model for a small beach house, demonstrating how Rudolph sometimes employed forms without regard for their appropriateness. Problems occurred during construction. Keeping the house's lightweight wood frame rigid and preventing it from shifting proved difficult. Wires strung in a crisscrossing fashion braced it, giving it a tensile quality, as did large plates of glass. Rudolph later said, "It crouches like a spider in the sand."[79]

Like Rudolph's previous houses, the Walker Guest House evoked many things simultaneously. Its white frame was balanced and symmetrical, like an abstract version of a temple; at the same time, it resembled a screened porch or an attenuated version of a columned Greek revival house from Rudolph's southern youth. Most significantly, it was both a tribute to and a critique of the white steel framework of Mies's iconic Farnsworth House (Plano, Illinois, 1946–51). Though the transparent house was one of the most famed domestic examples of the International Style, Edith Farnsworth had found its lack of privacy inhuman.[80] At his own Glass House (New Canaan, Connecticut, 1945–49), Philip Johnson solved this dilemma by pairing his glass-walled residence with an opaque, brick guesthouse; Rudolph knew this structure well from frequent visits.[81]

The enclosing shutters of the Walker Guest House were Rudolph's unique solution to the problems of the modernist all-glass house. The shutters, or flaps as Rudolph called them, were inspired by the vernacular, top-hinged hurricane shutters of the Caribbean. Rudolph enlarged this traditional form for the Walker building and made it from plywood, a

1.27 Shutters, Walker Guest House.

manufactured material not native to the region, thus exemplifying his statement in *Perspecta* that "true regionalism" was form, not materials. In addition to providing privacy, the shutters humanized the glass box by sheltering the inhabitants from the sun and rain. They could be bolted to protect the house from hurricanes and intruders, neatly transforming it into a closed box that could be left on the beach when the vacation season ended (figure 1.27).

Unlike Edith Farnsworth, who could not alter the architecture of her house, the Walker family could make themselves comfortable in accordance with the shifting sun, winds, and storms by adjusting the giant shutters with the system of pulleys, ropes, and weights. In fact, the Walker family affectionately called the house "Cannonball." The ingenious if difficult to manipulate arrangement required some upper body strength. Fascinated by the shutters, Rudolph attempted to use them in several other unbuilt, experimental houses of the 1950s.

With the shutters, Rudolph involved the inhabitants with the house in ways that could affect them physically and emotionally, making this another type of experiment with a humanism in which forms could stimulate the human body, as he explained in a 1953 talk for a conference about regionalism. Rudolph said of the Walker House, "With all the panels lowered the house is a snug cottage, but when the panels are raised it becomes a large screened pavilion. If you desire to retire from the world you have a cave, but when you feel good there is the joy of an open pavilion."[82] Rudolph's burgeoning interest in what he loosely called psychology belonged to a broader initiative discussed by many in the 1940s and 1950s from Langer to the abstract expressionist painters. They sought to humanize modernism by engendering emotion and subjectivity through explorations of the unconscious and stimuli of many sorts. Archetypal forms were just one way to achieve this.[83]

Light was a stimulus as important as space for Rudolph. With the exception of the carefully orchestrated spaces of Wright, Rudolph thought that modernism, particularly the International Style, had overlooked its importance. Rudolph said, "Indeed, the whole so-called International Style has, with a few exceptions, simply said 'let's have light' without controlling it psychologically. We need 'caves' as well as 'gold-fish bowls.'"[84] Rudolph repeated his phrase about caves and goldfish bowls for the rest of his career. Like the hearth, the cave was an archetype that summoned up associations with the origins of dwelling. It was a primitive but presumably comforting space, at least in Rudolph's mind. "Goldfish bowls" was a term commonly used to describe the bright transparent spaces of the International Style, exemplified by glass, curtain-walled buildings such as Lever House (Skidmore, Owings & Merrill, New York, 1951–52) as well as smaller structures such as the Farnsworth House.[85] With the Walker Guest House, Rudolph deftly combined cave and goldfish bowl into one flexible structure.

The Walker Guest House, the culmination of Rudolph's early work, was significant as his first outright critique of the International Style and also the first project where it was evident that he was deliberately trying to affect the bodies and minds of those experiencing his architecture. It would be the last design in which he permitted the user to adjust the building to such an extent. Rudolph continued to practice and build remarkable structures in Florida for the remainder of the 1950s, but he knew that if he was to achieve his great ambitions and challenge the International Style more directly, he needed commissions outside the state and larger than a tiny guesthouse.

Two
Challenging the
International Style

After emerging from the kindergarten of Sarasota, Rudolph entered an architectural adolescence. Between the mid- and late 1950s the themes and forms that would preoccupy him for a lifetime coalesced. Eager and restless, Rudolph maintained his Sarasota office and continued to build experimental houses in Florida, but he was omnipresent outside of the state, winning prizes, receiving new commissions, and cultivating a widespread network of support among his colleagues. The year 1954 saw a breakthrough for Rudolph. The Sao Paulo International Competition awarded him the prestigious Outstanding Young Architect Award for his work in Florida, and he received his most significant commission to date, a new U.S. embassy in Amman, Jordan.[1] It was his first notable project for a building larger than a house; others for a college arts center and office building in Massachusetts soon followed. Ambitious, complicated, and puzzlingly different in appearance from one another, each of Rudolph's projects challenged the International Style and often his clients as well.

"The Changing Philosophy of Architecture"

Forever establishing himself in the eyes of his contemporaries as a bright-eyed young maverick, Rudolph gave the defining speech of his career at the June 1954 annual meeting of the American Institute of Architects (AIA) in Boston. He appeared younger than his thirty-five years and was the most junior member of a panel called on to discuss "The Changing Philosophy of Architecture" (figure 2.1). His inclusion was a sign of his arrival in the front ranks of American architecture. The group included some of America's leading architects: Eero Saarinen, Josep Lluís Sert, Ralph Walker, and William Wurster.[2] These men would become Rudolph's friends, mentors, and rivals.[3]

The panelists discussed the new dilemma for modernism. After years of hostility toward it, modernism was becoming widely accepted in America. Nevertheless, each participant was dissatisfied with how it was being practiced, concerned that creativity was being neglected in favor of the utilitarian (in what amounted to a debasement of 1920s and 1930s functionalism) or the repetitive (the International Style's flat-roofed, glass-walled rectangular buildings).[4]

Rudolph was the speaker most vehement about the greater need for "expression." The word was used repeatedly in discussions of the period to describe the need for a more varied vocabulary and for architecture to represent or symbolize something, such as its function or structural qualities. In one of the most memorable passages from his speech Rudolph said, "Modern architecture's range of expression is today from A to B. We build isolated buildings with no regard to the space between them, monotonous

and endless streets, too many gold-fish bowls, too few caves. We tend to build merely diagrams of buildings." Rudolph called for a return to aesthetics, a subject downplayed by the functionalism of the 1940s, and pronounced that "the architect's prime responsibility is to give visual delight."[5] The architect could achieve this visual and spatial delight, said Rudolph, by reconsidering traditional urban forms. On a recent trip abroad, he had been impressed by the courtyards, squares, free-standing sculptures, arches, and gateways of the old cities of the Middle East and Italy and thought those elements could vary and enliven American cities.

Delivered with the passionate tones of his father's sermons, Rudolph's earnest words were understood by some younger listeners as an admonition to his elders on the panel and in attendance. Rudolph successfully channeled his innate contrarian attitudes into the maverick stance for which he would be known for many years. His slight stutter and a few witticisms softened his vehemence. Rudolph's comment on modern architecture's "range of expression" alluded to the often-repeated, barbed evaluation of Katharine Hepburn's acting ability attributed to Dorothy Parker: "She ran the gamut of emotions from A to B." Rudolph often made allusions in his talks and buildings that only he and a small circle around him could comprehend.

Though what he said was far from radical and indeed not entirely original, Rudolph articulated the anxieties and hopes of the discipline in an energetic, optimistic way that established him as one of its leaders. *Architectural Record* published excerpts from Rudolph's speech along with those by the other participants, and his entire talk appeared in *Architectural Forum*. Repeated by Rudolph many times afterward, his phrases serve as verbal blueprints for his projects of the mid- and late 1950s.

United States Embassy, Amman, Jordan

Rudolph received the commission for the new U.S. embassy in Amman, Jordan, in early 1954, several months before the AIA convention. He had long hoped for a commission for an important public building to demonstrate that he was more than just an architect of ingenious beach houses. Though never completed, the ambitious project was the source of many of Rudolph's later ideas and methods.

The embassy was part of an extensive, well-publicized campaign organized by the Foreign Buildings Operation (FBO) of the U.S. State Department to construct modernist diplomatic structures throughout the world.[6] Discomfort with the International Style motivated the campaign. Jane C. Loeffler has explained that in the early 1950s the U.S. government stopped commissioning classical style buildings because it was the style preferred by Fascism and postwar Soviet totalitarianism. Instead the preference was for International Style diplomatic structures, which possessed a transparency and aura of progress that symbolized the open, democratic image that the U.S. government sought to present abroad. However, modernist structures were soon considered unsatisfactory diplomatically because they were jarringly different from the stone and brick of the traditional cities where they were built.[7] Rather than "good neighbors," the new embassies were perceived as insensitive ones.

To remedy this, Congress formed the FBO to enlist prominent American architects to design embassies that would better relate to the architecture of their host countries and express a friendlier, more engaged policy, especially important in recently decolonized countries in the Middle East, Africa, and Asia where the United States was engaged in a struggle for influence with the Soviet Union. The FBO developed an extensive review system where committees of professionals and members of the State Department critiqued projects. The FBO's leading architectural advisor was the respected modernist architect and dean of the MIT School of Architecture and Planning, Pietro Belluschi.

Edward Durell Stone set the new standard for FBO buildings with his U.S embassy in New Delhi (1954–59). Expressing his own turn against the International Style, Stone reconciled the traditional and the modern by covering the glass walls of his imposing, symmetrical structure with screens emulating the ornamental stone jali screens of Indian Mughal architecture (figure 2.2). The screens became the hallmark of the historically informed, decorative "romantic modernism" developed by Stone, Minoru Yamasaki, and others. Its decorative qualities were considered to have a more popular appeal than the relative austerity of the International Style.[8] Romantic modernism's ornamental and historicist qualities, especially its screens, appealed to Rudolph to a certain extent.

Rudolph's Amman project, though called an embassy, was technically a chancellery because it housed the offices of the U.S. diplomatic mission. Belluschi, who became a mentor for Rudolph, probably selected him for the commission.[9] He was a good choice because of his interest in regionalism and experience in building in a warm climate. Beyond the mandates of the FBO, the site for the new structure itself raised questions about the relationship between traditional and modern architecture that Rudolph would return to repeatedly. It was a rectangular plot occupied by three old houses accommodating the offices of the U.S. mission and ambassador's residence; these were slated for demolition upon completion of the new building. The sloping site overlooked the old city from the Jebal Amman, one of the city's original seven hills, which during the twentieth century developed into the preferred neighborhood for government buildings, foreign embassies, and the residences of the royal and wealthy.[10] Rudolph found engaging the old

2.1 Rudolph at the American Institute of Architects Convention, Boston (1954).

2.2 Edward Durell Stone, U.S. Embassy (New Delhi, 1954–59).

Challenging the International Style   34

city's irregular streets, gateways, small squares, vaulted stone houses, massive citadel walls, Roman ruins of temples and amphitheaters, and minarets, all visible from the hillside site.

Ancient architecture of the region probably inspired Rudolph as well. In nearby Jericho, a large eighth-century Umayyad palace with many courtyards was under excavation.[11] Though Rudolph frequently said at this time that "true regionalism was form, not materials," the warm tones of the local stone enchanted him, and he decided to use this material for the embassy. While Rudolph was remarkably consistent in his views overall, there were exceptions to every rule he made for himself.[12]

The project was the first for Rudolph that was large enough to warrant in-depth collaboration with other design professionals, such as landscape architects and mechanical and structural engineers.[13] To prepare the numerous drawings needed, five to six architects from other Sarasota offices were pressed into service from time to time to assist the two men employed by Rudolph.

Rudolph quickly developed a design for an imposing structure built of the local limestone. Raised on a podium

containing a garage, it was sheltered by an "umbrella" roof of open vaults. With its heavy, monumental appearance, the building departed markedly from Rudolph's delicate, lightweight Florida houses. A double stair with a formal quality recalling that of an ancient palace led to a forecourt (figure 2.3). To give the building an interior focus like that of the traditional courtyard houses of Amman, Rudolph organized the rectangular building around two interior courtyards (figure 2.4).

The most remarkable feature of Rudolph's embassy was the free-standing roof of barrel vaults that hovered on multistory stone piers a few feet above the main body of the building. The roof shaded the building like an immense parasol, admitting refreshing air currents into the gap between building and parasol. In addition to providing a natural solution for cooling the building (it would have no air-conditioning), the vaults exemplified how for Rudolph regionalism could be inspired by local sources and yet related to the broader vocabulary of modernism. They recalled those found in the traditional houses of Amman and also those found by the mid-1950s in postwar modernist buildings from Mexico to Europe, including, of

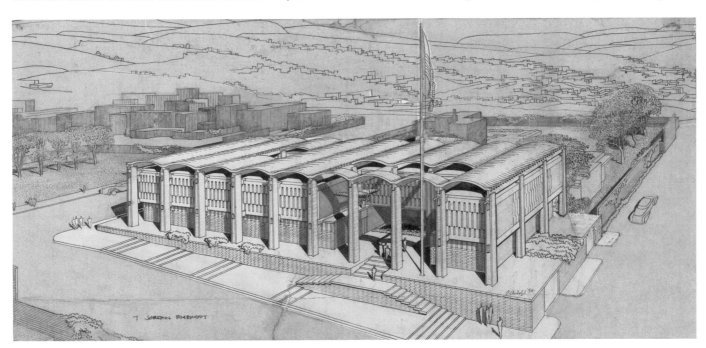

2.3 Rudolph, first scheme, U.S. Embassy (Amman, Jordan, project, 1954–58) .

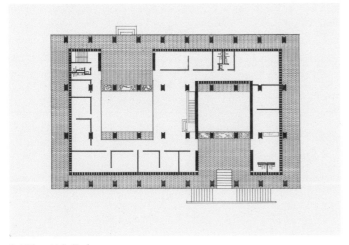

2.4 Plan, U.S. Embassy.

2.5 Rudolph, Hiss House (Sarasota, Florida, 1954).

course, Rudolph's own Hook House (Siesta Key, Florida, 1952–53). In Amman, the vaults of the embassy's umbrella were open frameworks of concrete staves that would have cast shifting shadows across the building, making a constantly changing pattern resembling ornament. Like the catenary roof, the umbrella was a concept developed by Le Corbusier, who employed it at his High Court at the new Indian capital of Chandigarh (1951–55).[14] Local sources also inspired the umbrella. Rudolph claimed that one model was the Middle Eastern "Arab tent" where one tent is sheltered beneath another to allow cooling air currents to circulate in between.[15]

Rudolph tested the umbrella concept in Sarasota, probably anxious that someone else might build one before he could, while he was designing the embassy. He sheltered the box-like dwelling and swimming pool of his Hiss "Umbrella" House (Sarasota, Florida, 1954) from the sun by means of a free-standing canopy made from local tomato plant staves (figure 2.5). One of Rudolph's most memorable, iconic Florida houses, it was the first project the architect built for Philip Hiss, the wealthy developer and modernist enthusiast who became Rudolph's most encouraging advocate and patron in Sarasota.

Building in Jordan was a challenge. Skilled construction labor was not available. In India, Le Corbusier had adroitly used local unskilled labor and traditional techniques, a choice that helped him to develop his profound monumentality of heavy concrete forms. Stone had also employed local labor to build his embassy in India. In Jordan, Rudolph learned from local contractors about an ancient Roman technique used in traditional buildings in Amman known as the *opus testaceum* in which concrete is poured between inner and outer limestone block walls to form massive supports. Like the umbrella roof, the *opus testaceum* was a practical, low-technology way to manage the building's temperature. Pierced only by narrow window slits like those in a castle, the eighteen-inch-thick walls of limestone and concrete would have kept interiors comfortable by absorbing heat during the day and releasing it at night.

Rudolph explained in a letter of 1954 to his friend the journalist Peter Blake that he employed the low-tech *opus testaceum* not merely out of necessity, but because he was moving toward aesthetics, forms, and techniques that would make his buildings part of the longer continuum of architecture. The narrow window slits also formed an ornamental pattern, making the walls a heavier version of the perforated screens that covered Stone's New Delhi embassy. Rudolph was proud that he had left behind the experimentation with new technology for which he had been known in Florida. Rudolph told Blake, "There is no structural innovation here at all."[16]

To give the limestone walls a textured and irregular quality similar to the ancient buildings of Jordan that he admired, Rudolph intended to have the local workers distress the walls using a bush hammer, a hammer with metal points on its end typically used to score masonry surfaces.[17] Marcel Breuer had already used the bush hammer to texture concrete walls in a few of his U.S. buildings.[18] Rudolph's employment of this surfacing technique for the embassy is particularly significant because it anticipated the famous corrugated or bush-hammered concrete he developed

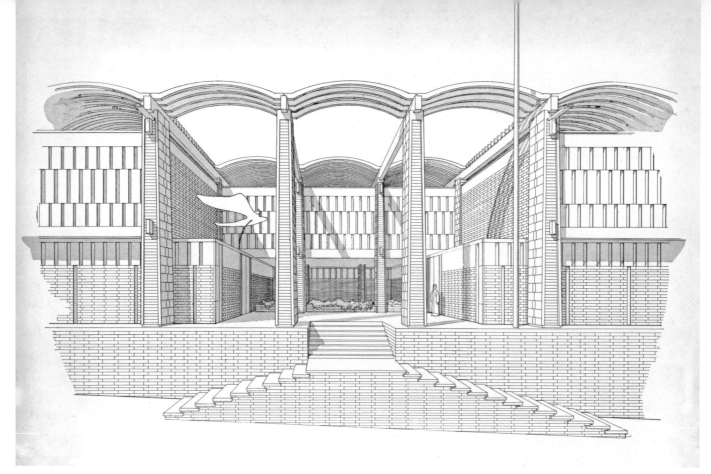

2.6 Entrance and eagle sculpture, U.S. Embassy.

for the Yale Art & Architecture Building (New Haven, Connecticut, 1958–63).[19]

Overall, the embassy would have had an ancient, formidable, and monumental character similar to the buildings of old Amman, which made it markedly different from most U.S. government buildings, most modern architecture of the time, and Rudolph's own projects in Florida. Thus the project was also notable as Rudolph's first attempt to revive heavyweight monumentality for modernism, an endeavor being pursued by Le Corbusier in France and India and by others. As Rudolph knew, European modernism had rejected monumentality after World War I as too traditional but reconsidered it in the early 1940s when Sigfried Giedion, Sert, and Fernand Leger proposed countering Fascist monumentality—the classically inspired buildings of Hitler's Germany and Mussolini's Italy—with a lightweight, transparent "new monumentality" that would draw people together.[20]

Rudolph was very conscious of the monumentality problem when he designed the embassy. In an article almost as significant for his thinking as his AIA speech, "The Six Determinants of Architectural Form" of 1956, Rudolph declared, "We must learn anew the meaning of monumentality." He outlined six broad determinants overlooked by modernism, ranging from site to the spirit of the times, but in what became a very important statement for him, Rudolph said, "Monumentality, symbolism, decoration, and so on—age old human needs—are among the architectural challenges that modern theory has brushed aside."[21]

Rudolph experimented with symbolic sculpture at the embassy (figure 2.6). Still drawn to sculpture as he had been during his youthful Alabama Polytechnic days,

Rudolph placed a large, awkwardly rendered eagle on a pedestal in the entrance forecourt to represent the United States. As Bert Brosmith, who ran Rudolph's Florida office, remembered, he was particularly interested in the eagle for his Amman project, drawing it himself many times and speaking of it as his "theoretical" gesture because it demonstrated how to return symbolism to architecture. In a letter to Blake, Rudolph also said that he increasingly looked for the "larger idea," or some type of theory, to guide his search for expression.[22] Like monumentality, symbolism was fraught with risks at this time. Traditional sculpture, especially of birds, had many negative associations with fascism and Soviet totalitarianism.

The appearance of Rudolph's embassy puzzled those unfamiliar with architecture's debates. Its monumentality particularly perplexed members of the military and the State Department who served on the FBO architectural advisory board. The FBO wanted diplomatic buildings that recalled the architecture of the region but that still seemed modern and representative of the open, democratic values of the United States. One committee member wondered if Rudolph was "out-Arabing the Arabs" by designing a structure that copied the older buildings of Amman too closely. Another thought it resembled "a fort, an outpost of the foreign legion" rather than a U.S. embassy.[23] As advisors to the FBO and Rudolph, Belluschi and Ralph Walker interceded regularly on Rudolph's behalf in what became a lengthy design and review process. Determined to express his own viewpoint, often careless about practicalities, and perhaps daunted by the prospect of his first large-scale building, Rudolph also made the project difficult because he disregarded many of its requirements, including those for

2.7 Embassy model with site's existing traditional buildings.

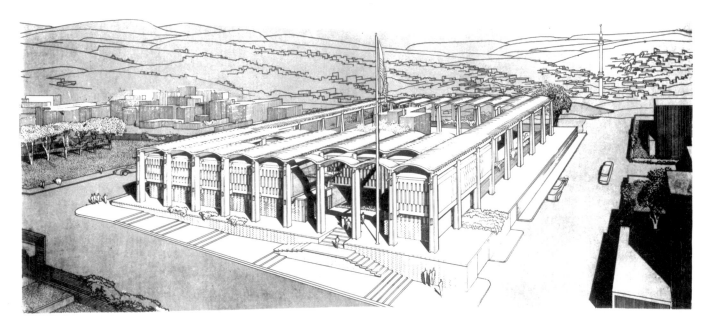

2.8 Late scheme, U.S. Embassy.

safety and security. Though he appeared confident, he was relentlessly self-critical of his own work, frequently changing course in already well developed schemes. Such apparent indecisiveness, or fecklessness, would be a continuing problem for Rudolph and his relationships with clients during the 1950s.

A significant change to the project occurred late in 1956 when the FBO decided to economize by incorporating into the complex, rather than demolishing, the three existing traditional houses on the site (figure 2.7). In a bold gesture that tied new and old together, Rudolph extended the canopy along the edges of the site, keeping the old houses intact and in effect transforming a solitary building into a compound. Small courtyards and fountains formed from the irregular spaces in between old and new recalled the twisting streets of the old city and the courtyards of its traditional palaces and houses—a reflection of Rudolph's

developing interest in urbanism (figure 2.8). Linking together new and old became a consistent theme of his large projects of the 1950s.

Though other U.S. diplomatic projects of this time were comparable, such as Sert's Baghdad embassy (1955–59), the Athens embassy (1956–59) by Walter Gropius and his firm The Architects' Collaborative (TAC), and Louis Kahn's consulate for Luanda, Angola (project, 1959–61), Rudolph's Amman structure was notable in its anticipation of directions that would not fully emerge in his own work or in modernism as a whole until the early 1960s, principally the heaviness of monumentality associated with brutalist architecture. The ancient building techniques, local materials, and direct engagement with traditional buildings on the site were also novel, sensitive for the time, and suggestive of a new direction for regionalism.

2.9 Rudolph, Jewett Arts Center, Wellesley College (Wellesley, Massachusetts, 1955–58).

Construction was set to commence in 1958 when a widespread outbreak of political unrest throughout the Middle East put the project on hold; Rudolph's embassy was never built. Given the uneasiness some advisory committee members had about the project, sidelining the embassy may have been the FBO's way of "being kind" to Rudolph, as Loeffler has suggested. Ironically, by the time a new U.S. embassy for Jordan was completed in 1992, security concerns made the massive stone building much more like "a fort, an outpost of the foreign legion" than Rudolph's scheme had ever been.[24]

The Jewett Arts Center

Rudolph elaborated on one of the primary themes explored in the embassy, relating old to new, in his first large-scale completed building, the Mary Cooper Jewett Arts Center at Wellesley College (Wellesley, Massachusetts, 1955–58). The arts center and the embassy were developed in parallel. Located in a Boston suburb on a beautiful campus of rolling hills designed by the Olmsted firm of landscape architects, Wellesley College is one of the foremost institutions of higher learning for women in the United States. Rudolph's building relates to a quadrangle of Collegiate Gothic buildings; its sun-protecting screens were inspired by the delicate forms of nearby windows (and Stone's screens), making this the architect's essay in romantic modernism. An elaborately choreographed

series of outdoor plazas and stairs, like those found in older European cities, suggests Rudolph's interest in urbanism (figure 2.9). Recognizing Rudolph's unusually sensitive response to architecture that most of his colleagues would have disdained as too traditional, James Marston Fitch, a key proponent for historic preservation during the postwar decades, said that architects "who are dropping their new buildings into old campuses with all the destructive power and malice of a bomb blast, could learn a lesson from Paul Rudolph at Wellesley."[25]

The Jewett Center was Rudolph's entry into academic architecture, which became a mainstay of his practice. A relatively new building type for higher learning, centers for the fine and performing arts proliferated across postwar American campuses. They were built to encourage students to study the arts, making them competitive with the sciences and technology, the fastest growing fields in higher education. The arts centers were also bulwarks against mass culture in the form of television and film. Further, arts centers that invoked archetypal urban forms became a way for architects to reassert the importance of the traditional city, albeit often in the incongruously low-density settings of Arcadian American campuses such as Wellesley's.

The college's administration and the building's donors, the family of Mary Cooper Jewett, the alumna for whom it was named, specified a structure with facilities for theater, music, studio art, and art history in the hope that these disciplines would enrich one another. Wellesley College art historian John McAndrew, a former MoMA curator familiar with Rudolph's work in Sarasota and the head of the college's building committee, selected Rudolph over better-known and more experienced architects, including Saarinen, Stone, and Hugh Stubbins.[26]

Rudolph had much assistance in designing the Jewett Center. Studies for the hillside site were conducted by architecture students from Yale, where Rudolph was serving as a visiting critic. Drawing on their research, Rudolph produced a detailed site plan showing how his building would form a new center for the campus, adjacent to its existing Collegiate Gothic administration buildings and overlooking the campus lake (figure 2.10). The landscape plan for the immediate area around the building was by Boston's Sasaki & Novak, which also was working on Rudolph's embassy project.

Because the project was larger and more complex than anything he had yet built or that his small Sarasota office could execute, Rudolph collaborated with the experienced Boston firm of Anderson, Beckwith, and Haible. Rudolph was credited as the project's designer; he produced the various schemes, including presentation drawings and a site model, with the help of three draftsmen in a small office he set up in Cambridge. Five draftsmen from Anderson,

Beckwith, and Haible translated Rudolph's plans into working drawings and specifications for construction. The firm's principals, Herbert Beckwith and Lawrence Anderson, also regularly met with Rudolph.[27]

In addition to his position at Yale, Rudolph taught at the Harvard Graduate School of Design (GSD) and at MIT in 1954 and 1955 and remained in Cambridge afterward because it was convenient to Wellesley. He maintained and visited his Sarasota office but preferred the collegiality of Cambridge and rented an apartment and office space near Harvard Square, at 26 Church Street. He kept in touch with Gropius and shared his office space with Serge Chermayeff, who was teaching at Harvard and had been profiled in Rudolph's special Gropius tribute issue of *L'Architecture d'aujourd'hui*. Rudolph also befriended and helped others who, like himself, were on the rise. He regularly discussed Le Corbusier's Chandigarh projects over breakfast with the Japanese architect Fumihiko Maki, who was teaching at the GSD in 1955.[28]

Rudolph and Philip Johnson, a regular visitor from New York, spent long hours in a Harvard Square Chinese restaurant giving each other advice about their careers. Seeing independence and individuality as more important than anything else for an architect, Rudolph advised Johnson

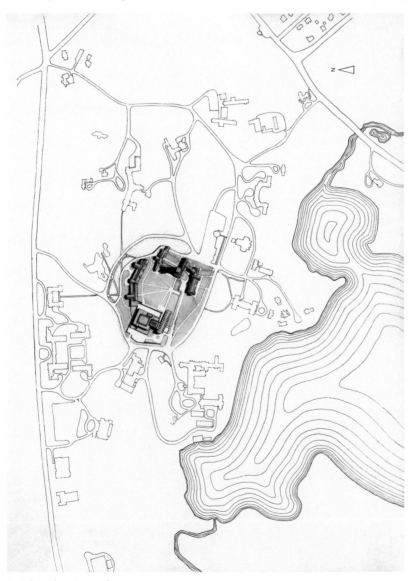

2.10 Site plan, Jewett Center.

2.11 Model, Jewett Center.

2.12 Venetian scheme for Jewett Center (c. 1955).

that he would never be remembered as anything more than Mies's underling if he collaborated with him on the Seagram Building (New York, 1954–58); Johnson did not take Rudolph's advice. Another topic was whether a position as an administrator or faculty member in an architecture school would help Rudolph's career. In addition, they also gossiped about colleagues, relishing news about the architecture department at their alma mater, Harvard. They frequently questioned William Morgan, a GSD student employed in Rudolph's office, about Dean Josep Lluís Sert. They found Sert's direction of the GSD autocratic, but his thinking about urbanism interesting.[29] In fact, this thinking would prove to be essential in Rudolph's conceptualization of the Wellesley project.

At Harvard under Sert and in the discipline as a whole, urbanism, formerly known as city planning, assumed a new importance after World War II. The reconstruction of war-torn and decaying cities was beginning just as suburbanization and decentralization were coming to be understood as detrimental. Elaborating on the communal aspect of the new monumentality, Sert and his fellow members of CIAM found a new prototype for urbanism in the dense, old centers of traditional cities, which they called "cores." They admired the cores, especially Italian ones, as strongholds of communal values and traditional culture. At CIAM 8 (the eighth meeting of the CIAM organization) in Hoddesdon, England, in 1951, Sert called for the separation of vehicles and pedestrians into distinct zones, a recommendation widely followed, and the building of urban spaces modeled on the piazzas of the past. Johnson attended the conference and talked about the qualities of Venetian piazzas. Rudolph could have encountered the same ideas at the first Harvard Urban Design Conference, organized by Sert in 1956.[30]

After some false starts because of changes that doubled the building in size, Rudolph's Jewett Center became an experiment in urban-inspired design, reflecting the discourse of the time and particularly his admiration for Italian cities. Rudolph decided to make his building the third side of an uncompleted quadrangle of Collegiate Gothic buildings by the firm of Klauder and Day; the fourth side was open to views of Wellesley's lake below (figure 2.11). In Rudolph's conception, the quadrangle became a new communal space for the campus, like a piazza, and its Gothic bell tower a campanile. A low building adjoined by a tower and piazza became one of Rudolph's preferred configurations, appearing repeatedly in his designs for large-scale complexes, even in his final skyscraper projects in Asia of the 1980s.

Rudolph's admiration for Italian cities was evident in numerous aspects of his schemes for the Jewett Center. Urbanistically, the radiating pathways he traced on the quadrangle recalled the fan-like pattern of the famous piazza in Siena, by far Rudolph's favorite. Topographically, Rudolph built his arts center into the slope of the existing hill, with brick retaining walls giving it a somewhat fortified air, like that of a citadel or Italian hill town. Formally, Rudolph initially conceived of the Jewett Center as a palazzo with a startling resemblance to Venice's fifteenth-century Doge's Palace, a building he greatly admired for its urban and decorative qualities (figure 2.12). (He had visited Venice while returning from Jordan that year.) Rudolph believed that the historic forms of the Italian city could serve as

models for contemporary urbanism and architecture. As for decoration, Rudolph covered his building with mosaic-like diapered patterning, similar to the distinctive exterior of the Doge's Palace, and he adorned it with poured concrete moldings as elaborate as those of Wellesley's neighboring Collegiate Gothic buildings.

Although the Venetian allusions may have seemed incongruous, Vincent Scully noted at the time that American architects, including Rudolph, increasingly employed the palazzo model in suburban American settings in order to bring "urbanity to the country" and therefore counter suburban decentralization.[31] However, the scheme inspired by the Doge's Palace puzzled Rudolph's Wellesley clients, who expected a more recognizably modern design. From that point on, the project became as difficult for Rudolph as the embassy project had been. In subsequent revisions, Rudolph attempted to make his allusions to the Doge's Palace more abstract; these efforts transformed the building into a disquisition about symbolism, decoration, and structure that drew on long-standing and new ideas from architectural discourse. Examining successive schemes shows how Rudolph attempted to give the project a theoretical basis. Finding theories to inform his architecture and for modernism as a whole was an endeavor Rudolph pursued in other projects that he was ambivalent about. He recognized the need for intellectually grounded and reasoned guiding principles but preferred responding to problems intuitively.

To preserve some resemblance to the Doge's Palace, Rudolph may have again turned for inspiration to Viollet-le-Duc, the great proponent of structural rationalism who showed how structure could be symbolic and decorative. In a way that would have appealed to Rudolph, Viollet-le-Duc explained how structure could be rational without being merely functional. He had admired the Doge's Palace as a particularly felicitous combination of structure and decoration that could serve as a model for the architecture of his day. In a diagram, he distilled the palazzo to its very essence: a series of Y-shaped supports derived from the lacy arcade of pointed arches at the base of the building (figure 2.13).[32]

Abstracting his design as Viollet-le-Duc had, Rudolph covered the facades of his next scheme for the Jewett Center with a series of large-scale, Y-shaped brick forms (figure 2.14). Applied externally like decoration, they did not constitute the building's structure but expressed it as what Rudolph called "symbols of structure." Rudolph often talked about this concept at the time. In his AIA talk of 1954, Rudolph said that a traditional Japanese house that had been constructed in the garden of MoMA that same year was admirable because "the actual structure is hidden and we are presented with a system of *symbols of structure* [Rudolph's italics]."[33] A large beam in the interior of the Japanese house appeared to support the ceiling but in fact was nonstructural. Present for aesthetic reasons, it was intended to symbolize the actual structure concealed in the ceiling above.

Rudolph borrowed the term "symbols of structure" from the influential architect and theorist Matthew Nowicki who in the early 1950s reiterated Viollet-le-Duc's ideas about structural rationalism when he said that not every element in a building had to be functional. Instead modern buildings

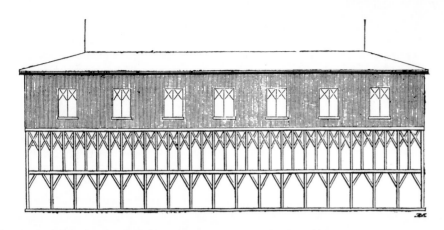

2.13 Eugène-Emmanuel Viollet-le-Duc, "Idea of the Venetian Palace" (1872).

2.14 "Symbols of structure" scheme, Jewett Center (c. 1955).

2.15 Late scheme, Jewett Center.

2.16 Sunscreens, Jewett Center.

could have elements that were symbols of structure, that expressed the theoretical, cultural, and historical meanings of construction in a symbolic and ornamental manner. In a way that seemed to anticipate Mies's famous use of the I-beam in a decorative fashion at the Seagram Building, Nowicki said in 1951, "The symbolic meaning of a support has also been rediscovered, and a steel column is used frankly as a symbol of structure even when it is not part of the structure itself."[34] Drawing on both Viollet-le-Duc's and Nowicki's thinking in this way, Rudolph's brick forms demonstrated a more sophisticated approach to the problems of symbolism than had the eagle in the entranceway of the Amman embassy.

The Y-forms and these concepts perplexed Rudolph's Wellesley clients as much as the original Doge's Palace–inspired scheme. Rudolph's decorative programs for the elevations struck some as "fussy" and overly ornamental in a way that violated the norms of good taste, which was always an issue at the class-conscious, elite college.[35] Rudolph discovered that institutional clients were not as open to his continuous experimentation as were residential clients in Sarasota, who allowed him to do much as he liked when designing a small guesthouse.

After prolonged revisions, Rudolph finally arrived at a solution acceptable to both him and his clients for the Jewett Center. He covered the art wing with light aluminum screens like those popularized by Stone at his New Delhi embassy, then at their most popular (figure 2.15).[36] Far more delicate and lightweight than Stone's screens, each of Rudolph's steel frames held hundreds of "vanes" of aluminum whose hand-sized scale related to the scale of the observer (figure 2.16). Deployed to control glare, reflection, sunlight, and heat, the screens looked like a series of giant, independent exoskeleton-like frames wrapped around the building. Rudolph derived their proportions from the dimensions of the window tracery of the neighboring Collegiate Gothic buildings, thus establishing a relationship between old and new largely based on scale. Echoing the character of the nearby ornament in modern terms, the screens were painted to match the limestone of the existing buildings. They were remarkably expressive structures that Rudolph referred to as "built-in ivy."[37] Again demonstrating the architect's fascination with effects of sun and shadow, they cast a rich play of shifting shadows across the facade throughout the course of the day, almost resembling the effect of sun and wind rippling across the ivy on nearby structures.

Though indisputably modern in appearance, the many different parts, spatial sequences, and decorative qualities of the completed Jewett Center recalled buildings that had grown over time in stages, like so many older buildings in Italy. Each wing had a distinct character and purpose (figure 2.17). The prominent four-story rectangular art wing held classrooms, faculty offices, studios, and an art library. It was crowned by pyramidal skylights that lit the top floor

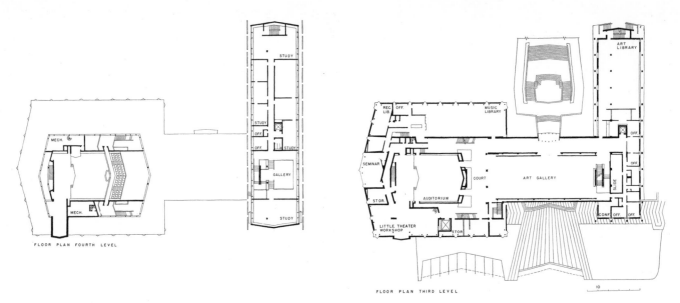

FLOOR PLAN FOURTH LEVEL

FLOOR PLAN THIRD LEVEL

2.17 Plan, Jewett Center.

2.18 Gallery, art wing, Jewett Center.

2.19 Staircase, Jewett Center.

art studios and echoed the pinnacles of the nearby bell tower. The multistory gallery, or sculpture court, in the art wing was a high, lofty space where student art could be displayed; a central seating area was adorned with sculpture from Wellesley's art collection and an ancient mosaic floor (figure 2.18). The art gallery, which was really the college's museum, connected the art wing to the wing for theater and music, which had an auditorium, music library, and practice rooms.

Rudolph gave the different-sized wings coherence by modeling the building as a whole on a gateway, which defined an elaborate outdoor spatial sequence. Rudolph invoked the gate archetype repeatedly, describing its possibilities for urban planning in his AIA talk. He had said, "Why do buildings always have to flank the street? Why can they not sometimes be placed over the street, thereby forming an enclosure and a focal point?"[38] Lines incised in the pavement led from the entrance plaza into a darkened passageway beneath the art gallery (the top of the gateway). From there, the pedestrian ascended an elaborate staircase, coming into the light of the interior courtyard and ultimately aligning with the Collegiate Gothic tower (figure 2.19). Rudolph had called for stimulating progressions deriving from those found in Italian cities in his AIA talk: "We need sequences of space which arouse one's curiosity, give a sense of anticipation, which beckon and impel us to rush forward to find that releasing space which dominates, which climaxes and acts as a magnet, and gives direction. For

instance, the Duomo in Florence is a magnet which dominates the whole city and orientates one."[39] Rudolph thought the bell tower at Wellesley could act as a similar magnet.

Most critics and fellow architects appreciated Rudolph's Jewett Center when it was completed in 1958, seeing it as another example of the romantic modernism of Stone and Yamasaki. Its decorative and urban qualities were understood to be alternatives to the prevailing International Style. Gerhard Kallmann said the screens projecting dynamically from beyond the ends of the building indicated the emergence of a new "action architecture" that was the architectural equivalent of action painting, or abstract expressionism.[40]

For Rudolph, however, the project had been a difficult one. His attempts to develop appropriate urban forms and decoration for Wellesley had led him down many different avenues, causing him misgivings even before the Jewett Center was completed. The transition from small houses to large buildings was proving to be tricky.

2.20 Rudolph, Blue Cross and Blue Shield Building (BC-BS) (Boston, 1957–60).

Blue Cross and Blue Shield Building

Rudolph's Blue Cross and Blue Shield Insurance Building (BC-BS) in Boston (1957–60) was his most direct challenge in the 1950s to the International Style.[41] Rudolph received the commission as a result of his work at Wellesley College. A member of the Jewett Center's building committee, the Boston investor Alexander C. Forbes, was also a trustee and head of the building committee for the Blue Cross and Blue Shield Insurance company. Though it is not as well remembered as other buildings by Rudolph, it was important for him because it was a tall building—a building type he found compelling.

Rudolph forthrightly challenged the hegemony of the glass curtain wall with the BC-BS Building. He wove together the building's structure and its heating and cooling systems into a basket-like exterior framework supported at its base by columns with Y-shaped capitals; these recalled the "symbols of structure" from an early scheme for the Jewett Center and Viollet-le-Duc's diagram of the Doge's Palace in turn (fig 2.20). The leaders of architectural discourse derided the glass curtain wall even as it had become the hallmark of the International Style in buildings such as the United Nations Secretariat Building (Harrison, Abramovitz and others, New York, 1948–52), Lever House (Skidmore, Owings, & Merrill, New York, 1951–52), and the Seagram Building (1954–58).[42] In lesser hands, the curtain wall had degenerated. Developers demolished blocks of masonry apartment houses along New York's Park Avenue and replaced them with office buildings sheathed in cheaper versions of Lever House's fine curtain walls, quickly creating a monotonous effect. Lewis Mumford lamented the resulting loss of "coherence and civic dignity" along the avenue and in midtown, and others who valued a humanism based on the individual, such as Scully, expressed uneasiness about the alienation that such repetition might induce.[43] "The Monotonous Curtain Wall," an article in *Architectural Forum* in 1959, pointedly summed up the negative consensus that was forming: "The standard curtain wall—perhaps America's single, most important building innovation in the past decade or so—is fast becoming, in the hands of less-than-sensitive architects and manufacturers, one of the most irritating eyesores on the U.S. scene."[44]

Consequently, the period saw a revived interest in Louis Sullivan. His seminal article "The Tall Office Building Artistically Considered" (1896) explained how a "sterile pile" of material could become a "proud and soaring thing" in part by articulating and adorning its structural systems with elaborate ornament. Sullivan was celebrated as the forefather of an American approach to modernism that emphasized individuality, and his pioneering development of the tall building and creation of his own ornamental systems would have appealed to Rudolph.

The BC-BS Building site was on Federal Street, near Boston's small financial district; no new structures had been constructed in the area since the stock market crash of 1929. Like many of its competitors, Blue Cross and Blue Shield of Massachusetts had considered moving to the suburbs, but after much study had elected to stay in the city for tax benefits, relatively inexpensive real estate, and ease of staffing. The building was also an important investment for the business, since insurance companies were prohibited from investing in the stock market. By the standards of the day, the Massachusetts headquarters would not be that large since the company had only a thousand employees. The majority were unmarried, city-dwelling women who performed clerical tasks.[45]

Dating back to colonial times, the neighborhood was about the closest Rudolph could have come in the United States to the irregular streets and dense urbanism of the Italian and Middle Eastern cities he admired. The narrow and irregular downtown byways offered the opportunity to create a building that was expressive rather than objective or neutral. In contrast to the embassy project or the Jewett Center, Rudolph had little trouble arriving at a design for the BC-BS Building. Beginning in 1957, he developed various schemes; the design he settled on was completed much as he had envisioned it by 1960.

As was typical for office buildings of the time, Rudolph placed a square surrounded by benches in front of the building. The relatively low cost of real estate in this district of Boston meant that leaving a portion of the site not built upon was not as extravagant a gesture as it was when Mies used a third of the expensive Seagram Building site for a plaza. Though owned by Blue Cross and Blue Shield, the plaza was a public space that brought the people of the city together. Raised on a podium that contained services and the employee cafeteria, the open area was also a quiet space slightly removed from the activity of the street. Skylights

2.21 BBPR, Torre Velasca (Milan, Italy, 1956–58).

2.22 Base and plaza, BC-BS Building.

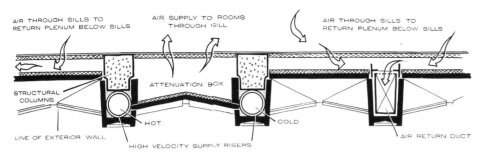

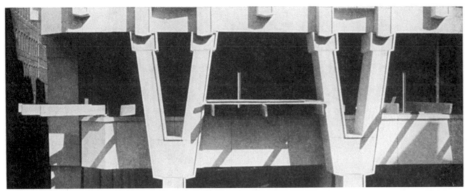

2.23 Systems and structure, BC-BS Building.

for the cafeteria—a group of curiously pyramidal crystalline forms that echoed the pinnacled skylights at Wellesley—punctuated the plaza.

As he had been at Wellesley, Rudolph was especially eager to forge relationships between new and existing structures to create discernible links to the past. He based the length and width of the BC-BS Building's 4-by-7-foot windows on the dimensions of existing apertures in nearby buildings. Unlike horizontally oriented modernist ribbon windows or flat curtain walls, these windows were vertically disposed (like a traditional window) and deeply recessed within the structure's framework. They formed a modular system derived from particular circumstances rather than from dimensions specified by a manufacturer, as was the case with many mass-produced curtain walls. For the exterior, Rudolph chose precast concrete panels with a stone aggregate to give his building a texture and solid appearance similar to the surrounding masonry buildings.

Rudolph was not the only one attempting to develop such relationships between new and old at this time. Several new American towers in the late 1950s suggested more traditional alternatives for the office building, even some by the International Style's greatest popularizer, Skidmore, Owings & Merrill.[46] If there was one tall building that especially inspired Rudolph, it was probably one from abroad: BBPR's Torre Velasca in Milan (1956–58) (figure 2.21). The tower exemplified the Italian neoliberty style, a term used derisively by the British critic Reyner Banham to describe what he considered the reactionary work of postwar Italian architects who were invoking, often in direct ways, historical forms inspired by the traditional architecture and urbanism of Italy.[47]

There is little evidence of direct contact between Rudolph and the members of BBPR, though the American architect probably met Ernesto Rogers and Enrico Peressutti when they taught at and visited American architecture schools where he taught—Princeton for example, during the 1950s. What is certain is that Rudolph and

BBPR shared many concerns. With its highly articulated reinforced-concrete framework and cast-in-place and pre-cast infill panels, the Torre Velasca was another experiment in structure and urbanism that polemicized against the architectural status quo and the typical glass-sheathed sky-scraper. It is notable that the almost muscular expression of the structural framework of Rudolph's BC-BS Building greatly resembled the Torre Velasca's external supports. In a way unusual for a postwar tall building, the lower twenty stories of the Milanese tower were devoted to offices and the upper six to apartments; the upper portion was a wider volume carried by prominent external brackets and topped by a hipped roof and chimneys.

The top-heavy mushroom-shaped profile of Torre Velasca resembled the outline of a traditional palazzo or townhouse with galleries projecting from its upper floors. Milan's Sforza Castle was said to be one of the inspirations for the tower as well. The building reflected BBPR's agenda of integrating modern architecture into the historical continuity of Italian cities. Rogers articulated this position very clearly when he said, "To consider the context, means to consider history."[48] There were numerous lessons to be learned from the Milanese structure. As Gerhard Kallmann observed, "The more closely the tower is studied, the more apparent its complex dialectic becomes—between function and form, construction and ornament, new technology and ancient forms."[49]

With the BC-BS Building, Rudolph explored these dialectics as well. He wove together mechanical and structural elements in a way that is most evident in the piers attached to the exterior (figure 2.22). Spaced at intervals of five feet, Rudolph's piers rose ten stories above the Y-shaped columns at the base to culminate in an opaque thirteenth-floor crown that housed the mechanical units. Though the piers appeared to be load-bearing elements, in fact they were not structural at all but fulfilled the concept of "symbols of structure." The hollow piers were simply attached to the facade rather like Mies's I-beam mullions at the Seagram

51

Building. However, Rudolph's piers also contained heating and cooling ductwork. In his AIA talk, Rudolph had speculated about whether ductwork could take on more organic and decorative qualities to become "a veritable tree inside, or a vine climbing over the façade."[50] Rudolph seemed to understand that the wall was no longer the stable entity of the past or the mere system of cladding of the International Style, but rather was a membrane of structure and meaning, more intricate than the screens of the Jewett Center and similar to the complexities perceived by Kallmann at the Torre Velasca.

In an article about innovative mechanical engineering, *Progressive Architecture* explained with a diagram how the heating, ventilation, and air-conditioning system worked at the BC-BS Building (figure 2.23).[51] On each floor, hot and cold air from supply risers in the exterior piers mixed in an attenuation box located between the interior building columns and expressed on the exterior. Interior panels made the mechanicals accessible. Air-return ducts were likewise placed within exterior piers. This difference was marked on the exterior: every third pier—those containing the air-return ducts—originated from a point higher than its neighbors. The dummy piers also helped emphasize the vertical aspect of the building, its "loftiness," as Sullivan would have referred to it. Exaggerating the vertical was important to Rudolph, since the thirteen-story building was short for the "tall building" type. Rudolph may also have been inspired by Sullivan himself, who had added false piers to the facades of his Guaranty Building (Buffalo, New York, 1894–95) to emphasize its vertical extension. The BC-BS and Guaranty Buildings were even the same height.

Though externally the facade employed the same grammar from bottom to top to create a uniform grid, the internal systems were not entirely consistent. Some pressure was taken off the air-conditioning apparatus by providing the eleventh and twelfth floors with a direct connection to the rooftop mechanicals. Thus the attenuation boxes on these floors were purely sculptural.[52] Explaining how the functional could become aesthetic, Rudolph had said in his AIA talk, "If we are to spend 60% of our budget on mechanical equipment we should derive more than physical comfort from it. Visual exploitation of it may become the sculpture of our time."[53] Such subtleties indicate that Rudolph had moved beyond a direct, unmediated representation of structure, which many thought was typical of his early Florida work, to an architecture that placed greater value on symbolism, aesthetics, and representation, thus returning the concept of structural rationalism to its nineteenth-century origins, as Nowicki had anticipated.

To enhance the sculptural qualities of the external piers and boxes, Rudolph clad them with a precast concrete made with a white quartz aggregate known by the trade name Mo-Sai. It was another of his experiments with materials, and it was further indication of a move away from the steel and glass of the International Style to a more malleable, plastic material. Rudolph had considered using Mo-Sai for the moldings and pillars in his Venetian-inspired scheme for Wellesley. The substance glittered in the sun and aged like traditional masonry. Free of the striations and marks of construction found in Le Corbusier's monolithic concrete forms, the precast cladding had a precision and elegance that resembled traditional ashlar (figure 2.24). The sparkling, white quartz aggregate, though inexpensive, created an aura of richness—in its more elaborate expression and simply by looking expensive—that was in keeping with Rudolph's attempts to engender these qualities in modernism.[54]

The BC-BS Building's novel structural framework created opportunities for spatial innovation. The office floors inside were desirable and flexible "open plans" almost entirely free of the internal columns that obstructed most office space in tall buildings (figure 2.25). Four concrete piers in the middle of the floors and an adjacent compact service core housing

2.24 Mo-Sai cladding, BC-BS Building.

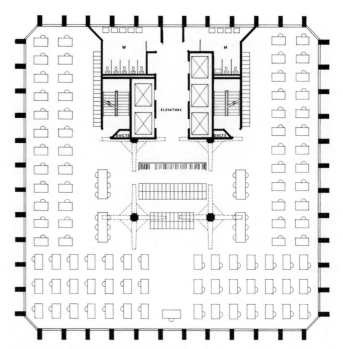

2.25 Typical floor plan, BC-BS Building.

Challenging the International Style

2.26 Cafeteria, BC-BS Building.

elevators and stairs within load-bearing reinforced-concrete walls provided additional support for each concrete floor. Noted structural engineer Paul Weidlinger devised this arrangement for the BC-BS Building; he formulated something similar for Eero Saarinen's headquarters for the Columbia Broadcasting System (New York, 1960–65), but it did not become standard practice.

Working for the first time with an interior designer, Bill Bagnall from the firm Contract Interiors, Rudolph achieved a cohesive set of interiors at BC-BS whose bold qualities complemented the expressive architecture of the building. Rudolph and Bagnall, who would collaborate on several projects, developed diagonally based geometries for the lighting systems and paving of the lobby, offices, and cafeteria of the building.[55]

The lobby was paved with a zigzagging pattern of bluestone that extended onto the outdoor plaza. The cafeteria aligned with Rudolph's concept of urban space, in which every detail was intended to enhance or alter the emotions of the user, and also with his dictum "we need caves as well as goldfish bowls." The subterranean cafeteria was clearly a cave that contrasted with the fishbowl-like glass-walled lobby above (figure 2.26). The cafeteria skylights—the unusual pyramids erupting into the plaza—were integrated into a ceiling whose diamond-shaped structural concrete ribs housed an elaborate system of artificial lighting. The lighting could be adjusted to create different moods, which was convenient in a space that could also be used as an auditorium or theater. Rudolph had admired how Johnson had achieved similar lighting effects with a dimmer in the 1953 renovation of the guesthouse bedroom at his Glass House.[56] The diamond pattern of the ceiling also mirrored the zigzagging pavement of the plaza above. Rudolph and Bagnall selected for the ceiling a bold shade of red whose hue changed as the lighting was adjusted (figure 2.27). Red surfaces were likewise used to punctuate the predominantly white and brown interiors elsewhere in the building.

Somewhat awkward and ungainly and therefore truly an adolescent effort, the completed BC-BS Building was anything but neutral, anonymous, or monotonous—qualities that Rudolph and some of his contemporaries associated with the International Style. From the sculpted quality of its exterior to the colorful geometry of its interiors, Rudolph showed how a new level of expression could create a more nuanced relationship between the tall building and the existing city. The innovative integration of services and structure and the almost barrier-free interiors at BC-BS offered new models for the office building.

Nevertheless, the desire to experiment often outweighed practicality for Rudolph, as it had in Sarasota. In the BC-BS Building, moving the services to the exterior had its drawbacks. Though loss of heat was not of great concern when fuel was inexpensive in the 1960s, heating ducts attached to the perimeter lost warmth and were difficult to repair despite access panels. Yet the building signaled that by the late 1950s, the themes that guided Rudolph's search for expression had coalesced, and he appeared to be at the forefront of practically every new development for modernism. He was ever eager for new projects and opportunities that would advance his architecture and career, and he found these at Yale University.

2.27 Ceiling detail, cafeteria, BC-BS Building.

Three
Humanism, Yale, and New Haven

For some time, Rudolph had considered how an academic appointment could make him better known and advance his career. For most of the 1950s, he taught at architecture schools across the country, where his pedagogical skills and forthright manner were admired. Several institutions considered him for an administrative position, and in 1958 Yale University appointed Rudolph chairman of its Department of Architecture. His seven-year tenure secured his place in the front ranks of his profession and brought him even greater attention in the architectural and popular press as the young maverick who was transforming modernism. Consequently the position led to many new commissions, notably ones for Yale and for the city of New Haven that were the most significant of his career.

Rudolph, in turn, transformed Yale's Department of Architecture. Galvanized by his energy and leadership, by the early 1960s it became one of the most important places in the world to study architecture, attracting students who became the profession's leaders over the next decades, including Charles Gwathmey, Robert A. M. Stern, Norman Foster, and Richard Rogers. To raise the level of architectural discourse at Yale, Rudolph invited guest critics and lecturers from around the country and abroad, especially Britain, such as James Stirling and the proponents of the "New Brutalism," Alison and Peter Smithson.

Yale extolled individuality, action, diverse expression, and aesthetics in ways that were compatible with Rudolph's existing beliefs. During his years at the school, his rhetoric and architecture took on a new grandiosity reflecting the position of the university's president, A. Whitney Griswold, who upheld humanism as the means for energizing American society and education. A figure just as influential for Rudolph at Yale, architectural historian Vincent Scully, believed in a comparable way that humanism could reinvigorate modernism.

Griswold became Rudolph's greatest patron and supporter. He commissioned buildings by the architect and others that made the campus an important site for postwar American architecture. New Haven mayor Richard C. Lee also involved Rudolph in the city's nationally acclaimed urban renewal efforts. These powerful patrons gave Rudolph opportunities to continue his explorations of monumentality, urbanism, symbolism, and decoration, as was evident in his projects for the city and university, including a parking garage, a laboratory, and student housing. The New Haven apartment and office Rudolph completed for himself and his firm by 1961 celebrated his successes. The culmination of these investigations would be the Yale Art & Architecture Building (A & A) (1958–63).

Yale

Rudolph first came to Yale as a visiting critic in the fall of 1955; he taught studio projects based on his own works. Students liked his energetic teaching style and admired his innovative Florida houses. He gave them his own commissions—such as the Jewett Center, the BC-BS Building, and even a project for a roadside Tastee-Freez ice cream stand based on one he had completed in Sarasota (1954–55)—as studio problems. Redolent of the mass culture decried by many of his senior colleagues and sometimes by Rudolph as well, the ice cream counter was an unusual choice for a student project and one of the typically brash gestures calculated to add luster to his reputation as a young maverick.[1]

Yale proved stimulating for Rudolph in part because the architecture department was part of a larger school of art and architecture with departments and programs for art, sculpture, and graphic design. Among its better-known faculty were Josef Albers, who chaired the art department; Alvin Eisenman of the graphic design program; and Christopher Tunnard, director of the city planning program, which was part of the architecture department. Rudolph formed friendships with some of the graduate students and young instructors, including the sculptor Robert Engman. Scully, a member of the art history faculty, was a regular presence in the architecture department.

Though well established, Yale's Department of Architecture was in disarray when Rudolph arrived.[2] To improve its standing, the school considered many of the most important modernist architects of the day—including Philip Johnson and Louis Kahn, who both were already affiliated with the department—in its search for a new chairman.[3] Powerful advocates at Yale supported Rudolph for the appointment. Scully, who was on the search committee, had referred to Rudolph's work favorably in some of his articles. Eero Saarinen, an admirer of Rudolph's who was Griswold's advisor on architecture, and the campus's master planner, probably recommended Rudolph for the appointment as well.[4] Thirty-nine years old at the time, Rudolph possessed youthfulness, skill at teaching, vigor, and a growing reputation, all of which made him the most attractive candidate.

Humanism

Griswold's and Scully's humanism inspired Rudolph greatly, elevating his rhetoric and giving direction to his search for expression. The term "humanism" had many meanings. Modernist architects had long talked about "humanizing" modernism, or bringing qualities to it that would allow humans to relate to it. In the 1930s, natural materials, such as wood and stone, humanized modernism and gave it a regional quality. In the postwar era, basing architecture on the form and proportions of the human body, following the example of the renaissance and classicism, was a way to humanize modernism often associated with Le Corbusier. Rudolph, Kahn, and many of their colleagues humanized modernism in the 1950s by invoking historical forms associated with renaissance architecture, such as the centralized plan. Humanism often referred to the "humanist" scholarship of renaissance Italy, but it could also mean the successive intellectual efforts since the Enlightenment to bring liberal, progressive values to society that for Griswold and Scully culminated in their efforts at Yale.

Griswold and many of his colleagues in architecture also thought humanism had a political dimension and could advance the dominant "liberal consensus" culture of the postwar era. The origins of this stance lay in Franklin Roosevelt's New Deal of the 1930s, when members of government, business, academia, and the arts from opposite ends of the political spectrum entered into an unusual accord to further the political, economic, and social development of the United States. Though agreement was not always apparent, and despite many crises, the liberal consensus endured until the late 1960s, providing financial and philosophical support for the type of large-scale civic projects that became Rudolph's specialty.[5]

Contemporaneous with the liberal consensus, the progressive humanism of the patrician Griswold pervaded academia and government in the 1950s and early 1960s, especially during the Kennedy administration, with which he was closely associated.[6] For Griswold, the arts embodied humanism. He published sweeping pronouncements calling for the bolstering of the arts and humanities at the university level in order to counteract mass and popular culture and perceived conformity in American society caused by overemphasis on technology, science, and business. To counter conformity, Griswold called for greater regard for aesthetics and creativity, which he described as the "subjective expression of the individual artist," employing terms very much like those used by Rudolph.[7]

Once introduced to modern architecture by Saarinen, Griswold immediately grasped its potential for expressing his humanism and his agenda for transforming Yale into a modern research university. In an example soon followed by other expanding educational institutions, he commissioned twenty-six new buildings by important American architects, remaking the campus into a veritable museum of modern architecture. Reflecting his humanist ethos, he said each was supposed to "come as close to the ideals for a building of its kind as the architectural genius of its era is capable of bringing it."[8]

Scully had much in common with Griswold, but his thinking about humanism pertained directly to architecture. A contemporary of Rudolph's in age, Scully was one of several powerful American critics and architecture school educators who advocated a historically informed, humanist modernism as opposed to one drawing on objective scientific and research-grounded approaches to modernism (the latter represented by Walter Gropius, Harvard's GSD, and those who advocated a machine-based modernism, such as Sigfried Giedion in the 1930s and the British historian and critic Reyner Banham in the postwar era).[9]

As influential at Yale as Giedion had been at Harvard, Scully had a great impact on students and on Rudolph as well through his eloquent lectures on history; his thinking about buildings, cities, and landscape; and his encouragement of design that was humane and imbued with human characteristics, such as dynamism and forcefulness. Rudolph regularly invited Scully to critique student work and was as familiar as the students with the ideas the historian expressed in his classes and writings.

Though tinged by French existentialism, especially Albert Camus, Scully's humanism derived from Geoffrey Scott's explanation of renaissance and baroque architecture set forth in Scott's 1914 book, *The Architecture of Humanism: A Study in the History of Taste*.[10] The text became equally important for Rudolph. Emphasizing taste and aesthetics above all else, Scott saw renaissance and baroque architecture as the intuitive, artistic personal expressions of great artists who contributed to the zeitgeist, or overall "spirit of the times." The architecture of the fifteenth, sixteenth, and seventeenth centuries was therefore not the product of theory, patronage, or science, as was often thought; it came from pure artistry and emotion. In a way that appealed greatly to Rudolph, Scott drew loosely on Theodor Lipps's ideas about empathy to explain how architecture both embodied the moods and feelings of its creators and strongly affected the bodies and minds of individuals who came into contact with it.

Scott's text was widely read and influential after World War II. Architects of the 1940s and 1950s found a parallel to their rejection of functionalism and its theory-based methods in Scott's dismissal of theory-based explanations of renaissance and baroque architecture. Johnson called himself a "Scott man," and it was just as likely that it was he who introduced Rudolph to Scott as that it was Scully.[11]

Scully drew on Scott when he defined his "architectural humanism" of the 1950s, or what he thought modern architecture should be, in a *Perspecta* article of 1957 that became the basis of his book *Modern Architecture: The Architecture of Democracy* (1961). The democracy of the title referred to a lecture by Frank Lloyd Wright, but it also suggested Scully's tacit commitment to the alliance between modern architecture and the American liberal consensus. Scully quoted Scott's definition of renaissance architecture as centered on the body and its emotions: "The centre of that architecture was the human body: its method, to transcribe in stone the body's favorable states; and the moods of the spirit took visible shape along its borders, power and laughter, strength and terror and calm."[12] For Scully, Le Corbusier's Unité d'Habitation and his other monumental, emotionally compelling buildings based on the human form exemplified the architectural humanism of the 1950s.[13]

What Rudolph hoped to achieve with his buildings in this period was also essentially summed up by Scott's definition. Rudolph often said *The Architecture of Humanism* was one of the books that influenced him the most, and he regularly quoted Scott in lectures and in introductory talks for his architecture studios at Yale. Though the book is a diatribe against theory, *The Architecture of Humanism* nevertheless gave direction to Rudolph's thinking, ironically supplying him with a theory, though this was not Scott's intention. It helped Rudolph further define his position as an upholder of aesthetics, individuality, and creativity in his teaching and justified his focus on stimulating physical and emotional responses in his architecture.[14]

"Architecture: The Unending Search"

Although he advocated the anti-theoretical position of Scott, Rudolph himself memorably suggested that theory was just what modern architecture needed in the first talk

3.1 Rudolph and students in studio (c. 1962) at the Yale University Art Gallery.

he gave to the Department of Architecture as its chairman in January 1958. In his speech entitled "Architecture: The Unending Search" Rudolph said, "Many have asked why I should come to Yale. It is because I believe that action has indeed outstripped theory and that it is the unique task and responsibility of a great university such as Yale to study, not only that which is known, but far more important, to pierce the unknown. My passion is to participate in the unending search. Theory must again overtake action."[15]

When Rudolph said "action has indeed outstripped theory," he was referring to the many architects who paid little regard to ideas or theory as they pursued every opportunity to build. As Rudolph well knew, this criticism could be leveled at him as well, though his allusions to Viollet-le-Duc's structural rationalism and his grappling with symbolism suggest that theory was one of the things he was searching for during the 1950s. The speech had the earmarks of Rudolph's earlier talks and writings, such as his phrase about his passion for participating in an unending search, but it had a new, more urgent, elevated tone to it, similar to the sweeping, humanist rhetoric of Griswold, Scully, and Scott.

Rudolph identified four "forgotten fundamentals" that he believed the Department of Architecture should concentrate on. None were radical or unique to him, but all were evident in the buildings he designed at the time. The first was developing an urbanism of diverse spaces and buildings. The second was emphasizing materials and structure to express "age-old concepts, such as fine proportions, how to get into a building, relationships of volume to volume, how to relate a building to the ground, the sky, and so forth."[16] The third was heeding visual perception, or how a building looked at different times of the day, during rain or in sunlight, and by the individual from different perspectives. The fourth was cultivating visual delight, or aesthetics.

The aesthetic aspect of architecture had long been derided by advocates of functionalism and was feared by some who thought it encouraged formalism. Rudolph, however, in his 1954 AIA speech, had said that architects had been overly apologetic about aesthetics. Clearly, this would not be the case at Yale. Adding a new note, again unmistakably reflecting the humanism of Griswold, Scully, and Scott, Rudolph said that only creativity could foster aesthetics. He declared at the end of the speech that the department's first concern was to make sure that the student was "acutely, perceptively and incessantly aware of the creative process."[17] Nearly everything Rudolph did at Yale as an architect, teacher, and administrator was intended to foster this creativity.

Administration

The Yale administration and faculty strongly supported Rudolph in the early years of his chairmanship of the architecture department. Griswold increased the department's budget and scholarship funds and promised improved quarters for the school. Rudolph ran the department like he ran his architectural practice: delegating administration to others and concentrating on design and teaching. Capable, experienced men, such as the dean of the school Gibson Danes and architectural historian Carroll Meeks, helped

Rudolph with administration, allowing him to concentrate on reinvigorating the department by raising its profile and by teaching.[18] Rudolph galvanized the many young instructors (called visiting critics) who were hired on a yearly basis to supplement the small permanent faculty of about six professors. Among the visiting critics were architects who went on to become significant figures, such as Robert Venturi and John Hedjuk. Often hand-picked by Rudolph to teach at Yale, the younger men found Rudolph an inspiring, if demanding, master.

William de Cossy remembered Rudolph going around a table during regular monthly faculty dinners at Mory's, Yale's famous club, and in his officer's manner upbraiding young instructors for their shortcomings.[19] Rudolph believed his unvarnished directness demonstrated his honesty in dealing with people. To symbolize his openness to others, there was no door to his office in the Yale A & A Building. Scully found Rudolph's leadership refreshing after a period of difficult administrative politics and called him "a straight shooter."[20]

Pedagogy

Students experienced Rudolph's intense tutelage in creativity in the loft-like studios of the fourth floor of Louis Kahn's acclaimed Yale University Art Gallery (1951–54), where the architecture department was housed until it moved across York Street to Rudolph's completed A & A Building in 1963 (figure 3.1). During his first years, Rudolph taught undergraduates. In 1959, when the School of Art and Architecture became a fully accredited graduate professional school, Rudolph turned his attention to the master's degree candidates, as their numbers increased and more talented students—some from abroad, such as Englishmen Foster and Rogers—were attracted by his presence and joined their ranks.

In the studio, Rudolph drew attention to subjects he believed modernism had overlooked and that he was exploring in his own projects, principally urbanism, monumentality, and aesthetics; he frequently referred to Scott and to Camillo Sitte, the nineteenth-century urban theorist. He insisted that students present their projects in the manner in which he presented his own, favoring the perspective section and highly finished, compelling presentation drawings.[21] In fact, drawing was the skill most emphasized. Though Rudolph and Yale insisted on individuality and Rudolph never worked for a large firm, the department paradoxically had a professional emphasis, preparing students for careers in large firms where hierarchy and collaboration were prized.

Rudolph's emphasis on diligence, individuality, competition, and speed reflected his own values and working methods and resulted in an intensely competitive atmosphere that led to some isolation among students.[22] Rudolph occasionally and unexpectedly pitted students against one another by posing a twenty-four-hour design problem to the whole student body. He regularly reviewed projects just days before end of semester presentations, requiring sometimes that students completely reconceive their projects. Students, however, understood that Rudolph cared deeply about architecture and their work. He often visited

3.2 Philip Johnson (left foreground), Rudolph (center, seated), and Scully (standing right with folded arms) review student work (c. 1960) in a snapshot taken by Stanley Tigerman (Yale BArch 1960, MArch 1961).

the studios late at night, staying for many hours to help students resolve problems with projects.

Rudolph transformed the jury system, an established tradition in architectural pedagogy, into the most important ritual of the department. Three or four jurors, often drawn from the well-known visitors Rudolph invited to Yale, publicly critiqued the students' studio projects at the end of the semester. Rudolph's criticism could be devastating, but he was also fiercely protective of the students. He became annoyed if jurors dismissed the student's point of view.[23] Though spirited exchanges between the jurors often outshone the work presented, Rudolph believed that this was how architectural discourse developed and that students would learn by absorbing it (figure 3.2).[24]

Discourse

Rudolph made the Department of Architecture at Yale one of the most stimulating places for architectural discourse in the early 1960s by inviting important figures to lecture, serve on juries, and sometimes stay on as visiting critics, just as he had done when he first came to Yale.[25] These "stars" exposed him and his students to diverse points of view, which often contrasted with those of the faculty and with his own as well. This open-mindedness to different approaches became the defining characteristic of Yale during Rudolph's chairmanship. Despite his criticism of the International Style, Rudolph greatly respected Ludwig Mies van der Rohe, who was a visiting critic at Yale in December of 1958 and was honored with a student-organized exhibition of his work. Though Rudolph had left their sphere of influence, Gropius and Josep Lluís Sert visited Yale in 1960. Jane Jacobs, the author of the important critique of modernist urbanism *The Death and Life of Great American Cities* (1961) spoke in 1959. Her celebration of small-scale urban neighborhoods, in formulation at that time, challenged Rudolph's large-scale monumentality and urbanism. Reyner Banham, who thought Yale's and Rudolph's aesthetics to be as reactionary as those of the Italian neoliberty, nevertheless visited Yale in 1961.

Influential editors and writers from American architectural journals often served as jurors and critics at Yale, for example Peter Blake, Douglas Haskell, Thomas Creighton, and Walter McQuade. They reported on the department and Rudolph extensively but not always positively, to his chagrin. Theory and philosophy were increasingly emphasized during Rudolph's chairmanship, reflecting architecture's awakening interest in them. One visitor (1960–61) was the theorist Bernard Rudofsky, best known for his research on vernacular architecture, an interest Rudolph shared. The philosopher Susanne Langer lectured (1964) about how forms and symbols could stimulate feelings, which was significant for Rudolph and also for Scully. Architectural historians, such as Rudolph's long-time friend Henry-Russell Hitchcock (visited 1959–60), who wrote with sympathy about Rudolph's latest work, were regularly present at Yale. Rudolph's close friend and ardent supporter architectural historian and critic Sibyl Moholy-Nagy from the Pratt Institute in Brooklyn, New York, was a frequent visitor known for her forceful personality. Philip Johnson was a strong presence, and Yale students were regulars at the salons on architecture he held at his Glass House in nearby New Canaan.

Public and Private Life

Rudolph's complex persona was part of his attraction. Though enigmatic about some things, he was unusually direct and open in his professional life about his views and dealings with others in the department and in his architectural practice. He cut a recognizable figure on campus, and his every move and utterance at Yale was noted. Students analyzed and repeated his words and even emulated his stutter out of admiration. A graduate student at the time, the architectural historian Kurt Forster said Rudolph's distinctive rolling gait and clipped manner had the masculine decisiveness of a sailor.[26]

Despite intense scrutiny, Rudolph successfully compartmentalized his professional and personal life, an arrangement respected by those around him. He was discreet about his homosexuality, which was known but never openly discussed. He socialized outside the Department of Architecture with faculty and graduate students from different fields. Though it was not well known, he maintained a romantic relationship with Ellis Ansel Perlswig, a young professor of psychiatry at the Yale School of Medicine, from 1963 until 1967. They occupied separate residences in New Haven, advisable since exposure as a homosexual often ruined lives and careers. Homosexual "witch hunts" were common in the 1950s;[27] both Bruce Goff and Charles Moore were to varying degrees forced from important academic positions.[28]

Addressed as "Mr. Rudolph" by most of his office staff and students, Rudolph was sometimes intimidating and often remote and reserved. Impish humor and wit, manipulative at times, leavened his serious demeanor. For all his professional transparency, Rudolph also liked secrets and mystery. In architecture and in life, he enjoyed staging situations that would stimulate reactions from others, with a trip into the unknown being one of his favorites. Without explaining where they were going, Rudolph took Robert A. M. Stern, then a student, out for a stroll; the destination turned out to be dinner at the New Haven home of Serge Chermayeff, a faculty member in the architecture department at Yale whom Stern did not care for, as Rudolph well knew. Chermayeff was a former GSD faculty member and long-time friend of Rudolph's whom he hired to teach at Yale.

Though he moved in sophisticated circles, Rudolph never entirely learned their ways. Stern thought he remained curiously naive about how others saw and perceived him.[29] Norman Foster said Rudolph was a "solitary figure with a side that could be touchingly awkward and shy." Foster recalled Rudolph being lost for conversation on one of the few occasions when he invited students to his home.[30] Robert Engman, a sculptor from the department, remembered Rudolph as an aloof but regular member of an informal group of faculty who gathered for long lunches and lively but often critical conversation about each other at a diner near the Yale University Art Gallery. Rudolph became notably cooler toward Engman after he called Rudolph's Greeley Laboratory "structurally irrational."[31]

Greeley Laboratory

Even before naming him chairman of the Department of Architecture, Griswold had showed that he favored Rudolph by awarding him the commission for the William B. Greeley Memorial Forestry Laboratory (1957–59), one of the president's modernist projects for the Yale campus. The research facility for the forestry school was named after one of its distinguished alumni. Rudolph designed a low, one-story, flat-roofed glass pavilion on a podium built into a hillside, north of the main campus and adjacent to older forestry school buildings. Respecting the existing character of the site, Rudolph located the laboratory between ancient specimen trees that towered over it and left undisturbed the gentle slope of the hill on which it sat (figure 3.3).

Structurally and stylistically, the building was a transitional one for Rudolph. Expanding on the "symbols of structure" concept, Rudolph melded decoration and structure into one with the laboratory's striking, Y-shaped capitals,

3.3 Rudolph, William B. Greeley Memorial Forestry Laboratory (New Haven, 1957–59).

3.4 Construction, Greeley Laboratory.

more sinuous versions of those at the Blue Cross and Blue Shield Building. The elegant curves reflected the decorative spirit of romantic modernism that still held Rudolph under its sway. He clad Greeley Lab's podium base with Mo-Sai panels and manufactured off-site its precast concrete posts and capitals. To make the impressive ceiling of mixed precast and monolithic concrete elements inside, Rudolph topped the columns with massive concrete beams poured in place on the site; these anticipated the heavier, more monumental concrete aesthetic he became known for in the 1960s (figure 3.4).

It was the malleability of concrete that made such expressive forms possible. The material transformed architecture in the late 1950s and early 1960s. In a special 1960 issue of *Progressive Architecture* devoted to concrete, the critic Ada Louise Huxtable said that architects were turning away from the steel and glass of the International Style to concrete because it could be shaped in any way they liked. Huxtable wrote, "A unique material, concrete is formed in the most literal sense by the architect. Unlike wood and stone, . . . concrete is a viscous mass turned into substance by design and engineering."[32]

Greeley Labs was the largest project Rudolph's office had undertaken without the assistance of another firm. Immersed in his Boston and Florida projects and still teaching at Yale, Rudolph brought William Grindereng from his Florida office to serve as the project manager and pressed Yale faculty into service as well. Faculty member Charles Brewer assisted Rudolph with the intricacies of design, construction, and management. To develop the remarkable ceiling, columns, and capitals, Rudolph collaborated with another faculty member, Henry A. Pfisterer, an experienced structural engineer. Pfisterer had helped Kahn develop the famous tetrahedral concrete ceiling for the Yale University Art Gallery, which Rudolph saw every working day in the architecture studios.[33]

To observers such as Engman, Greeley and its expressive concrete capitals and beams seemed like a marked departure from the structural rationalism associated with Rudolph's Florida houses. In his own take on this direction, Johnson, in a spring 1958 lecture for Scully's modern architecture class, called Rudolph a "decorative structuralist"

3.5 Interior, Greeley Laboratory.

3.6 Roof, Greeley Laboratory.

who "takes his structures and makes beautiful decorations out of them".[34] Some critics thought the forms of the building were related to its function as a forestry school. The many columns with their curvaceous branch-like capitals had an organic character recalling a "concrete orchard," *Architectural Forum* observed.[35] But *Architectural Forum* also noted that the sinuous forms resembled the gestural qualities of the whiplash lines of the art nouveau style. Long despised by modernists for its decorative qualities, the style was to some extent rehabilitated during the 1950s as architects such as Rudolph began sifting through the recent past to find forms for the present.[36] The curving capitals of Greeley suggested yet another new direction for modernism: one journalist who was regularly present at Yale, Thomas H. Creighton, called this emergent direction the "new sensualism," explaining that it was a more plastic elaboration on romantic modernism so pronounced that it could produce a "tingle of sensual pleasure" in the viewer.[37]

However, the sinuous forms and patterns at Greeley were, according to Rudolph, not merely exercises in surface aesthetics but expressive of the structural and material properties of the building. The undulating pattern of the precast and poured-in-place ceiling beams expressed "the nature and direction of the roof stresses," or internal forces. Rudolph said they were widest "where the shear stresses are greatest and narrowest at the center of the bay."[38] The architect integrated function and decoration, housing light fixtures, wiring, and cables in cavities between the beams, this novel configuration making a striking overall pattern conceptually comparable to the concrete ceiling of Kahn's Yale University Art Gallery. To make the entire ceiling visible from all vantage points within the building, interior partitions richly paneled with grained walnut (again appropriate for a forestry school) were topped with transom-like glass panes (figure 3.5). Celebrating the ceiling further, Rudolph repeated the pattern of the curvilinear beams in gray and white marble chips on the building's roof. The gigantic decorative pattern could be seen from a hillside staircase, confirming Johnson's observation on Rudolph and his "decorative structuralist" approach (figure 3.6).

Although its columns, capitals, and ceiling were admirable, Greeley Laboratory had many of the problems common to laboratory buildings designed by modern architects at the time. Among the greatest drawbacks were temperature fluctuations and not enough storage space. Cracking of windows and transoms was blamed on everything from strong winds to contraction. Nevertheless, the building is still used for its original purpose well into the twenty-first century. Greeley Labs was significant as a transition for Rudolph from the lighter, decorative forms of romantic modernism to the heavier, more monumental vocabulary of monolithic concrete for which he is best known and that was further developed in his remarkable parking garage for New Haven.

Temple Street Parking Garage

Not long after Rudolph became chairman of the Yale architecture department in 1958, Mayor Richard C. Lee and his redevelopment director Edward J. Logue commissioned him to design the Temple Street Parking Garage

3.7 Rudolph, Temple Street Parking Garage (New Haven, 1958–63).

(1958–63), a monument key to New Haven's renewal. One of Rudolph's most compelling buildings, the 760-foot-long structure extended two city blocks, spanning George Street like a bridge. Its powerful, elongated concrete arches gave it an ancient and rhythmic quality that observers likened to Roman structures (figure 3.7).[39] The design and development of the garage, dedicated in February 1963, paralleled and informed Rudolph's other great, monolithic, concrete project, the Yale A & A Building, completed in November 1963.

With the garage, Rudolph left behind the delicate forms of Greeley Labs for the bolder, more expressive, and monumental aesthetic that he became known for in the 1960s. Poured-in-place concrete was critical in generating this new aesthetic; the technique was used for floor plates, parapets, columns, and arches, whereas at the laboratory it had been employed for just the larger ceiling beams. The rough-edged striations from the formwork, left visible in the concrete, caused journalists, such as Walter McQuade in his *Architectural Forum* article about the garage, to suggest that it was also an experiment in combining decoration and structure to make more powerfully expressive sculptural forms.[40]

The garage was Rudolph's introduction to federally funded urban redevelopment. Such projects transformed American cities during the postwar decades and became a mainstay of Rudolph's practice. During the 1950s and 1960s, Mayor Lee secured for New Haven more federal funding for urban redevelopment on a per capita basis than any other city in America. Redevelopment was intended to fix New Haven's ills, which were symptomatic of urban decline nationally: loss of industry, changing demographics, and suburbanization. In an effort paralleling Griswold's transformation of the Yale campus, Lee enlisted Rudolph and other modernist architects to remake New Haven into a nationally recognized laboratory for urban renewal called the "Model City," a name President Johnson later adopted for his Great Society urban renewal initiative.[41] An enthusiastic supporter of Lee's redevelopment efforts, Rudolph told the *New Haven Register* in 1963, "In a few years, New Haven will have more significant architecture than any other city its size."[42]

A vital component of downtown renewal, the garage was part of a larger mall, hotel, and office complex called Church Street Redevelopment, which was intended to lure commercial life back to New Haven's downtown.[43] Lee wanted the garage to be spectacular, to make it clear to suburbanites leaving Interstate 91 or 95 (part of the national network of interstate highways built with funding from the Federal Highway Act of 1956) and driving into the city on the newly built Oak Street Connector (also a part of the redevelopment scheme) that this was the place to park and shop in New Haven (figure 3.8). Drivers could enter the garage and shop in the new mall without ever setting foot on the city's streets, which were being disdained more and more as decrepit and disorderly. Calling it the "cornerstone" of New Haven redevelopment, Lee stressed repeatedly that the garage was a symbol of civic and commercial rejuvenation for New Haven.[44] To clear the site for the new complex, blocks of vibrant existing businesses and residences were appropriated.[45] Whether such drastic means had to be

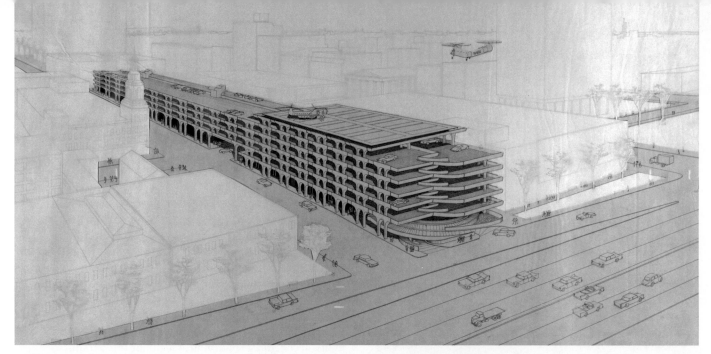

3.8 The Temple Street Parking Garage adjoined the Oak Street Connector. The rooftop heliport was never built.

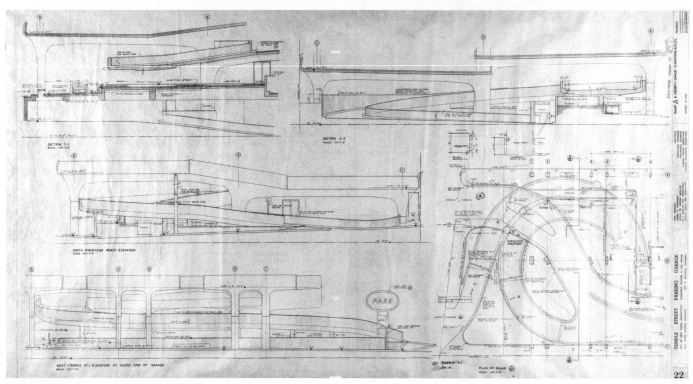

3.9 Ramp details, section and plans, Temple Street Parking Garage.

taken to reinvigorate the city was a question raised at the time and later.

After some exploratory discussions with Lee and Logue, Rudolph came up with a design in just ten days. The program—parking for 1,280 cars, some office space for the garage managers, and a street-level row of shops—was developed for the city by parking and economics consultants. Rudolph's scheme was immediately accepted by the mayor, Logue, and the chairman of the parking authority. However, completing the garage was a lengthy process, complicated by two and a half years of delays ranging from site flooding during excavation to revisions made to working drawings. Rudolph still had no office in New Haven, but he quickly assembled a staff of about six men who became the kernel of his expanding practice in the city. They carried out a tremendous amount of work, including everything from specifications to working drawings. Pfisterer again provided engineering expertise, notably improving Rudolph's designs for the curving ramps (figure 3.9). Grindereng was in charge of the staff and executed many of the construction drawings with Ulli Scharnberg and John Damico. Experienced with the supervision of a building project, Andrew Nastri oversaw construction and worked with the builders Fusco-Amatruda of New Haven.[46]

Rudolph conceived of the garage as an extension of the new highways and as an expression of the movement of the automobile, whose role in the city he discussed often. He said, "Most parking garages look like office buildings with glass. I wanted to make it look like it belonged to the automobile and its movement, . . . a system of bridges over large open spans."[47] Rudolph said he had considered making the garage into a 1,700-foot-long bridge spanning the sunken Oak Street Connector, a bridge that would rejoin the portions of the city that the new road had separated.[48] Spanning the highway would also make the garage into a monumental gateway to the city, one of the urban archetypes Rudolph consistently invoked. In describing his garage as expressive of movement and seeing it as something that could create new urban relationships, Rudolph probably had in mind Kahn's plans of the 1950s for center city Philadelphia, which suggested erecting raised highways for traffic to create an "architecture of movement" or "viaduct architecture."[49]

Though he never gave up hope that it would one day be completed as he envisioned, Rudolph's highway-spanning structure was deemed unfeasible even before he presented his first scheme to the city, so he reduced the garage in length and moved it back to the edge of the Oak Street Connector.[50] The garage was still an immense structure, a half block wide and two blocks long, that stretched 760 feet from the edge of the Connector toward the New Haven Green. It retained something of the gateway-like aspect by virtue of bridging over George Street, a surface street parallel to the Oak Street Connector. The completed garage consisted of four levels of concrete trays for parking supported by regularly spaced rows of double columns and another two subterranean levels. Driving beneath immense, moving, arcing shadows while following the curving ramps was an exciting spatial and visual experience for the motorist (figure 3.10).

Every element in the building was calibrated to produce expressive effects of light, shadow, and movement. Rudolph extended the horizontal trays of the garage beyond their supporting columns so that they cast horizontal shadows the entire length of the building. The paired columns cast contrasting vertical shadows. The parapets attached to the edges of the trays alternated between long and short lengths to mark the bays and cast more shadows, forming another series of rhythms along the facade. To further suggest movement, Rudolph joined the columns with elongated, parabolic arches, like those of the art nouveau style, imbuing the building with a greater sense of dynamism than could have been conveyed by the more typical round arch.

All the concrete was poured in place which, as had been the case with the Greeley Laboratory, called for particularly precise construction. Rudolph was frustrated by the builders' many delays in beginning work, but to his surprise and delight Fusco-Amatruda brought in boat builders to construct the curved formwork, which came to resemble the hull of a ship (figure 3.11). Rudolph often avoided building sites, finding the building process troublesome. But for the garage, perhaps because it reminded him of his days in the Brooklyn Navy Yards, Rudolph supervised the assembly of the three-inch boards into the formwork.[51] The precision of the formwork resulted in masterfully cast concrete forms of unusual power and plasticity with well-defined edges and few flaws.

Pfisterer's engineering skills helped Rudolph achieve this powerful expression in concrete by means that might have troubled a purist committed to the rational expression of structure. McQuade, generally supportive of Rudolph if often skeptical about his increasing grandiosity, pointed out in his assessment of the project for *Architectural Forum* that although it appeared to be an arcuated structure—that is, one with a structural system of supporting arches like a Roman viaduct—the garage was in fact a trabeated structure—that is, post and beam, more like a Greek temple. And though the building seemed as if it was entirely cast in monolithic or poured-in-place concrete with steel reinforcing rods, it was in fact also pinned together at its center with 300 tons of concrete-covered steel plates and girders so that it could span George Street.[52] Rudolph was untroubled that the building was not what it appeared to be structurally; his goal was to express the powerful qualities of monolithic concrete, through the dynamic forms of the arches and parapets, rather than the actual structural system of the building. This approach was in keeping with his thinking about "symbols of structure."

Rough striations left on the concrete when the wood forms were stripped away further expressed the titanic forces of construction that had forged the arches and columns. In the past, these marks would have been sanded or covered over with a veneer of plaster or masonry, but Rudolph appreciated the texture they gave the surface of the building. He had been inspired to emphasize the marks of construction after seeing Le Corbusier's work in Chandigarh, India, in May 1960 on his way back from Tokyo's World Design Conference. Experiencing Le Corbusier's Chandigarh, which he had long admired,

> 3.10 Ramps, Temple Street Parking Garage.

3.11 Construction, Temple Street Parking Garage.

was an important turning point for Rudolph, consequential for the garage and other contemporary projects. He told *Architectural Forum* that seeing the monumental, rough-hewn concrete buildings of the new Indian city had transformed his thinking about concrete and that he only wished the marks on the garage could be more pronounced because "Chandigarh is rougher still."[53]

Other architects of the time who were experimenting with concrete, such as Marcel Breuer and Kahn, were also leaving or emphasizing marks of construction. But there was a great difference between their thinking about these striations and Rudolph's. While for Kahn the imprint of the wood forms on the concrete stair silos of his Yale University Art Gallery revealed the building process and suggested authenticity and realness, for Rudolph at the parking garage the additional texture and shadows the striations gave the surface of the buildings were another type of decoration. The decorative character of Rudolph's striations was much noted at the time. McQuade said they created a pattern "which, close up, sometimes produce odd visual effects."[54] *Architectural Record* compared the effects of the regular striations and their shadows on the ramps, arches, and columns to the fluting found on classical columns.[55]

In emphasizing the striations—integrating his ornament into the very fabric of the garage to create an overall pattern—Rudolph may have been alluding to a larger theoretical point about the making of architectural ornament long discussed by architectural theorists and reinvoked by Scully. The nineteenth-century British architect and theorist A. W. N. Pugin had said that the ancient practice of making ornament part of the substance of a building, "the construction of decoration," was typical of classical architecture and the Gothic revival architecture of the nineteenth century that he deplored. Pugin thought it an inappropriate and dishonest method that concealed structure and thus violated the precepts of structural rationalism. Pugin instead advocated "the decoration of construction," following what he believed were the methods that had been used in the medieval Gothic architecture he admired. Pugin thought ornament was not to be applied, sculpted, or incised upon a building merely for the decorative effect, but should be applied to it in order to enrich or express structure in what was a more honest or authentic approach to the problem.[56] This approach would turn out to be especially appropriate for the nineteenth century, which increasingly emphasized a building's frame.

Scully had brought these seemingly arcane arguments into currency at Yale. In his lectures and writings of the 1950s about Louis Sullivan, Scully said that the Chicago architect should be admired because he decorated construction in the manner recommended by Pugin—sheathing his buildings with decorative terra cotta tiles, thus articulating the frame and imbuing it with a masculine "forcefulness."[57] Rudolph did something like this with Mo-Sai panels at the Blue Cross and Blue Shield Building, but at the Temple Street Parking Garage he instead constructed decoration when he adorned it with nonstructural arches and patterned the building with striations, thus returning to more traditional and less rational ways. In Rudolph's thinking, constructing decoration allowed for more opportunities for making the type of textured surfaces that he liked,

evident in the Atkinson House and the Amman embassy years before, among other projects.

More significantly, the bold plasticity of Rudolph's garage and its striations indicated that, for him, sculpture, structure, and decoration were becoming one. Confirming this (and using language similar to Scully's in his assessment of Sullivan), McQuade wrote of the garage, "Herein lies its immense force: this is an enormous, unabashed piece of sculpture."[58] Beginning in the mid- and late 1950s, making buildings into sculpture was a significant tendency of American modernism, one that was not unique to Rudolph, as could be seen in important works by Saarinen, Breuer, and others of Rudolph's contemporaries.[59]

Unfortunately, the garage's marvelous sculptural and decorative qualities were not fully apparent to passersby because the impressive eastern facade, which would have greeted drivers on the Oak Street Connector, was soon obscured by a newly built home for Malley's department store, one of the adjacent mall's anchor tenants. The fact that the garage was not visible enough from the city and highway, and was thus unable to become the prominent monument for New Haven that Lee, Logue, and Rudolph had intended it to be, was the building's greatest shortcoming.

On the whole, however, the garage was a success for Rudolph. A breakthrough in his experiments with concrete, the Temple Street Parking Garage prepared the way for the large-scale monumentality that he became known for in the early 1960s and also for more elaborate experiments with the construction of decoration. At the dedication in February 1963, Mayor Lee, his administration, the newspapers, and most of the architectural press admired the garage as a "tour-de-force" exemplifying Rudolph's virtuosity and individuality. A financially remunerative commission despite some setbacks along the way, the garage helped Rudolph buy, appropriately enough, a new Jaguar sports car.[60] Some observers, however, thought the garage's sheer grandness contradicted Rudolph's repeated declarations about the need to sensitively relate old to new through scale. The shopping mall designer Victor Gruen, who had been a consultant for the Church Street Redevelopment mall project, said the "glory, bulk and impressiveness" of Rudolph's garage reduced everything around it to "complete insignificance."[61]

Yale Married Student Housing

As he had in Florida, Rudolph simultaneously investigated many different forms and ideas during his years at Yale, and as a result buildings he designed at the same time could look very different from one another, to the confusion and dismay of his critics. The tight massing of Rudolph's Yale Married Student Housing (New Haven, 1960–61) demonstrated the high density he favored for urban housing. The project's block-like forms and brick walls edged with precast concrete coping suggested that Rudolph was also engaging with the vocabulary of British brutalist architecture, if not its ideas.

Rudolph's first scheme for the Married Student Housing (1960), which was located adjacent to Greeley Laboratory on the same sloping hillside site, consisted of a dense grouping of overlapping, two- to three-story cubic structures sheltered by a canopy of trees that formed an informal grid organizing the complex's many patios and courtyards. With its hazily rendered trees, the presentation drawing by John Fowler, one of the best draftsmen in Rudolph's office, departed from Rudolph's precisely rendered line work, but it was recognized by him and everyone in the office as a masterful image and was reproduced many times (figure 3.12).[62]

The low-rise complex was an alternative to the high-rise towers or superblocks that many universities were building for student housing at the time. Often poorly related to their surroundings, these tall structures were frequently criticized as inhuman and alienating. In contrast, Rudolph's complicated stacking of staircases, bridges, and terraces gave his project a city-like or urban quality, reflecting both his admiration for the city as a diverse series of spaces expressing different characters and his preference for density rather than the stark openness often favored in planning at the time.

The complex also recalled an Italian hill town, an important model for architecture and urbanism in the early 1960s. Architects began looking to these ancient, vernacular villages because the hill town's consistent yet varied vocabularies, materials, and shared walls and outdoor spaces were thought to engender community, something that architects and pundits feared was disappearing from American life. Hill towns appealed to Rudolph for their communal values as well as their picturesque qualities, and in fact he had invoked this precedent in advance of the general preference in his Jewett Arts Center at Wellesley College. The units in Rudolph's Yale housing were bound together in a reciprocal fashion: the rooftop of one apartment block was a private terrace for the block above. Lanes and small areas recalling intimate piazzas formed shared communal spaces between the buildings. A favored model for such housing at the time, Le Corbusier's terraced Roq et Rob Housing (project, Cap Martin, France, 1949) probably inspired Rudolph's arrangement to some degree, as did Saarinen's Morse and Stiles Colleges at Yale (1958–62), then being built and noted for the picturesque or romantic qualities of their irregular passages and courtyards and the unusual, concrete, rubble-wall construction.

Rudolph's Married Student Housing was also an experiment with concrete, but in this case with far more mundane, unadorned concrete blocks, a material he used in his early Florida houses and that he was reinvestigating in other projects at this time. In the first scheme, Rudolph proposed load-bearing walls of concrete block to give the buildings a more solid, weighty appearance, in keeping with traditional architecture and with the monumentality that he hoped to bring back to modern architecture.

Other influences informed the Married Student Housing complex as well. With its rough surfaces, humble materials, and cubic forms, the first scheme closely resembled the rough brick walls and concrete details of Ham Common Housing in England (London, Stirling and Gowan, 1955–58); James Stirling was one of several young British architects Rudolph brought to Yale as visiting critics (figure 3.13). The similarities between the two housing complexes are likely due to Rudolph's ongoing explorations of new architec-

tural tendencies, in this case British brutalism; in the end, however, Rudolph's approach was quite different.

The small group of avant-garde British architects and artists led by Alison and Peter Smithson, which included Stirling, rejected functionalism and sought new directions in the early 1950s. Stirling, probably the most aesthetically inclined of the group of Britons, described the emergence of a new, plastic "alternative architectural expression" built with rough, simple materials and inspired both by Le Corbusier's postwar work and by historical examples ranging from vernacular buildings to the seventeenth-century high-style Blenheim Palace to twentieth-century industrial buildings.[63] A roughness philosophically reflective of existentialism was synonymous with authenticity, and the Smithsons spoke of dragging "a rough poetry out of the confused and powerful forces" of the mid-twentieth century.[64] The British critic Reyner Banham enthusiastically named, endorsed, and promoted the "New Brutalism" because he believed it was an architecture of ethics rather than aesthetics (unlike neoliberty, which he thought was a regression) and recalled the honesty of expression advocated by Pugin, John Ruskin, and designers of the early twentieth century.[65] Scully, Johnson, and many other Americans believed the proponents of the brutalist approach were at the forefront of a breakthrough for modernism.[66]

Rudolph may have thought he had much in common with the brutalists, but their attitudes turned out to be markedly different from his own and from the thinking of his American colleagues, which became apparent when he invited the Smithsons to review student work at Yale in late 1960 and early 1961. Yale students greatly admired the Smithsons' buildings, but they were surprised to find that the visitors considered their studio projects too monumental and grandiose, demonstrating an aesthetic rather than an ethical approach to architecture—much like that of their department chairman. Alison Smithson found a student's studio project for a natatorium, a swimming pool complex, in New Haven "heavy-handed and grim," showing little regard for the users.[67]

Other Britons at Yale questioned Rudolph's ways. The British students admired Rudolph's virtuosity, quickness, and industry, but were skeptical about his aesthetics and disregard for functional requirements. Rogers, for instance, was dismayed by a conversation with Rudolph about how parked cars should be arranged in a decorative pattern that could be admired from an overlooking building. The British found Rudolph's desire to elevate even the most ordinary things by drawing on aesthetics, art, and sculptural form impractical and ridiculous.[68]

Rudolph's drastically revised final scheme for the Yale Married Student Housing complex confirmed that his approach to brutalism tended toward the aesthetic (figure 3.14). Both informal and yet unified and coherent, the completed grouping consisted of five staggered, two- and three-story cubic buildings linked together by a multilevel staircase with broad landings for sitting and for playing (figure 3.15). At Yale's request, Rudolph had reduced the project in size and resorted to conventional American wood stud wall construction, forgoing the load-bearing walls of concrete block. To make it similar to Stirling's Ham Common (in appearance at least), Rudolph clad the

3.12 Rudolph, first scheme, Yale Married Student Housing (New Haven, 1960–61), John Fowler, delineator.

3.13 Stirling and Gowan, Ham Common Housing (London, 1955–58).

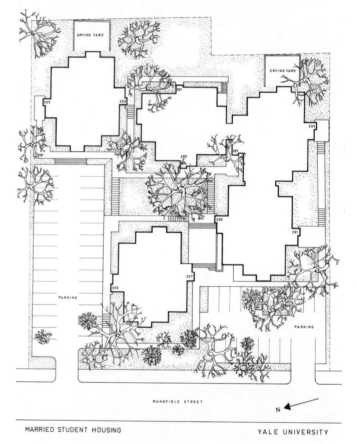

3.14 Plan, final scheme, Yale Married Student Housing.

3.15 Staircase, Yale Married Student Housing.

buildings with a red brick veneer speckled with white and black bricks to give a variety to the surfaces; further, he outlined the buildings' edges and fenestration with light-colored, precast concrete coping. Though typical of American construction, the brick veneer, according to brutalism's ethics, could be seen as a dishonest, even unethical, approach to construction because it was not load-bearing.

Residents found some aspects dismaying. Parents feared their children might fall off the rail-less platforms of the outdoor staircase.[69] Safety codes of the time did not require railings, and leaving the landings open to enhance the complex's multilevel qualities again demonstrated that, for Rudolph, the aesthetic outweighed the practical, yet another factor in what some observers considered an unethical approach to architecture. In addition to answering to an aesthetic rationale, the open landings pointed to a newly dangerous spatial quality found in some of Rudolph's other works of this time, such as his own New Haven apartment, recently completed.

The boxy forms of the Married Student Housing would reappear in a few other projects, and their cubic patterns were certainly reiterated in Rudolph's later prefabricated projects, but his interest in brutalism soon dwindled. The design approach did not live up to anyone's expectations. To Banham's dismay, by the mid-1960s his original hopes that brutalism might put architecture on a more ethical basis were entirely overlooked whenever the term was employed. Misunderstood and misused at first by journalists who employed it in a sensational fashion to criticize modernism, and then by everyone else, the term "brutalism" became

associated during the 1960s with the large-scale, rough-surfaced concrete buildings designed by the "Johnsons, Johansens and Rudolphs of the American scene," as Banham explained, most often with the Yale A & A Building by Rudolph.[70] Although Rudolph never used the term to describe his large-scale monumentality, "brutalism" was nonetheless forever used to characterize his buildings.

Apotheosis

The years between 1960 and 1963 were Rudolph's apotheosis at Yale. He dominated the reinvigorated architecture department, and, as he had hoped, the university's imprimatur brought him accolades, publicity, and jobs. Russell Bourne reported in *Architectural Forum* in 1958 that Rudolph's office "handled nearly $2.5 million worth of business" in 1957, though it is not clear how much of this was profit; this number probably grew steadily.[71] Rudolph celebrated his successes by buying a nineteenth-century house near Yale (figure 3.16). The first residence he owned, it was at 31 High Street, just a few hundred feet from the architecture department's studio spaces and the site of its future home, the Yale A & A Building. For the most part, Rudolph's daily existence in New Haven was lived amid these few blocks in a shabby, downtown neighborhood at the edge of the campus. Though he was known for his houses, it was revealing that he never designed one for himself, and always preferred the city over the suburbs and country.

Appreciative of traditional buildings and how they related to their surroundings, Rudolph left intact the facade of the

3.16 Rudolph House, 31 High Street, New Haven, Connecticut.

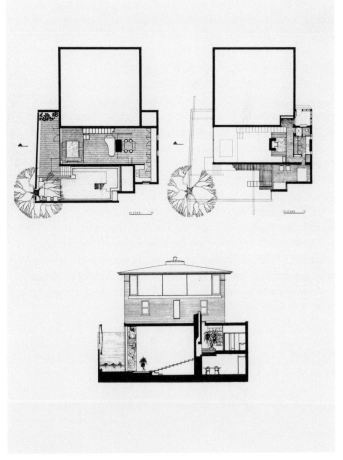

3.17 Plan, additions to 31 High Street.

79

3.18 Rudolph meeting with his office staff at 31 High Street (1962); left to right: Frank Chapman, Jonathan Hall, James Weber, Rudolph, John Damico, Bill Bedford, Andrew Nastri.

square, brick, flat-roofed Italianate-style house from the 1850s. Inside, he constructed an office for his expanding practice and an apartment for himself (1961), carving out an attic studio for the office and adding a rear wing for his residence. Rudolph made the remainder of the building into rental offices and apartments (figure 3.17).[72]

By 1960, Rudolph had shut down his Sarasota and Cambridge offices, consolidating his practice in New Haven. It grew to about ten architects and draftsmen; students, some of whom later became famous in their own right, such as Charles Gwathmey, provided additional help as needed. Some Florida office employees, such as Grindereng, came to New Haven and worked for Rudolph in his practice, and others, for example Rudolph's first employee, Bert Brosmith, worked for Rudolph at Yale, becoming visiting critics. For the first time, Rudolph hired a secretary to organize his business affairs. But he was uncomfortable with transforming his experimental practice into a professional one and resisted appointing an office manager until Grindereng and Ulli Scharnberg, a recent Yale graduate, installed themselves in the position.

Rudolph's dislike of hierarchy and organization was evident in the design of the office. His desk was next to those of the draftsmen. There were no doors in the one big room and every conversation with clients was carried out within hearing and sight of everyone in the office. Rudolph presided with military curtness over meetings held in a conversation pit in the center of the office beneath an open raftered ceiling (figure 3.18).

In the office, Rudolph could be friendly, but his style of management was distant. Despite receiving an almost

unmanageable number of new commissions, he was involved in nearly every aspect of every project. Rudolph moved energetically about the office like "a ball of fire," often exhausting, but also inspiring, everyone present. The atmosphere alternated between intensity and quiet. The moment Rudolph left town, the staff relaxed, took a break from work, and went out to get haircuts.[73]

Since Rudolph rarely took the lead in organizing a project, staff members typically appointed themselves project managers and divvied up duties. After Rudolph conceived the design, the staff wrote specifications, made working drawings, and oversaw construction; he carefully reviewed and revised all their work. Rudolph closely supervised the making of presentation drawings, doing a surprising amount of the work himself because drawings for clients and publication mattered greatly to him. Few remembered seeing him lay out the basic framework of these drawings, which he preferred to do after everyone had departed for the day.[74] Rudolph often worked at his drawing board late into the night, leaving little sketches on his staff's desks to be developed into larger drawings the next day. As he had with earlier projects, Rudolph partnered with associated firms who also produced working drawings and oversaw construction, supplementing his few staff. Collaboration with outside firms allowed Rudolph to complete a remarkably high number of projects for someone with such a small practice.

The other side of 31 High Street was Rudolph's apartment. A world almost entirely its own, the residence centered on the double-height living room in the discrete, two-story wing he added to the house's rear. He lived there

3.19 Living room, 31 High Street.

3.20 Party at 31 High Street (1962).

by himself, employing a man named Jeff Meekins to maintain the building and office and act as a valet. Meekins remained with Rudolph when he moved to New York in 1965.[75] Rudolph entertained only a few friends at the house, considering it a personal retreat. Staff members who wandered into the office on weekends could sometimes overhear Rudolph playing the piano in the apartment below, but they never saw him perform.[76]

An experiment in interior architecture, the apartment was the first of several similarly impressive domestic interiors Rudolph designed for himself and others that he invested with qualities of drama, sensuality, and danger (figure 3.19). The living room was beautiful, but perilous. Everything in the windowed, fishbowl-like space was white, except for the black grand piano. The rail-less staircase that hugged one side of the room terrified visitors. Its open risers appeared to float in the air without any means of support, giving it a sculptural quality. The staircase exemplified how Rudolph began at this time to stage situations in his architecture that stimulated strong, though not always positive, emotional and physical reactions from users. Such reactions were in keeping with Rudolph's developing ideas about architecture. Scott had said that renaissance architecture reflected all the varying moods of the body, including terror. According to several of his friends, Rudolph himself was afraid of heights but enjoyed the feeling of safety that came after an adrenalin-stimulating descent of a rail-less staircase or a crossing of a precipitous drop on a catwalk.[77]

In the fall of 1962, Elliott Erwitt, known for his iconic photos for *Life* and other popular magazines, photographed a black-tie cocktail party and concert staged in Rudolph's living room for an article profiling the architect in the fashion magazine *Vogue* (figure 3.20).[78] Erwitt's photo of men and women in evening dress seen through the living room's wall of windows and an elaborate play of reflections conveys the qualities of drama, elegance, and aesthetic richness found in Rudolph's architecture in the early 1960s. Rudolph's most steadfast supporter at Yale, Griswold, appears in the foreground of the photo on the far right, sitting alongside Yale University Art Gallery director Andrew Ritchie. The photograph testified to Rudolph's success, recording an evanescent moment when both the architectural profession and the wider world of media, culture, academia, and government looked to him for the buildings that would express the energy, prosperity, and optimism of America in the early 1960s. Of course, not all was as ideal as it appeared to be in this picture. For the first time, critics were beginning to write negatively about Rudolph's latest works, expressing dismay about how each of his new buildings appeared to be entirely different from the last. Rudolph, however, believed that his Yale Art & Architecture Building (New Haven, 1958–63), already rising nearby, would demonstrate his maturity and therefore refute all their charges.

Four
The Yale Art & Architecture Building

Few architectural events in the postwar United States were as eagerly awaited as the completion of Rudolph's Art & Architecture Building at Yale University (1958–63). Known as the A & A, the structure was heralded as the solution to modernism's major problems. In her review of the building, *New York Times* critic Ada Louise Huxtable said, "It asks and answers some of the major questions facing the art of architecture today, at a time of crisis and transition in the development of the contemporary style."[1]

Designing the A & A Building was Rudolph's greatest challenge up to that time, and with it he seemed to find, as Huxtable suggested, answers to some of the questions about urbanism, symbolism, decoration, and monumentality that had long preoccupied him and the discipline. The building was intended to stimulate students' creativity with its staggered towers, roughened, corrugated concrete surfaces, and complex interior spaces adorned with artifacts and art works carefully selected and arranged by Rudolph. The product of much agonizing, the A & A was Rudolph's true masterpiece, displaying his virtuosity to his fellows, in this case the growing number of critics who wondered what to make of the broad range of expression in Rudolph's work. The issue of whether the building was all too personal an effort by the architect was one that would be raised repeatedly.

The A & A Commission

Rudolph received the commission for a new arts facility in 1958 but did not begin design work on the A & A Building until late 1959 after a false start. Able as usual to perform several tasks at once, Rudolph completed the building while designing other projects and supervising students and faculty as well as the staff of his growing practice. Rudolph was in the unusual position of designing a building to house the department he chaired, to some degree acting as his own client, as Reyner Banham noted at the time.[2] Rudolph thus joined a select company: Karl Friedrich Schinkel with his Bauakademie in Berlin (1832–36), Walter Gropius with his Bauhaus in Dessau (1925–26), and Ludwig Mies van der Rohe with his Crown Hall for Chicago's Illinois Institute of Technology (1950–56). Frank Lloyd Wright's drafting room at Taliesin (Scottsdale, Arizona, 1937–38) might also be included on this list.

University president A. Whitney Griswold gave Rudolph considerable freedom to design the A & A in keeping with his policy of fostering the "genius of the architect." He reviewed each stage of the project for practical matters but left decisions about design and aesthetics to Rudolph. Little remains in writing about how such determinations were made because the design process consisted mostly of spoken exchanges between the principals.[3] Architecture department faculty, including structural engineer Henry A. Pfisterer, were part of the design team as well. All involved knew each other well, and this "clubbishness," typical of Yale, may have been why Rudolph was allowed so much leeway and why aspects such as the design of studio spaces for artists were not considered more carefully. Rudolph's thinking about the A & A, on the other hand, is more readily traced because he published and discussed his successive schemes for the project at the time and afterward.[4]

The new arts building was intended to bring together Yale's roughly 60 faculty and 300 or so students in architecture, urban planning, painting, sculpture, and graphic design; previously their quarters were in and around the Yale University Art Gallery. Griswold and Rudolph believed that consolidating the departments would spark the creativity of the students and encourage interdisciplinary exchanges. The legacy of Gropius's Bauhaus, which had fostered a synthesis of the arts, was tangible at Yale in Rudolph, Gropius's student, and in Josef Albers, the chair of the art department, who had been a Bauhaus student and instructor. In addition, just as the Bauhaus building had become an iconic paradigm for modern architecture, Rudolph believed that students would learn from the architecture of the A & A Building itself, especially his carefully crafted and decorated interiors.

In 1958, the Yale administration initially had Rudolph develop schemes to renovate the school's existing quarters in Street Hall and Weir Hall and to design an addition in order make a new fine arts facility. Finding it difficult to improve these old structures adjacent to the Yale University Art Gallery (which also housed some of the architecture studios), they decided in May 1959 to construct a new building on a new site at the corner of York and Chapel Streets opposite the Art Gallery.[5] Preoccupied with his many other commissions, teaching, and administration, Rudolph did not give the project his full attention until the end of the year. In December 1959, Rudolph quickly developed a first scheme for a five-story building with a street-level portico of smooth surfaced, multistory, regularly spaced concrete piers that supported a projecting, cornicelike series of box-shaped studios (figure 4.1). Rudolph focused the interior on a double-height exhibition room with a sunken area resembling an amphitheater that would host juried reviews of student work from all disciplines, much like the conversation pit in the center of Rudolph's office at 31 High Street. Above the exhibition room was a similarly configured, double-height drafting room for the architecture students. Classrooms, offices, studios, and other facilities were distributed in balconies and wings around these two central spaces.

Especially in its projecting cornice of artists' studios, the first scheme was clearly inspired by the top-heavy massing of Le Corbusier's monastery at La Tourette (Eveux-sur-Arresle, France, 1957–60), whose monumentality would inspire many brutalist buildings in the 1960s. The first scheme for the A & A also resembled one of Rudolph's last important projects for Florida, the Sarasota Senior High School (1958–60). It too had smooth panels of white painted concrete and regularly spaced sunscreens (figure 4.2). The thinness and regularity of the piers in

4.1 Rudolph, Yale University Art & Architecture Building (A & A), first scheme (c. 1959).

4.2 Rudolph, Sarasota Senior High School (Sarasota, Florida, 1958–60).

both the Sarasota and Yale structures were redolent of the decorative, lightweight qualities of romantic modernism, still significant for Rudolph.

There were other similarities between the Sarasota school and the Yale building. In Florida, an imposing, central, open-air entrance lobby formed a meeting place, like a piazza, that brought an urban dimension to this project, something that Rudolph wanted to foster no matter where he was building. He later said it was his first truly urban design and the basis for all that followed.[6] Breezes circulating through the lobby and adjoining open-air corridors cooled the building naturally. Some of this openness to the elements and monumental, urban grandeur was retained in the A & A Building, though the open-air spaces proved ill-suited to the cooler New England climate.

Increasingly critical of his own work, Rudolph was probably more dissatisfied with the first scheme for the A & A than his clients were, feeling that it did not adequately respond to its corner site and the larger urban context of the campus and city.[7] In what became a prolonged design process, Rudolph continued to revise schemes for the A & A over the next several years and even after ground was broken in December 1961. He largely retained the configuration of two central stacked, double-height chambers, but he elaborated on the overall form to give it a more monumental character recalling the solidity of Le Corbusier's La Tourette and other buildings of the past and present that he admired.

Rudolph published successive schemes for the A & A Building in architectural journals, the *Yale Daily News*, and the *New York Times*. He probably intended to attract attention to his work and practice, but in fact he raised expectations that put him under intense pressure to produce something extraordinary, something that would demonstrate his maturity as an architect. Rudolph's anxiety was heightened by a wave of criticism about his latest works and pedagogy that appeared in print just as he developed the final scheme for the A & A in 1960 and 1961. The A & A Building therefore became important for Rudolph as the justification to his critics for his search for expression.

Criticism

By 1961, critics were frequently asking what Rudolph stood for. His large-scale projects, both recently finished and nearing completion—the Jewett Arts Center (Wellesley College, 1955–58), Blue Cross and Blue Shield Building (1957–60), Greeley Laboratory (Yale University, 1957–59), Temple Street Parking Garage (New Haven, 1958–63), and Yale Married Student Housing (New Haven, 1960–61)—all appeared markedly different from one another.[8] The Sarasota Senior High School and the first scheme for the A & A Building suggested still another new direction. The criticism reflected a growing uneasiness about the eclectic range of sources referenced by modernism, especially by the practitioners of romantic modernism.

Echoing his criticism of the Italian neoliberty movement, British critic Banham warned that romantic modernism's eclectic use of historical models and decoration represented a regression from modernism's ethical stance, especially its defining break with historical forms, which pandered to popular tastes uncomfortable with modernism. Particularly put off by one of Philip Johnson's early schemes for his theater for the New York City Ballet at Lincoln Center (New York, 1959) inspired by art nouveau, Banham coined the derogatory term "Ballet School" architecture, thus characterizing romantic modernism as effete and even effeminate, associating it with the way that ballet was often stereotyped. Banham implicitly compared it to the forthright, authentic, and presumably masculine qualities of the "New Brutalism" he advocated.[9] Believing that ethics rather than aesthetics should inform architecture, the British were the most critical of romantic modernism. In a 1959 postcard, James Stirling told Colin St. John Wilson, another British instructor at Yale, that Yale students were interested in what was going on in Britain "and reacting against, ballet arch: i.e. Johnson, Saarinen, Rudolph etc."[10]

Rudolph experienced the first negative criticism of his career in 1960 because of his association with romantic modernism and also because of his perceived eclecticism. The British-born McGill University architectural historian Peter Collins was the first to question Rudolph's principles and pedagogy, in a November 1960 article for the *Manchester Guardian,* which was reprinted in the American journal *Progressive Architecture* in August 1961. Like Rudolph, Collins was interested in new directions for modernism and also shared with him a fascination for concrete, but his aversion to the aesthetic approach practiced by Rudolph put him squarely in the British camp.[11] Collins said Rudolph's work defied "classifiability" because each

of his buildings looked different from the others. Collins wrote, "On what principles, it is frequently rhetorically asked, are his designs based?" Collins said that to keep up with his reputation for innovation and the inexhaustible demands of the architectural journals, Rudolph had been "forced by the spirit of Madison Avenue to be a Form-Giver; to be a leader of fashion when he still confesses that he does not know the right direction to take."[12]

Among academics and cultural commentators, there were few more negative characterizations than to be associated with the advertising firms of Madison Avenue or with mass culture, the forces that many felt were destroying American culture and its prized individuality. For Rudolph, Collins's characterization must have been particularly galling as mass culture and the conformity it engendered were, in his mind, anathema to his expressive architecture.

American critics also questioned Rudolph's credibility and viability as a leader of the discipline. In a December 1960 assessment of his recent work for *Architectural Design,* another British journal, the MIT architectural historian Henry Millon wrote, "There is no absolute way to know if Paul Rudolph is a man of great genius, a better-than-mediocre figure, or, perhaps, a charlatan. But it seems to be clear that he is entering a profoundly different phase of his career that might be a more mature phase or might, equally, signal his collapse as a notable figure."[13]

Stung by these criticisms, Rudolph defended himself in the pages of *Perspecta* with an adamant statement about his beliefs accompanied by six successive schemes for the Yale A & A Building and other recent works. The seventh scheme for the A & A—the final one—was still being refined. Somewhat bombastically, Rudolph justified his search for his own means of expression with passionate phrases recalling Griswold's humanist rhetoric and Geoffrey Scott's thinking about the individual and the zeitgeist:

> The architect must be uniquely prejudiced. If his work is to ring with conviction, he will be completely committed to his particular way of seeing the universe. It is only then that every man sees his particular truth. Only a few find themselves in such a way. . . .
>
> Our commitment to individualism is partially a reaction to growing conformity in the 20th century, but more importantly an excitement when we sense magnificent new forces and their possibilities. There are too many new worlds to explore, too many new problems crying for solutions, for there to be a universal outlook (every critic implores the gods to make us the same) in an age of profound transition.
>
> An age expresses through its artists certain preferences and attitudes which are inherent to that age, but no man can ascertain at the time those which have validity.[14]

Rudolph was not safe from criticism, however, even in Yale's student-run journal. *Perspecta 7* was an assessment of the state of architecture in 1961. Critics described how modernism was splintering apart after the collapse of functionalism and other modernist institutions, including CIAM, which had disbanded by 1960. Instead of representing new directions, neoliberty, romantic modernism,

Project stages. The architect did not consider the first version suitable for the corner site. All subsequent plans are variations of the 'windmill-plan'. Stage 1: The corner is not particularly emphasized. Stage 2: Rounded shapes begin to appear in the horizontal elements. Stage 3: The corner grows in importance. Stage 4: Corners of the building gain 'weight'. Stage 5: Facades become transparent. Stage 6: The overall form becomes more refined.

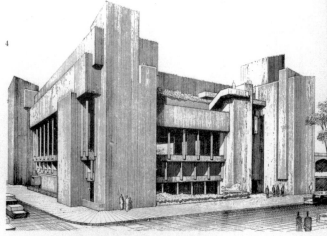

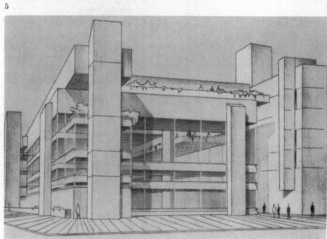

4.3 Schemes 1–6, A & A Building (1959–61).

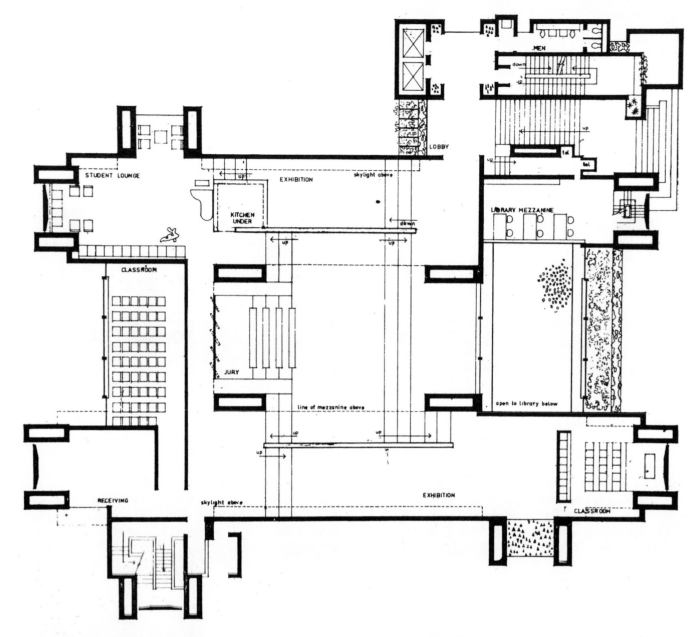

4.4 Final plan, A & A Building (c. 1961).

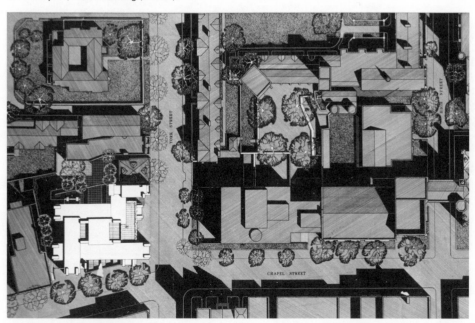

4.5 Site plan, A & A Building (c. 1961).

brutalism, and the different ways in which Americans including Eero Saarinen, Rudolph, and Johnson were each pursuing their own paths were all symptoms of a crisis that might lead to modernism's end.[15] Journalist Walter McQuade memorably described Rudolph as the architect searching most earnestly for a new means of expression in the "exploded landscape" of the post-functionalist era. McQuade painted a dramatic verbal portrait of a Rudolph possessed of great discipline and talent who seemed to be cracking from the strain of searching for a unique means of expression. He believed that Rudolph completely identified with his architecture: "Rudolph is so tense I think he may yet maim his talent. He is perhaps the most disquieting of all these architects. This may be because he has inserted himself so ruthlessly into his work, has been so recognizable personally in it. No matter how he varies the recipe for facades, I can see the faultless young crew cut head, the glinting-eyed face peering out of the windows; I can hear the quiet commanding voice. He is such a gifted, disciplined architect that he is going to destroy himself—or go bad—if he does not find a personal answer in the rubble of the exploded landscape."[16]

McQuade's description shows how Rudolph's buildings were believed to reflect his character to the point where he was "recognizable personally in it." It may be taken as a depiction of Rudolph in the throes of working and reworking the design of the A & A Building.

Between 1959 and 1963, Rudolph and his office staff, assisted by students from the architecture department, produced more than 1,000 drawings for the A & A, virtually all drawn by hand.[17] Rudolph's critics may have thought that his search for expression seemed directionless, but the six schemes for the A & A published in *Perspecta 7* (and presented on a single page in Rudolph's 1970 monograph) show a consistent development of symbolism, urbanism, decoration, and monumentality—his constant preoccupations—that can be traced through the design process (figure 4.3). The many buildings and forms that informed the A & A also illuminate the formalist perspective of Rudolph and those close to him, such as Johnson. The appreciation of pure form made examples from disparate eras comparable in their eyes.

Symbolism

To give the building a sense of coherence and dynamism, Rudolph developed the plan of the first scheme as a pinwheel, or a windmill as he sometimes called it. The pinwheel was a favorite form of Rudolph's because it suggested movement. This form and the related spiral, along with the gateway and the amphitheater, became part of Rudolph's vocabulary of symbolic forms.

Though Rudolph considered the pinwheel formally, or as a discrete piece of geometry, it was also symbolic, rich in associations with the past and full of suggestions for the present. The pinwheel was an ancient symbol associated with everything from the sun to movement. For Rudolph, the pinwheel was also a symbol of modernism itself. This figure became the basis of the plan of the A & A's primary public floor (figure 4.4). The long arms of the pinwheel housed classrooms, lounges, and services, such

as stairs and bathrooms, defined the exhibition room and drafting room at the building's center, and rose into towers at the ends that reached outward toward the surrounding city and campus.

As he developed the plan, Rudolph turned for inspiration from Le Corbusier's La Tourette to another landmark structure, Wright's Larkin Building (Buffalo, New York, 1904–06, demolished in 1950). For Rudolph, the office building's massive, opaque brick towers were another model for a new monumentality; additionally, invoking Wright's structure suggested his realliance with the origins of American modernism, as would be apparent elsewhere in the A & A. Wright organized the Larkin Building into a main block adjoined by a nearly independent entrance and service wing; at the A & A, Rudolph placed the stairs, elevators, and bathrooms in an almost free-standing service tower on the north side. Rudolph's stacked central exhibition and drafting rooms corresponded to the memorable, multistory interior atrium at the center of the Larkin Building.[18] Rudolph intended his tower to serve the future additions that might be constructed to the north along York Street. Allowance for growth was a quality that Rudolph would frequently emphasize in his architecture in the coming years.[19]

Urbanism

In addition to its formal and symbolic role, the dynamic form of the pinwheel, Rudolph believed, could also help engage the building with the city. Rudolph's site plan depicts how he aligned the arms of the pinwheel to parallel the streets of New Haven, turn the corner from York Street to Chapel Street, and reach out toward the Yale campus and the city (figure 4.5). The exactness with which the existing campus was rendered in the site plan attested to Rudolph's admiration for Yale, an urban university thoughtfully integrated into the colonial street grid of New Haven. Though most modernists were dismissive of the eclectic academic architecture of the 1920s and 1930s, Rudolph often told students that Yale's Collegiate Gothic and Georgian revival courtyards revealed much about how to knit together structures of different periods and styles to form a diverse yet cohesive whole.[20]

In a way that recalled the methods used by earlier campus architects to foster cohesion, Rudolph steadily enlarged and defined the tower at the corner of Chapel and York Streets until it became almost freestanding; the concrete shaft was visible down the length of Chapel Street all the way to the historic New Haven Green, a distance of several city blocks. Rudolph envisioned the A & A as a landmark for New Haven as well as for Yale probably because of his familiarity with the blocks where he lived and worked and his knowledge of Lee's and Logue's plans for the city.

Rudolph's understanding of the A & A Building as part of New Haven's elaborate and varied cityscape suggests his awareness of the aesthetically based urbanism of Gordon Cullen, British architect, illustrator, and urbanist. Instead of advocating modernism's functionalism-derived and tabula rasa planning, where everything was cleared from a site in order to build anew in a consistent way,

4.6 A Street in Shrewsbury, England, from Gorden Cullen, *Townscape* (1961).

4.7 Rudolph, elevation of Chapel Street, New Haven (c. 1961).

Cullen, like Rudolph, emphasized the aesthetic or visual over other considerations and, more specifically, analyzed how urban spaces affected pedestrians. Cullen's illustrations in his book *Townscape* (1961) showed how buildings of different eras accrued along the irregular streets of an English town, resulting in a pleasing whole (figure 4.6). Rudolph's drawing of the north side of Chapel Street showed in detail how the pedestrian could experience the street and the diverse, historic buildings of the campus on the approach to the A & A. It is as careful as one of Cullen's townscape drawings, though more sharply delineated (figure 4.7).

It is no surprise that Banham saw Cullen's conceptions as formalist and reactionary.[21] But by the early and mid-1960s, a range of studies looked beyond the functionalist-based city planning of the immediate past. Kevin Lynch, Jane Jacobs, and Christian Norberg-Schulz, though varying in perspective, attempted to explain the reactions of individuals to environments that had grown over time by considering the ways in which passersby perceived details such as streets, pavements, and lamp posts.[22]

It is notable that Rudolph had listed visual perception as the third of his "forgotten fundamentals" in the very first talk he gave to the Department of Architecture as its chairman in January 1958.[23] Aesthetics and personal experience colored the ways Rudolph's cohort at Yale discussed urbanism during those years. Vincent Scully, in his lectures, narrated his own experience of exploring ancient Greek temple complexes such as the Acropolis. Johnson, using similar personal terms in his 1965 *Perspecta* article "Whence and Whither: The Processional Element in Architecture," described how the pedestrian encountered real buildings in real time, most memorably along the

route to his own Kline Biology Tower at Yale (New Haven, 1964–65).[24]

Rudolph's drawing of Chapel Street called attention to the various structures built for the study of art at Yale, demonstrating how he thought about the A & A Building as a culmination in the evolution of the university's facilities for the arts. Originally a Ruskinian Gothic edifice of 1864 called Street Hall, the Yale University Art Gallery had been expanded along Chapel Street in 1927 with a romanesque addition and in 1954 with Louis Kahn's addition. An imaginary line from the top of the main block of the A & A to the top of the 1927 addition shows that Rudolph calibrated his structure to the existing ones.[25] Rudolph related his building to the campus in many other spatial and visual ways, also evidenced in his drawing. In addition, the varied heights of the terraces and towers of the A & A gave it an irregular silhouette similar to the picturesque skyline of Yale with its many towers of different styles and periods. Rudolph also showed how the A & A belonged to the campus's tradition of monumental masonry edifices by including in his drawing buildings blocks away from Chapel Street, such as the Gothic bell tower of Branford residential college and the tower-like, blocky masses of the Collegiate Gothic Sterling Library and the Graduate School.

Rudolph admired Kahn's architecture greatly, and he wanted to forge a close relationship between his A & A Building and Kahn's adjacent Yale University Art Gallery addition (1954), which he knew so well. Rudolph said the openness of the transparent banks of windows at the center of the A & A complemented Kahn's blank masonry wall expanse along Chapel Street in what he called a "reciprocal relationship" (figure 4.8). Further, Rudolph said that the two buildings together marked the edge of the campus

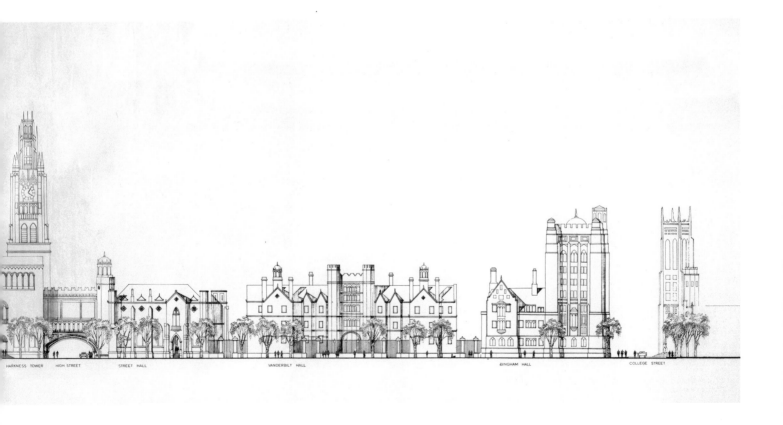

HARKNESS TOWER   HIGH STREET   STREET HALL   VANDERBILT HALL   BINGHAM HALL   COLLEGE STREET

4.8 A & A Building, and Louis Kahn's Yale University Art Gallery (1954).

like a gateway.[26] His A & A towers also resembled the towers of Kahn's laboratory at the University of Pennsylvania (Alfred Newton Richards Research Buildings, Philadelphia, 1957–64).

Concrete and Decoration

The A & A Building marked the first appearance of the corrugated concrete that would become Rudolph's signature. Corrugated concrete walls, which signal the relationship between the A & A and Yale's monumental masonry buildings, appear in the second scheme for the building in 1960. Though often referred to as bush-hammered or corduroy concrete, Rudolph called it corrugated concrete because its ridged and furrowed surface resembled cardboard packing material.[27] He did not invent corrugated concrete but adapted it for his own use in collaboration with Charles Solomon of the Macomber Company, the Boston construction firm that built the A & A and several other modernist buildings at Yale. Treating most interior and exterior walls the same way gave Rudolph's A & A Building a consistency that answered his critics' concerns about the range of details and finishes he employed in single works. The corrugated surface consisted of parallel, closely spaced vertical ridges of cast concrete, one-half inch at their narrowest, that were broken by masons with a heavy three-pound "bush hammer," that is, one with with a grid of pyramidal points (figure 4.9). Aligning the corrugated ridges from the different horizontal pours was a considerable technical feat, a demonstration of Solomon's and his workmen's skills.

Hammering the concrete exposed an aggregate of stones, micas, and seashells that glittered and shone in the sunlight (figure 4.10). Some of these unusual ingredients had a symbolic value for Rudolph; in the walls of one of the subterranean corridors, Rudolph encased half of an iridescent nautilus shell whose shape echoed the spiraling form of the pinwheel plan of the building. The small shell also suggested how Rudolph's building related to others he admired. The nautilus shell had been an inspiration for Wright's Guggenheim Museum (New York, 1943–59), and the crab shell had influenced Le Corbusier's chapel at Ronchamp (Notre Dame-du-Haut, Ronchamp, France, 1950–55).[28]

Corrugated concrete represented the end product of Rudolph's years of investigations into how to produce complex, shifting patterns of light and shadow and give texture and depth to the surfaces of his buildings. He had first thought of using bush-hammering in 1954, for the limestone walls of his unbuilt U.S. Embassy in Jordan (project, 1954–58). He had achieved similar effects of light and shade by means of shadow-casting devices, such as the latticework umbrella of the Hiss House and the decorative screens of the Jewett Arts Center. As Rudolph himself later suggested, the multiple, closely spaced vertical lines that became dominant in his presentation drawings of this period—a technique he developed to evidence texture and surface variety—may also have suggested to him the corrugated concrete.[29]

Though he never acknowledged Kenzo Tange as an influence, Rudolph's walls at the A & A resembled the

4.9 Bush-hammering the corrugated concrete, A & A Building.

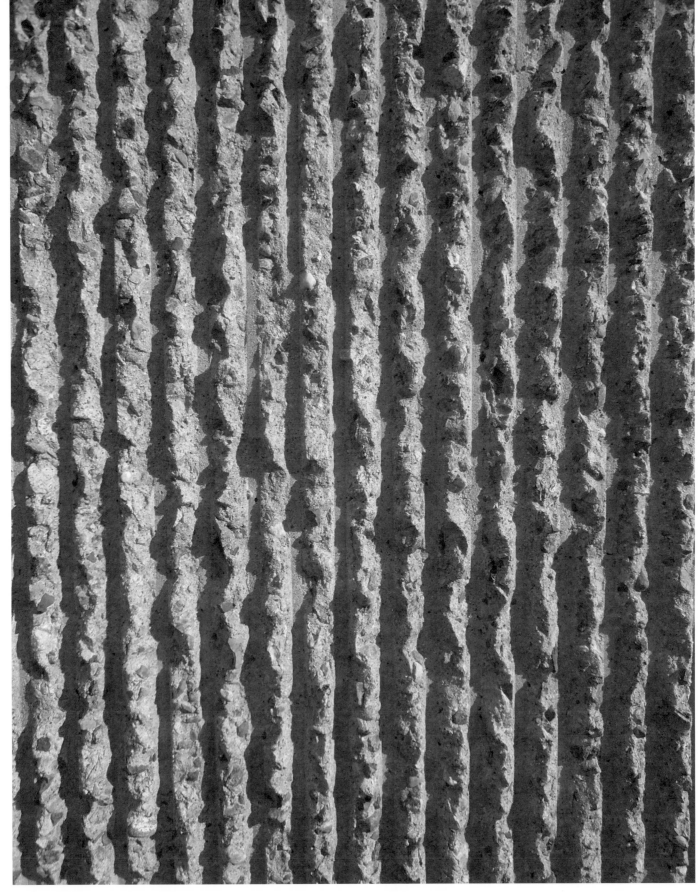

4.10 Corrugated concrete, A & A Building.

bush-hammered, raised ridges at Tange's Administration Building for Kagawa Prefecture in Takamatsu, Japan (1955–58), which Rudolph saw during the World Design Conference in May 1960 in Tokyo (figure 4.11).[30] Another similarity between Rudolph's second scheme for the A & A (published in the *New York Times* in June 1960) and Kagawa Prefecture was the suggestion of a giant post and beam building in concrete.[31] Rudolph saw more concrete buildings in Japan and in India, where he stopped on the way home, that would influence his other buildings. He said that the *beton brût* (raw concrete) of Le Corbusier's Chandigarh projects in India had inspired the striated, concrete walls of his Temple Street Parking Garage.[32]

Other projects at Yale supervised by Charles Solomon and built by Macomber anticipated the A & A's corrugated concrete walls. For his Morse and Stiles Residential Colleges at Yale (1958–62), Saarinen was working with the firm to develop roughened, monolithic concrete walls studded with large pieces of rubble, which resembled the varied textures and random arrangements of block and brick of the campus's traditional buildings (figure 4.12). In the 1920s and 1930s, masons had deliberately distressed or antiqued the masonry walls of Yale's Collegiate Gothic buildings to make them look old, like the walls of a college at Oxford or Cambridge, a treatment that probably inspired Saarinen and Rudolph.

How to make modern decoration was much discussed in architectural circles at Yale at the time. Saarinen commissioned Constantino Nivola to make abstract, decorative, concrete sculptures and light fixtures for Morse and Stiles, some of which protruded from the walls like gargoyles. Rudolph's concrete surfaces were similar in intent and can be understood as part of his larger effort to "construct decoration," as he had in the Temple Street Parking Garage. His ridges, an all-over form of decoration covering every wall surface, are integrated into the building's structure. Rudolph had written about the possibility of "completely ornamenting buildings" with all-over patterning in an article in 1958.[33] The moving shadows cast from the concrete ridges and the shining, glittering aggregate added ornamental complexity.

Like the parking garage, the A & A Building blurred the line between decoration, sculpture, and structure, thus reiterating the basis of Rudolph's program for the building: to bring about a synthesis of the arts. To memorialize this agenda, Rudolph commissioned Robert Engman, a friend and the chairman of Yale's sculpture program, to design a twenty-foot-high cast-concrete sculpture entitled *Column*. The vertical form, penetrated by groupings of voids arranged rhythmically, echoed the building's towers.[34] Rudolph called it a "totem" and said that for him it recalled the past, when decoration was "much more a part of the building."[35] Seemingly an integral part of the building and constructed at the same time (though cast independently), the sculpture appeared to grow out of the corrugated concrete perimeter wall on the south side of the A & A (figure 4.13). *Column* was an extension of the building like Nivola's sculptures for Morse and Stiles. It was another example of how Rudolph attempted to construct decoration. Engman inscribed the piece with the names of faculty

4.11 Kenzo Tange, Kagawa Prefecture Building (Takamatsu, Japan, 1955–58).

4.12 Eero Saarinen, Morse and Stiles Residential Colleges at Yale University (1958–62).

4.13 Robert Engman, *Column* (1963), A & A Building.

from different departments of the school, including Albers, Rudolph, and himself, commemorating the collaboration among the arts at Yale. Like the eagle in Rudolph's Amman embassy, symbolic of the United States, or the nautilus shell that referred to the pinwheel plan, *Column* encapsulated the subjects Rudolph investigated in the design of the A & A Building.

A marked departure from the delicacy of the ornament of romantic modernism, the roughness of the corrugated concrete walls of the A & A transformed the character of Rudolph's architecture. The breaking of the ridges with a hammer imbued the corrugated concrete with a masculine forcefulness, like that attributed by Scully to Louis Sullivan's architecture, that was characteristic of the building as a whole.[36] Such forcefulness was, of course, considered one of Rudolph's chief personal characteristics. The photographer Robert Damora suggested that Rudolph and his building, particularly its prickly exterior, were one and the same when he superimposed a photo of the architect across the corrugated surface of the A & A for the February 1964 cover of *Progressive Architecture,* surely one of the most remarkable portraits ever of an architect and his building (figure 4.14).

Monumentality

With the Yale A & A Building, Rudolph redoubled his efforts to revive monumentality, an investigation begun with his proposed U.S. Embassy in Amman, Jordan (project, 1954–58). Rudolph's visit to Le Corbusier's government buildings at Chandigarh provided lessons about monumentality, but his sustained interest in the subject was not solely a result of this encounter. In 1961, the competition for the Franklin Delano Roosevelt Memorial in Washington, D.C.—Rudolph was a juror—had renewed interest in this subject, long of concern for architectural discourse. Rudolph participated in the final reviews that selected a monumental Stonehenge-like arrangement of steles by Pederson and Tilney just as he was reworking his final schemes for the A & A in 1961 to give them a heavier, more forceful character.[37]

Rudolph made monumentality the subject of a colloquium for Yale alumni that he organized in April 1963, just six months before the November dedication of the A & A Building. Studio art, graphic design, and city planning faculty members spoke about their respective discipline's approaches to monumentality in front of prominent graduates, all leaders in government, business, and education.[38] Rudolph himself led tours of the unfinished A & A for distinguished guests such as August Heckscher, the Kennedy administration's special consultant for the arts. Heckscher was already well disposed toward Rudolph's monumentality: he had discussed how new monumental buildings for the arts could improve American life in his 1962 book *The Public Happiness.*

The title of Rudolph's unpublished lecture for the colloquium, "Monumentality Versus Humanism in Architecture," suggests that he wanted to pre-empt interpretations that might find the heavy forms of his A & A Building authoritarian, always a problem for monumentality.[39] In 1962, Pederson and Tilney's competition entry

for the FDR memorial had in fact been rejected by the Commission of Fine Arts and the Roosevelt family because they found its monumentality inappropriate and oppressive.[40] Rudolph prepared for his talk by reading about a 1948 symposium on the new monumentality, participants in which had included Gropius, Sigfried Giedion, and Henry-Russell Hitchcock.[41] The new monumentality of the 1940s attempted to recover monumentality from the totalitarian regimes that had made it their own during the 1930s by outlining steps for creating large-scale, lightweight, and transparent civic buildings that would foster democratic communities.

In his talk Rudolph explained that despite monumentality's recent associations with authoritarianism, large-scale, public structures were necessary for civilization as symbols of public life. In heroic tones similar to Griswold's grandiloquence, Rudolph concluded that monumentality could only be redeemed by a humanist architecture where "the human being" could "recognize himself, his experience, what he feels in the structures which surround him." Buildings would have to be active and dynamic, like human beings, and their bold forms would move those encountering them. Unlike the monumentality of the recent past, which was intended to appeal to the masses or a community, Rudolph's monumentality was intended to stimulate the individual, presumably a Yale student or passerby from New Haven, and reflected mid-century America's emphasis on individuality.

The completed A & A Building—bold, dynamic, and calibrated to elicit responses from individuals—fulfilled the program for monumentality that Rudolph described in his talk (figure 4.15). Dramatic juxtapositions prompted reactions from observers. The architecture was heavy and solid but varied; massive but dynamic. Transparent surfaces alternated with opaque ones. Towers appeared to advance toward the pedestrian and reach out to the city in a gestural manner. Radiating lines in the pavement, like those at the Jewett Arts Center at Wellesley, drew pedestrians up Chapel Street past Yale's buildings.

The approach and entrance to the A & A Building demonstrated how Rudolph's monumentality could affect minds and bodies, or transform them (figure 4.16). In effect announcing this intention, Rudolph installed a metal sculpture whose title was *Transformation* by Josef Albers consisting of overlapping parallelograms, above the front entrance. The sculpture's presence proclaimed the agenda of the building: to bring about a fruitful interaction between art and architecture. To reach the entrance and raised public floor housing the exhibition room, corresponding to what was known as the *piano nobile* in Italy, pedestrians ascended a grand staircase that rose in the chasm formed between the main block and the service tower to the north. Rudolph's staircase was the first of a series of staged experiences in the A & A intended to affect the user in a theatrical manner, like the choreographed journey through the Jewett Center's tunnel. Such movements through buildings had been characteristic of the monumentality of the past, as for example in baroque architecture. In her review of the A & A, Sibyl Moholy-Nagy in fact compared the entrance stair to the Vatican's Scala Regia (1635), or Royal Staircase, a similarly configured

February 1964 **PROGRESSIVE ARCHITECTURE**

4.14 Robert Damora, cover of *Progressive Architecture*, February 1964.

4.15 A & A Building (New Haven, 1958–63).

and dramatic baroque staircase designed by Gian Lorenzo Bernini.[42] In Rudolph's narrow, high space at Yale, climbers were compressed between the building's textured walls and its massive piers, which themselves seemed active. A concrete beam levitated above the stairs and appeared to reach out toward the street. Promising spatial release from this constricted area was a patch of distant sky visible through the open-air landing at the top of the stairs, though wind and rain whistling through it chilled climbers on New Haven's many cold and inclement days.

Despite Rudolph's concern about fostering better urban relationships, raising the primary entrance and public rooms above the ground isolated the building from its immediate surroundings, an approach that would prove problematic in a number of Rudolph's projects of the time. To better accommodate those entering the A & A, Rudolph provided a more convenient and humble doorway at the foot of the stairs, thus giving the building a human dimension that was a relief from its powerful immensity.

The Interior

Rudolph believed that he particularly excelled at designing interiors, a subject of sustained interest for him since his undergraduate days. Interiors offered opportunities for complete control. He could design everything inside a building, manipulating space, objects, and color in order to affect users, which was increasingly the goal of his architecture in the early 1960s. To create stimulating situations within the A & A Building, and to fulfill his dictum "we need caves as well as gold-fish bowls," Rudolph orchestrated narrow hallways, projecting balconies, changes in floor level, and juxtapositions of lightness and dark. Within the primary floors of the building (more or less seven to nine including mezzanines and basement), there were an astonishing thirty-seven variations in floor level, ranging from terraces at the top of the building to changes of just two to three steps within different rooms. The complex, multistory interior was exciting, and yet it was daunting for a generation accustomed to the easily traversed open floor plans of International Style buildings. Press accounts continually mentioned the thirty-seven different levels in amazement.

Walking through the building was a journey with exciting views at every turn. Glass interior walls opened up vistas and deep sightlines, making it possible to look through several levels and from one room into the next. Vivid orange carpet flared dramatically and contrasted with the concrete walls. To make the interior even more compelling and stirring, Rudolph adorned the corrugated concrete walls with architectural fragments and Beaux-Arts plaster casts, which were themselves a form of commentary about subjects, such as decoration and pedagogy, that concerned him greatly. The cumulative effect was powerful and surreal. In its 1964 assessment of the building, *Progressive Architecture* said that, though many found the interiors impractical, "few who visit this building can resist the mnemonic quality of its spaces, its light, its inventive furnishings, its use of art work."[43]

Widely published by architectural journals, Rudolph's masterful perspective section of the A & A Building seen from the Chapel Street side explained the completed

4.16 Staircase and entrance, A & A Building.

building's diverse spaces (figure 4.17).[44] Rudolph had used this drawing format on occasion in the early 1950s, but by the early 1960s began to employ it regularly because it expressed the growing spatial complexity of his buildings better than any plan could have. He closely supervised the making of the section drawing in his High Street office, even sketching the top-shaped human figures that balance precariously, as though buffeted by the active flow of space through the building. Thirty by forty-eight inches, the original drawing has both a commanding and a surprisingly crafted appearance (many portions were patched to reflect changes in the ever-evolving design). Architecture students, including Charles Gwathmey, helped in the laborious process of drawing the thousands of closely spaced lines that suggested the qualities of shadow and depth produced by light shining across the building's corrugated walls. Rudolph himself could draw the lines faster than anyone else.

The perspective section remains the best guide to the building. Studios for sculpture and the graphic arts are housed in two levels beneath the street; ingeniously configured lightwells and skylights admit sunshine into these subterranean caverns. The sculpture studios are wrapped around Hastings Hall, the auditorium, a shadowy, mysterious cave in itself (figure 4.18). Though the hall was not large, Rudolph divided it into several platforms and suspended small balconies from its sides so that it resembled a miniature theater. Ionic capitals from a demolished New Haven church, mounted on pikes at the front of the room, floated like disembodied heads. The canvas curtain across the stage was painted by abstract expressionist Willem de Kooning. Its title, *Labyrinth* (1946), was appropriate for such a spatially complicated building, and its presence suggested that the A & A was the architectural equivalent of abstract expressionism. As with elements of Rudolph's architecture, the gestural strokes of action painting were often intended to affect the viewer and express the individuality of the artist.[45]

In contrast to the darkened cave-like auditorium, the art and architecture library one floor above was a goldfish bowl. Light, space, and ceilings of different heights alternated with one another, forming bright areas for interaction and darker ones for solitary study. In its upper story, glass walls brought in light from the street and allowed views into the exhibition room at the same level (figure 4.19). Increasingly interested in lighting for its effect on the emotions, Rudolph designed for the library a metal framework with bare, incandescent light bulbs that appeared to float independently from the walls. Bright orange carpet—a hue which, according to Rudolph, reflected light—made the floor appear to rise or float in contrast to the heavy corrugated concrete walls and stimulated the eyes and emotions of the viewer.[46]

Knowing that the impact of color was difficult to predict, Rudolph generally restricted his palette to white and gray, as in his own apartment at 31 High Street. Many of his projects were finished in a unifying and unobjectionable white. Occasionally, he punctuated his interiors with bright colors, for example the red ceiling in the Blue Cross and Blue Shield Building. At the A & A, he believed more vibrant colors were appropriate. Rudolph found in the theories of his colleague Albers an obvious source of inspiration, but they were difficult to apply, so he returned to the architects who had long inspired him, including Wright, Le Corbusier, and De Stijl designers.[47]

For help with the interior color choices, Rudolph again turned to the interior designer Bill Bagnall from the Boston firm Contract Interiors, who had designed the brightly colored interiors of the Blue Cross and Blue Shield Building. Bagnall selected red and yellow as the basic palette; when mixed, they yielded orange, the color used for the library carpet and elsewhere. The choice of hues reflected generally accepted ideas about the perception of color. In his book on what he called "color therapy," Faber Birren, one of the foremost color theorists of the postwar years, said that red "stimulates the organism to action" and historically symbolized "fire and blood" and nobler attributes such as charity and generosity.[48] Cool colors such as the blues and greens that could calm the observer were not found in the A & A.

Inside the A & A Building, Rudolph curated a collection of art and objects intended to stimulate the mind, body, and eye. Collaborating with Carroll Meeks, a Yale architectural historian, he selected the de Kooning curtain in the auditorium and commissioned the Albers sculpture above the entrance. He also chose works by his favorite architects, such as sketches by Le Corbusier. To once again symbolize the interaction of the school's different departments in the structure, Rudolph installed large-scale murals by Yale faculty members Norman Ives and Sewell Sillman in office areas and in the drafting room.[49]

In what was considered his most provocative decorative gesture at the A & A, Rudolph installed in various places Beaux-Arts plaster casts of ancient reliefs, such as those from a Hellenistic or Roman sarcophagus hung on the far wall of the library. He scattered them throughout the building, so that they were often encountered unexpectedly, like the theatrically lit reliefs found in the darkened stairways (figure 4.20). Their appearance was surreal and mnemonic, as *Progressive Architecture* suggested, causing wonder in those observers who had not seen them before and eliciting memories in knowledgeable viewers.[50]

Rudolph's display was a disquisition about architectural pedagogy and history as well as scale and ornament. Rudolph explained, "These works have been used to reduce the scale of the interiors, which is, I believe, the basic relationship between all ornament and architectural space."[51] Students educated in the Beaux-Arts system had drawn from plaster casts, but most art and architecture schools had discontinued this practice after adopting modernist curriculums in the 1930s and 1940s. Rudolph recovered the casts from Yale's basements to indicate his openness to different approaches to teaching and his interest in learning from history. Though he did not espouse a revival of Beaux-Arts practices or architecture, he often stated that there was much to be learned from Beaux-Arts architecture, especially its approaches to urbanism, a view usually expressed only by the more architecturally conservative.[52]

Scully said the installation of the casts made some members of the architecture faculty "mad with rage," seeing it as a validation of the Beaux-Arts system that they

4.17 Perspective section, A & A Building.

4.18 Auditorium, A & A Building.

had fought hard to overthrow.[53] Rudolph admitted that the display had a polemical or contrarian edge to it, no doubt intended to stimulate debate or strong reactions; the casts also demonstrated Yale's commitment to history. The arrangement may in fact have reflected how Rudolph began to question the methods of the GSD, where he had been educated. By the early 1960s, Gropius's students who had repudiated his functionalism believed that he had repudiated history as well, symbolized at the GSD by the banishment of the Beaux-Arts plaster casts. Rudolph's comments to *Architectural Record* suggested that he wanted to correct this perceived wrong: "When Gropius came to Harvard, he threw out all the plaster casts. Now we are bringing them back again."[54] Responding to those who saw the display of casts as a traditionalist gesture, Rudolph emphasized their pedagogical qualities: "It is, of course, easy to criticize the use of the plaster casts, but I believe that the purist arguments against using them are outweighed by the effect of their 'presence' in a building devoted to learning."[55]

The display in Rudolph's office suggests that his deployment of the casts was also a form of exegesis about the ornamental qualities of his corrugated concrete walls. Plaster copies of Louis Sullivan's intricate terra cotta panels from the recently demolished Schiller Building in Chicago (1891–92) were hung on a beam above Rudolph's office door (figure 4.21). The proximity of casts and corrugated walls invited comparison, suggesting an equivalence or dialogue between Rudolph's raised relief walls, Sullivan's ornament, and other Beaux-Arts architectural

relief sculptures and ornament of the past. Sullivan's low-relief panels cast ever-shifting shadows across his building's facades in a manner similar to the raised ridges of Rudolph's corrugated concrete. On the other hand, the juxtaposition of Sullivan's casts and Rudolph's walls was a lesson about contrasting approaches to decoration. Sullivan's panels demonstrated the decoration of construction while Rudolph's corrugated concrete exemplified the construction of decoration, the opposite approach.[56]

Despite these differences, Rudolph found in Sullivan's work numerous qualities that appealed to him as he repudiated Gropius and reembraced the origins of American modernism. Sullivan was an American architect from the early years of modernism who had successfully invented new systems of decoration for his buildings. He had advocated subjectivity, action, and masculinity in architecture, all things that appealed to Rudolph. Perhaps Sullivan also appealed to Rudolph because of his rumored homosexuality or "sex troubles," which is how Philip Johnson alluded to it in print at the time.[57] Rudolph incorporated other architectural fragments from Sullivan's structures into the A & A Building. He used decorative ironwork elevator grills from Sullivan's Chicago Stock Exchange (1893–94, possibly designed by Frank Lloyd Wright) as entrance gates to the faculty offices and to the library, suggesting once more that Rudolph was realigning himself with American modernism's lineage.[58]

Rudolph's admiration for Wright was apparent throughout the building as well. In addition to the A & A's overall resemblance to the plan and massing of Wright's Larkin

4.19 Library, A & A Building.

4.20 Stairway, A & A Building.

4.21 Rudolph's office, A & A Building.

Building, Rudolph's exhibition room recalled the sanctuary of Wright's Unity Temple (Oak Park, Illinois, 1905–08), one of the first modernist experiments in monolithic poured concrete. Located at the center of the A & A's pinwheel plan, the double-height chamber was the school's primary public space for receptions, exhibitions, and juried reviews of student work (figure 4.22). Like Unity Temple's sanctuary, it featured four rectangular piers at its corners; at the A & A, these supported balconies for faculty offices. With the piers, Rudolph elaborated on his earlier attempts to integrate services and structure, as he had done for the Blue Cross and Blue Shield Building. The piers at the A & A rose through the structure from bottom to top and contained heating and cooling ducts, as did several perimeter piers attached to the towers.

One of the most charged places in the building, the alcove located between the piers on the west side of the exhibition room, was where architecture students displayed their work for critique by juries and spectators. Known as the "jury pit," it was intended by Rudolph to be an especially stimulating area, like the entrance to the building. The review process had previously been a nomadic affair; Rudolph made reviews in the jury pit into a theatrical ritual complete with a stage-like area, revolving panels for display, and a series of stepped platforms for seating. The alcove was similar to an amphitheater, which was becoming one of Rudolph's favorite archetypes, and

also reiterated the form of the auditorium several floors below. The position of the pit, in the school's primary public space, was intended by Rudolph to encourage members of other departments to use it for juries or to watch or listen to the architecture critiques in a way that would encourage interaction between the arts.[59]

The architecture students produced their projects in the drafting room above the exhibition room. In contrast to the smaller, nearly windowless exhibition room, the drafting studio occupied the entire floor of the building and was far brighter (figure 4.23). Like the exhibition room, it was a double-height chamber with balconies supported by the four great piers that rose through the building. It was both contained and inward looking, in ways that fostered concentration, yet also expansive and outward looking. Wall-size expanses of glass on the south, east, and west flooded the room with light and offered views of the surrounding city and campus. Multistory lightwells illuminated the center of the room naturally, while metal frameworks with exposed bulbs lit it artificially. About 150 to 160 undergraduates and 12 to 20 master's students occupied five platforms. The city planning department had its own separate mezzanine. The platforms of different heights beneath ceilings of different levels gave the room an internal topography, opening up sightlines that made it possible for students to see exchanges between peers and

The Yale Art & Architecture Building

4.22 Exhibition room with "jury pit," A & A Building.

4.23 Drafting room, A & A Building.

4.24 Artists' studios, A & A Building.

4.25 Penthouse, A & A Building.

faculty. Rudolph's multiple levels challenged the universal spaces and open plans of the International Style yet again.

Every element of the drafting room was intended to stimulate and instruct the student. A fourteen-foot-tall, second-century Roman statue of Minerva borrowed from the Yale Art Gallery presided over the room as a reminder of the importance of the past. Rudolph incised the proportional system derived from Le Corbusier's Modulor man on one of the room's enormous piers and complemented it with a relief of Leonardo's Vitruvian Man, providing another lesson about scale and how the human form could humanize modernism. Carrels with adjustable dividers screened the desks from one another, providing students with a degree of privacy. The bright red dividers punctuated the room with intense, floating fields of color, as might be seen in a De Stijl interior.

Rudolph placed the studios for the art students in the uppermost stories of the A & A Building to take advantage of the natural light at the summit of the building (figure 4.24). But he was surprised that the artists thought that their studios were too small and low ceilinged. Rudolph had not anticipated that studio spaces would have to become bigger to accommodate large-scale canvases, in part because of the delayed introduction of abstract expressionism to Yale. Albers, the chair of the art department, had resisted its introduction. After he retired in 1958, the department was leaderless for several years; interim chairs had little to say about the design of the studios. It was not until 1963 that a chair familiar with the New York art world, Jack Tworkov, would arrive, and by then the A & A was nearly completed.

The most talented students of the time, such as Richard Serra, Nancy Graves, and Chuck Close, never painted in the A & A Building, decamping to more generous studio spaces. Inadequate facilities became a long-standing source of disgruntlement about the A & A, and the goal of bringing under one roof all the members of the school was never truly achieved.[60]

At the very top of the A & A was a glamorous penthouse where Rudolph entertained and housed the school's most important guests (figure 4.25). Reiterating the primary spatial configurations and decorative effects of the building, the penthouse featured orange carpet, multiple levels, and plaster casts (in this case of Egyptian hieroglyphic reliefs) on its corrugated concrete walls. An antique candelabrum gave the room a curiously sacerdotal or gothic character, exemplifying the "mnemonic quality" of the interiors noted by Progressive Architecture. The room was the building's grand finale. Sweeping views from the penthouse and adjacent terraces again reminded viewers of the role the building played in the greater urban context of the campus and city.

Critical Response

The Yale Art & Architecture Building was dedicated on November 9, 1963, at a gala event attended by 2,300 guests. The ceremonies were tinged by somberness because of the death in April of the building's patron, President A. Whitney Griswold. Rudolph gave a brief presentation about the A & A to the large audience assembled in the exhibition room. The new Yale president, Kingman Brewster, formally accepted the building from Rudolph, and other dignitaries made pronouncements.

The keynote address was delivered by distinguished British architectural historian Nikolaus Pevsner. To Rudolph's chagrin, he advised students not to imitate the building because it was too individualistic. Pevsner thought that Rudolph's individuality and interest in aesthetics and historical forms were a reactionary undermining of modernism, which Pevsner believed was predicated upon the teamwork, objectivity, functionalism, and machine-inspired vocabulary of the 1920s.[61] This viewpoint reiterated the opinions being expressed by some of Rudolph's critics at this time. One witness said that Rudolph grew "pinker and pinker" as the full import of Pevsner's words, delivered in a room containing members of the Yale faculty and his friends Johnson and Henry-Russell Hitchcock as well as other luminaries of the architectural world, dawned on him.[62] Journalists reported that Pevsner's remarks were surprisingly negative for a keynote address.[63]

Reactions to the building varied. The three leading American architectural journals, Architectural Forum, Architectural Record, and Progressive Architecture, featured the A & A Building on their covers in January and February of 1964—an unprecedented concurrence—and described it in favorable terms, voicing only a few reservations about the internal complexity. The mainstream press also gave a great deal of favorable attention to the building. Articles appeared in the New York Times and Time magazine. The New York Times architecture critic Ada Louise Huxtable praised Rudolph and his building for daring to "question the rules that have become the established basis of most contemporary practice" such as the "ban on decorative enrichment" and "the validity of less is more."[64] Those who questioned the International Style and the still lingering legacy of functionalism admired the A & A, seeing it as a statement about the importance of history and aesthetics. In Architectural Forum, Sibyl Moholy-Nagy enthusiastically described the building as a much needed return to architecture as art.[65]

Surprisingly, some critics close to Rudolph were not so positive. In an astute but critical assessment that appeared in the British journal the Architectural Review, Vincent Scully praised the A & A Building's urban qualities but expressed strong reservations about its corrugated concrete. With some hyperbole, Scully wrote, "the slotted and bashed surface is one of the most inhospitable, indeed physically dangerous, ever devised by man. Brushing against it can induce injuries roughly comparable, one supposes, to those suffered in keelhauling. The building repels touch; it hurts you if you try."[66] Scully addressed the adverse effects of the increasing spatial complexity in Rudolph's buildings in an essay for an exhibition of Rudolph's work at the Yale University Art Gallery, organized to accompany the A & A Building's dedication. Scully noted that in Rudolph's new buildings, "a will towards sculptural body sometimes puts demands upon the individual user which not every psyche will be able to meet."[67] Scully's remark suggested the primary problem with Rudolph's approach to architecture: imagining

that reflecting the experiences of the user would humanize monumentality. But because it was difficult for him
to imagine any user other than himself, his buildings
nearly always reflected his subjectivity. After the review
appeared, Rudolph's relationship with Scully was never the
same.[68] Scully continued to describe Rudolph's projects
over the next decade, but never entirely positively. And he
would not champion Rudolph the way he would Kahn or
Robert Venturi.

Despite the mixed response, the A & A Building was a
success for Rudolph in its demonstration to his critics and
contemporaries that he had at last matured and achieved
a recognizable "Rudolph style." The signature corrugated
concrete was quickly imitated internationally. Beyond
advancing Rudolph's personal style, the A & A suggested
new directions for urbanism and the interior, and especially for monumentality. Rudolph had addressed that final
issue in a way that would inspire and instruct others for
the rest of the decade.

Five
Scenographic Urbanism

Rudolph enjoyed fantastic success in the early 1960s. It was impossible to open a newspaper, magazine, or architectural journal in the United States or abroad without seeing one of his projects or reading his opinions about the state of modernism. In 1963, the year the Yale A & A Building was completed, Rudolph was working simultaneously on six governmental, five academic, and three corporate projects.[1] He had nearly abandoned private houses, once his mainstay, for larger works.

Of the various building types, Rudolph most wanted corporate commissions, especially skyscrapers; however, he was least successful in this field, probably because businesses found his increasingly personal vocabulary ill-matched to their organizational ethos. Rudolph's few commissions for business were not office buildings but corporate research laboratories that he made as monumental as his public projects, for example the IBM Research and Manufacturing Facilities (East Fishkill, New York, 1962–66) and the Endo Laboratories (Garden City, Long Island, 1960–64).

Rudolph's monumentality and urbanism were better suited to the public realm. Beginning in the 1950s in cities such as New Haven and accelerating in the 1960s under the Kennedy and Johnson administrations, government-supported redevelopment transformed America's cities and provided Rudolph with numerous new commissions for civic buildings.[2] The building of new academic campuses and the expansion of existing ones, often publicly funded as well, also provided Rudolph with many jobs. His most significant public projects of this decade, the Boston Government Service Center (1962–71) and the campus for the Southeastern Massachusetts Technological Institute (Dartmouth, Massachusetts, 1963–72), elaborated on the signature monumental style that he had arrived at with the Yale A & A. To critique what he considered the banality and incoherence of contemporary approaches to urban renewal and campus design, Rudolph imbued them with a scenographic quality fit for the set of an opera, with swirling staircases, colorful, multistory, balconied interior spaces recalling baroque architecture, and great plazas resembling amphitheaters inspired by the ideas of nineteenth-century city planner Camillo Sitte.

Boston Government Service Center

Although in a project model the Boston Government Service Center (BGSC) (1962–71) appeared to be one massive structure, in fact it consisted of two connected low-rise buildings of corrugated concrete that formed a courtyard punctuated by a twenty-three-story office tower (figure 5.1). The BGSC was not completed as depicted in the model. The low-rise buildings and courtyard pavings were finished, but the tower and spiraling staircase at its

foot were never built. Originally to have been the work of three different firms, the complex was planned to house state and federal offices and facilities for physical and mental health, education, welfare, and social security. The Kennedy and Johnson administrations' New Frontier and Great Society programs funded the substantial expansion of these services through the 1960s.[3]

The complex was an integral part of one of the largest, most discussed redevelopment projects of the decade, Boston Government Center, which replaced sixty acres of commercial and residential buildings with a master plan by I. M. Pei & Associates (1961–62) (figure 5.3) Part of a larger effort to revive the stagnating city, similar to what was being done in New Haven, Government Center was the keystone for the "New Boston," Mayor John Collins's vision of a city whose renaissance would be symbolized by new modernist landmarks.[4] Rudolph had no interaction with Pei, whom he knew only slightly, or with Pei's partner, Henry Cobb. He was, however, friendly with one of the project's primary administrators, Edward T. Logue, the director of the Boston Redevelopment Authority (BRA); Logue had been deputy director for redevelopment in New Haven when Rudolph designed the Temple Street Parking Garage (1958–63) there.

The Government Center master plan exemplified one of the strategies typical of American city planning in the 1950s and early 1960s for redevelopment projects with many buildings: different architects were given separate commissions in the hope that the results would approximate the urban diversity of the past. The centerpiece for Boston was Kallmann, McKinnell and Knowles's acclaimed new Boston City Hall (1962–68) (figure 5.2). Rudolph admired the building, a landmark example of brutalist architecture, and was friendly with the members of the firm.[5] The other important buildings in the master plan were the John F. Kennedy Federal Office Building by Walter Gropius and TAC (1967); the Government Center Garage by Kallmann, McKinnell, and Wood with Samuel Glaser and Partners (1970); and a large office building, One Center Plaza, by Welton Beckett and Associates (1966–69).

Although critics praised individual buildings in Government Center, it was apparent even in its earliest stages that the complex would have a piecemeal, disjointed feeling, jarringly different from the historic brick and stone buildings and streets that had been demolished. In fact, Government Center represented many things Rudolph thought wrong with urban planning and redevelopment in the early 1960s. The enclosed, sheltered plaza of his BGSC was a contrast to the large, open City Hall plaza, and encapsulates Rudolph's perspective on city planning at the time.

Sitte's Influence

For the most part, modernists had favored openness in twentieth-century urban planning, maintaining that undue density caused social problems and that expansiveness and green, park-like spaces were healthful and therapeutic. The early 1960s saw a shift away from this type of thinking, and Rudolph, representative of this shift, had concluded

5.1 Rudolph, coordinating architect, model, Boston Government Service Center (BGSC) (1962–71).

5.2 Kallmann, McKinnell and Knowles, Boston City Hall (1962–68).

5.3 I. M. Pei and Associates, Boston Government Center, master plan (1961–62), model.

that open spaces caused alienation. Instead he advocated enclosure, believing that it stimulated strong, positive, emotional responses from individuals and the community. Rudolph's notion of what constituted community was unclear, however, perhaps because of his intense focus on individuality. Rather, his notions about urbanism, enclosure, and communal space—mostly an appreciation of the traditional city's formal, aesthetic qualities—were drawn largely from the late nineteenth-century Austrian planner Camillo Sitte's book *City Planning According to Artistic Principles* (1889).[6] Rudolph frequently referred to Sitte in articles and lectures and in discussions about urbanism for his studios at Yale. Like Sitte, Rudolph believed that buildings that shared walls exemplified tighter, more cohesive urbanism.

Famously employing the term "agoraphobia" to describe the alienating effects of vast open urban spaces, Sitte criticized the psychological impact of conventional approaches to planning in the nineteenth century.[7] His proposal for enclosing the plaza in front of the Votivkirche in Vienna showed how arcades and gateways could be used to shape the open expanses of the new Ringstrasse extension to the city into more psychologically comforting, enclosed spaces based on the traditional squares and piazzas of Italy that he admired (figure 5.4).

In a way that appealed to the musician in Rudolph, Sitte thought the city should be like the stage set for an opera. It would be a Wagnerian *Gesamtkunstwerk*, a total work of art, with squares and piazzas for civic activities such as parades and communal festivals, that would have the emotional impact of theater directed by a great conductor.

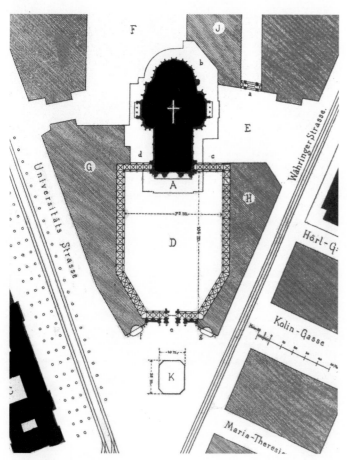

5.4 Camillo Sitte, Votivkirche Plaza, *City Planning According to Artistic Principles* (1889).

These views confirmed Rudolph's own, and he found especially appealing Sitte's criticism of conventional planning strategies, collaboration, and bureaucratic organization. Sitte said, "Works of art cannot be created by a committee or through office activity, but only by a single individual; an artistically effective city plan is also a work of art and not merely an administrative matter. That is the crux of the whole matter."[8] Though Sitte was sometimes criticized for favoring traditional architecture, modernists—among them Le Corbusier and postwar architects and urbanists ranging from Gordon Cullen to Josep Lluís Sert and Eero Saarinen—had long been inspired by his writings.[9]

Rudolph's suggestions for "Sitte-esque" improvements for Washington, D.C., made at the behest of *Architectural Forum* in 1963, indicate that his BGSC was indeed a critique of conventional approaches to redevelopment. Rudolph never cited Sitte in the *Architectural Forum* article, but the influence of the Austrian planner's concepts is apparent in Rudolph's sketch proposing an arcaded forecourt for the U.S. Capitol; the arcades would link to nearby structures, including the Supreme Court and the Library of Congress. On the opposite side of the Capitol, infill buildings, often in the form of gateways, would define the amorphous spaces of the National Mall (figure 5.5).

Rudolph said in *Architectural Forum* that most recent modern civic architecture in Washington, in comparison to government buildings of previous eras, was inappropriately scaled and "anemic." He may have had in mind the romantic modern, neoclassically inspired porticoes of Edward Durell Stone's National Cultural Center, one of the largest, most high-profile projects for the city, which became the Kennedy Center (1958–71). The Jewett Arts Center had been Rudolph's own essay in romantic modernism, but, like many of his contemporaries, he too reacted against the style by the early 1960s. Calling for bolder, more expressive, and more powerful forms, Rudolph said, "Virility, strength, spirit, and the dynamic—these are the qualities to be sought in the capital of democracy, not prettiness." Echoing Sitte's criticisms of planning by committee, he wrote in the heroic tones of the early 1960s, "The planner's approach is insufficient to accomplish that which is worthwhile. Finally, only art can move men to action."[10] Rudolph's suggestions never yielded commissions for Washington, as he had probably hoped, but his BGSC and many of his other projects of the early 1960s represent his attempt to use Sitte's concepts to enliven the banal redevelopment projects of the era.

Capturing the Commission

The story of how Rudolph came to design the BGSC is one about the architect at the height of his powers, when his virtuosity enthralled his colleagues and appeared to channel the political and economic forces of urban redevelopment into compelling civic forms. As originally conceived, the complex consisted of three independent structures on a boomerang-shaped site cleared by the BRA and bounded by Staniford, Merrimac, and New Chardon Streets. In keeping with its policy of promoting diversity of expression, the BRA assigned each building to a different Boston architectural firm: M. A. Dyer with Pedersen and Tilney Company

Applying these principles, Mr. Rudolph has roughed out (below) some of the possible results: **(A)** The Supreme Court is relocated and placed over existing bridges, to form terminus for Maryland Avenue and a southern entrance to the city. **(B)** Maryland Avenue is architecturally defined, and given a "Madison Memorial Gateway" **(C)** at its Capitol end. **(D)** The Mall is also given more decisive form. **(E)** Pennsylvania Avenue is defined by buildings of uniform height, with plazas forming alcoves on alternating sides. **(F)** Pershing Square becomes an important terminus, the other one, at the Capitol end **(G)**, being a proposed "FDR Memorial Gateway." The entire area around the Capitol **(H)** has been scaled down and defined with buildings that link existing structures and spatial sequences that add drama to the approach to the Capitol. The gaping hole **(I)** toward Union Station has been closed off, but vistas remain toward the station. Gateways and plazas **(J)** around the Supreme Court and the Library of Congress are scaled to fit those existing structures.

5.5 Rudolph, improvements for Washington, D.C., *Architectural Forum* (1963).

drew Health, Education and Welfare; Shepley, Bulfinch, Richardson and Abbott received Employment and Social Security; Desmond and Lord were given Mental Health.[11]

Hoping to capitalize on Rudolph's reputation, the chairman of the established firm Desmond and Lord, Richard R. Thissen, Jr., hired Rudolph as a design consultant. Thissen, a businessman and not an architect, believed that Rudolph's affiliation with Yale and reputation and design skills could raise the profile of the firm. In effect, Rudolph became the firm's chief designer for the Mental Health building (and other projects) because there was no one of his caliber at the firm.

Although the role of design consultant may have seemed inimical to an upholder of individual genius—and indeed it eventually proved to have its drawbacks—Rudolph was initially enthusiastic because Thissen granted him almost complete design autonomy. Additionally, the firm's thirty or so members provided him with more assistance than his own staff could provide. Rudolph drew a regular salary from Desmond and Lord, which he liked because it gave him some financial stability.[12]

Each firm participating in the BGSC project produced its own design for a freestanding building, but they soon realized that the structures were poorly related. Rudolph took this moment as an opportunity to expand his involvement. He convinced all three firms to meet in New Haven (his home ground) on June 13, 1962. After the members of each firm debated different approaches to their collaboration, Rudolph seized their attention theatrically; in a virtuoso display of his design skills and leadership, he took just seconds to sketch a plan in which the buildings would be joined to form a roughly triangular complex enclosing a central courtyard focused on a twenty-three-story tower. Essentially, Rudolph had combined three separate buildings into one large structure (figure 5.6).[13]

Published in many journals along with accounts of the anecdote about its creation, the sketch was celebrated as the mark of Rudolph's consummate design skills. Though the concept was no doubt thought out well in advance, Rudolph appeared to have arrived at a solution intuitively, in the manner expressive of genius celebrated by Geoffrey Scott and Sitte. He was admired for taking action, after study and reasoning—the methods he thought most modernist planning emphasized to too great an extent—had failed. The final plan for the complex was almost identical to the original pen and ink sketch (figure 5.7). Rudolph said of his solution, "Too many specialists and bureaucrats with overlapping authority created a vacuum which left the way open for an idea."[14]

Rudolph consolidated his control of the project in subsequent meetings in an equally dramatic and calculated manner. Charles G. Hilgenhurst, director of the BRA's office of Planning, Urban Design and Advanced Projects, recalled that, at the next meeting in Boston, Rudolph deliberately upstaged the other firms by arriving late and with fully realized drawings. Hilgenhurst recounted, "Twenty minutes late, Paul Rudolph walked onto the stage followed by his crewcut entourage from Yale. After a few brief apologies he unrolled a series of black line prints. . . . The effect was immediate, and he seized advantage of the moment and

began to expound the 'philosophy' of his design. The plan was unchanged—but now the architecture had emerged."[15]

Swayed by Rudolph's ideas, conviction, reputation, and showmanship, the other firms embraced his plan. Logue named him coordinating architect, granting him the authority to supervise the design of all exteriors. Overseeing the project in much the same way that he performed his studio critiques at Yale, Rudolph reviewed each firm's contribution during weekly visits to Boston between 1962 and 1965. To assist him, Rudolph had a recent Yale graduate, James McNeeley (Yale class of 1960), appointed as his liaison at Desmond and Lord. It was a position of some responsibility that might have gone to an older man, but Rudolph often chose young, inexperienced architects to work for him, perhaps because he was accustomed to a student-teacher relationship, or perhaps because a young architect would not challenge his decisions or authority.

To further facilitate the completion of the BGSC, Rudolph also set up a small Boston office of his own.[16] He gave his architects weekly assignments, usually leaving them rough sketches on yellow tracing paper that they would develop into larger drawings "in a way that Rudolph would do it himself," recalled William Grindereng, the office manager in New Haven. Rudolph reviewed his staff's work carefully, remembering every detail and elaborating on them himself. He was "very demanding," and the one day a week that he visited Boston to meet with the other firms and his staff was known as "ogre day."[17]

The tenor of Rudolph's relationships with the different firms varied. He worked well with the designer of the Employment Security Building, Jean Paul Carlhian from Shepley, Bulfinch, Richardson and Abbott, though they frequently got into heated discussions. Rudolph urged Carlhian to make his portion of the complex more sculptural and plastic, like Rudolph's own Mental Health Building. On the other hand, Rudolph found Dyer, Pedersen, and Tilney's scheme for the tower inconsistent with the other parts of the complex. They were dismissed, and Rudolph redesigned the tower himself.[18] The project developed quickly, assuming almost its full form between June 1962 and spring 1963, though construction was delayed until the spring of 1967 because of funding problems.

Design Criteria

At the meeting in Boston that led to his appointment as coordinating architect, Rudolph outlined five design criteria for the BGSC. Though he would have resisted following anyone else's guidelines, he had no problem prescribing his own. The five criteria shed light not only on the Boston building complex but also on the increasing dramatic qualities of his other contemporary projects and also the emergence of a vocabulary common to the large-scale concrete brutalist buildings of the time. The application of these criteria is evident in the portion of Rudolph's Mental Health Building visible from the corner of Staniford and Merrimac Streets; this was the portion of the complex he designed entirely himself (figure 5.8).

The first benchmark of the five was a common material and surface treatment for all the buildings. Rudolph chose the corrugated concrete that he had developed for his

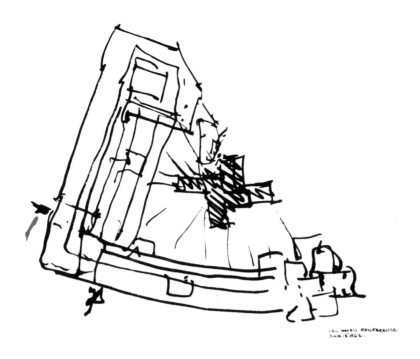

5.6 Rudolph, sketch, BGSC (1962).

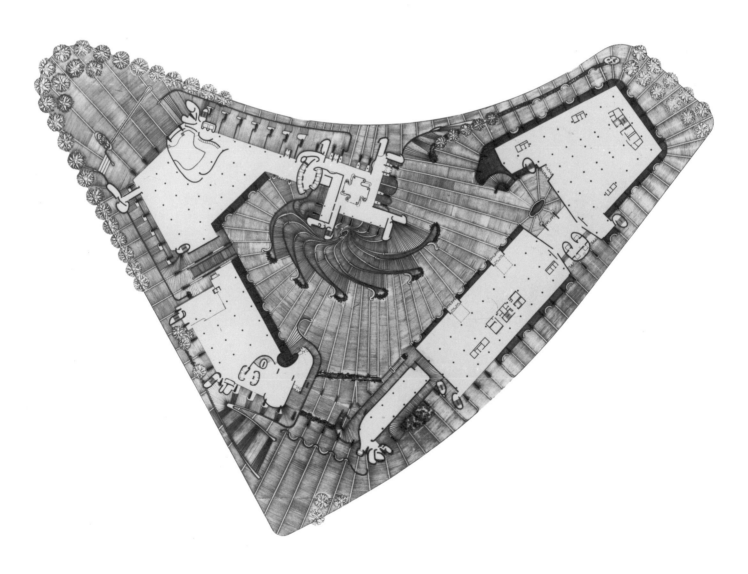

5.7 Rudolph, coordinating architect, plan, BGSC (c. 1963).

5.8 Rudolph, Mental Health Building, BGSC.

A & A Building at Yale, which was then under construction. Vappi Construction of Boston executed the high-quality monolithic corrugated concrete walls at the BGSC. Though the A & A's corrugated concrete had been developed by Macomber Construction for the particular context in New Haven, the medium quickly became virtually a trademark for Rudolph, employed by him for a range of projects in different settings and emulated by others internationally.

The second criterion was massive rectangular piers with rounded corners at the periphery of each structure. These were to vary from three to twelve feet in diameter and four to seven floors in height. The piers imparted a sense of rhythmic order that helped unify the complex. For Rudolph, these elements made the large scale of the building comprehensible in the context of the city. He believed that passing pedestrians would be able to understand the dimensions of the complex by comparing the size of their bodies to the buildings' piers.

The third standard was a deep cornice that would unite the rooflines of all three structures. The cornice consisted of one or more projecting floors, similar to the studio floors atop the A & A Building, that conferred on the complex a top-heavy silhouette like that of the Boston City Hall. This profile, which became typical of brutalist monumentality, derived from Le Corbusier's postwar creations, such as his monastery of La Tourette (Eveux-sur-Arresle, France, 1957–60).

The fourth criterion was the articulation of all service areas, such as elevators, stair towers, and even toilets, with curvilinear shapes and towers. Such articulation would heighten the complex's expressive character. Rudolph's turrets gave the building a medieval or baroque character, a quality prevailing among his other contemporary projects.

The fifth specification was stepped interior facades. The inward-looking facades were required to consist of setback terraces that as a whole would form a bowl- or amphitheater-shaped central courtyard. Rudolph favored this amphitheater-like configuration and setback terraces in other projects of the time, as did his students at Yale and other architects (figure 5.9).

Topography

By the mid- and late 1960s, Rudolph would often speak of the possibilities of what he called a "topographical architecture," a concept whose origins lay in the Boston project. Looking for inspiration outside of Pei's master plan, Rudolph explored ways to give the complex a strong presence in the context of the existing city by making far-reaching connections between old and new. Again demonstrating his formalist way of looking at architecture—that is, seeing forms of disparate size and meaning as related by appearance—Rudolph claimed that the concave "bowl" of the courtyard was conceived as the inverse of the convex form of nearby Beacon Hill itself, as well as the gold dome atop the historic statehouse at the summit of Beacon Hill by Charles Bullfinch (1795–97), a landmark and symbol of the city.[19] Rudolph's thinking about how the complex would be perceived visually and spatially probably owed something to the concepts of architect

5.9 Courtyard, BGSC, model.

and planner Kevin Lynch, a contributor to the master plan for Government Center. Lynch explained, in his 1960 book *The Image of the City*, that pedestrians navigated urban terrain using landmarks both humble and grand that they perceived as "images." An "image" of immense size, Rudolph's proposed twenty-three-story tower would have identified the Government Service Center in the city (figure 5.10). Its anticipated role in the skyline recalled a 1961 proposal, by a design committee appointed by Logue and including Lynch, for a "high spine" of towers across the city that would create more meaningful and legible landmarks for the "New Boston."[20] To win support for his tower from the BRA, state and city officials, and the public, Rudolph hired Helmut Jacoby, one of the leading architectural renderers of the day, to make a presentation drawing that was more festive than his own impressive, but somber delineation. (Usually preferring to rely on his own singular way of rendering, Rudolph rarely employed professional renderers.)[21]

Jacoby's rendering shows Rudolph's poured-in-place concrete shaft rising twenty-three stories to terminate in a series of cornice-like projecting floors and turrets. Fulfilling one of Rudolph's design standards, the cornice gave the tower a memorable silhouette distinctive among the flat-roofed tall buildings nearby. A pinwheel-shaped plan provided numerous corner offices for managers and central work areas for clerks and secretaries. Notably different from Government Center's other tower, Gropius and

TAC's rectilinear twenty-six-story Federal Office Building, Rudolph's tower was a critique of the status quo in tall building design. It was the successor to his nearby Blue Cross and Blue Shield Building (1957–60), the parallel to his powerfully plastic Crawford Manor housing for the elderly (New Haven, 1962–66), and the progenitor of his Tracey Towers, two publicly funded middle-income apartment towers in the Bronx, New York (1967–74).

At the foot of the proposed twenty-three-story structure was what would have been one of Rudolph's most compelling but unfortunately never built pieces of stagecraft: a series of curving staircases resembling a giant spiral or nautilus shell that would have linked the plaza to the parking garage beneath it. Rudolph admired the nautilus form and had encased such a shell in the walls of the A & A Building. In the Boston proposal, the swirling series of stairs resembled a giant nautilus construction and would have exerted a powerful draw, pulling pedestrians toward the tower as though they were caught in a whirlpool. The courtyard paving was completed, and it had similar drawing properties. In a more subtle attempt to bring pedestrians to the tower, Rudolph sloped the surface of the courtyard gently downward and incised radiating lines recalling those at the Piazza del Campo in Siena, a similarly configured, amphitheater-shaped urban space with theatrical qualities long admired by Rudolph. To further foster community in this outdoor space, Rudolph proposed adorning the courtyard with the flags of the fifty

5.10 Helmut Jacoby, rendering of Health, Education and Welfare Tower, BGSC (project, 1963).

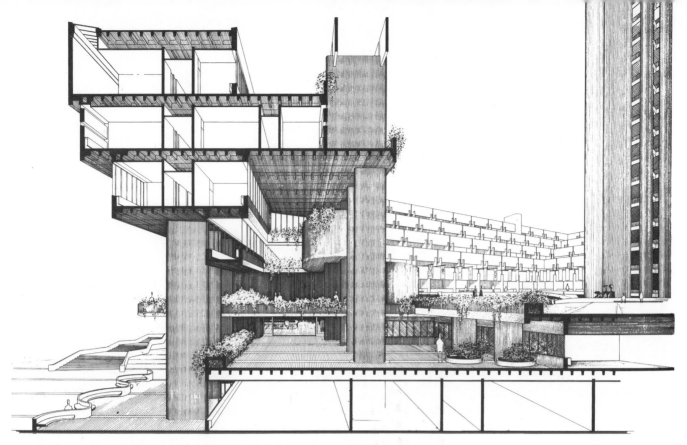

5.11 Perspective section, Mental Health Building, BGSC, William Grindereng, delineator.

5.12 Staircase, Mental Health Building, BGSC.

states to evoke the Sienese piazza, which was bedecked for festivals with flags representing the city's guilds and leading families.[22]

Scenography

Rudolph's decision to model his civic space in Boston on an amphitheater was justified by Sitte, who had asked "What is a forum but a type of theater?"[23] The amphitheater-like shape and dramatic qualities of the courtyard of the BGSC were also evidence that scenography, or the art of making stage scenery, especially in perspective, was of growing importance for Rudolph's architecture at this time. Rudolph regularly attended film, theater, classical music, and opera performances in New York, all of which informed his projects. In 1962, he collaborated with theater set and lighting designer Ralph Alswang on a scheme for an experimental theater where slides and films projected in rapidly changing combinations would create instant stage scenery.[24] Stage sets and theaters that affected and transformed users were powerful models for Rudolph during these years—for instance, the theater-like jury pit of the A & A Building made those using it into actors and spectators.

Another equally impressive piece of stagecraft devised by Rudolph for the BGSC was the lengthy staircase that he threaded through a covered portico or gateway at the center of his Mental Health Building. A perspective section of the gateway-like configuration demonstrated Rudolph's skill at integrating horizontal and vertical spaces (figure 5.11). Sitte had recommended employing "flights of stairs, balconies, gables, and whatever else make up the picturesque trappings of stage architecture" to make the modern city a more engaging place.[25]

Recalling the dramatic staircases of opera sets, Rudolph's concrete stair wound its way sinuously between the piers of the portico to a plaza at the corner of Staniford and Merrimac Streets (figure 5.12). Serpentine concrete benches on the plaza sustained this sense of momentum, breaking down into low steps and radiating lines that fanned out across the pavement (figure 5.13). The extraordinary curving forms of the stair and plaza, a vocabulary Rudolph elaborated on throughout the complex, marked an even more expressive turn in Rudolph's vocabulary, one inspired by baroque architecture, which was itself noted for stagy qualities derived from theater.

For Rudolph to turn to the baroque was not surprising, since the theorists he admired most, notably Scott and Sigfried Giedion, extolled baroque buildings as models for monumentality and urbanism. Giedion explained in *Space, Time and Architecture* how the undulating walls and flexible floor plans of the late baroque fostered emotional responses to architecture that he thought modernism could learn from. The modernist stalwart's description of the creative ways in which baroque architect Francesco Borromini drew on the classical past without copying it directly probably inspired Rudolph as well.[26]

Rudolph elaborated on the curving forms of the baroque inside the Mental Health Building to support its social mission. The Community Mental Health Act of 1963, which reflected revolutionary changes in the care of the mentally ill, made it possible to release the mentally ill from full-time residency in state-run institutions into communities.[27] The Mental Health Building was intended to be a way station where the deinstitutionalized could acclimate to Boston. Relatively free to come and go, clients could sleep in the building's wards, take their meals, socialize, use the gymnasium, swim in an Olympic-size pool, make art in studios, and receive therapy and treatment. Outpatients could use the building's facilities as well.

Putting into practice his conviction that nonorthogonal geometry was beneficial and even therapeutic, Rudolph enclosed the patients within oval-shaped rooms and curving corridors lined with corrugated concrete. Community rooms featured curving built-in leather banquettes and wood bookcases. One even had a stage and dressing room for amateur plays, again demonstrating Rudolph's belief in theater as a way to stimulate people and bind them together. Obviously the product of great care and expense, such carefully conceived facilities (and the complex, dramatic architecture of the entire complex) contrasted visibly with the bare-bones functionalism typically considered adequate for most public facilities. Though easily discounted as an example of Rudolph's desire to show off his design skills, such attention to the patients' environment suggested he felt a true regard for them.

The building's two most memorable interior spaces were extravagantly theatrical in a way made possible by the plastic properties of poured-in-place concrete. The first was a stair hall housing a curvilinear staircase, recalling the outdoor ones but shaped like a corkscrew, that connected the different floors. With its corrugated concrete walls and dramatic lighting, it was tremendously expressive and, again, atypical for a building housing health services (figure 5.14).

The second and even more remarkable interior was the interdenominational chapel perched in a turret high atop the Mental Health Building (figure 5.15). Completely curvilinear, it bore an unmistakable resemblance to a giant concrete nautilus shell. Rudolph embraced the worshippers in an oval sanctuary, recalling the elliptical baroque chapels of Borromini and Gian Lorenzo Bernini, lit by an oval skylight. The pattern of bush-hammered ridges around the oval altar was the most openly ornamental example of Rudolph's corrugated concrete. Archetypal in feeling, like a cave, it was one of several churches Rudolph designed in the early and mid-1960s that demonstrated his affinity for the emotionally charged interiors of religious buildings.

With the Boston Government Service Center, Rudolph raised his expressive vocabulary to a more elaborate pitch, which had both positive and negative consequences. It demonstrated the maturity of his architecture and of modernism as it moved beyond its "classical" phase of the 1920s and 1930s, just as the renaissance had evolved into its mannerist and baroque periods. The BGSC also demonstrated how to make a powerful, monumental civic architecture. Rudolph and many of his contemporaries imagined that there would be more and more such civic commissions to keep pace with the growth of big government.

Yet the BGSC had many drawbacks as well. Despite Rudolph's belief that variety was therapeutic, the open stairwells, roughened surfaces, labyrinthine circulation, and dramatic interiors did not provide a conducive setting

5.13 Plaza, Mental Health Building, BGSC.

5.14 Interior staircase, Mental Health Building, BGSC.

for mental health services.[28] The complex as a whole did little to remedy the limitations of Pei's Government Center master plan, nor was it successful urbanism. It was difficult to imagine Bostonians or the poor, unemployed, and mentally ill who received assistance at the Government Service Center gathering there for communal celebrations. The plaza was too high above the existing streets and secluded from them, and the service center was more of an enormous barrier than a waypoint for pedestrians. (This problem was not unique to Boston's Government Center. Despite the best intentions, many of the large-scale modernist projects of this period cut pedestrians and autos off from existing neighborhoods, streets, and waterways.) But the BGSC's greatest drawback was that it was never completed because of lack of funding and changes in attitude. The two low buildings and much of the courtyard plaza surface were finished by 1971, but for many years a vast, weed-choked expanse enclosed by chain-link fencing took the place of the tower until a courthouse was constructed in its place in 1999.

Southeastern Massachusetts Technological Institute

Rudolph amplified the dramatic, scenographic qualities of the BGSC in the second project he designed for Desmond and Lord, the Southeastern Massachusetts Technological Institute, known as SMTI (Dartmouth, Massachusetts, 1963–72), which later became the University of Massachusetts, Dartmouth. Rudolph considered it to be

the most complete realization of his experiments with urbanism and monumentality. Architects of the 1960s found college campuses to be ideal places for experimenting with urbanism because of their size, complexity, and possibilities for continuous growth and funding. At SMTI, Rudolph again looked to baroque scenography for ways in which to stimulate the students, but his efforts were also informed by two notable examples of what is known as the single-vision campus, that is, one campus entirely designed at one time by one architect: Frank Lloyd Wright's Florida Southern College (Lakeland, Florida, 1939–58), an inspiration for him since his earliest Florida days, and Thomas Jefferson's University of Virginia (Charlottesville, 1817–25), which had in turn inspired Wright.

Rudolph's investigations resulted in a new campus whose bold concrete block buildings and towers were indisputably modern and yet were imbued with curiously ancient or archetypal qualities. Like a small city or world complete unto itself, SMTI would rise from the woods and suburban streets of southeastern Massachusetts, its monumental buildings like the impressive relics of some ambitious but forgotten civilization, in this case the postwar United States (figure 5.16).

The Commission

The creation of SMTI resulted from the merger in 1960 of two technical schools, one in New Bedford and one in Fall River, Massachusetts. Local and state political leaders believed that a new institution could reinvigorate the

5.15 Chapel, Mental Health Building, BGSC.

5.16 Rudolph, Southeastern Massachusetts Technical Institute (SMTI) (Dartmouth, Massachusetts, 1963–72).

5.17 Rudolph, master plan, Tuskegee Institute (Tuskegee, Alabama, project, 1958).

declining textile industry of the area. Federal and state monies funded the building of the new campus on seven hundred acres of former pasture and woodlands between the two cities near Interstate 195, one of the new highways transforming the nation.[29] In the postwar era, the highway and the automobile gave rise to a new building type exemplified by SMTI: the commuter campus.[30]

The Commonwealth of Massachusetts awarded the commission for SMTI to Desmond and Lord, and in early 1963 Richard Thissen turned the project over to Rudolph. He would design the master plan and at least one building for the school; the structure would serve as a prototype for additional buildings to be executed by other architects. Grattan Gill and Jan Heespelink from Desmond and Lord acted as job captains and themselves designed numerous buildings based on Rudolph's model.

Although the months leading up to the completion of the A & A Building was a busy time for his office, Rudolph quickly developed the master plan for SMTI. He derived

the design in part from his master plan for the Tuskegee Institute (Tuskegee, Alabama, 1958), which expanded an old campus by means of a mall lined with arcades. These covered paths tied together existing and proposed new structures, including an amphitheater, campanile, and monumental chapel; the chapel was the only portion executed (Interdenominational Chapel, Tuskegee, 1960–69) (figure 5.17).

Tuskegee, and thus SMTI as well, were inspired by Wright's Florida Southern College, which also featured a central mall crisscrossed by protected walkways leading to a chapel built of concrete block and a waterside amphitheater. Wright, and therefore Rudolph too, drew from Jefferson's University of Virginia campus, where the "academical village," as it was known, had a central mall defined by linked arcaded buildings, a configuration that made the complex seem like one large building. Rudolph's office completed a master plan and an enormous model less than a week before the dedication of the A & A

Building at Yale, just in time to present to the governor of Massachusetts and state and SMTI officials at a luncheon held in Boston on November 3, 1963.[31]

Collaboration between Rudolph and his client was more apparent at SMTI than in his other projects of the time. He worked closely with the institute's first president, Joseph Driscoll, who was as committed to the humanities and humanism as President Griswold had been at Yale. Unlike state politicians, who saw SMTI as little more than an elaborate technical school improved for future mill workers by the addition of some college-level humanities courses, Driscoll envisioned the new institution as nothing less than a catalyst for the "economic, cultural and educational renaissance" of the financially depressed region. Rudolph and Driscoll agreed that the first new building for the campus would be for the humanities.[32]

State officials projected an enrollment of twenty-five hundred by 1966, but Driscoll had grander plans: he imagined a future university of twenty-five thousand. To be convincing, SMTI would have to look imposing, like an established university, even before it became one. Rudolph deployed his stagecraft to this end. His easily expandable master plan suggested inevitable growth, and he continually pressed Desmond and Lord's Thissen to make SMTI bigger and grander. After the state chose Franchi Construction to build the first building, Humanities 1, Rudolph sent a postcard to Thissen from Venice, his favorite vacation spot, asking if three million dollars was available to build a 450-foot-high poured-in-place concrete campanile, taller than the one in St. Mark's Square depicted on the card, as was proposed in the master plan (figure 5.18).[33] Rudolph's words are breezily confident, and it is not clear whether he is joking.

The Master Plan

SMTI was one of Rudolph's few tabula rasa projects. The flat, undeveloped site in Dartmouth afforded the architect

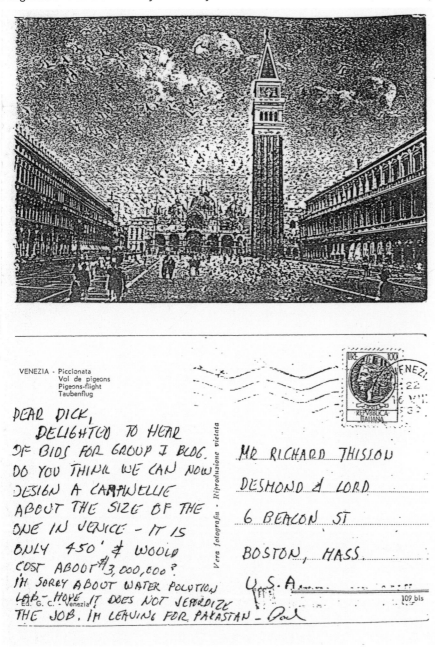

5.18 Postcard from Rudolph in Venice to Richard Thissen of Desmond and Lord in Boston, August 1964.

131

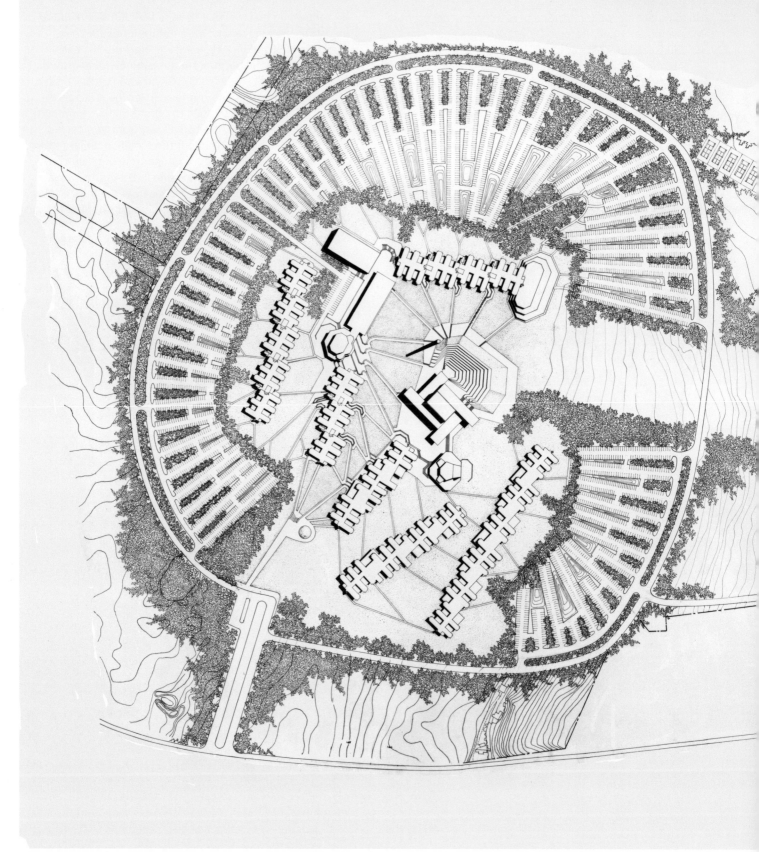

5.19 Rudolph, master plan, SMTI (1963). The outer buildings were not completed.

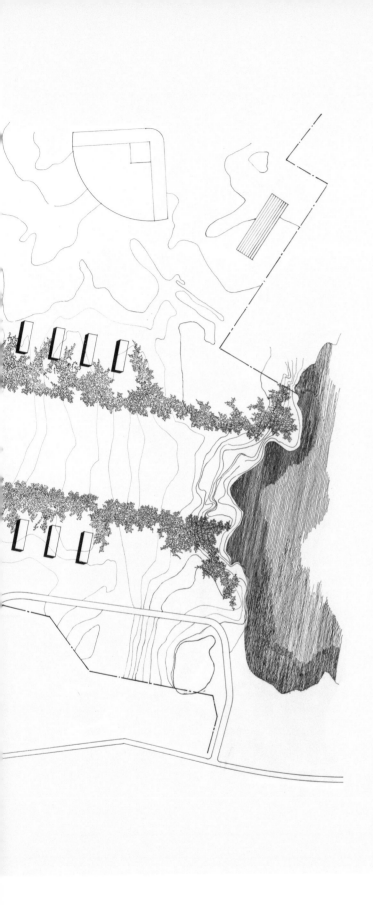

considerable freedom, allowing him to shape the master plan to accommodate both the automobile and the pedestrian (figure 5.19). In a 1966 article describing the most innovative new campuses of the 1960s, the sociologist and urban theorist Oscar Newman said that the circulation of automobiles and pedestrians, especially on the commuter campus, appeared to generate the bold forms of the new buildings, imbuing them with a symbolic value as the "embodiment of the mobile society or the personification of progress."[34]

To accommodate the automobile, Rudolph defined the perimeter of the campus with a ring road, uninterrupted by stop signs or traffic lights, that kept traffic moving smoothly. The ring road strategy was adopted at many other postwar campuses, such as the new University of California, Irvine (William L. Pereira & Associates, master plan, 1964) or the greatly expanded University of Massachusetts, Amherst (Sasaki and Associates, 1962). The ring road was adjoined by parking lots for five thousand cars, double the predicted student body for 1966. The parking lots were screened from view by an earthen berm that formed a second giant circle, like a prehistoric earthwork, within the ring road; administrative and academic buildings were inside the area enclosed by the berm. At SMTI, Rudolph moved and molded the earth in both noticeable and imperceptible ways that demonstrated his largely unremarked-upon skill with landscape. The berm may have recalled primitive earthworks, but the arrangement of the lots was a practical response to the modern problem of parking, which Rudolph had taken into consideration beginning with his first large-scale projects, such as the Jewett Arts Center at Wellesley (1955–58). Unlike at other campuses, at SMTI no one had to walk much more than a few hundred yards from a parking lot to the central buildings. Additional ranges of buildings in the master plan showed how the campus could be expanded at some future date.

Within the berm, plantings of trees and wide lawns recalled the expansiveness of traditional American campuses; the buildings themselves evoked the picturesque towered skylines of the Collegiate Gothic. Two long ranges of turreted buildings, Humanities 1 and its virtual twin, Science and Technology, circumscribed the primary communal space at the campus's center, a spiral-shaped outdoor mall that widened, pivoted, and changed direction at the foot of a concrete campanile and an adjacent amphitheater to lead out to pastoral views of a pond. An unusual shape for such a space, the spiral was increasingly significant for Rudolph's ever more expressive vocabulary. Diagonally aligned walkways guided pedestrians across the mall.

To create an illusion of greater length for his open space and to make the buildings flanking it seem larger, Rudolph angled the ranges and raked the surface of the mall so that it sloped downward to the amphitheater and campanile, subtly creating a forced perspective. Such effects, fundamental to scenography as it had developed since the renaissance, were advocated by those writers to whom Rudolph regularly turned for advice.[35] Sitte favored trapezoidal plazas resembling stages that made the buildings behind them seem like theatrical backdrops, such

133

5.20 View drawing of mall, SMTI (c. 1963).

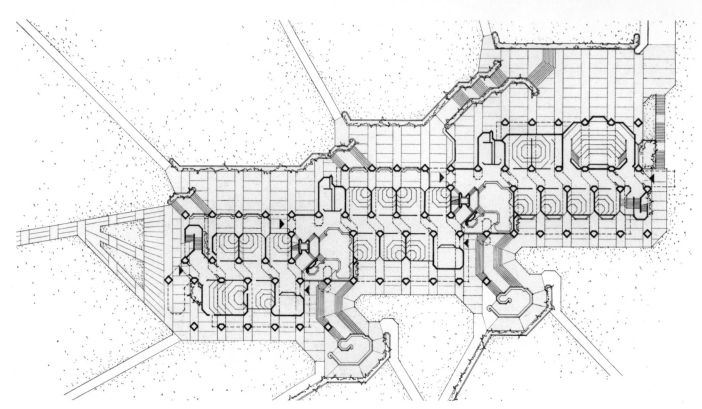

5.21 Ground floor plan, Humanities 1, SMTI (1963–66).

as the forecourt of Bernini's piazza in front of St. Peter's Basilica.[36] Giedion appreciated the baroque's ability to make things seem bigger and more compelling than they really were. In *Space, Time and Architecture,* he wrote of the baroque that "in painting and in architecture the impression of infinity—the infinite in a linear sense, as an indefinitely extended perspective—is being used as a means of artistic effect."[37]

Rudolph's forced perspective at SMTI suggested this type of infinity, but not in a way that was perceptible to the conscious mind or eye. The effects are hinted at by a presentation drawing that shows the view up the mall from an airborne vantage point near the campanile (figure 5.20). Illusionary in nature, aesthetics of this type distinguished SMTI from many of the new campuses being built at the same time. One architectural journal pronounced that catching glimpses of the turreted silhouettes of the SMTI campus core while circling it in an automobile amounted to an exciting new type of aesthetic experience.[38] Rudolph was at his most masterful at SMTI, deftly orchestrating his master plan to heighten anticipation for drivers who left their parked cars behind and became pedestrians caught up in the architectural drama at the center of the campus.

Humanities 1

When Rudolph first began work on SMTI in 1962, his office was so busy that he did not have time to design each of the new buildings. Instead he developed a system for design and construction—exemplified in Humanities 1 (1963–66)—that Desmond and Lord and their successors could follow for new buildings. Integrated ground-floor arcades would connect all of the buildings along the mall, recalling those of the University of Virginia and Florida Southern. This organization created the impression of one vast building,

an approach used for a number of the innovative new campuses of the time.[39] Rudolph summed up his intentions for SMTI in a single sentence: "The campus is intended to be a single building utilizing a single structural mechanical system to be constructed of one material."[40]

Rudolph's building system was based on an underlying rectangular grid of 28-by-14-foot modules, a standard that suggested limitless possibilities for expansion. The basic element of the "single structural mechanical system" was a giant hollow pier that formed the framework for the building and contained all the heating, ventilation, and air-conditioning ductwork. The component was an elaboration on the four giant piers in the center of the Yale A & A Building, which also contained services. Rudolph rotated the piers on a 45-degree angle to contrast with the underlying grid and inject a quality of motion into the building (figure 5.21).

The use of the same material for all buildings, a rectangular 8½-by-16-inch concrete block, also imposed coherence. The manufactured "fluted" block, which featured semicircular raised ridges, was a less expensive alternative to Rudolph's corrugated concrete. Not as plastic as the poured-in-place corrugated concrete used for the curving stairs and turrets of the BGSC, the block gave SMTI a different, but still powerful character. Rudolph's use of the block, the 45-degree angle, and the diagonal axis, for example in the walkways crossing the mall, invested the campus with a markedly vibrant, staccato quality in comparison to the almost sensual sinuousness of the BGSC. In Humanities 1, rotation of the giant piers eliminated conventional right-angled corners and made many rooms nearly octagonal. The faceted spaces were ideal for ground-floor amphitheater-like classrooms or lecture theaters, thus reiterating the leitmotif of theater throughout the campus, especially the great amphitheater adjoining the mall.

5.22 East facade, Humanities 1, SMTI.

Approaching from the parking lots, visitors to Humanities 1 ascended an impressive zig-zagging staircase to the main level, passing the angled piers that supported a series of staggered bays forming a projecting upper floor, and a projecting cornice similar to that of the BGSC (figure 5.22). The angular vocabulary and nonrectilinear spaces of Humanities 1 were intended to stimulate students, helping them engage with the place and each other. Humanities 1 had few of the monotonous corridors typical of institutional buildings. Rudolph said, "Circulation twists and turns are calculated to bring people together, for alienation is a major problem in commuter campuses."[41]

The articulated corridors brought students, staff, and faculty to the multistory "common rooms" Rudolph placed at regular junctures in the classroom buildings. Many new campuses of the time had similar communal spaces, always intended to foster community and identity among students who did not live on campus. The common rooms in Humanities 1, some of the most impressive interior spaces designed by Rudolph, were places for students to eat lunch and organize activities, to stage theatricals, including an amateur opera, and, at the end of the 1960s, to paint anti-war protest banners.[42]

The two common rooms in Humanities 1 and in its twin on the opposite side of the mall, the Science and Technology range, were light-filled, spacious multilevel spaces, different in tone from the complicated interiors of the BGSC or the A & A Building. In accordance with Rudolph's precept "we need caves as well as gold-fish bowls," each Humanities 1 common room had an enclosed cave-like area on the ground level lined with banquettes and focused on a hearth. An unusual feature for a commuter college, to say the least, the hearth was the basis for community in the room, recalling Wright's conception of the hearth as the foundation of family life. Rudolph transformed the space above the darkened ground floor into a goldfish bowl lit by enormous glass windows. Balconies appeared to float in the air, supported by only a single pier. Each balcony formed a lounge space for the adjacent floor; the topmost level was reserved for faculty.

Carefully chosen, brightly colored textiles and carpeting acted as vibrant, stimulating foils to the omnipresent, gray concrete. In a 1965 photo (figure 5.23), a red banner tied the balconies together visually. Rudolph again collaborated with the interior designer Bill Bagnall. Together they chose to upholster the common room banquettes in orange and carpet the floor with a pattern of orange, red, and purple stripes. The banded carpet echoed the raised ridges of the concrete block and the striations on the poured-in-place structural beams and balconies. Rudolph had no plaster casts, architectural fragments, or curtains by de Kooning to adorn the interiors of SMTI; he opted instead to use stripes and lines to make the type of all-over patterning or decoration for the interior that in the mid-1950s he had prescribed

5.23 Common room, Humanities 1, SMTI.

5.24 Grattan Gill and Jan Heespelink of Desmond and Lord, amphitheater, library, and campanile, SMTI (1972).

for the exteriors of buildings. The pervasive decoration also recalled his signature corrugated concrete.[43]

Rudolph had been drawn to interior design since his undergraduate days, and his regard became more pronounced in the mid-1960s just as new materials and avant-garde ideas were reinvigorating the field. Rudolph's New York apartment was close to the city's Upper East Side interior design district; Bagnall kept him informed about new developments as well. Rudolph's interest is evidenced by the curtains in the SMTI common rooms. The curtains, made of small silver-colored aluminum disks, typified the "silvery look" popular among New York interior designers in the mid-and late 1960s; the designers were inspired in part by Andy Warhol's famous aluminum-foil-lined Factory studio.[44]

An ephemeral decorative scrim, the metal curtains rippled continuously, filtering and reflecting sunlight and projecting changing shadows across the fluted concrete-block walls. Philip Johnson had achieved similar effects at the Four Seasons Restaurant at the Seagram Building in New York with chain-link curtains (Mies van der Rohe with Philip Johnson, 1958). At SMTI, Rudolph brought effects conceived for a four-star restaurant to a room where students might be eating brown-bag lunches. In their original state, the multiple plays of lines, light, shadow, and color in Rudolph's SMTI common rooms must have been mesmerizing and, on sunny days, almost kaleidoscopic. Though the brightly colored carpets, curtains, and upholstery are long gone, the common rooms remain sturdy and intact, some of Rudolph's most successful interiors.

Dismissal

Humanities 1 was an architectural success but a professional fiasco. The building impressed those who attended its spring 1966 dedication, but unfortunately, its magnificence, even though achieved by fairly economical means, dismayed state officials. Citing excessive costs for the next phase, the nearly identical Science and Engineering range opposite Humanities 1, state officials called Rudolph an expensive architect and reprimanded Joseph Driscoll, whom they held responsible for encouraging such grandiosity.

In what became a prolonged drama reported in the local and national press, Rudolph was fired in 1966 and then rehired and dismissed several more times. Thissen of Desmond and Lord adroitly held on to the project despite the political firestorm, and his firm was retained to complete the campus without Rudolph. Local newspapers repeated state officials' claims that Rudolph was an expensive architect who paid little heed to budget, anticipating similar charges that would soon begin to diminish his reputation. Ada Louise Huxtable, however, rose to Rudolph's defense in the *New York Times*, telling a national audience that Massachusetts officials had little appreciation for great architecture.[45]

There was not much Rudolph could do about his dismissal. He had made himself dispensable by creating a standard system for design and construction on the campus. However, he had come to care greatly about SMTI and wanted to complete the project himself, even without credit or compensation. Rudolph conducted "backstairs" reviews with Gill from Desmond and Lord of the Sciences and Humanities range and other buildings. At the same

139

time, Rudolph, still under contract to complete the BGSC for Desmond and Lord, had to walk a delicate line with the firm.

Rudolph enjoyed such intrigue. The buildings he critiqued in the stairwell between his office and Desmond and Lord's premises, especially the library by Gill and Heespelink, are some of the most powerful and convincing essays in Rudolph's style: for all his emphasis on individuality and virtuosity, Rudolph could be successfully imitated. Gill and Heespelink displayed considerable ingenuity in completing the campus according to Rudolph's master plan. Gill was able to build the campanile, telling the state that it was a communications tower for broadcasting lectures and performances (figure 5.24).[46]

Rudolph made many comebacks at SMTI. In 1972, he returned and completed the Student Union Building. Driscoll left the institution the same year, forced out by state officials who distrusted his ambitions and students unhappy that he had not supported their anti–Vietnam War protests. Rudolph cultivated a relationship with SMTI's administrators and faculty, resulting in the Norman Dion Science and Engineering Building (1985-89). By that time, SMTI had grown, student housing had been built, and the school had been absorbed by the state university system. Grand and resilient, the campus continues to serve students and faculty well half a century after its conception.

Six
Prefabrication and the Megastructure

As Rudolph was working on his monumental projects for Yale, New Haven, and Boston, he was also, as was typical since his Florida days, pursuing several other directions. Beginning in the early 1960s and well into the early 1970s, he concentrated on developing manufactured building components—ranging in size from individual concrete blocks to an entire modular residential unit he called the "twentieth-century brick"—in order to lower costs, improve quality, build at a larger scale, and, as ever, make his buildings more dramatic and expressive.

Experiments with manufactured, or prefabricated, building elements, usually for residential construction, had their origins in the nineteenth and early twentieth centuries. The architects Rudolph admired most, Frank Lloyd Wright and Le Corbusier, had long considered building homes from manufactured elements, such as slabs, panels, or blocks, or mass-producing an entire house in a factory. From his time at Harvard's GSD in the 1940s, Rudolph was familiar with Walter Gropius and Konrad Wachsmann's unsuccessful efforts to develop a home made from mass-produced panels.[1]

Rudolph's own investigations began in the early 1950s in Florida, a fecund period of experimentation that he drew on continually. His first houses with Ralph Twitchell had employed a manufactured concrete block made from local Ocala sand. Once he established his own practice, Rudolph attempted to develop a prefabricated panel system. Recalling Gropius and Wachsmann's efforts, he built his Wilson House in Sarasota (1953–54) from prefabricated cardboard panels. He did not pursue the experiment further, concluding that developing a new system was inefficient in comparison to adapting existing means.[2]

Rudolph discovered one of these existing means in his own backyard: the low-cost, factory-made trailers or mobile homes that were proliferating in Florida and across America in the 1950s. The rectangular units of wood and aluminum evolved from the mobile caravans or campers that had become popular in the 1930s. In fact, when Rudolph arrived in Sarasota in 1941, it had the "world's largest trailer city," the Sarasota Tourist Park, a community complete with its own police and firefighters, post office, and water and sanitation facilities.

Given the trailer home's growing presence in postwar Florida, it is not surprising that in 1954 Rudolph sketched an apartment tower for Sarasota made of prefabricated, trailer-home-like modules suspended from a central mast (figure 6.1). Rudolph's first design for a tall building, it was developed in response to a query from William Rupp of his Sarasota office: Rupp had asked Rudolph what he thought a tall building should be like since he found most of them objectionable.[3] Though he did not publish the Trailer Tower project until 1967, when interest in prefabrication was peaking, it anticipates later, better known, conceptually similar projects, namely Kisho Kurokawa's famed Nakagin Capsule Tower (Tokyo, 1970–72).[4]

In the 1960s Rudolph and many of his contemporaries reconsidered manufactured elements and prefabrication in part because they were seeking economical ways to construct the large-scale public housing schemes of the period. His "twentieth-century brick," a prefabricated, mobile-home-like housing module—the title was coined with Le Corbusier's "Dom-ino" and Wright's "American System-Built Houses" in mind—demonstrated that his architecture was not merely aesthetically driven, but part of a larger, more consistent set of concerns. He foresaw fashioning vast, mountain-range-like structures for Manhattan from the twentieth-century bricks, recalling his Sarasota trailer tower and exemplifying what he called "topographical architecture," an elaboration on his interest in scenography.

Rudolph's experiments with prefabrication spanned a tumultuous period in his career, from the early 1960s, when he was an acknowledged star of the architecture profession, to the early 1970s, when he was increasingly beleaguered and criticized, especially for such large-scale experiments. Implementing prefabrication indeed proved more difficult than Rudolph and his contemporaries anticipated. He built only one project using the twentieth-century brick, Oriental Masonic Gardens (New Haven, 1968–71), but poor construction and maintenance resulted in its demolition just a decade later.

Concrete Block

Almost as soon as soon as he developed it, Rudolph realized that the formwork and bush-hammering of corrugated concrete made it too expensive for most projects, especially for the new, often publicly funded, commissions that he was receiving at the time. Bill Bedford, an architect in Rudolph's New Haven office, suggested to Rudolph in early 1962 that a factory-made but customized concrete block could be a viable alternative.[5] Ordinary block was often used for foundations and painted or covered with a veneer because it was considered unsightly; Rudolph, however, sought to dignify the material, much as Wright had with his patterned concrete blocks at Florida Southern College (Lakeland, Florida, 1938–59).

By 1963 Rudolph was able to achieve the aesthetic qualities of corrugated concrete at a lower cost by using two types of block—fluted block and split rib—that he developed with Plasticrete, a New Haven manufacturer of masonry building materials. The fluted block was an 8½-by-16-inch concrete block made from a mold in a factory; six to eight raised convex ridges recalled the ridges of Rudolph's corrugated concrete. Customized for each project, the fluted block came in as many as thirty different configurations. Though conceived for Crawford Manor (1962–66), an apartment block for the elderly in New Haven, Rudolph first employed the fluted block at the Humanities 1 building at the SMTI campus (1963–65) (figure 6.2).

Rudolph did not invent the split rib block, but he certainly popularized it. Less expensive and labor-intensive to work with than the fluted block, it consisted of a block cut in half

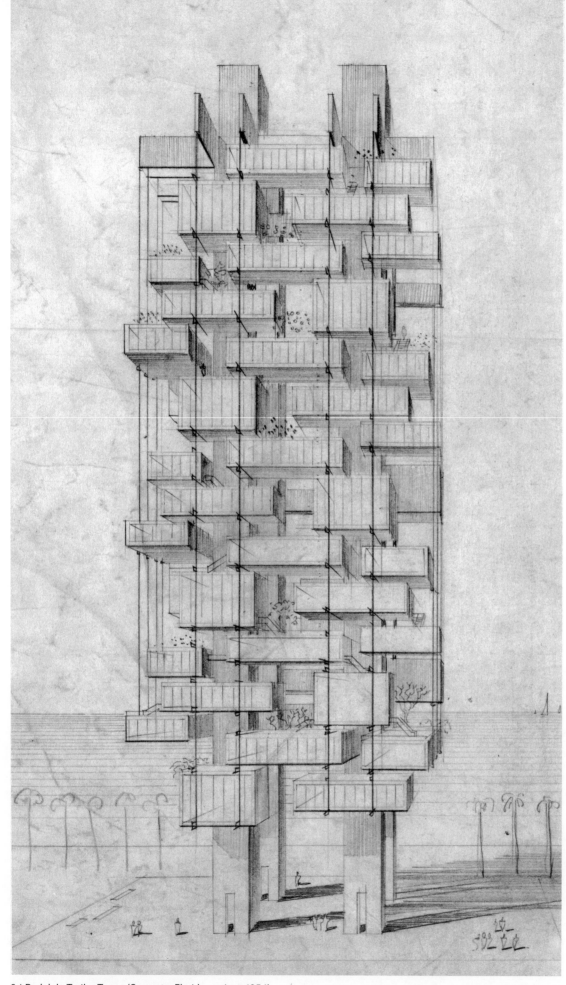

6.1 Rudolph, Trailer Tower (Sarasota, Florida, project, 1954).

to reveal two roughened surfaces with raised broken ridges; these ridges were far rougher than those of the fluted block and more like those of corrugated concrete (figure 6.3). The split rib block proved adaptable for many settings and purposes. Rudolph first used it for the Charles A. Dana Creative Arts Center at Colgate University (Hamilton, New York, 1963–66). He also used it for civic projects including his Orange County Government Center (Goshen, New York, 1963–71) and often for large publicly funded housing such as the Waterfront and Shoreline Apartments (Buffalo, New York, 1969–77). The split rib block could also be configured to make an entire tower with rounded bays, such as Tracey Towers in the Bronx (New York, 1967–74). Rudolph's precedents made the everyday material acceptable for significant civic buildings by other architects, such as the New Haven Department of Police Services (Orr, De Cossy, Winder and Associates, 1973). It was used for more ordinary purposes as well: split block became part of the late twentieth-century vernacular, ubiquitous in every strip mall and warehouse district across the United States and beyond.

Mannerism

Rudolph's use of the term "flutes" for the features of his factory-made blocks was an apparent allusion to the fluting of classical columns. Using the vocabulary and forms of classicism to explain modernist elements was typical of the architectural discourse of the time. Scholars likened Ludwig Mies van der Rohe's use of the I-beam to classical pilasters, and one journal compared the two-inch-wide marks left by the wood forms at Rudolph's Temple Street Parking Garage to the flutes of classical columns.[6]

It is worth noting that classical fluting is concave; Rudolph's raised ridges were convex. It would have been more accurate to call the raised ridges reeding or gadrooning. Rudolph may have been using the term incorrectly, or he may have deliberately inverted the classical flute to invoke the spirit of sixteenth-century Italian mannerism. By the early 1960s, theorists, historians, and architects looked to the architecture of the renaissance, mannerism, and the baroque to explain modernism's growing complexity.

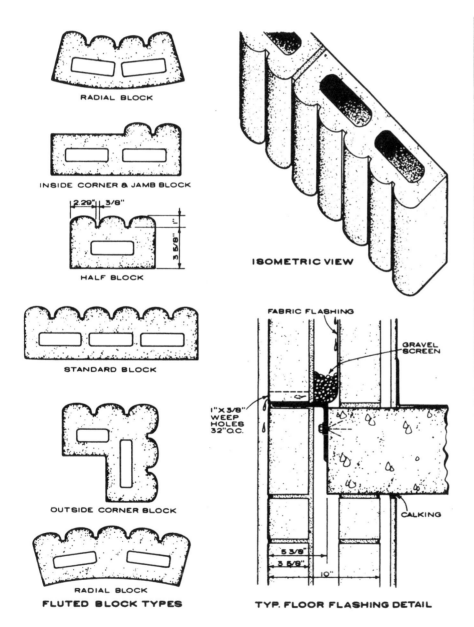

6.2 Rudolph, "fluted" block configurations.

6.3 Rudolph, split rib block, Charles A. Dana Creative Arts Center, Colgate University (Hamilton, New York, 1963–66).

Some academics and architects whom Rudolph knew were especially drawn to mannerism.

An influential theorist and historian of the time and an occasional visitor to Yale, Colin Rowe had turned to mannerism to explain how modernism had become more formally complex. He explained that modern masters, like the mannerist ones of the past, often made historical references ironically. Of Le Corbusier, he wrote, "there is always an element of wit suggesting that the historical (or contemporary) reference has remained a quotation between inverted commas, possessing always the double value of the quotation, the associations between old and new context."[7] His adroit analysis informed the thinking of architects who were coming to prominence in the early 1960s, as was evident in Robert Venturi's important 1966 book *Complexity and Contradiction in Architecture*, which used examples of Italian mannerism to explain how modernism could take on more complex qualities. Reflecting the emphasis on history of his Princeton education, Venturi had a deeper understanding of mannerism than Rudolph.[8] The book was already in manuscript form when Venturi co-taught with Rudolph a masters' studio on precast concrete in 1963, just as Crawford Manor (1962–66), Rudolph's best known experiment with fluted concrete block, got under way. Venturi even quoted Rudolph in the book. Though the relationship between the two was amicable, and in 1963 their fascination with mannerism appeared to indicate they had much in common, Venturi would famously use Crawford Manor to explain how painfully labored postwar modernism had become in his, Denise Scott Brown, and Steven Izenour's influential *Learning from Las Vegas* of 1972.[9]

In the early and mid-1960s, some observers were applying the term "mannerism" to Rudolph's work, but in a more particular way. His increasingly elaborate architecture was becoming "mannered," or overwrought, as in the curvilinear staircases and dramatic chapel of the Boston Government Service Center. In 1965, Philip Johnson suggested that there was a "mannerist (do we dare use the word Mannerist?) play of spaces" in the interior of the Yale A & A Building "which baffles and intrigues."[10] To achieve greater expression, Rudolph himself called for "an enrichment of architecture at the brink of mannerism."[11] Qualities both mannered and mannerist that baffle and intrigue are apparent in Rudolph's experiments with manufactured and prefabricated building elements of this period.

Crawford Manor

Crawford Manor (New Haven, 1962–66), the final New Haven project Rudolph began while still chairman of the Yale architecture department, was a publicly funded 109-unit, fourteen-story apartment building for people over sixty-five years of age. Another of Mayor Richard C. Lee's redevelopment projects, it was named in honor of George W. Crawford, New Haven's leading African-American lawyer and a long-time friend of Lee's. For Rudolph, it was an experiment with the fluted block and another attempt to transform the expressive qualities of the tall building. Though the structure was in fact a rectangular block, it

appeared from many angles to be a series of clustered towers of varied heights (figure 6.4).

Crawford Manor's exterior cladding consisted entirely of fluted blocks. No seams were visible between the individual units, so the building looked as though it had been cast in one piece like a sculpture. As in a giant classical column, the flutes rose from the bottom to the top of the building without interruption, forming walls of all-over patterned decoration, another example of Rudolph's attempts to construct decoration. The flutes cast shifting shadows across the facades, recalling those at the rougher-edged A & A Building.

An arresting piece of urban scenography, like the nearby Temple Street Parking Garage and the A & A Building, Crawford Manor had a dramatic silhouette that Rudolph called "a stalk, a landmark" immediately visible to drivers as they exited the nearby Oak Street Connector. One journal described it as a building that a resident could "point to and say that's home" because it stood apart from the other buildings in the city and also from the banal apartment towers and homes constructed for the elderly at the time.[12]

Crawford Manor's balconies, arranged in a staggered fashion, were responsible for its distinctive profile. They heightened its strikingly plastic character, which was similar to that of the unbuilt tower of the Boston Government Service Center (1962–71). Of two different sizes, the balconies were platforms for an individual or couple within the larger framework of the community. Small balconies are typically known as "Juliet balconies," but Rudolph called these "Romeo and Juliet" balconies; perhaps it was a slip, or perhaps, as a lover of the theater, he imagined residents in dialogue with one another like Shakespeare's famous lovers (figure 6.5).[13]

The fluted block enabled Rudolph to achieve a remarkable degree of plastic expression at Crawford Manor despite the limited budget. However, all was not what it appeared to be. The building exemplified Rudolph's increasingly elaborate scenographics, his prioritizing of the overall appearance of the building over everything else, and his penchant for ambiguity in the spirit of mannerism. Revisiting his earlier observations about symbols of structure, Rudolph said in 1965 that "pure structure" could be "relegated to a relatively unimportant role" in order "to achieve the desired environment."[14]

Crawford Manor had many visual and structural ambiguities. Though the fluted blocks appeared to form solid, monolithic, load-bearing walls, they were in fact a cladding wrapped around a typical poured-in-place concrete frame (figure 6.6). The towers appended to the main block mostly contained galley kitchens and closets, rather than the type of services usually placed in vertical volumes (stairwells, elevators, heating and cooling ductwork). Rudolph had been criticized for breaking the rules of structural rationalism in this fashion at the A & A Building as well.[15] At the A & A, however, the towers contained fairly large rooms, whereas the closets at Crawford Manor were more difficult to justify.

Crawford Manor's twisting hallways of fluted block, like those of SMTI, and its varied apartment configurations were intended as spatial antidotes to the endless corridors and repetitive interiors of most publicly funded housing (figure 6.7). The floor plans are virtual ideograms for Rudolph's

6.4 Crawford Manor (New Haven, 1962–66).

6.5 Balconies, Crawford Manor.

6.6 Construction, Crawford Manor.

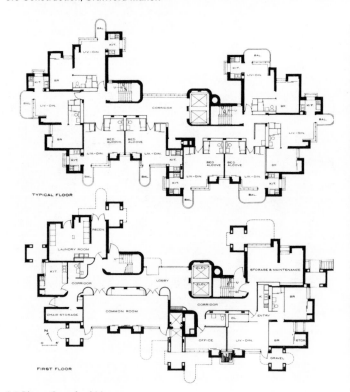

6.7 Plans, Crawford Manor.

6.8 Crawford Manor and Oak Street Connector, 1966.

6.9 Charles A. Dana Creative Arts Center (Colgate University, Hamilton, New York, 1963–66).

thinking about spatial complexity and reflect the increasingly mannered qualities of his architecture, which may have confused as much as stimulated the building's inhabitants.

The expressive and innovative exterior of Crawford Manor was not matched on the interior. Budget and ingenuity appeared to run out at the building's unwelcoming, nearly hidden, poorly defined entrance and in the small and banal lobby and common room. The fluted block may have enlivened Crawford Manor with shifting shadows, but it also retained moisture, and on inclement days, large unsightly wet stains appeared, a problem at the A & A as well. Certain negative aspects of the building were beyond Rudolph's control. The building's surroundings were disquieting and even alienating, and redevelopment in New Haven was already faltering by the time the building was completed because of lack of funding and stirrings of organized opposition. Crawford Manor stood virtually alone among the desolate, open spaces that had been cleared to make way for the never-completed Oak Street Connector (figure 6.8).

Charles A. Dana Creative Arts Center

Rudolph had first employed split rib block at the Charles A. Dana Creative Arts Center at Colgate University (Hamilton, New York, 1963–66) (figure 6.9). The program for the center, a building for the study of art history, studio arts, and the performing arts, was similar to that of Rudolph's Jewett Arts Center, his A & A Building, and numerous other arts centers on college campuses. Rudolph used split rib block

as infill for an exposed concrete framework; the walls had a rough, textured, and almost wavy appearance suggestive of rusticity. The earthen tones of the block were as compatible with the bucolic setting deep in the New York State countryside as they were in other milieus.

Another building that was not exactly what it appeared to be, the Dana Center had an ambiguous spatial complexity recalling that of mannerist structures. It was located at the entrance to the campus, like a gateway, and on approach it looked like a thin, rectangular building with a projecting drive-through entrance porch that provided a public entrance to the building and framed views of the chapel on the hill at the campus's center. Rudolph liked making such long-distance visual connections. From the side, however, the building revealed its true bulk (figure 6.10). The dramatic architecture suited the happenings within the building (figure 6.11). The primary interior space is a theater, and there is barely a right angle among the Dana Center's practice rooms and performing halls, again demonstrating Rudolph's belief that spatial variety engendered creativity (figure 6.12).

Rudolph's skill at siting was evident at Colgate, where the center was built into a hillside. The location offered a private entrance for students and faculty. After following a path from the center of campus, members of the Colgate community could enter the building via a rooftop terrace adjoining the hill and then descend to their classrooms through an open, multistory interior hall ringed by stairs, balconies, and glass-walled fishbowl-like faculty offices. The hall recalled the complexity of the common rooms at

6.10 Eastern elevation, Dana Center.

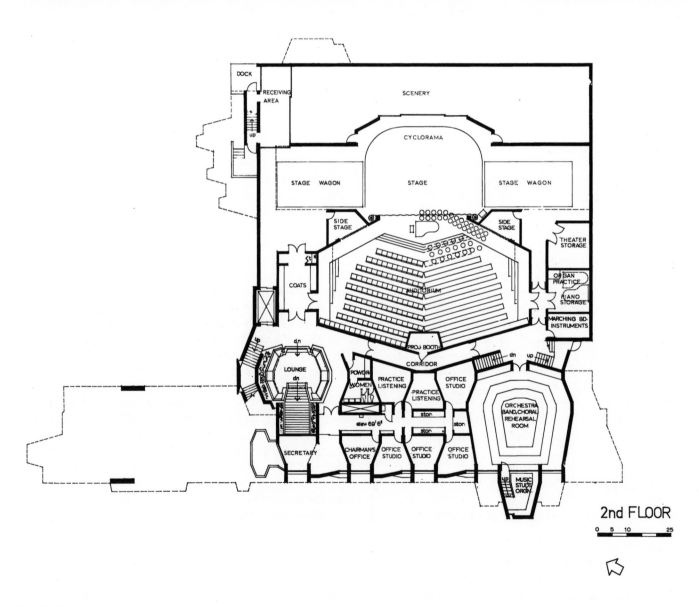

6.11 Plan, Dana Center.

SMTI. The hall also accommodated members of the public who were attending performances. These visitors made their way from the entrance porch to a lounge at the hall's bottom via a grand stair. The lounge was raised one level above the ground, like an Italian *piano nobile*, and also served as a lobby for the adjoining theater. A space that seemed as if it should have been surmounted by a dome, the interior hall recalled mannerist or baroque precedents in its complexity. In fact, historian Kurt Forster, then a graduate student at Yale, researched the baroque churches of Germany for Rudolph at this time (figure 6.13).[16]

Rudolph used brown split rib block on the interior and exterior of the building, giving consistency to the varied chambers but also making the interiors dark and somewhat oppressive. The split block, like Rudolph's fluted block and corrugated concrete, was affected by environmental conditions. Dust, grime, and soot adhered to its ridges.

Rudolph pointed to the blocks when he replied to charges that he was careless about costs, which he heard frequently after he was fired by SMTI in 1965. His favorable image in the press as an innovator and maverick was beginning to slip. Increasingly defensive when speaking with journalists, Rudolph said that he used low-cost materials such as the concrete block to keep costs down. He preferred the humble block to more expensive materials, even if some found it too utilitarian for a civic or academic structure. He said with some vehemence in a 1966 interview, "I use inexpensive materials, concrete block for example, . . . but then I *like* concrete block."[17]

The Twentieth-Century Brick

Rudolph believed that building costs could be reduced even more if architecture utilized another mass-produced element, the trailer home. After World War II, trailer homes evolved from the wheeled camping caravans pulled by automobiles into larger, permanent residences manufactured in factories. Made of lightweight wood and aluminum, these structures were sited, sometimes on foundations, on private property or in trailer parks, where occupants paid a fee to park and to connect to water, electricity, and other services. Rudolph had the opportunity to see one of the nation's first planned communities for such manufactured dwellings, "Trailer Estates," which opened adjacent to Sarasota in Bradenton, Florida, in 1955. During the 1950s, standard ten- to twelve-foot widths were adopted for the "mobile home"— a new term—and the length varied to accommodate one to three bedrooms. Mobile homes also appealed to Rudolph's contemporaries because of their interest in prefabrication, though they disapproved of how the units, complete with shutters and siding, aped traditional homes.[18] By the early 1960s, the term "mobile home" had acquired negative connotations, so Rudolph called his large-scale manufactured housing unit the "twentieth-century brick." He thought that its rectangular form resembled a traditional brick and that its bigger scale made it the appropriate size for building the increasingly large structures of the twentieth century. The term exemplified Rudolph's efforts to organize his ideas systematically and to devise a lexicon to describe his experiments, just as Wright and Le Corbusier had done.

Rudolph believed that the twentieth-century brick would serve as the basic unit of a new vernacular that would provide a universal architectural order for the country, similar to the use of the tatami mat in traditional Japanese architecture. Striking a defiant tone, which reflected an increasing sense of beleaguerment, Rudolph said in 1969 that the dimensions of his manufactured units were derived from the nation's infrastructure—the width of highways—and were therefore destined to dominate residential construction. He said, "Out of the American road is emerging a series of dimensions, which will be as powerful in the United States as the three-foot-by-six-foot module is in Japanese tradition. That is American domestic architecture of the present and future as far as I'm concerned."[19]

Winning acceptance for the twentieth-century brick, however, was not easy. Popular because they were inexpensive, mobile homes were at the same time scorned for their often shoddy construction and design that recalled traditional architecture, among many other reasons. Unions feared that the mass-production of mobile homes would result in fewer construction jobs, and municipalities thought they lowered real estate values and did not contribute enough to the tax base. Also, the parks were considered an aesthetic blight on the landscape.[20] Such objections did not deter Rudolph. Just as he hoped to dignify concrete block, Rudolph aspired to elevate the mobile home. It would be affordable, practical, and attractive, and it would transform the American housing industry.

Oriental Masonic Gardens

After several attempts, Rudolph finally succeeded in using the twentieth-century brick for Oriental Masonic Gardens (1968–71), a publicly financed housing cooperative in New Haven.[21] Rudolph's long-time friend Mayor Lee was instrumental in getting construction approved. Rudolph said, "Unions and codes made it excessively difficult to get these units built. That they have been built is due to a great deal of finesse and to the extraordinary efforts of Mayor Richard C. Lee of New Haven."[22]

Oriental Masonic Gardens was innovative as an experiment in prefabrication, in urban redevelopment, and in social policy. Unlike most "housing projects" of the time, where occupants rented their homes, this was a low-income cooperative where residents could buy their units. Housing projects were usually located in dense urban centers; in this case, New Haven redevelopment administrators deliberately sited the Gardens at the edge of the city near its East Rock Park. As he had with Crawford Manor, Mayor Lee attempted to use the project, begun in the aftermath of the race riots that devastated New Haven and many American cities in the summer of 1967, to strengthen his relationship with the city's politically nascent African-American community.[23]

The popular and architectural press covered development of Oriental Masonic Gardens extensively, believing it a step toward solving the interrelated problems of racial segregation, poverty, and sub-standard housing that troubled urban America in the late 1960s. New experiments with prefabrication, such as Moshe Safdie's Habitat for Expo '67 in Montreal, a prototype for mass housing

6.12 Perspective section, Dana Center.

6.13 Multistory hall with lounge, Dana Center.

assembled from concrete modular units, attracted wide-spread favorable attention and affected national policy around this time. In July 1969, Lee publicly unveiled Oriental Masonic Gardens in the presence of George Romney, Secretary of Housing and Urban Development for the Nixon administration. Romney had recently announced an ambitious national plan to transform the housing industry called Operation Breakthrough. Intended to revolutionize American residential construction with high-quality, but inexpensive, manufactured housing units, Operation Breakthrough called for rapidly eliminating slums by inserting massive amounts of prefabricated housing built by private industry. Representing a consequential policy shift, it was part of recently elected Republican president Richard M. Nixon's attempts to move the country away from the public initiatives favored by the Democratic Kennedy and Johnson administrations toward private ones.[24] Though never a part of Operation Breakthrough, Rudolph's project bolstered the government's plan.

Rudolph clustered the units at the Gardens in informal groupings that related to the site's natural slope (figure 6.14). Units were roofed with arched plywood vaults that resembled those of Rudolph's Hook House (Siesta Key, Florida, 1952–53). All of the vaults faced the same direction, recalling Le Corbusier's similarly configured terraced and vaulted Roq et Rob housing (project, Cap Martin, France, 1949), a widely influential housing model in the 1960s. This uniformity gave the complex an impressive consistency, like that of an Italian hill town, that was particularly apparent against the forested hills of New Haven's East Rock.

Each rectangular module measured twelve feet wide and thirty-six or forty-eight feet long, dimensions similar to conventional mobile homes (figure 6.15). Rudolph built his modules of wood to make them light and easy to transport; it was also appropriately rustic for the wooded site. Safdie's units at Habitat '67 had been made of concrete and were therefore heavier and harder to move. The Eastern Portable Buildings Corporation manufactured the modules complete with wiring and plumbing in its Maryland factory and transported them by ship and highway to the site. Yuji Noga, a former Yale student, was Rudolph's project manager, assisting the builders, the Macomber Company from Boston. Cranes stacked the modules into 148 pinwheel-shaped, two- to five-bedroom, duplex units (figure 6.16). The doors and details were painted in bright primary colors to impart some lightheartedness and to contrast with the wood siding. Walled courtyard gardens offered to the duplex apartments the privacy and individuality of a single-family house (figure 6.17).

Oriental Masonic Gardens opened in 1971 to a mixed reception. The *New York Times* reported on the new owners joyfully decorating their homes.[25] However, the prefabricated modules had not been built well, and the apartments were more expensive than anticipated. The units sold for $21,000 to $23,000, which was not so different from the price of conventionally built housing.[26] Moving residential construction toward prefabrication proved difficult, and the complex was in fact one of the few large-scale projects made from manufactured units to be completed in the United States.

6.14 Rudolph, Oriental Masonic Gardens (New Haven, 1968–71).

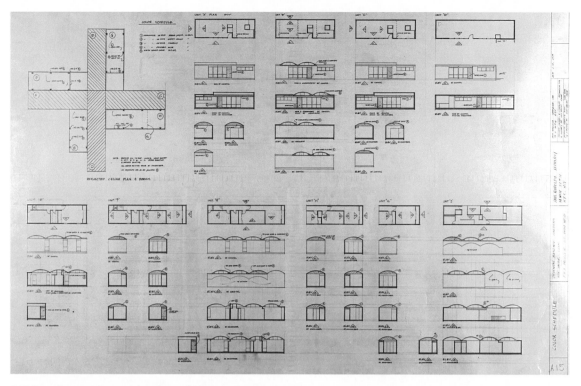

6.15 Specifications for modules, Oriental Masonic Gardens.

6.16 Construction, Oriental Masonic Gardens.

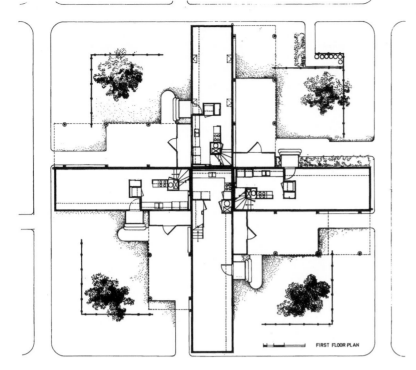

6.17 Unit plan, Oriental Masonic Gardens.

Rudolph insisted that the true innovations at Oriental Masonic Gardens were political rather than technological, in particular because it overcame many of the barriers that municipalities and unions employed to prevent the erection of prefabricated housing.[27] For Rudolph, the Gardens exemplified what prefabrication could achieve on a large scale; the immense megastructures made from twentieth-century bricks that existed on his office drawing boards at the time were further demonstrations.

Megastructures

In a 1973 interview, Rudolph said that the megastructure was among the most important recent developments for modern architecture.[28] The concept had many antecedents. Projects by the Russian avant-garde and Le Corbusier from the 1920s and 1930s informed it, but it did not fully cohere until the 1960s. Fumihiko Maki defined the megastructure in 1964 as "a large frame in which all the functions of a city or part of a city are housed."[29] The framework could be endlessly expanded, and elements within, including prefabricated residential modules, could be replaced as needed, giving the megastructure an almost organic character that defined it more than any formal quality. Different configurations were possible. The overall form could be bridge-like, as in the case of Kenzo Tange's famous project for Tokyo Bay 1960, or it could resemble a Mediterranean hill town or even a natural geological formation such as a mountain range.

By the mid- and late 1960s, new proposals for urban planning regularly referenced the megastructure in some way. Avant-garde architects such as Yona Friedman and groups such as Archigram and Superstudio envisioned fantastic constructions, spanning cities and entire continents, that would solve housing shortages and accommodate expanding populations through sheer size. These schemes were generally conceptual, critical in nature, and frequently unrelated to site or realities of construction. Several of Rudolph's projects had anticipated the enthusiasm for the megastructure. Both the Boston Government Service Center (1962–71) and the SMTI campus (1963–72) were conceived as great single buildings, though they in fact comprised several, and his Sarasota Senior High School (1958–60), Temple Street Parking Garage (New Haven, 1958–63), and Yale A & A Building (1958–63) were all designed to be expandable as well.

Developing these qualities further in light of the experiments of Tange and Archigram, Rudolph's two visionary megastructures proposed for Manhattan in the late 1960s, the Graphic Arts Center (project, 1967) and City Corridor or Lower Manhattan Expressway (project, 1967–72), were thought out in their specifics, in contrast to the conceptions of the avant-garde. Though he believed in aesthetics above all else and often had difficulty engaging with the practical and social aspects of architecture, Rudolph had a pragmatic strain, and his Manhattan projects showed how megastructures could be accomplished in real places for real clients in response to real problems. The culmination of Rudolph's thinking about urbanism and prefabrication, these unbuilt projects served as touchstones, inspiring the Asian buildings of his late career.

Graphic Arts Center

Rudolph's 1967 designs for the Graphic Arts Center, for the west side of downtown Manhattan, proposed an artificial peninsula of towers composed of twentieth-century bricks. Providing living and working accommodations for the members of the Amalgamated Lithographers Guild of America, it would be their very own hill town in the city (figure 6.18).

The Graphic Arts Center was conceived by the guild in 1961; the group asked Le Corbusier to design the new complex, but he declined the commission.[30] In 1967, after several changes in site and architect, the union asked Rudolph to design a workplace, residence, and real estate investment at the edge of lower Manhattan's printing district. The lithographers would inhabit self-contained quarters, like the members of a medieval guild, on a site bounded by the Hudson River, the adjacent West Side Highway, and Harrison, Greenwich, and Hubert Streets (figure 6.19). It was just blocks from the Holland Tunnel and the interstate highway system that would deliver the modules for the construction as well as the paper and supplies for the printing industry.

As was often the case, Rudolph's project was a critique of what he considered conventional practices. He included the nearby towers of Minoru Yamasaki's World Trade Center (1962–75) in the models, plans, and renderings of the Graphic Arts Center to illustrate the profound differences between the schemes. Rudolph had long objected to the rectilinear form typical of American tall buildings, which was exemplified by the Twin Towers. The immense hundred-plus-story Trade Center towers also exemplified the enormous jump in scale and size that, according to Rudolph and others, was transforming cities at the time. Rudolph believed that standard approaches to the tall building and city planning were ill-equipped to handle this change. In contrast to the isolated and monolithic forms of the Trade Center towers, Rudolph's Graphic Arts Center was a wondrous, expressive cascade of irregular towers reaching out like a gesturing arm toward the river. This craggy, crystalline peninsula exemplified what Rudolph called "topographical architecture." Related to the scenographic tendencies that were becoming apparent in his projects, topographical architecture was both a response to natural terrain and a development of constructed terrain.

To some degree, the Graphic Arts Center also reflected the influential Lower Manhattan Plan, commissioned by the city of New York in 1966 but never realized. To infuse life into the moribund lower part of the island, the plan recommended developing residential buildings, esplanades, and marinas along the rivers, which had been neglected after the decline of commercial shipping in the early 1960s. Unlike typical redevelopment proposals of the time, the Lower Manhattan Plan proposed leaving streets intact.[31]

Rudolph intended the Graphic Arts Center to be a self-contained city within the city. Its peninsula-shaped platform connected to nearby streets, bridging the West Side Highway and extending over the river, where it was supported on pylons. The platform housed loading docks for trucks and a parking garage for 2,100 cars. Atop it was work and office space for the lithographers, a million square feet of steel-and-concrete-framed stacked open lofts. Residential towers complete with shops, schools, and social services were connected to the commercial components and descended to the river in a dramatic arc. Along the river were terraced esplanades for strolling, a marina, tennis courts, and a pool.

In what would have been a novel structural system for a tall building, the residential towers consisted of prefabricated twentieth-century bricks suspended from central concrete masts containing services, elevators, and fire stairs; the composition recalled Rudolph's 1954 Trailer

6.18 Rudolph, model, Graphic Arts Center (New York, project, 1967).

6.19 Site plan, Graphic Arts Center.

Tower proposal for Sarasota. The pinwheel-shaped base and floors of Rudolph's towers also recalled the configuration of Frank Lloyd Wright's St. Marks-in-the-Bouwerie Tower (New York, project, 1928–30) and Crystal Heights mixed-use project in Washington, D.C. (project, 1940), a series of connected, polygonal towers. Rudolph also looked to Le Corbusier for inspiration. Just as Le Corbusier's Unité d'Habitation (Marseilles, France, 1946–52) had shopping and other amenities at midheight, each tower at the Graphic Arts Center provided shops, kindergartens, and other services on its tenth floor.

The dense stacking of units would have given the complex a fantastic quality, again almost mannered in its complexity and ambiguity, but also recalling science fiction's fantasy cities, a quality found in many of the era's megastructures (figure 6.20). Even so, Rudolph believed that his proposal was pragmatic. Compared to the concrete modules of Safdie's Habitat, Rudolph's units would have been relatively lightweight, easier to transport and lift into place. The 12-by-60-foot steel units would have arrived from the factory complete with plumbing and wiring; workers would have hoisted them into place and expanded their width to twenty-eight feet by unfolding panels from their sides. Units could have been added and removed to create new living configurations.

Had it been built, the Graphic Arts Center would have provided spacious, inexpensive apartments with plentiful outdoor space, a precious commodity in the dense city. The floating city would have added a new dimension to the urban experience, anticipating the type of access to the river achieved by riverfront projects initiated almost forty years later. Most strikingly, the complex would have been a captivating landmark amid the almost uniformly rectilinear buildings of Manhattan. Certainly there would have been drawbacks, notably an isolation as a city within the city characteristic of large-scale housing complexes of this period.

The Lithographers Guild canceled the project in 1968. Rudolph said that the powerful New York City unions of plumbers, carpenters, and masons persuaded the lithographers to halt the project because they believed that prefabrication on such a large scale would hurt their livelihoods. Given the many problems with prefabrication encountered at Oriental Masonic Gardens, it was unlikely that a project of such enormous scale could have been built anyway. Rudolph, however, believed that a prefabricated megastructure like the Graphic Arts Center would be built some day, if not in Manhattan then in some far away place.[32]

LOMEX and City Corridor

Rudolph had commenced work on a still-larger megastructure for Manhattan even before the Graphic Arts Center work was canceled. If the latter resembled a peninsula, then City Corridor (project, 1967–72) was a mountain range that would have stretched across the New York island from east to west with a spur that linked it to the Manhattan Bridge. Rudolph used the City Corridor designs to elaborate on the forms and ideas of the Graphic Arts Center at a grander scale, making it another example of his topographical architecture and the culmination of his investigations into the megastructure (figure 6.21).

Although doubts were already beginning to emerge about such immense projects, the belief that the future of architecture lay with the megastructure was not uncommon in the late 1960s. Rudolph had long thought that immense structures could bring order to haphazardly planned American cities. Coherent physical forms could presumably also help inspire social order, a concern in 1967 when race riots broke out in many of the country's increasingly poor, racially divided, and crime-ridden cities. Architects responded differently to these seismic events, some thinking that designers must work in more socially responsive ways and thus gearing their efforts to small-scale community-based projects. Rudolph, however, still believed that

Prefabrication and the Megastructure

6.20 Suspended units, Graphic Arts Center.

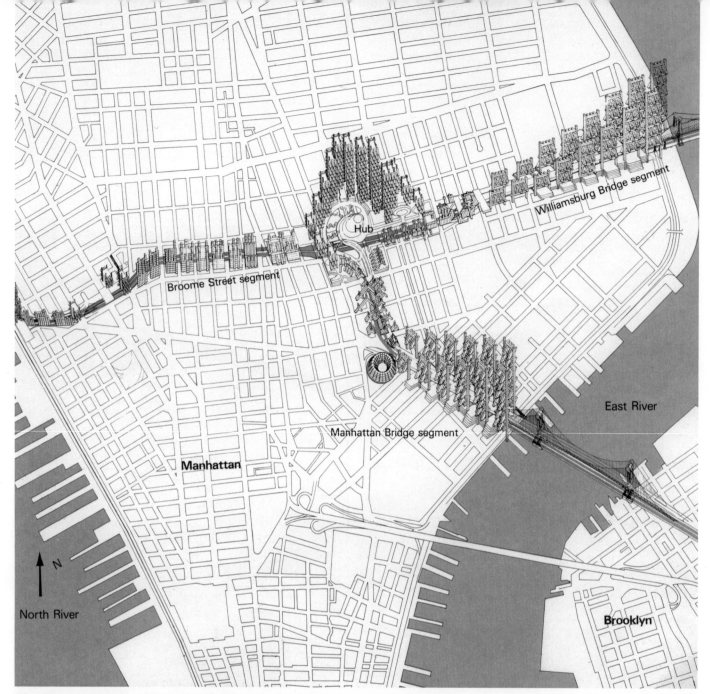

Labels on image: Williamsburg Bridge segment, Hub, Broome Street segment, Manhattan Bridge segment, East River, Manhattan, North River, Brooklyn, N

6.21 Rudolph, City Corridor (New York, project, 1967–72).

the designer of a city should act like a conductor or artist. In its grandeur, City Corridor was Wagnerian, recalling Camillo Sitte's recommendations that the city should be like a symphony or great work of art that affected the viewer emotionally. As critic Paul Goldberger later suggested, City Corridor's mountainous heights and precipices would have inspired intense reactions recalling those that Edmund Burke said were stirred by natural landscape when he theorized the sublime in the eighteenth century.[33]

Rudolph imagined building City Corridor on top of the proposed Lower Manhattan Expressway (LOMEX), concealing the roadbed from view entirely with buildings from end to end. The LOMEX project was one of the last spearheaded by Robert Moses, the autocratic administrator who built most of New York City's highway system and many of its parks and other amenities between the 1930s and the late 1960s.[34] Rudolph was no friend or ally of Moses, and in fact, the former's hypothetical project was an intervention

intended to heal the enormous rift that Moses's expressway would have created through Soho and the Lower East Side. Though the Y-shaped LOMEX would have allowed vehicles to flow across Manhattan without interruption, relieving congestion on the city's streets, the thoroughfare exemplified the worst, most imperious aspects of postwar redevelopment and highway building. Hundreds of buildings would have been demolished, neighborhoods altered, and people and businesses displaced; the expressway would have divided the island in two.

Many were horrified by LOMEX's potential impact on the city, and especially by the destruction of Soho's nineteenth-century cast-iron industrial buildings and the vibrant new arts community they housed. A coalition of urban activists and preservationists led by Jane Jacobs defeated Moses's expressway in a highly publicized battle in 1969. By 1971, LOMEX was officially "demapped," or removed from the official list of city projects,[35] and was therefore a dead project

6.22 Model, City Corridor.

6.23 Bridge Apartments (Brown & Guenther, 1963) and George Washington Bridge Bus Terminal (Pierluigi Nervi, 1965–66) atop Interstate 95 leading to George Washington Bridge, New York.

for almost the entire time Rudolph was working on his City Corridor plan. However, LOMEX was not dead in the imaginations of some architects. Although they understood how damaging Moses's expressway would have been for the city, Rudolph and some of his young contemporaries were fascinated by how the unbuilt highway could make Manhattan an even more complex urban environment. It provoked them to envision fantastic hypothetical projects for New York that would advance thinking about urbanism.

For Rudolph, City Corridor became a purely academic venture, supported by a grant from the Ford Foundation and the American Federation of the Arts, that allowed him to bring together in one project his investigations into prefabrication, urbanism, and the megastructure. He constructed an enormous model of the project in a downtown studio space in Manhattan rented expressly for this purpose and worked on it for nearly five years with a team of model-builders led by Donald Luckenbill, who became a key member of Rudolph's office over the next decade (figure 6.22). In addition to the model, the research resulted in the book *The Evolving City*, which illustrated Rudolph's City Corridor and another urban proposal for Manhattan by Ulrich Franzen, an old friend of Rudolph's. Texts by the urbanist Peter Wolf explained both projects.[36]

Though City Corridor's size and boldness may seem extraordinary, Rudolph's project had much in common with other projects of similar magnitude. In his book *The Metropolis of Tomorrow* (1929), architectural renderer Hugh Ferriss envisioned a Manhattan-like future city with mountain ranges of art deco skyscrapers clustered in gateway-like groupings around bridges and on top of multilevel highways. Ferriss's immense formations prefigured Rudolph's topographical architecture and typified a romantic admiration for Manhattan's skyscrapers characteristic of the 1920s and 1930s, an attitude shared by Rudolph. City Corridor also elaborated on Kevin Lynch's 1961 suggestion for a "high spine" of skyscrapers across Boston, which may have been a reference point for Rudolph's Boston Government Service Center (1962–71).

Contemporary structures in Manhattan inspired Rudolph as well. His City Corridor resembled a new urban configuration in Upper Manhattan, the recently built Bridge Apartments, a series of towers by Brown & Guenther (1963), that connected to an adjacent bus terminal by the Italian engineer Pierluigi Nervi (1965–66); the complex covered a new submerged highway across the narrow upper end of the island that extended Interstate 95 across the George Washington Bridge (figure 6.23). Building on top of a highway provided new opportunities to exploit air rights not often used for development in the past. However, rising noise and exhaust made such structures difficult to inhabit.[37] The potential of air rights, the necessity of ventilation, and the dramatic possibilities of bridge approaches were all lessons that Rudolph likely learned from this project.

City Corridor also had much in common with other hypothetical projects of the time for New York City. Rudolph's former Yale students Jacquelin Robertson and Jonathan Barnett proposed enclosing the exposed railway viaduct along upper Park Avenue in Harlem with a concrete tunnel and then building housing and mixed-use high-rises on top of it. Their project appeared in the 1967 Museum of Modern Art exhibition *The New City: Architecture and Urban Renewal*. The show of speculative projects reflected the late-1960s' great interest in urban redevelopment and the megastructure. A project that in 1967 was still slated to be built but already controversial, LOMEX represented a presence in the urban landscape so potentially transformative for Manhattan that it spurred architects to design new, visionary projects related to it. In Linear City (1967), also shown in the exhibition, McMillan, Griffis & Mileto put forth the idea of covering the Long Island Railroad in Brooklyn with a new highway joined to Moses's LOMEX; atop the route was a megastructure containing housing, parking, industrial buildings, and an arts center, all aligned along a lushly planted, linear pedestrian walkway.[38] Rudolph's City Corridor had many qualities similar to those of Linear City, but it would be even bolder.

Design

City Corridor was a series of closely spaced but freestanding buildings that formed three portions. The Williamsburg and Manhattan segments were named for the bridges they joined LOMEX to; the Broome Street segment in Soho was a low-rise series of A-frame structures. Towers also encircled a transportation "HUB" located where the three segments converged. As an ensemble, City Corridor formed a mountainous configuration that both impressed the viewer through sheer scale and suggested order and symbolic meaning. Wolf's text for *The Evolving City* explained how the buildings had been arranged in a scenographic and symbolic fashion in accordance with Rudolph's concept of topographical architecture: "In this proposal, buildings through the modulation of their scale, form hills and valleys rather than standing free in meaningless juxtaposition. The hills signify locations of intensive use or special symbolic importance and the valleys indicate areas of less intensive uses or places of calm. Thus, at the bridge approaches, the gateway to the city, the ceremony of entering which traditionally received great attention in urban design is again expressed by the continuous massing of tall structures."[39]

Rudolph framed the two bridge approaches from Brooklyn with apartment towers made from twentieth-century bricks (figure 6.24). His perspective section of one of these vast gateways was an exciting image of urban complexity—not unlike a Ferriss rendering—that again could have been a depiction of some futuristic city from the cover of a science fiction magazine. Attached to a structural lattice containing services, the slope-fronted, trapezoidal apartment modules introduced a diagonal-based geometry to the project, imparting a feeling of direction, dynamism, and energy. The apartments were perilously suspended in the air, recalling the smaller-scale dangers of the rail-less stairs and vertiginous drops of Rudolph's New Haven apartment and New York interiors of this time.

Rudolph often used the perspective section to explain internal complexity, and the depiction of City Corridor revealed the many stacked layers of transportation and pedestrian spaces he wrapped around Moses's expressway to form the corridor that gave the project its name. Rudolph placed parking garages beneath the expressway and incised the pavement of the pedestrian mall above it

6.24 Perspective section, City Corridor.

6.25 HUB, City Corridor.

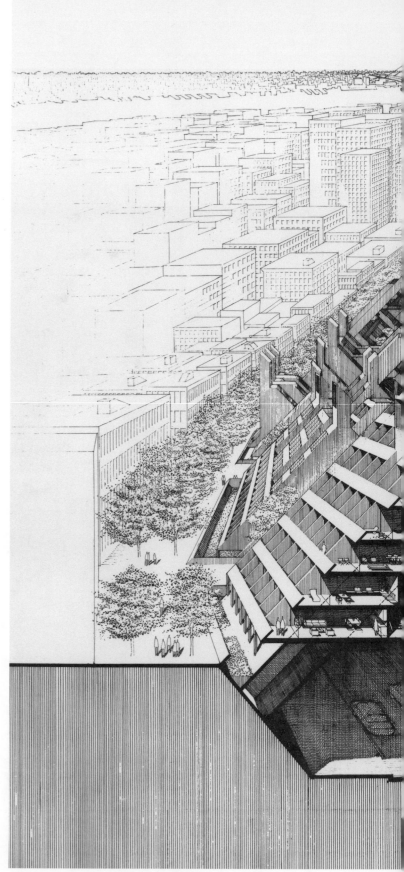

6.26 Broome Street segment, City Corridor.

with his characteristic radiating lines to draw pedestrians to features, such as sculptures and smaller plazas, that humanized its enormous scale. A monorail and concrete tubes containing walkways also connected the entire complex internally.

Rudolph was specific about City Corridor's relationship to the city and its construction, but not about much else. Unlike many urban studies of the day, City Corridor was not informed by research about the city's inhabitants developed with the rational methods and statistical data of the social sciences. Nor did Rudolph greatly emphasize community or civic life, which were among the primary themes of urbanism for architects from Kahn to the members of CIAM during the postwar years. Other than saying that offices and apartments were mixed together, Rudolph did not specify exact uses for the structures or how they would be financed, implying that it was another effort to build low-cost housing. As was consistent with his thinking, Rudolph instead focused on the aesthetic experience of the individual, seeing the megastructure as a series of opportunities to create visually thrilling experiences for New Yorkers. *The Evolving City* explained that City Corridor "seizes the necessity of a major public works project to propose some urban design organizing principles that could benefit the experience of the individual in the city and the visual-aesthetic quality of the city itself."[40] Rudolph often pointed to the experience of emerging in a speeding automobile from the darkened, enclosed portions of Manhattan's FDR Drive near his own Beekman Place apartment into the sunlight near the United Nations building as the type of exciting, visually "kaleidoscopic" occurrence that mid-twentieth-century urbanism should strive to emulate.[41]

Such experiences could be had at the intersection of Chrystie and Delancey Streets, City Corridor's most significant crossing. Rudolph marked the convergence of the

two branches of the highway coming from the Manhattan and Williamsburg Bridges with a domed structure called the HUB. (He capitalized the term though it was not an acronym) (figure 6.25). The HUB was a key transportation node where City Corridor dwellers could leave the internal monorail and walkways to connect with the subway system and with Moses's highway or to follow the wavy pedestrian walkways, themselves expressive of motion, that linked the HUB to the surrounding buildings of City Corridor and to the city's streets.

Inside the HUB, the dimensions of the city's infrastructure were revealed from a different angle than usual. From escalators and elevators and through transparent walls and floors, the traveler could see the convergence of expressway, subways, monorail, and walkways coursing through City Corridor, an experience similar to looking at one of Rudolph's perspective section drawings. Wolf wrote, "A deep, multimodal sinew of transportation ways and systems is revealed to the spectator, to the person in the city."[42]

City Corridor engaged directly with Manhattan's existing streets and buildings in its lower portions. In Soho's Broome Street segment, instead of towers, two parallel sets of A-frames containing apartments, schools, and small-scale commercial and social facilities framed the pedestrian mall. The height of these structures matched the five- and six-story historic buildings along Spring and Broome Streets (figure 6.26).

Among the many precedents for the A-frame were Tange's Tokyo Bay project and other megastructures of the late 1950s and early 1960s.[43] At City Corridor, the A-frames consisted of stacked twentieth-century bricks. Their sides and fronts unfolded to make them larger and form the slope-fronted profile that gave City Corridor its aesthetic unity (figure 6.27). To keep vehicular fumes

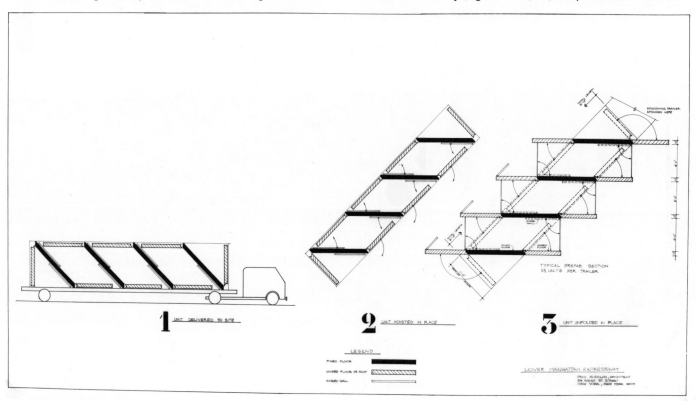

6.27 Construction diagram, City Corridor.

out of the buildings, Rudolph vented exhaust through stacks aligned like chimneys along a ridge crowning the A-frames.

In contrast to LOMEX, which would have cut many of the city's streets in two, City Corridor was penetrated by several of the existing roads; they were transformed into bridges over the highway that gave pedestrians views of the traffic and people-movers below. In another gesture toward the existing city, Rudolph preserved Soho's cast-iron lofts by inserting the low-rise A-frames between Spring and Broome Streets; many of the existing facades would have been saved, though they would have been reduced to something like false fronts in a frontier town.

A bold and sincere proposal to mitigate the high-handed destruction that would have been wrought by Moses's LOMEX, City Corridor was impressive, aesthetically memorable, and carefully thought out in many of its details. Providing Soho with improved affordable housing might even have contributed to its long-term viability as a neighborhood for artists. However, it is impossible to think that it would have improved the city overall. City Corridor embodied the overwrought or mannered quality, reflective of Rudolph's romantic admiration for the city's skyscrapers, increasingly evident in his work by the mid-1960s. He paid little or no attention to the realities of living and working, and his preservation of just the fronts of Soho's cast-iron buildings was an approach preservationists later found facile. Most disturbing, though it maintained the existing streets and avenues, City Corridor still divided Manhattan in two, perpetuating the most detrimental aspect of Moses's expressway.

The investment that Rudolph made in studying prefabrication and the megastructure did not pay off for him in the long run. In fact, his advocacy of both tendencies would contribute to his sinking reputation. Although Rudolph's visionary megastructures for Manhattan informed other projects—the Earl W. Brydges Library (Niagara Falls, New York, 1969–74) and the Burroughs Wellcome Headquarters (Research Triangle Park, North Carolina, 1969–72), as well as his later Asian projects—such schemes had fallen out of favor by the time *The Evolving City* was published in 1974. In his comprehensive history of the megastructure, critic Reyner Banham called it a "whitening skeleton on the dark horizon of our recent architectural past."[44] Though *Architectural Record* had celebrated similar megastructures in the late 1960s, the journal's review of *The Evolving City* in 1975 called City Corridor's modular units "repetitive trapezoidal pigeonholes" and concluded that it was "incredibly limited in its vocabulary and horrendous in its inhumanity."[45] These views represented a marked shift of opinion about Rudolph's architecture; though its origins were complex, the alteration was reflective of the enormous transformations society underwent in the late 1960s and early 1970s.

Prefabrication fared no better, either as a technique of construction or in the court of public opinion. The units were difficult to build and widely opposed by unions and municipalities. The recession of the 1970s was the final blow to such efforts. The fate of Oriental Masonic Gardens exemplified prefabrication's problems; the units were poorly manufactured, and the complex decayed soon after it was completed. It fell prey to the crime and other social problems often endemic to low-income housing at the time. Efforts to renovate the housing cooperative failed, and it received little support from the Federal Department of Housing and Urban Development, which had taken over its management. Oriental Masonic Gardens was finally demolished in 1981, yet another blow to Rudolph's reputation, by then in steep decline.[46]

Seven
Reversal of Fortune

Few architects had brighter prospects than Rudolph in the early 1960s. By the end of the decade, however, his reputation was in decline and his masterpiece, the Yale A & A Building, in ruins. The fire that gutted the A & A in 1969 is often thought of as the catalyst for this unforeseen reversal of fortune, but it was just one of a series of related events at Yale that altered attitudes toward him and his architecture in New Haven and beyond.

Rudolph faced increasing difficulties at Yale even before the dedication of the A & A Building in November 1963. The beginning of the end of his time there can be dated to the death of Yale president A. Whitney Griswold in April 1963. The loss of Rudolph's greatest supporter meant the loss of university support as well. Rudolph said Yale "was never the same" for him after Griswold's death.[1] Kingman Brewster, Yale's new president, presided over the dedication of the A & A Building, but he was not as interested in architecture or as supportive of Rudolph as his predecessor. Brewster's primary focus became keeping the campus peaceful as it was engulfed by the protest movements of the late 1960s.[2]

At the same time, Rudolph was losing support among faculty and students in ways that portended broader shifts within architecture. His sometimes close, sometimes contentious relationship with Serge Chermayeff exemplified the different era. Rudolph had introduced his long-time friend Chermayeff—they shared office space in Cambridge in the 1950s—to the Yale faculty in 1962. Though in retrospect many of their positions seem similar, in the early 1960s they appeared to be diverging markedly. Chermayeff championed an updated functionalism, the very thing that Rudolph had long inveighed against, in ways that proved attractive to faculty and students who were beginning to react against Rudolph's heroic aesthetics. Chermayeff inscribed a copy of the book he wrote with Christopher Alexander, *Community and Privacy: Toward a New Architecture of Humanism* (1963), to Rudolph with the words, "To Paul, with warmest regards from the other end of the architectural spectrum."[3] Rudolph and Chermayeff both believed in humanism, but the latter thought it could be achieved using familiar, humble, small-scale forms that balanced the communal with the individual—patios, for example—rather than the monumental ones favored by the former. Instead of aspiring to build grandiose civic structures, some Yale students began to design and build modest, quirky houses in rural places such as Vermont, a tendency in keeping with the back-to-the-land environmental movements and counterculture of the 1960s.[4]

Rudolph had reinvigorated Yale during his seven years as chairman of the Department of Architecture and built a landmark new structure to house the program. In return, the university's prestige had bolstered his reputation, and his practice had flourished. But the loss of support at Yale

7.1 Coffee house, Yale A & A Building.

PLEASE CLEAR TABLE
AS YOU LEAVE

7.2 Supergraphics, graphic design studios, A & A Building.

made it a less attractive place for Rudolph. He resigned and by fall 1965 had moved his office and residence to New York.

Charles Moore

The tenor of the Yale Department of Architecture changed greatly after Rudolph left. If Rudolph epitomized the orderly "liberal consensus" culture of the 1950s and early 1960s, then his successor as chairman, Charles Moore (1925–1993), represented its virtual opposite, the free-wheeling "social activist" culture of protest movements and community-focused activities that had developed at places such as the University of California, Berkeley, where Moore had been a faculty member before coming to Yale.

Moore's architecture likewise reflected the zeitgeist of the 1960s. In his small, vernacular-inspired houses and his academic buildings, he employed pop art imagery and colorful cutout forms to create stimulating interior environments more whimsical in tone than those of Rudolph. Moore shifted the pedagogical emphasis of the architecture department from Rudolph's aesthetics, individuality, and fostering of the professional skills of design at the drawing board to social activism and hands-on building skills. This was most apparent in his introduction of the Yale Building Project, for which students designed and built structures for poor communities in New Haven and elsewhere.[5]

Moore transformed not just the department but the Art & Architecture Building. Upon his appointment in 1965 (he would serve until 1970), Moore declared that he was opposed to Rudolph's approach to architecture. He told the Yale Daily News in September 1965, "Mr. Rudolph is an important architect who works as an individual and ran the

school that way. He did things by himself and seemed to make people like it." Adroitly mixing criticism and praise, Moore added, "I disapprove of the Art and Architecture Building whole-heartedly because it is such a personal manifestation for non-personal use. However, I enjoy very much being in it."[6]

Moore also seems to have enjoyed altering the A & A. It became a hands-on, exploratory laboratory for students reflecting the playfulness and "contagious excitement," as one student remembered it, that Moore brought to Yale.[7] He converted Rudolph's elegant rooftop penthouse into a coffee house for students and faculty (figure 7.1). Experimental structures were built in the exhibition room. Inspired by pop art, students remade the A & A's interiors with enlarged and colorful graphic images exemplifying the "supergraphics" movement, making the building its epicenter (figure 7.2).[8] Supergraphics intrigued Rudolph, but he avoided the building when in New Haven, seeing its transformation only during a rare studio review in 1967.[9]

Despite the lively events within, the physical condition of the A & A quickly declined under Moore. The building filled with trash and litter because of inadequate maintenance, a growing problem across the Yale campus. Increasing crime, a phenomenon common to many cities throughout the nation, made the streets around the structure feel unsafe and, at times, found its way into the building itself. The art students and faculty, dissatisfied with their cramped studios since the building had been inaugurated, blamed the design of the building. An article about their unhappiness appeared in the Yale Daily News in May 1967; a letter followed from a senior faculty member of the art department calling the building a "total failure," an appraisal that would soon be much repeated.[10]

7.3 Graffiti, Yale A & A Building.

7.4 Minerva, drafting room, A & A Building.

7.5 "Favelas" in drafting room, A & A Building.

"A Building As a Teacher"

By 1967, only four years after its completion, the A & A Building was in a distressed state and attracted the attention of the press beyond New Haven. More articles were written about Rudolph's numerous projects in the architectural and popular press that year than in any year previously, and they were not all positive; in fact, they contributed to his fall as they chronicled it. In March 1967, the *New York Times Magazine* profiled Rudolph and put his picture on the cover. While such attention from the nation's newspaper of record appeared to be a sign of Rudolph's success, the article questioned his virtuosity even as it appeared to celebrate him. Writer David Jacobs, who toured the A & A in its modified condition, wondered if it had deserved the accolades it had received on its completion.[11]

More negative appraisals from the press soon followed. Journalist Ellen Perry Berkeley suggested that the design of the A & A Building was largely responsible for its poor condition and the way in which its users were altering it in an article entitled "Yale: A Building As a Teacher," which appeared in the July–August 1967 issue of *Architectural Forum*.[12] It was a turning point for the reputations of Rudolph and his building. Under the editorship of Rudolph's friend Peter Blake, *Architectural Forum* had abandoned the celebratory style typical of most postwar architectural journalism by sometimes taking an investigative approach, reflecting the late 1960s' questioning of established ways. Berkeley, a successful journalist and *Forum* editor who had studied at Harvard's GSD, employed the rhetoric of student protests, describing her article as a "live-in and a speak out" because it quoted the users' opinions extensively, if anonymously. She later said she felt no animosity toward Rudolph and had long admired his buildings.[13]

Berkeley scrutinized Rudolph's claim that the building would instruct and stimulate Yale students. Maintaining an objective tone, she speculated about the various factors—including Moore's presence, Yale's maintenance of the building, and larger social problems and differences in attitude—that could have caused changes at the

A & A. Berkeley interviewed Rudolph, Moore, and numerous students and faculty, who were quoted anonymously. She also stayed for five days in the guest bedroom attached to the former penthouse with her husband Roy, a professional photographer whose photographs of the interior in its altered state accompanied her article.

The photos were especially surprising because they appeared alongside Ezra Stoller's shots of the building in its original, pristine state in 1963; the juxtaposition clearly manifested the changes in the building and the attitudes of its users. Graffiti, including graffiti that mocked Rudolph, had spread through the building in a way that delighted some with its irreverence and troubled others who saw it as sign of unrest and decay (figure 7.3). In the drafting room, students hung clotheslines from the statue of Minerva and painted her eyes white (figure 7.4). They hung large sheets of paper from clotheslines to shade themselves from the sunlight that flooded the room and cast distracting shadows across their drawing boards. Berkeley reported that students and faculty considered the A & A's interiors cramped, poorly lit and ventilated, noisy, and ill-equipped for their needs.

Additional alterations in the drafting room revealed that it was not only the art students who were disgruntled. Having become as unhappy with their quarters as the artists had long been, many of the architecture students found Rudolph's presence, or point of view as an architect, too palpable. They countered it by transforming his grandly proportioned drafting room, the pedagogical heart of the building, into their own personal, private spaces with makeshift partitions of used wood, cardboard, and other materials (figure 7.5). Moore and the Yale administration appeared to have given up jurisdiction over the drafting room. Although the 1967 photographs were surprising, it is worth noting that even during Rudolph's chairmanship the room had often been fairly crowded and disorderly in appearance, as indeed was typical of studio spaces where architecture was taught and practiced.

Nevertheless, the language Berkeley used to describe these modifications was damning. She said the structures students built in the drafting room resembled "favelas,"

7.6 Fire, June 14, 1969, A & A Building.

the shantytowns surrounding Rio de Janeiro, Brasília, and other urban areas of Brazil. Using the term to describe the constructions in the A & A implied a failure by Rudolph, and modernism as well, to acknowledge basic needs.[14] Like squatters who built favelas, the Yale students appeared to have taken matters into their own hands in order to shelter themselves within what they considered an inhospitable modernist environment.

Berkeley noted that economies, such as a lack of air-conditioning and window-washing equipment, contributed to the occupants' discomfort and the unkempt appearance of the A & A. Never openly condemning the building or Rudolph, Berkeley even suggested that the students' reworkings of it and its disorderliness demonstrated its success as "one of the most stimulating environments for the study of environment." Nevertheless, she found the building unsatisfactory, and she concluded, "Perhaps the most serious shortcoming on this long list is the fact that the entire building essentially represents one person's approach."[15] The charges that Rudolph was largely unable to conceive architecture from viewpoints other than his own, despite his attempts to take the user into account, would be heard again.

When Berkeley interviewed Rudolph, he told her that he was "pleased" about the changes. He said in the article, "People should do as much as they want to."[16] Privately, Rudolph was furious about the article. He published no public retort, but he wrote Blake, *Architectural Forum*'s editor in chief, that the article was unfair and would cost him clients. More and more often in the late 1960s,

Rudolph would withdraw rather than confronting his critics. He stopped speaking to Blake, one of his oldest friends, for a decade after the article was published.[17]

Rudolph's greatest champion, Sibyl Moholy-Nagy, denounced the article in a letter to the editor, calling it a "mean and in the long run suicidal death sentence on architecture whose argumentation has nothing at all to do with architecture." Moholy-Nagy maintained that the students' alteration of the building reflected disenchantment with the architectural profession and the architecture department during troubled times, not with Rudolph's architecture. The Yale administration's inability to keep order in the building showed that it had not fulfilled its basic administrative responsibilities, she claimed.[18]

It is indeed difficult to understand why Yale allowed the building to physically decline so quickly, especially when basic measures such as improved maintenance, security, and relief from overcrowding could have easily improved conditions for all inhabitants. There had been some criticism of the building's functional drawbacks when it was completed in 1963, but the notion that the A & A and Rudolph had failed was one that arose subsequently and only after the building's interiors had been significantly altered under Moore. The idea that the building symbolized failure also took hold because of the political and social context in which the article appeared in July 1967. The smell of urban decay was palpable as American society failed not only to achieve social, political, and economic equality but to disengage itself from a worsening war abroad.

Fire

The historian William H. Chafe called 1968 the "watershed" year that effectively brought to an end the postwar period and the liberal consensus that shaped it in the United States. Among other events, 1968 saw violence at the Democratic National Convention; race riots and arson in cities; the assassinations of Martin Luther King and Robert F. Kennedy; some of the most intense campaigns of the Vietnam War; and massive student protests against the conflict. Chafe said, "The nation seemed to come apart as, one blow after another, it reeled from psychic and emotional wounds unprecedented in the modern era."[19] Similar turmoil occurred around the world, much of it on college campuses, including Yale. Columbia University virtually shut down for nearly a week in late April 1968 when armed student activists occupied its administration buildings. The academic discipline of architecture was also attacked. The May 1968 student strikes in Paris resulted in the dismantling of the long-established pedagogical system of the École des Beaux-Arts, one of the oldest architecture schools in the world.

Given this charged atmosphere, it is not surprising that many believed the fire that consumed the interior of the A & A Building in June 1969 was deliberately set. That spring, radicalized students began to openly challenge Yale, and President Brewster began a struggle to maintain control of the campus.[20] At the A & A, a group of students and faculty from the city planning department accepted minority students into the department without

7.7 Drafting room after 1969 fire, A & A Building.

administrative approval in order to make Yale a more diverse place; in response, Brewster almost dissolved the program. To protest against his disciplinary measures, an anonymous handbill, written in uppercase letters, appeared at graduation in early June. "WHY HAS YALE NOT GONE UP IN SMOKE?" it asked. "SEE THE A & A BUILDING, SEE EVERY BUILDING, SEE THEM SOON."[21]

The warning was prophetic. In the early morning of June 14, 1969, a fire gutted the drafting room of the A & A Building (figure 7.6). Smoke and water damaged the sixth-floor painting studios and seeped into other floors and rooms as well. The damage was estimated at $900,000, and the building was uninhabitable. The *New York Times* and *New Haven Register* reported that New Haven fire chief Francis Sweeney suggested that the fire might have been deliberately set or the building bombed, given the speed and intensity of the fire. They published photos of the ruined drafting room still presided over by the statue of Minerva, a miraculous survivor (figure 7.7). The fire and rumors about it were reported nationally. Shocked by the catastrophe, Rudolph made no comments to the press.[22]

By late June, New Haven fire marshall Thomas Lyden dismissed the possibility of arson, concluding that the fire had been accidental, most probably caused by a combustible mixture of the favelas, paper used for drawings, and open cans of chemically based glues, rubber cement, and paints. Lyden noted that both the massive amounts of flammable materials present and the neglected building maintenance could have caused the fire.[23] Yale exercised little control over the building even after the fire. Banners supporting political causes appeared on it while it was being repaired. The School of Art and Architecture was relocated, not returning until fall 1971. Once the smoke had cleared, the lively atmosphere fostered by Moore was gone as well. Moore left Yale in 1970, and Brewster reorganized the School of Art and Architecture, by 1972 splitting it into separate schools for art and architecture. Though Moore had been in charge of the architecture department when the building burned, the disaster was never associated with him.

Despite Lyden's statement that the fire was not caused by arson, the story that the A & A Building was deliberately burned by students circulated anecdotally in architectural circles; similar conspiracy theories arose to explain other events of the 1960s, such as John F. Kennedy's assassination. Ultimately, whether the fire was deliberately set or not, the impact the conflagration had on Rudolph's career was devastating.

Aftermath

The fact that the A & A Building continued to deteriorate over the next thirty years was taken as confirmation of the notion that Rudolph and his architecture had failed. The corrugated concrete walls of the structure survived the blaze largely undamaged, but renovations by Douglas Orr Associates of New Haven did not restore or improve the A & A. Indeed, the repairs seemed almost like further punishments for the building. Ironically one of Rudolph's instructors at Yale, William de Cossy, carried out the awkward renovations; he later apologized to Rudolph for how they compromised the building.[24] New partitions blocked open vistas. The jury pit was filled in. The corrugated concrete retained the smell of smoke long after the fire. Measures that could have improved the building, such as the installation of air-conditioning, were not undertaken. Overcrowding persisted. Trash accumulated and graffiti spread once more. Though most evident in the A & A, these conditions were prevalent throughout Yale because of the university's deferred maintenance, caused in part by the recession of the 1970s.[25] The popular and architectural press that had once praised the building continued to report on its decline.[26] Although Ada Louise Huxtable voiced her ongoing admiration for the A & A in a 1971 New York Times article about the building's continuing problems, the article and those of her successor Paul Goldberger about its dire state perpetuated into the next decades the idea that the A & A was a failure.[27] Traumatized by the fire, Rudolph refused to speak about what had happened to the A & A Building until many years later. For some time, he could not even talk about his years at the university. Finally, in a 1988 interview, Rudolph said, "I've never worked on a building that affected me as much as that one does. I'd like to think that, in spite of everything, it says something about the nature of architecture."[28] Though the building's renown had largely turned to notoriety, the sustained attention substantiated Rudolph's wish that the A & A convey "something about the nature of architecture." The building would remain important as a symbol—a symbol with an ever changing meaning—even as it continued to decline physically.

Postmodernism

Many factors led to Rudolph's downfall, although the fire is often thought to be the sole cause; high among them were the transformations that architectural discourse underwent in the early 1970s. By that time, Rudolph, the maverick of the 1950s, was seen as a member of the "Establishment"; his buildings appeared excessive, outdated, and irrelevant to an influential segment of the discipline. Marking the decline of postwar modernism and the rise of postmodernism was the landmark 1972 book Learning from Las Vegas by Robert Venturi, Denise Scott Brown, and Steven Izenour. This volume summed up the prevailing attitude toward Rudolph and had implications for his type of expression—and for him personally—more significant than any alteration of the A & A Building or article in Architectural Forum.

The best known of the book's three authors, Venturi had been acquainted with Rudolph long before its publication, though they were never close friends. They met in Eero Saarinen's Detroit office in 1954—Venturi worked there and Rudolph briefly consulted on a project—and Venturi was a visiting critic at Yale in 1963. That spring, Venturi and Rudolph co-taught a studio on precast concrete just as Rudolph's Crawford Manor (New Haven, 1962–66) got under way.[29] The two architects appeared to have had much in common in the early 1960s, agreeing that greater complexity and even mannerist-inspired contradiction would enrich modern architecture. However, compared to the increasingly grandiose Rudolph, Venturi was refreshingly direct and modest.

Venturi developed the ideas in his seminal Learning from Las Vegas from studios focused on the casino city that he and his wife, Denise Scott Brown, co-taught at Yale in 1968; Rudolph's A & A Building during its most radically altered period under Moore was therefore the book's incubator. Learning from Las Vegas proposed an architecture of flattened one-dimensional signs inspired by neon casino displays and billboards as an alternative to Rudolph's and his contemporaries' conception of buildings as concrete sculpture with a strong, but often inchoate symbolism. Rudolph's plastic Crawford Manor was unflatteringly compared to Venturi's Guild House (Venturi and Rauch, Cope and Lippincott Associates, Philadelphia, 1960–63), an apartment building for the elderly adorned with signs.

A major point in Learning from Las Vegas expanded on the different approaches to construction and decoration discussed by A. W. N. Pugin and John Ruskin in the nineteenth century. Venturi, Scott Brown, and Izenour asserted that Rudolph's sculptural approach demonstrated the "construction of decoration" while their sign-based one represented the "decoration of construction" advocated by Pugin. Rudolph's labored way of making architecture was irrelevant for a society being transformed by late 1960s social activism, the automobile, and popular culture. Invoking Pugin's name, the authors concluded their book with words that could have been meant specifically for Rudolph: "It is all right to decorate construction, but never construct decoration."[30]

An astute, powerful, and consequential critique of postwar modernism, Learning from Las Vegas was a seminal work. The system of signs and legible historical allusions proposed by the authors led to postmodernism, which proved more attractive to architects and architectural discourse than Rudolph's expressionism in concrete, in part because its methods of representation were flexible, resonant, and less expensive in difficult economic times.

Rudolph never replied to Venturi, Scott Brown, and Izenour in print. After the fire at the A & A, he was heard from less frequently in public. Though he had refuted his critics in the past, in the early 1970s Rudolph did little to defend himself against the growing number of them. Moholy-Nagy probably would have written some sort of rebuttal to the authors of Learning from Las Vegas on Rudolph's behalf, but she had died in 1971. Never finding another supporter so eloquent or vehement, Rudolph mourned her passing with a remembrance published in Architectural Forum.[31] At a party in the early 1970s, Rudolph briefly confronted Venturi and Scott Brown about their explication of Crawford Manor in the book, but he quickly backed down, and the encounter ended amicably. Years later, understanding the consequences of Learning from Las Vegas for Rudolph, Venturi wrote him a letter of apology.[32]

Even if they had come earlier, apologies would have done little to help Rudolph. A small but influential cadre of architects in the early 1970s picked up on the idea that Rudolph's architecture was "irrelevant." Many were still students at architecture schools, and their political awareness had been raised by the era's social movements and war protests. They no longer admired Rudolph as a bold figure who was challenging modernism's verities; rather they disdained him as a member of the Establishment. By the late 1960s and early 1970s, the hegemony of the Establishment and its partnership between government, business, and academia began to crumble; consequentially, support for Rudolph's type of monumental, high-minded architecture eroded.[33] The reputations of Rudolph's contemporaries also declined at this time. In the fall of 1970, Ada Louise Huxtable wrote in the *New York Times* that the Museum of Modern Art's exhibition of recent work by Philip Johnson, Kevin Roche, and Rudolph was the "season's most fashionably hated show" because the buildings were considered "Establishment architecture."[34]

Rudolph vehemently denied that he was a member of the Establishment, but it is certainly the case that by the early 1970s few thought of Rudolph as the maverick he once had been. Though he was only in his early fifties, the generation gap between those who matured before and after World War II made differences in age seem greater. Rudolph had little interest in subjects of importance for the younger generation, such as the environment or a community-based architecture. Conversely, young people confronted Rudolph about the subjects he had sought to recover for modernism, especially monumentality. In a 1973 interview, he was dismissive when John W. Cook and Heinrich Klotz asked if monumentality was synonymous with authoritarianism and fascism.[35] He reacted defensively to questions about whether his monumentality was overly self-expressive, a charge that was leveled with increasing frequency. Attempting to justify the monumentality of his Boston Government Service Center (1962–71) to another young interviewer the same year, Rudolph lashed out, retorting, "If you think that I built it like this in order to project myself, in order to puff up myself, in order to express myself in this building—then you are mistaken; that wasn't the reason at all, just forget about me; it was built for the city! It is always time for monumentality, when we are interested in the total design of a city."[36]

Rudolph's Books

Rudolph attempted to demonstrate his continuing relevance with books published in 1970 and 1972. *The Architecture of Paul Rudolph* (1970) catalogued his work from his Florida days to the late 1960s by means of drawings, photographs, and concise and sometimes rueful captions by Rudolph. An introduction by Sibyl Moholy-Nagy explained Rudolph's architecture well and comprehensively. *Paul Rudolph: Architectural Drawings* (1972) compiled the architect's compelling presentation drawings. Fated to appear the same year as *Learning from Las Vegas*, it received little critical recognition; still, the intricate drawings were widely admired around the world by many outside the upper echelons of architecture in the U.S. Northeast.[37]

Nevertheless, the focus in both books on Rudolph's projects from the 1950s and 1960s unintentionally confirmed that he was a figure of the past. The books also lacked theoretical insights, a lacuna particularly notable in the years following the publication of *Learning from Las Vegas*, when theory and theoretically driven accounts dominated architectural thinking. Rudolph did not adequately discuss his long-term attention to specific subjects such as monumentality. Nor did his brief references to topographical architecture and the twentieth-century brick amount to a truly coherent theoretical standpoint.

Decline of the Liberal Consensus

Coinciding with the shift of opinion about Rudolph's work was the decline of the liberal consensus. This political and social accord had supported Rudolph's architecture politically and financially, and its dissolution was a phenomenon that hurt his practice directly. In the 1970s, several of his large-scale civic projects were canceled or curtailed because of policy changes. Republican Richard Nixon, elected U.S. president in 1968, supported those who called for the dismantling of the social and educational programs of the New Deal, New Frontier, and Great Society over the next several decades.

Among other efforts, Nixon advocated cutting funding for urban redevelopment and reallocating some monies from cities to suburbs, where his constituents were. Other factors, chiefly the recession and oil crisis of the 1970s, also dealt blows to the large, government-funded civic and academic projects that had become the focus of Rudolph's practice. The *Boston Evening Globe* of February 6, 1970, featured a photo of Rudolph's Boston Government Service Center, still under construction, beneath the headline "Nixon Seen Switching Plans for Cities."[38] Rudolph's central tower, which would have housed Great Society programs for health, education, and welfare, remained a vast empty hole at the edge of the complex's crumbling concrete courtyard for almost three decades, virtually symbolizing the collapse of the liberal consensus and its unfilled ambitions. A courthouse by Kallmann, McKinnell & Wood was built in place of the tower in 1999.

Along with this curtailing of ongoing projects and lack of new commissions, Rudolph lost the support of several of his leading patrons; like him, they were casualties of the political and social changes of the late 1960s. New Haven mayor Richard C. Lee did not run for reelection in 1970 because the city's race riots of 1967 had damaged his political standing. Joseph Driscoll stepped down from the presidency of Southeastern Massachusetts Technical Institute in 1972 because his handling of anti-war protests on campus satisfied neither students nor his superiors in state government; the latter were, in any case, uneasy with his grand ambitions for the school.

Rudolph was not alone among architects in losing his way amid the turmoil of the late 1960s and 1970s. The architectural profession contracted in the 1970s because of the recession and resulting lack of work, affecting notable figures including Louis Kahn and Marcel Breuer. Critical vagaries afflicted the reputation of Philip Johnson, among others, who was lambasted as an Establishment figure and, like Rudolph, seemed unable to respond to the younger generation's calls for a more socially inclusive, community-based architecture.[39]

Somehow, these architects and firms were to recover and even thrive by the end of the 1970s, but Rudolph never regained his footing. While other designers faced just one or two career challenges, Rudolph encountered nearly all of them within a short span of time: a decline in reputation, a shift in architectural thinking and taste, and a falloff in commissions, not to mention the calamitous fire at the A & A Building. Rudolph's reserved personality and tendency to shut down when confronted put him at a great disadvantage. Traumatized by the cumulative impact of these vicissitudes, in the 1970s he retreated from the center of architecture into an interior world of his own making.

Eight
Turning Inward

Beginning in the mid-1960s, Rudolph turned his attention to domestic projects and related investigations in furniture and lighting, the type of commission that had dominated the early years of his career. In projects for himself and for a newly acquired group of affluent clients (many of them in New York City), Rudolph manipulated space, light, materials, and found objects to make interiors with a strong physical and emotional impact. Rudolph initially undertook residential interiors because they offered an opportunity for experiments with interior, furniture, and lighting design, but they became a mainstay for his practice when the flow of new commissions slowed in the 1970s.

These projects had a markedly more sensual and at times dangerous quality to them, different in tone from the joyful explorations of the 1950s Florida houses. Rudolph involved himself in their every aspect. Interested in interior design since his undergraduate days, he often selected paint colors and finishes and designed furniture for projects himself, rather than working with interior designers.

Demonstrating yet again his virtuosity and impressive productivity, Rudolph designed these apartments, townhouses, and freestanding residences in New York and elsewhere while simultaneously completing his civic and academic complexes and envisioning his vast, prefabricated megastructures for Manhattan. Though lesser known, these domestic projects played an important role in Rudolph's late career. His remarkable white villa, the Bass House (Fort Worth, Texas, 1970–72), became the prototype for his houses of the 1970s and 1980s. And sustained experimentation, again typical of his approach, resulted in one of the most significant projects of Rudolph's final decades, his own penthouse at 23 Beekman Place (New York, 1977–97). Although these works and others merited critical attention,

Rudolph seemed to nearly disappear from contemporary discussions, especially once postmodernism became dominant in the 1970s.

New York Practice

Rudolph had great expectations when he resigned from Yale and moved to New York in 1965. He told friends and students that he was at last going to become a "skyscraper architect," a life-long dream.[1] Establishing a New York office would put him on the same path as his contemporaries who had left academia and big firms to start their own successful practices, such as Marcel Breuer and I. M. Pei. Rudolph gave up teaching entirely, shut down his New Haven office, sold his house there, and, at age forty-seven, anticipated entering the most productive years of his career. Exhibiting his often characteristic secrecy, Rudolph told Ellis Perlswig, his companion, that he was leaving for New York only after he made these arrangements. Though surprised, Perlswig remained committed to the relationship and they commuted back and forth between New York and New Haven for nearly two years.[2]

Desiring an impressive setting for his burgeoning practice, Rudolph leased and renovated the top floor of a six-story building at 26 West 58th Street, near the Plaza Hotel. Over the next few years, he staffed it with some of his New Haven employees, including Bill Bedford, who served as office manager; his best students from Yale, including Der Scutt; other architects with whom he had a rapport, such as Grattan Gill from Desmond and Lord; and a constant stream of young men recently graduated from architecture schools. The talented younger architects in the office kept Rudolph up to date about new directions for interiors, especially since some, such as Peter Hoppner, designed original, experimental Manhattan apartments for themselves. By 1969, Rudolph's office expanded from the ten or so of his New Haven days to between twenty and thirty.

Although new commissions flowed in at the start, Rudolph was ill-equipped to make the transition to the large-scale practice of a "skyscraper architect." He continued to run his office like an experimental atelier centered

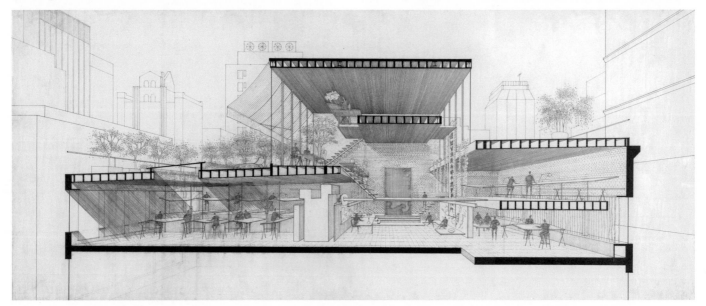

8.1 Rudolph, perspective section, Rudolph's 58th Street Office (New York, 1965).

8.2 Reception area, Rudolph Office.

8.3 Employee stepping between desk platforms in the Rudolph Office.

around himself, believing that this was the only way to maintain his vision of architecture. He had no partners or associates. In a 1966 interview, he said, "Architecture is a personal effort, and the fewer people coming between you and your work the better."[3] The office was often chaotic, and the lack of trusted delegates limited the firm's growth. Rudolph never hired a business manager or anyone other than a secretary or bookkeeper to manage finances. The practice made money in the boom years of the mid-1960s, allowing Rudolph to continue to indulge his passion for sports cars, but income was not steady, and staff were paid little.

These problems were typical for architectural practices, but Rudolph's personality exacerbated them. Unskilled at office management and dealing with people, he alternated between being affable and cold. His humor turned wryer. He disappeared into Times Square movie houses for hours when he could not cope with a problem, and for the most part continued to supervise his staff with the commanding manner of his Navy days. To clients, however, Rudolph could be charming and persuasive when necessary.

With renovation carried out under the supervision of Der Scutt in 1965, Rudolph's 58th Street office became a dramatic showcase for his architecture, one that anticipated impressive interiors laced with danger that he would design in New York over the next few years. Attaining new levels of virtuosity as a manipulator of form, Rudolph overturned conventions of up, down, horizontal, and vertical. He transformed the rented loft space into a spectacular three-level penthouse, his favored form for urban living, by raising ceilings and adding mezzanines and a terrace (figure 8.1). He centered the office on a multilevel, atrium-like central area surrounded by a pinwheel of precarious catwalks and rail-less staircases, resembling the stair in his New Haven house (figure 8.2, compare figure 3.19). Everything was painted white, making the office appear cohesive and disguising the makeshift construction and various violations of building codes. Hanging plants with long drooping tendrils, drawings of Rudolph's better-known projects, and an immense topographical model of his unbuilt new town in Virginia, Stafford Harbor (project, 1966), suspended vertically like a relief mural, created a dense, multilayered, almost jungle-like atmosphere at the office's center. It was apparent to any visitor that this was not a large corporate office but the artistic atelier of a master.

In a 1969 article describing the office, Rudolph's friend the journalist C. Ray Smith said it was "immediately impressive" but also "confusing, disconcerting, dizzying and vertigo-producing." Smith believed that the protest movements, sexual revolution, and general loosening of traditional strictures all contributed to a renaissance for the interior in the mid- and late 1960s, especially in design-conscious cities such as Milan and New York. Experimental interiors for everyone from avant-garde artists in downtown lofts to the very rich in Fifth Avenue apartments reflected a complex and at times ambiguous confluence of sources ranging from Italian mannerism to pop art–derived supergraphics.[4]

Rudolph was unapologetic about the experimental qualities of his office. He said, "It was usually disconcerting on first visit because suddenly, after being in the elevator, the space was not defined. And when people know the definite

limitations of a space they are more happy. This space was free flowing vertically, like a Mies plan turned on edge."[5]

Rudolph perched at a drawing board that was cantilevered from the top level, some twenty feet above the reception area. Others in the office—staff and visitors—had to be fearless and sure-footed. Employees occasionally lost their footing and fell when they stepped or hopped over gaps between the large flat file cabinets on which Rudolph had mounted their desks to make a space-saving mezzanine (figure 8.3).[6] Rudolph's spatial manipulations were dangerous and no doubt in part responsible for the high staff turnover. He also took a mischievous delight in how the office sometimes frightened potential clients, though he lost a few as a result. Rudolph said he replaced a catwalk's rope railing with a more substantial banister after "the look on a certain mayor's face said that was one civic center I wasn't going to do."[7]

Like many of Rudolph's New York interiors, the office was ephemeral. In 1969, the building was demolished to make way for a new office tower, and Rudolph moved his office to a more conventional space nearby at 54 West 57th Street above Hacker Art Books. He occupied this office, which gradually became cluttered with his ever-growing archive of drawings and the curling green tendrils of potted plants, until the late 1980s.

23 Beekman Place

Like his first Manhattan office, Rudolph's Manhattan apartment served as a laboratory for his experiments with interiors. In 1961, he had rented a one-bedroom apartment in a Georgian revival townhouse at 23 Beekman Place as a weekend refuge from Yale's hothouse environment. For over three decades he conducted some of his most innovative investigations with interior space in this East Side building, eventually topping the townhouse with a spectacular penthouse after buying it in 1977.

An apartment on Beekman Place was a sign of success. The two-block stretch of apartment buildings and townhouses overlooking the East River was considered one of the best addresses in Manhattan. Living there brought Rudolph into proximity with the rich, artistic, and famous of the East Side, some of whom would become his clients. He also associated with the neighborhood's well-to-do, artistic, homosexual men who lived in apartments they designed for themselves. On one weekend visit to see Rudolph, Perlswig recalled, they encountered Edgar Kaufmann, Jr., who had curated the *Good Design* exhibition that Rudolph designed for MoMA in 1952, outside of Billy's, an established neighborhood restaurant. The three went back to Kaufmann's nearby Sutton Place apartment for drinks served from opalescent Tiffany glasses.[8] For decades, Rudolph dined at Billy's weekly, often with longtime friends Philip Johnson, the architect Robert Rotner, Sibyl Moholy-Nagy, the journalist Mildred Schmertz, or Joanna Steichen, the therapist and widow of the photographer Edward Steichen, for whom Rudolph had designed the installation for the *Family of Man* exhibition at MoMA in 1954.

> 8.4 Rudolph, living room, 23 Beekman Place (New York, 1967).

8.5 Bedroom, 23 Beekman Place.

During a lull at the office after the Stafford Harbor project was canceled in late 1966, Rudolph renovated his 800-square-foot apartment in a way that reflected his personal tastes. The fourth-floor rental was a typical New York City townhouse apartment consisting of a large living room overlooking the East River and a bedroom facing the street. Along the connecting hallway was a tiny bathroom and a galley kitchen, which Rudolph used little. Rudolph left intact the configuration of the rooms, but he transformed the interiors by means of built-in and custom-designed furniture, raised platforms, and decorative effects. A young architect and Yale graduate who had been Rudolph's project manager for Stafford Harbor, John Pearce, built and installed most of the woodwork and Lucite furniture for the apartment.[9]

The living room was cool, white, and surreal in feeling (figure 8.4). To take advantage of the prospect over the East River, Rudolph installed an expansive glass window in the living room that afforded views of passing ships, July 4th fireworks, and Roosevelt Island. A narrow balcony, like a diving board with a floor of steel grating, levitated several stories above the rear garden and frightened visitors with vertigo.

Rudolph curtained the window with hundreds of mirrored plastic disks threaded on invisible nylon fishing line. The disks resembled the coin-size mirrors the fashion designer Paco Rabanne used to make dresses at the time, or perhaps small dental mirrors, which Rudolph employed in other interiors of this period. The curtain construction, which moved and shimmered with the slightest current of air, reflecting light from the sky, the river, and the all-white interior, recalled the silvery curtains of Rudolph's common rooms at the Southeastern Massachusetts Technical Institute.

The idea of using "found" objects for a domestic interior demonstrated a revived interest among artists and architects in the 1960s in Marcel Duchamp's concept of the readymade, which had been important for surrealists in the 1920s and 1930s.[10] Rudolph liked employing found objects, often taken from his own architectural projects, because they added just such a surreal note to his interiors. In his living room, as he had in his office, he transformed a topographical model of Stafford Harbor into a low-relief mural. Plaster panels of Louis Sullivan's decorative ornament, which Rudolph had used in the Yale A & A Building, formed a low room divider separating a black grand piano from the seating area. Rudolph manipulated light to give the room an unearthly quality. Banquettes low to the floor were illuminated from beneath, creating what Rudolph described as the illusion of a "floating platform."[11] Transparent plastic and Lucite furnishings of Rudolph's design were also subtly lit from beneath so that they appeared to glow from within. Rudolph further stimulated physical and emotional responses by covering floors and other surfaces with soft wall-to-wall carpeting, thus blurring conventional boundaries between walls and floors.

The bedroom's sensual qualities were readily apparent (figure 8.5). Rudolph installed curtains of plastic, amber beads that screened the windows from outside viewers, amplifying the emotional qualities of the room. A row of exposed tubular light bulbs at ceiling level reflected light across the curtains, suffusing the room in an amber glow that was warmer than the arctic whiteness of the living room. In its insularity and use of controlled lighting, the room recalled the vaulted, windowless bedroom of Philip Johnson's brick guesthouse (remodeled 1953) at the Glass House (New Caanan, Connecticut, 1949), a setting for erotic play where Rudolph and Perlswig often spent a weekend.[12] Rudolph and Johnson enjoyed reminiscing about Frank Lloyd Wright's 1956 visit to the Glass House, when he had called the guesthouse bedroom a "fuck studio."[13]

Rudolph's bedroom was no doubt conceived as a setting for sex as well, as suggested by its striking wall mural. Above his bed Rudolph had hung a large advertising billboard for deodorant featuring a bare-chested, hirsute man surrounded by towel-clad women—another ready-made. The image was reflected in a mirror on the opposite wall so that it was visible from any angle. The mirrored wall also made the 9-by-14-foot room appear larger. It was the first time Rudolph had incorporated a mural into one of his interiors since he had made the stylized mural of nude men fishing for his very first built work, the Atkinson House in Auburn, Alabama (1940).

As Duchamp had shown, a ready-made object could take on a new meaning from a new context. Rudolph drew a homoerotic quality out of the billboard by placing it in his bedroom—the architect and his sexual preferences provided the context. Anyone in the room became caught in a series of exchanged looks with the powerful gaze of the man who stared outward from the mural, creating a charged sexual atmosphere for Rudolph and perhaps for his guests. Simultaneously before and behind the spectator, the mural was the theatrical backdrop for the fur-covered bed, itself a staged setting for sexual activity. The arrangement was redolent of voyeurism and scopophilia, where the hirsute man, and the women as well, were additional players, or spectators, in the activities unfolding in the room like a scene from a pornographic film.

Rudolph amplified the homoerotic aura of the mural by placing a small, male nude Roman torso in the corner of the room, artistically juxtaposed with a Josef Albers print. Visitors to the apartment understood these cues. In the increasingly sexually liberated New York of the late 1960s, Rudolph found greater opportunities for erotic encounters, especially after his relationship with Perlswig ended amicably. His libido strong in midlife, Rudolph dated many young men during the 1970s.[14]

Although the Beekman Place mural might be interpreted in various ways in light of later critical theory, Rudolph rationalized it as an experiment in decoration, pop art, and supergraphics.[15] Showing his familiarity with supergraphics as current at Yale and elsewhere, Rudolph recommended using advertisements, enlarged photographs, and billboards as inexpensive interior decor when the apartment was published in the New York Times Magazine in July 1967.[16] The reactions of some in New York's architectural community reflected how opinions were shifting about Rudolph. While the mural could be understood in the context of pop art or supergraphics, some also saw it as an imprudent revelation of his homosexuality, which was well known among architects, but certainly never openly discussed or written about. Though the article implied nothing, Rudolph's mural spoke of what the era's homophobia kept silent for the architectural profession and indeed for most of America. To some,

8.6 Rudolph, Hirsch House (New York, 1966–67).

Rudolph's decision to publish the project showed poor judgment, causing them to wonder if his architecture was becoming entirely about self-expression and ask whether he could be trusted with large-scale public projects.[17] Publication of the apartment became an embarrassment rather than a triumph. On top of it all, Perlswig remembered, were newspaper stories about the male model from the billboard suing Rudolph for improper use of his image.[18]

The *New York Times* article reflected Rudolph's naïveté about how he was perceived. It is unlikely that he intended to declare his sexuality through the mural or its publication, and it is equally unlikely that he saw it as a gesture of solidarity with the nascent homosexual rights movement of those years, in which he showed no interest. Further, the July 1967 publication coincided unfortunately with Ellen Perry Berkeley's *Architectural Forum* article about the shortcomings of the Yale A& A Building.[19] Together they confirmed the growing perception that Rudolph's architecture was self-indulgent or mannered and that, despite allusions to new trends such as supergraphics, he was losing his bearings as a leader of the discipline.

Hirsch House

The spatial and emotional qualities of Rudolph's office and apartment were the foundation of the residential projects he designed for others, as was demonstrated with his elegant Hirsch House on Manhattan's Upper East Side (New York, 1966–67). The house is one of the few modernist townhouses built in New York after World War II. Though it is among Rudolph's most compelling residential projects of the late 1960s, it was also a project where at times he seemed to go too far.

The commission originally belonged to Philip Johnson, who was intrigued by the possibility of creating a house for the couple Alexander Hirsch and Lewis Turner, who were members of the elite homosexual circles he frequented. But Johnson was too busy for the job, and he recommended Rudolph to Hirsch. The wealthy real estate attorney and investor built and owned unremarkable apartment and office buildings in New York but wanted something of a higher caliber for his own residence. Turner was a noted amateur chef and collector of fine eighteenth-century French furniture; although Turner preferred traditional interiors, Rudolph won him over by tutoring him about modernism and working closely with him on the design of the house. The two reviewed fabrics and finishes together and considered using exotic animal skins, including lion skin. Rudolph designed a decorative mural and much of the furniture himself, the principal pieces being a monumental Lucite dining room table and a chromed subway grating used as a coffee table. For the most part, Hirsch and Turner found Rudolph easy and agreeable to work with, and the architect often spent weekends at their East Hampton house.[20] Located on a desirable block adjacent to Park Avenue at 101 East 63rd Street, the Hirsch House occupied a 25-foot-wide, 100-foot-long site, formerly a nineteenth-century carriage house. Rudolph designed a steel frame in the spirit of Mies van der Rohe—similar to but more nuanced than the iteration Johnson had employed in his nearby Rockefeller Guest House (New York, 1949–1950)—subtly outlining four floors with set-back, recessed frames made from steel I-beams painted brown (figure 8.6). He glazed the frames with fixed brown-tinted glass panels and casement windows screened by interior shutters; the ambiguous pattern made it difficult to discern what was wall and what was window. Rudolph said the house was "a world of its own, inward looking and secretive."[21] It would be easy to see this as Rudolph's attempt to construct a protective environment for a homosexual couple, even a "closet," but many of his residential projects displayed this reserved and even defensive attitude toward the street, a quality often found in Wright's houses as well.

The dramatic interior spaces were revealed gradually (figure 8.7). After entering a small entrance hall and traversing a long low-ceilinged corridor, visitors stepped into an all-white, 27-foot-high living room, one of the loftiest, most impressive private interiors in the city (figure 8.8). Instead

8.7 Perspective section, Hirsch House.

of the usual townhouse garden, Rudolph developed at the rear of the room a two-story greenhouse planted with large palms. Shielded from the street by the spaces at the front of the residence, the living room was extraordinarily peaceful for Manhattan. In fact, spaciousness and quiet were the house's true luxuries.

However, the living room, and even the house as a whole, were not for those susceptible to vertigo. A rail-less staircase with floating risers, similar to the one in the living room of Rudolph's New Haven house, hugged the west side of the room and led up to a book-lined balcony and adjacent master bedroom suite overlooking the street. A catwalk with only the flimsiest of railings hovering two levels above the living room connected the third floor to a guest suite overlooking the greenhouse. Another self-contained suite with a large terrace on the house's fourth floor was a gallery for Turner's collection of French furniture.

In the immense living room Rudolph found another opportunity to include a mural. Created around the time his Beekman Place mural was published and recalling the one he made many years before for the Atkinson House in Auburn (1940), Rudolph's wall-size composition depicted stylized men in tight-fitting renaissance costumes with leggings and codpieces. Like the mural in Auburn, it is a puzzling scene of men engaged in some sort of struggle, here hurling stones in a landscape of mountains, streams, and trees. A man in the center of the group appears to collapse, though he is actually stooping to pick up a stone. Using the same technique and materials as the Atkinson House work, the mural was incised on Homasote boards painted white. The incised lines were filled with silver paint to give it a reflective quality and make the figures stand out.

The best depiction of the mural is a snapshot of Hirsch standing in front of it (figure 8.9). The mural itself is long gone, and only a portion of Rudolph's cartoon for the scene survives in the Rudolph Archive. In Ezra Stoller's 1969 photograph of the room, the center of the mural is blocked from view by a small sculpture (figure 8.8). The blockage suggests that the mural was considered unsatisfactory, as was in fact the case. Rudolph had proposed the installation of a mural to his clients in the summer of 1967 and executed it when they were away for several months in Puerto Rico later in the year. Hirsch and Turner were surprised by the results when they returned to their newly completed house. Turner found it to be a violent scene and saw the stooping man as a fallen martyred saint.[22]

Turner was not far wrong, for the origins of the image are found in a biblical story featuring violence, sexuality, wrongful accusations, and revenge; themes that may have been on the troubled Rudolph's mind in the summer of 1967 as he cast about for a large-scale, dramatic, and decorative element to finish the Hirsch House living room. His rather obscure source for the composition was a full-page color illustration torn from a French art journal showing a panel painting from a fifteenth-century Italian marriage chest by the Florentine artist Domenico di Michelino (1417–1491) (figure 8.10).[23] The painting illustrated a biblical subject often taken up during the renaissance: Susanna, a virtuous Hebrew wife, is falsely accused of adultery by priests; the

8.8 Living room, Hirsch House.

Turning Inward

8.9 Alexander Hirsch and mural, Hirsch House (1967).

8.10, Domenico di Michelino, detail from *The Story of Susanna*, reproduced in *Connaissance des Arts,* February 1964.

accusing priests are stoned by Susanna's avengers. The journal illustration, like Rudolph's mural, shows only the stone-throwers.

It is hard to know exactly what Rudolph intended with his artwork. The son of a minister, he was probably familiar with the Bible story. The scene of vengeance may have appealed to the beleaguered architect, who was feeling increasingly under attack from negative press accounts of his A & A Building and other projects. He also sensed that he was losing his colleagues' high regard. While he had not been falsely accused of adultery, his sexuality had become a subject of gossip and derision in architectural circles after he had imprudently revealed himself by publishing the mural in his bedroom in the *New York Times Magazine*.

The Hirsch mural, an odd choice for an Upper East Side living room, is another of the missteps made by Rudolph at this time, exemplifying the curious blind spots he had about his work and its reception. He believed himself to be a great designer of interiors, but his decorative experiments sometimes went too far for his clients. Rudolph probably believed that the depiction of human figures would humanize the enormous room. The mural probably also evoked the type of historical and archaic associations that he liked to make in his interiors, akin to those put forth by the Beaux-Arts plaster casts in the A & A Building. He may also have thought that such masculine imagery was appropriate for a same-sex couple.

Unfortunately, it was satisfactory in none of these ways. The scene instead expressed an awkward current of struggle and sexuality. The stylized figures and landscape were crude and stiff rather than dramatic or sensual; it is not surprising that Stoller blocked the wall piece when he photographed the house for publication. It may have been the last of Rudolph's mural experiments, because he too recognized how unsatisfactory it was.

And the episode epitomized an often characteristic strain of high-handedness in Rudolph's attitude toward his clients. Having been reassured by Rudolph that the mural would be the finishing touch for their new house, Hirsch and Turner were disappointed when they saw it completed after returning from their Caribbean sojourn. The client-architect relationship and friendship quickly soured when differences arose about reimbursing Rudolph for $1,500 in expenses he had incurred in fabricating it. The mural was not the house's only drawback. Hirsch and Turner found it impractical and hard to heat. The catwalk above the living room terrified Turner, who refused to cross it even after an elegant, but flimsy, velvet and leather cord was installed.[24]

Despite these problems, the Hirsch House proved to be one of Rudolph's most memorable domestic projects. Important for his development as a residential architect, the building was the prototype for other steel-framed townhouses he built in his last decades. And it established Rudolph as an architect who could design exciting, high-end interiors and houses for the well-to-do. Hirsch and Turner sold the house in 1974 to the fashion designer Halston, who had always coveted it and in any case was not afraid of heights. Halston commissioned Rudolph to renovate the house, and one of the first decisions was to eliminate the mural. In the living room, Rudolph upholstered

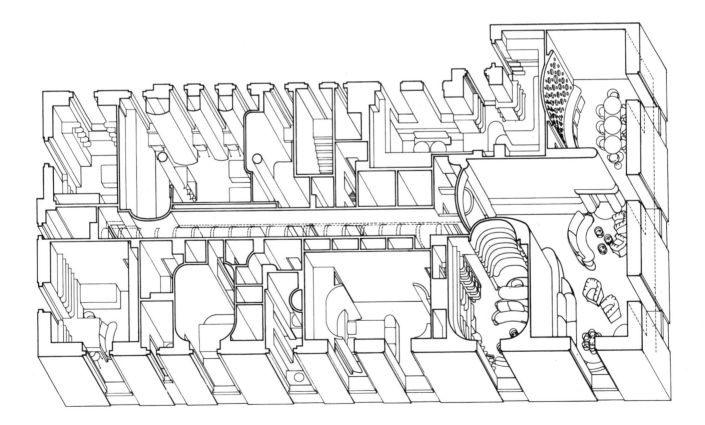

8.11 Rudolph, plan oblique, Edersheim Apartment (New York, 1970).

8.12 Living room, Edersheim Apartment.

chairs and a sofa he had designed in the flannel knit jersey fabric Halston used for dresses.

Edersheim Apartment

In the late 1960s and early 1970s, Rudolph received a number of commissions for glamorous New York apartments; these clients appreciated him even as his reputation was declining in the architectural world. High-end fashion and home design magazines, including *Vogue* and *House and Garden,* gushed about his works. Rudolph's characteristic idiom of Lucite and reflective surfaces was admired and imitated. It was his contribution to an innovative, experimental phase for interior design in the mid- and late 1960s. Rising young architects in New York, such as former Yale students Charles Gwathmey and Robert A. M. Stern,

began to design experimental apartment interiors similar to Rudolph's.[25]

The Edersheim Apartment on Fifth Avenue (1970), complete with custom-designed furniture, demonstrated both the all-encompassing quality of Rudolph's vision and its suitability for families and socialites alike. The Dutch-born Maurits Edersheim was a senior executive at the financial services company Drexel Burnham Lambert. Edersheim and his wife, Claire, bought a large apartment in a traditional prewar building to accommodate their family of seven children, several of whom were away at boarding school.

During the late 1960s and well into the 1970s, Rudolph alternated between a vocabulary of hovering planes and right angles, evoking the geometry of the De Stijl movement, and a language of curvilinear forms, recalling his baroque-infused projects or the later works of Frank Lloyd Wright. Either vocabulary could stimulate the user. For the

8.13 Dining room, Edersheim Apartment.

Edersheim Apartment, Rudolph explained that curves utilized the existing space better than right angles, "mold[ing] it to the human need" and providing "a sense of intimacy."[26] Rudolph rounded many of the grand apartment's existing corners and replaced conventional walls with gentle arcs, creating a series of embracing, cocoon-like spaces for the family (figure 8.11).

In what was a notably harmonious collaboration, the Edersheims gave Rudolph free rein to orchestrate mesmerizing effects recalling the scenographic qualities of his larger-scaled projects. He roofed the corridor connecting the bedrooms with a silver-mylar-papered barrel vault; the arch reflected those walking beneath it and made the hall seem longer in an ambiguously mannerist way. Rudolph was not the first to use silver mylar in an interior space; its avant-garde associations evocative of Andy Warhol's famous foil wallpapered studio (New York,

1963), the material became fashionable in mid- and late-1960s Manhattan.[27]

Some of the aesthetic predilections of Rudolph's earlier work manifested themselves in the apartment in new ways and in different materials. For instance, he upholstered some walls with a tweedy, beige shag carpet; Rudolph claimed that the covering would absorb sound from the children, but knobbly stripes in the weave recalled the vertical ridges of his corrugated concrete. Mirrored strips on the living room walls reflected light from the windows overlooking Central Park; the dimensions recalled those of Rudolph's fluted concrete block, again showing both a sustained attraction to specific forms and a marked, if perhaps unconscious, desire to render them in different materials (figure 8.12). The mirrors distorted the image of visitors to the room, breaking them into a series of moving silvery shards, almost like images in a Cubist painting

195

8.14 Isometric aerial view, Bass House (Fort Worth, Texas, 1970-72).

or in a funhouse. To make the room shimmer even more, Rudolph lacquered the ceiling bright blue and mirrored the window surrounds. These reflective effects anticipated trends of the 1970s and 1980s, as for example the mirrored interiors Warren Platner designed for corporate and commercial clients.

In the dining room, round niches in a curving wall housed the Edersheims' objets d'art and porcelains, many of Dutch origin. Rudolph designed all the lighting and furniture for this area. In place of a conventional chandelier, Rudolph fashioned a starburst-shaped arrangement from off-the-shelf light bulbs. Lighting was, in fact, a developing interest for Rudolph (figure 8.13).[28] The architect also created a series of circular white, single-pedestal, formica-topped tables resembling Eero Saarinen's famed Tulip tables. They could be used to enlarge the dining room table or set up independently in other rooms for larger parties.

Although it is not well known, Rudolph often turned his attention to furniture during these years. He worked with New York craftsmen on custom furniture of Lucite and Plexiglass, materials that he first contemplated in his undergraduate thesis at Alabama Polytechnic and then employed in his *Family of Man* exhibition installation at MoMA in 1954. Rudolph also transformed manufactured or industrial objects into furniture, as he had with the subway grating coffee table in the Hirsch House. Rudolph often combed the shops along Manhattan's Canal Street for plastic, chrome, and stainless steel industrial hardware and furniture components; he would combine these in his own furniture and lighting creations. Rudolph was credited in part with inspiring the "high tech" style of the late 1970s that used industrial, ready-made elements for domestic interiors.[29]

Rudolph's striking residential projects put him at the forefront of experiments in interior design in the late 1960s

8.15 Entrance court, Bass House.

and early 1970s, even though he was no longer considered one of modernism's leaders. The Edersheims became Rudolph's most faithful patrons, choosing to live entirely in a world of his making. The architect renovated their country house in Westchester, built a guest house for the property, and designed an office suite for Maurits Edersheim in New York's World Trade Center (the last was destroyed in the terrorist attacks of September 2001). Firm friends and supporters, the Edersheims endowed a lectureship in Rudolph's honor at the Yale School of Architecture in the 1990s.

Bass House

In addition to luxurious apartments and townhouses, in the 1970s Rudolph designed many private houses. He had made his name designing houses in Florida after World War II, but the new residences were of a different caliber, varied in appearance and often for clients far richer than his Florida patrons. The Bass House (Fort Worth, Texas, 1970–72) served as the prototype for an important series of white, villa-like houses. The grandest, most important house of Rudolph's later career, it was built for the Fort Worth, Texas, multimillionaire Sid Bass and his wife, Anne. Sid Bass became another of Rudolph's most supportive and important patrons.

Only in his late twenties when he inherited a fortune in oil and real estate, Bass commissioned Rudolph to design a house because he had a deep regard for the Yale A & A Building, which was completed when he was an undergraduate at the university. Vincent Scully's lectures augmented Bass's interest in modern architecture. To his friends, Rudolph referred to Bass as "my Renaissance prince," realizing that the Texan, who also painted and collected art, was the kind of educated, affluent patron he needed.[30]

Bass introduced Rudolph to Texas at a time when the state's wealth was making it an important locus for modern architecture. Oil and real estate speculation enriched the state, providing northeastern architects such as Johnson and Pei with commissions for corporate headquarters and cultural institutions. The Basses planned their house to accommodate a growing collection of significant postwar painting and sculpture (though, prudently, they did not let Rudolph arrange it).[31] Aware that giving Rudolph free rein over all aspects of a project had on occasion resulted in unsatisfactory outcomes, the Basses hired professionals from interior designers to landscape architects to allow Rudolph to focus on what he did best, the architecture.

This was a wise choice. Rudolph saw all commissions as opportunities to be original. He initially conceived of making a massive post and beam structure out of opalescent, plastic logs, but he quickly realized that it was unfeasible. Relieved that Rudolph had given up the experiment, the Basses encouraged him to invest their house with a rigor and precision that would reflect their refined approach to living. In an early meeting, Anne Bass asked, "Do we have to have curves, or could we just have straight lines?"[32] Sid Bass gave Rudolph a diagram suggesting the uses for each room and the relationships between them.[33] These ground rules led to a fruitful collaboration. The Basses were closely involved with the commission and committed to high-quality materials and construction; in the end, their house had none of the sometimes makeshift qualities typical of Rudolph's other projects, even those with significant budgets.

More than any other type of client, Rudolph enjoyed

> 8.16 Garden elevation, Bass House.
>> 8.17 Living room, Bass House.

197

spending time with sophisticated women like Anne Bass, and the two remained friends after the project was completed. She was trained in ballet; dance both served as one of Rudolph's inspirations and brought its disciplined qualities to the project. In terms that could have described a ballet dancer *en pointe*, Rudolph later explained that "the genesis of the dwelling" was "the ideal of weight and counterweight (similar to the movement of the human body)."[34] An isometric aerial view of the house depicts it as a pinwheel of intersecting and overlapping planes levitating amid expanses of greenery. The site was an eight-acre lot of rolling hills edged by woods and a stream in a neighborhood of estate-like houses (figure 8.14).

More ambitious in concept and size than Rudolph's other residences of this time, it was truly within the tradition of the villa, a concept that stretched back to antiquity and possessed an importance for modernism. To suggest discipline and rigor, Rudolph framed the Bass House with steel beams enameled white and paneled it with white porcelain aluminum panels, a cladding associated with Richard Meier's architecture (figure 8.15). The Bass House is indeed comparable to the "white villas" built by Meier and some of his contemporaries, a group known as the "Whites" for their elaboration on the vocabulary of Le Corbusier's white villas of the 1920s.[35] Rudolph's Bass House may have shown his determination to keep up with the "Whites." It also recalled Mies's Farnsworth House (Plano, Illinois, 1949–51), which had been a point of departure many years earlier for Rudolph's Walker Guest House (Sanibel Island, Florida, 1952–53).

Frank Lloyd Wright's Fallingwater (Mill Run, Pa., 1934–37) was another obvious precedent for the Bass House. Just before receiving the commission Rudolph wrote an essay about Wright's house for a special issue of a Japanese journal. He described Fallingwater as "that rare work which is composed of such delicate balancing of forces and counterforces, transformed into spaces thrusting horizontally, vertically and diagonally, that the whole achieves the serenity which marks all great works of art."[36] Rudolph intended the Bass House to be an homage to Fallingwater that would bring him fame equal to Wright's. Rudolph aligned the primary axis of the Bass House with the crest of the ridge it sat on and cantilevered its terraces and balconies above the descending slope in a way that recalled Wright's famous siting of his many-leveled house above a waterfall (figure 8.16).

For Rudolph, the Bass House was a welcome return to building in a warm climate. He centered the house on a courtyard that was like an outdoor room in itself, open on one side to views of the extensive grounds. The interior of the house was impressive and complex. Rudolph said that anyone journeying through the house would make eight turns and rise fifteen feet along the stair from the entrance hall to the vast white and gray living room.

Perched above the hillside, the living room had its own internal topography.[37] A sheltered cave-like conversation pit contrasted with an adjacent fishbowl-like double-height seating area presided over by large-scale canvases by Morris Louis and Frank Stella (figure 8.17). The interior designers who consulted on the project helped choose fabrics and finishes that resulted in interior spaces throughout the house of greater subtlety than those designed entirely

by Rudolph at this time. On the grounds of the house, Rudolph worked with modernist landscape architect Robert Zion and British garden designer Russell Page, acclaimed for perpetuating a tradition of grand formal landscape gardening. Though both Page and Rudolph were strong willed, Rudolph appreciated the classical order Page brought to the project, and the two collaborated successfully. Rudolph's cantilevered terrace became an extraordinary mid-air vantage point for viewing Page's allée of pleached oaks (figure 8.18).

Conceived and built during a troubled time for Rudolph, the Bass House was among his most beautiful houses, perhaps even more impressive than the white villas built by his younger colleagues. It demonstrated that Rudolph was capable of designing rigorous, disciplined works, especially in conjunction with committed patrons. Unfortunately, few people in the architectural community saw the Bass House when it was completed in 1972. It was not published until 1991 because of the Basses' security concerns.[38] The friendship between the couple and Rudolph—which resulted in a commission for a pair of office towers in Fort Worth (1979–83) among other things—compensated for the little recognition he received for the house.

Theory Considered

Despite success with the Bass House and other residences, the 1970s were difficult for Rudolph. Many works designed during this time remained unbuilt, and of the few buildings that were completed, several were commissions that had been initiated in the early 1960s. The lingering recession that began in 1973, ensuing inflation, and oil crises all meant fewer projects for architects; Rudolph suffered more than most because of his declining reputation and professional problems.

Rudolph's ceaseless experimentation and inattention to the details of construction caught up with him in the 1970s. Structural problems with his Earl W. Brydges Library (Niagara Falls, New York, 1969–74) resulted in litigation that was lengthy, expensive, and professionally damaging. Yet this was just one of many legal battles of the time. On one of the few occasions when he discussed such matters, Rudolph told a friend, Robert Rotner, in the mid-1970s that he had at least seven ongoing lawsuits, but left it to his lawyers to worry about these problems.[39]

Rudolph attempted to keep pace with new developments in architecture, but many of his colleagues considered him irrelevant during the 1970s. Those who led architectural discourse were perplexed as to the position of this still-working and important figure for modernism. In 1974, Rudolph's significance was debated in *Oppositions,* the newly founded but already influential journal of the Institute for Architecture and Urban Studies (IAUS). The Rudolph coverage was part of *Oppositions*'s plans to assess the "major philosophical currents in American architectural education over the past twenty-five years" with a series of articles over the course of several issues. Essays by the leading figures of opposing factions in architecture—Peter Eisenman, the organization's director and the journal's editor, and Robert A. M. Stern, the advocate of historically informed postmodernism—suggested that Rudolph was

8.18 Terrace, Bass House.

either the progenitor of the new theory- and form-driven direction for architecture (Eisenman's position) or a largely historical figure of the recent past (Stern's attitude).

Both had studied with Rudolph and knew his work and ideas well. An architecture student at Cornell University in the 1950s, Eisenman had encountered Rudolph when he was a visiting critic; Stern had been Rudolph's student at Yale in the early 1960s. Both saw Rudolph regularly in New York during the early 1970s. Stern remembered lunches with Rudolph that became painful if Yale was mentioned. Traumatized by the transformation of the A & A Building and the fire and its aftermath, Rudolph could not speak about his years at the university.[40] Eisenman became close to Rudolph at this time, looking to the older architect as a mentor for design. Rudolph visited and favorably appraised Eisenman's House VI (Cornwall, Connecticut, 1972–75), one of the best known of the white villas of the 1970s.[41]

Included as part of the *Oppositions* coverage was Rudolph's first speech as chairman of the architecture department at Yale in 1958, in which he declared, "Theory must again overtake action." Eisenman wrote a preface to the speech, noting that Rudolph at that time had been asking questions about theory and education "which only now seem to have come into focus for many of us."[42] Eisenman found Rudolph's architecture to be full of implications for the present. He believed architecture could evolve into an autonomous formal language with its own internal rules derived from linguistics and semiotics; he did not find relevant the demands in the late 1960s and early 1970s for a social component. Fascinated by Rudolph's formal inventiveness, Eisenman lectured at the IAUS about the forms Rudolph had used in his Florida houses, exhaustively working through their permutations to show how they related to one another and would lead to the Yale A & A Building. He believed Rudolph anticipated fruitful directions for modernist architecture and pedagogy that could be taken up again at the IAUS.[43]

Stern felt differently, reflecting more widely held opinions about Rudolph. In his 1969 book *New Directions in American Architecture,* Stern had written admiringly of his former teacher's virtuosity, but declared that the dramatic vocabulary of the Boston Government Service Center (1962–71) showed that his architecture was becoming "overwrought."[44] In *Oppositions*, Stern offered a carefully researched historical account of how architecture was taught at Yale from 1950 until 1965, Rudolph's final year as chairman of the architecture department. Employing the oral history methods of the time, Stern quoted at length from interviews and correspondence with his classmates. Because Rudolph avoided speaking about his years at Yale or about the A & A Building, he was never quoted, which made him seem curiously absent or even obsolete. It was remarkable that Stern discussed Rudolph as a historical figure only nine years after he had left Yale. To Stern and most of his classmates, the early 1960s already seemed like a distant era.

Stern was more critical of Rudolph than Eisenman was, which reflected the way opinions about Rudolph had changed in the early and mid-1970s. Stern saw Rudolph's emphasis on individuality and empathy as more of an attitude than a coherent approach, and concluded that Rudolph did not "have a theory of architectural education."[45] For Stern, Rudolph's championing of form and architectural expression had become megalomaniacal and harmful to the urban environment. Like many others, he was dismayed by Rudolph's proposed City Corridor for Manhattan, published in *The Evolving City* in 1974, shortly before the *Oppositions* articles. Stern considered the gargantuan size of the project to be indifferent to New York, out of step with present thinking, and a reversal of the sensitive attitude toward the existing city that Rudolph had fostered at Yale. For Stern, City Corridor and Rudolph represented everything that had gone wrong with modernism.[46]

Though Rudolph was no longer the important figure for the discipline that he had been, Eisenman's and Stern's strong but diverging viewpoints suggest that 1974 represented a time when Rudolph could have become more involved with both and thus bolster his reputation. Philip Johnson, twelve years older than Rudolph, engaged deeply with these younger men not only out of friendship, but in order to revive his career. Like Rudolph's, Johnson's practice and reputation had faltered at the end of the 1960s, but Johnson revitalized himself in part by absorbing new ideas from these young practitioners and their successors. Enjoying his role as patron and Svengali, Johnson used his connections to secure commissions for the younger architects.[47] He himself emerged as a leading advocate of postmodernism by the late 1970s, and his AT&T Building (New York, 1978–84) was one of the most often cited examples of the style.

Rudolph, by contrast, was not as suave or perspicacious as Johnson, nor was he interested in power or patronage. In fact, even if Rudolph had not experienced considerable misfortune, it would have been unlikely that he could remain a maverick at the forefront of his profession as he aged, as it would have been for anyone. Indeed, Rudolph's introversion became all the more pronounced during the difficult years of the 1970s. Though in the past he had been able to integrate new tendencies in architecture into his work, from prefabrication to supergraphics and the white villas, by the mid-1970s Rudolph had become uncomfortable with architecture's new theoretical emphasis and balked at the widespread acceptance of postmodernism.

Nevertheless, though he had misgivings about its direction, Rudolph clearly recognized theory's importance for the 1970s. He attempted to catch up with his younger colleagues by summarizing his ideas in what he intended to be a theoretical book, with a text by his friend Carl Black. Though the text was completed, the book was never published. Its numerous illustrations made it an expensive undertaking, and Black's Jungian-influenced interpretation, which emphasized the archetypal qualities of Rudolph's architecture, may also have seemed out of date to publishers in the early 1970s. Excerpts on the Boston Government Service Center and Tuskegee Chapel were published in 1973.[48] Rudolph continued to collect materials and to look for potential collaborators for many years.[49] But he never succeeded in publishing another book.

Rudolph came closest to summarizing his thinking with the essay "Enigmas of Architecture," written for a special 1977 issue of the Japanese journal *A + U*, which documented his most important works from 1946 to 1974.

Though Rudolph's work had fallen out of favor in the West, in Asia his architecture was still appreciated and published. In the essay, Rudolph reiterated his basic principles using lines and entire passages from his talks of the 1950s and early 1960s. It appeared that very little had changed in his thinking since his heyday. For Rudolph, maintaining his views was a way of maintaining his integrity.

He did, however, strike a new and more thoughtful note when he admitted to some disappointments in his search for expression. He wrote, "The results of the search never match what had been imagined. This is not to say that imagination is imprecise; rather that one's mind is obsessed with recurring references, equations, visions, the unknown. The reality never matches the imagination. Complex emotional responses play on directions of thought (the essence of the project). This dilutes the ultimate goal of thought and imagination. In this sense, all mistakes, failures, confusions are completely the architect's own, never caused by the owner, or even by outside rules."[50] With these poignant remarks, which showed a new level of self-awareness, Rudolph also acknowledged the drawbacks of his architecture. He still, however, considered a building to be largely the product of the architect's viewpoint rather than an entity shaped by the "outside rules" of society. Rudolph's interiors of the time embodied this solipsistic attitude.

Beekman Place Penthouse

"It's hard to be depressed in here," Rudolph said of the bedchamber in his Beekman Place apartment, renovated in 1975. The offhand remark in *House and Garden* suggested that the interior had become a refuge from Rudolph's professional difficulties.[51] Perhaps because of its obviously erotic content, the advertising mural had long since been removed. Abandoning the mural form altogether, Rudolph instead channeled his decorative impulses into increasingly complicated effects of light, reflection, and surface. In the renovation of the bedroom, Rudolph mirrored both end

8.19 Rudolph, Bedroom with light curtain, 23 Beekman Place (c. 1975).

walls and the ceiling and hung a "light curtain" of miniature bulbs reminiscent of Christmas tree lights; the reflected grid of lights suggested that space extended to infinity beyond the 9-by-14-foot room (figure 8.19). Rudolph said that every room had such "implied spaces," a concept he associated with Mies's architecture, paralleling "the nine-tenths of the human brain which makes up the subconscious and the imagination."[52] Rudolph cobbled together his apartment renovation in his typical makeshift way. Rotner remembers Rudolph proudly showing him the renovated bedroom, only to have one of the strings of lights fall and short out all the electricity in the apartment.[53]

Shortly afterward, Rudolph embarked on a major renovation of the Beekman Place house itself, building a four-story penthouse of plexiglass, steel, and other materials. Its illusionary, enigmatic quality raised the level of danger and stimulation found in his earlier interiors to new levels of intensity. Interior elements big and small—the refinement of a fireplace surround, the replacement of a floor with stainless steel panels—were part of an ongoing architectural experiment nearly impossible for the historian to track. Rudolph would quickly sketch a detail as inspiration seized him; it would be executed by workmen just as quickly, giving the penthouse a remarkable improvisational and homemade character, quite different from the sleekness often associated with modernism. The two-decade-long, continuous renovation was Rudolph's late career masterpiece.

Although the economic recession impacted Rudolph's practice, it also made it possible for him to undertake this project. Real estate values declined precipitously when New

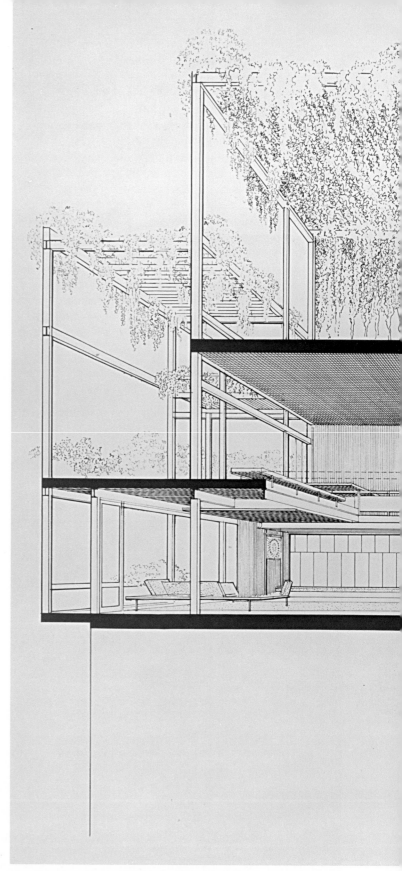

8.21 Perspective section, Penthouse, Beekman Place.

8.20 Rudolph, Penthouse addition, Beekman Place (New York, 1979–97).

Turning Inward

206

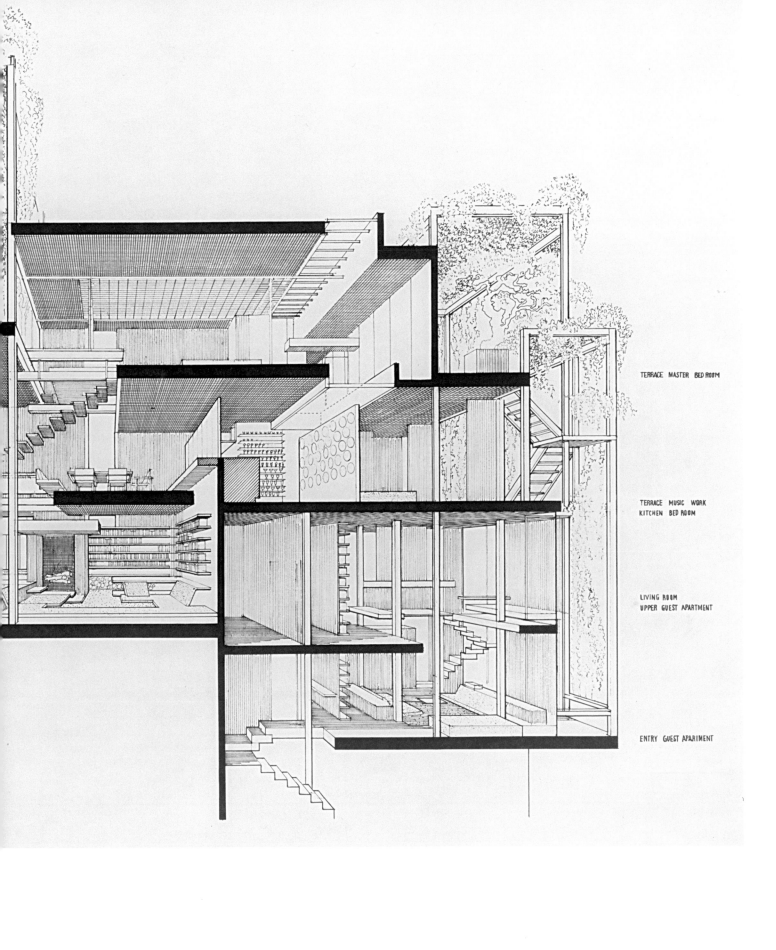

TERRACE MASTER BED ROOM

TERRACE   MUSIC   WORK
KITCHEN   BED ROOM

LIVING ROOM
UPPER GUEST APARTMENT

ENTRY GUEST APARTMENT

8.22 Living room, Beekman Place.

York City's government neared bankruptcy in 1975, making it feasible for Rudolph to buy 23 Beekman Place in 1976 for a reasonable $300,000.[54] Rudolph was never skilled at managing money, but he had saved enough for the down payment because he was frugal in the way he lived and practiced. Rudolph renovated the townhouse's additional apartments with his own details and finishes and then rented them out. The rentals paid the building's mortgage and supplemented Rudolph's income in lean times.

Work began in 1977, when Rudolph demolished his fourth-floor apartment (it was too idiosyncratic for a rental unit) and began building the rooftop addition. Rudolph's office manager, Donald Luckenbill, who had worked on the City Corridor project, supervised construction. Rudolph carried out the work with the encouragement of Ernst Wagner, a young Swiss man whom he had met in 1975. Wagner occupied the guest apartment, also known as the library, of the Beekman Place Penthouse. The two traveled together to places Rudolph enjoyed visiting, including abroad to such architecturally significant sites as the Acropolis in Athens, Greece.

Rudolph and Wagner embarked on various endeavors that contributed in one way or another to the evolving design of the penthouse. Though he cared little for the everyday workings of business, Rudolph could be quite entrepreneurial. In 1976, Rudolph and Wagner founded Modulightor, a firm that sold lighting they designed together and produced in small quantities in Manhattan, initially by a few skilled workmen from Wagner's native Switzerland and later by unskilled workers from Eastern Europe, who also carried out many of the changes being made to the penthouse.[55] Rudolph had long been interested in lighting, designing his own fixtures for the Yale A & A Building and experimenting with it in the apartments he designed for clients in Manhattan. He intended to have Modulightor manufacture the lighting for his projects, thus generating even more income, but it took the firm many years to make a profit.

Like the Hirsch residence, the Beekman Place Penthouse was a steel-framed structure painted brown; here Rudolph clad the frame with metal and precast concrete panels (figure 8.20). In the summertime, lush plantings softened its many cantilevered terraces and balconies, giving it the appearance of a hanging garden; the apartments Rudolph had envisioned for the New York Graphic Arts Center and the open terraces of the skyscrapers he began to build in Asia in the early 1980s presented a similar aspect.

Rudolph split the penthouse between public rooms, which were centered on a double-height living room overlooking the East River, and private chambers, which consisted chiefly of the guest apartment or library, which had its own double-height living space, facing Beekman Place (figure 8.21). A small, Plexiglass elevator at the center of the apartment rose through the four levels, treating visitors to a unique and terrifying experience of surfaces and spaces appearing and receding simultaneously above their heads, below their feet, and all around them. Plexiglass hallway floors and staircase treads formed a transparent series of bridges in the apartment's center, filtering sunlight into it and affording fascinating and complex views through multiple levels. The transparent materials confused visitors,

and not everyone reacted positively to these spaces. To Rudolph's amusement, guests at his occasional parties sometimes had vertiginous reactions; one woman fainted and was removed on a stretcher. Wine glasses set down on what appeared to be solid surfaces often plunged and shattered on distant floors below.[56]

The penthouse was Rudolph's summary statement about his work, reiterating his belief that it was worth taking risks to make architecture and urbanism that provoked strong reactions. It recalled aspects of some of his most compelling projects. Looking at multiple levels through the transparent floors at the house's center approximated the experience of seeing subways, people-movers, and highways conjoin through transparent surfaces beneath the HUB in the City Corridor scheme. He also evoked some of his most memorable interiors. The all-white, double-height living room resembled the exhibition room and drafting room of the Yale A & A Building and the living rooms of Rudolph's New Haven house and his Hirsch House. It was illuminated by dazzling rays of sunlight that reflected off the East River and were then refracted across the marble floors and in the mirrored surfaces of the columns and beams (figure 8.22).

Certain objects evoked Rudolph's past (figure 8.23). Occupying a corner of the living room was one of the plaster panels of Louis Sullivan's decorative ornament he had displayed in the A & A Building. Rudolph still played the piano daily and, in a gesture that defied gravity, hired a crane to hoist his grand piano from his previous apartment onto the living room balcony. Across from it, Rudolph drew in midair at a cantilevered drafting table.

The Beekman Place Penthouse had many surprises. A combination shower, bathtub, and Jacuzzi in Rudolph's top-floor master bathroom had a clear, Plexiglass bottom that formed the ceiling of the two spaces below: the kitchen and the bedroom of the guest apartment (figure 8.24). The Plexiglass bottom funneled light into the center of the apartment like a skylight, but it also presented opportunities for taking in "mesmerizing visual juxtapositions," as the critic Michael Sorkin politely put it in his 1988 article about the penthouse, of one or more bodies in the Jacuzzi, which may have delighted or disconcerted anyone beneath it, especially amid the prosaic pots and pans of the kitchen.[57] Rotner remonstrated with Rudolph, telling him the transparent bottom was both impractical and unconventional, but Rudolph thought bathrooms afforded opportunities for pleasure and sensuality.[58]

The penthouse also had many of Rudolph's almost secret "implied spaces." Shielded from the street by shutters, the guest apartment or library was accessible by many different entrances, staircases, hidden doors, and fire escapes, allowing occupants to come and go freely. A brushed-steel floor, mirrored ceilings, and columns clad in mirrored laminate reflected in a hauntingly blurred fashion the dark, shadowy, and mysteriously beautiful double-height living room at the guest apartment's center and anyone in it. In contrast to the white hues used elsewhere in the penthouse, Rudolph upholstered the low sofas in black leather. Sorkin declared the room "masculino."[59] The guest apartment had some

> 8.23 Living room, upper level, Beekman Place.

8.24 Bathroom, Beekman Place.

8.25 Guest suite, Beekman Place.

surreal touches of its own. The clear bottom of a Plexiglass sink formed part of an overhead soffit; viewers below could see water pooling when the faucet ran. A rail-less, steel staircase—a striking piece of folded sculpture—led from the sitting area to the bedroom, small study, and bath on the upper level (figure 8.25).

Such dream-like chambers were a retreat for Rudolph— an insular, sybaritic, aesthetically rich sanctuary from the tribulations of the real world. With Rudolph's late residential works, especially the Beekman Place penthouse, the architect came closer than ever before to achieving the psychologically and physically stimulating environments, laced with traits from playfulness to danger and eroticism, that he had always sought to build.

Aesthetics Reconsidered

In his 1988 article about the Beekman Place Penthouse, Sorkin praised it as "one of the most amazing pieces of modern urban domestic architecture produced in this country."[60] Although Rudolph created the penthouse in Manhattan, one of the centers of American architectural culture and his own home base, few of Rudolph's colleagues acknowledged the residence. It was notable that Sorkin's article appeared in *House and Garden,* a consumer publication, rather than in an architectural journal, which would have been the venue of choice just a short time earlier. An important critic, Sorkin was searing in his denunciation of the status quo in architecture during the 1980s. He called for overturning postmodernism by reinvigorating modernism and its aesthetics; his admiration for Rudolph was sincere, if polemically driven.

Celebrating Rudolph as modernism's forgotten hero, Sorkin wrote in a 1986 article entitled "The Invisible Man," one of his regular columns for the *Village Voice,* that although the once omnipresent Rudolph was now nearly invisible to his fellow architects, he was admirable for standing by his unfashionable modernist beliefs at a time when postmodernists changed their architecture to suit the every passing whim of their predominantly corporate clients.

Sorkin found Rudolph's adherence to his own aesthetics admirable and even ethical, not self-indulgent. He said of Rudolph, "At a time when the artistic may be the only viable domain left for architecture, its only visible point of resistance, there's a stampede to sell out. Paul Rudolph is not for sale."[61] Celebrating Rudolph's aesthetics for their ethical stance was a remarkable turnabout: he had been castigated for that very thing not long before. Sorkin called Rudolph the best designer of his generation and published humorous poems praising him.[62] The critic was one of a small but growing coterie of young admirers of Rudolph in the 1980s who were also seeking alternatives to postmodernism. Working with Rudolph, Yale architecture students organized an exhibition of drawings of the A & A Building in 1988, helping initiate a favorable reappraisal of the building. Rudolph's rapprochement with Yale had begun in 1985 when his former student Thomas Beeby became dean of the school of architecture.[63]

For the most part, however, Rudolph's profession ignored him. He was mentioned infrequently in the academic literature and the architectural press other than for remarks on the failure of his work. His long time supporters, led by Edward Logue, tried repeatedly to nominate him for the American Institute of Architects Gold Award, but they never succeeded. Though bitter about the rebuff, Rudolph remained resilient. He had found new patrons in Asia and during his last years would work indefatigably in the belief that his final works would validate his views about architecture and restore his reputation.

Nine
Asian Finale

From 1979 until his death in 1997, Rudolph turned his focus eastward. Postmodernism had less of an impact in Asia than in the West, and Rudolph and modernism were still respected there. Though he was building little in the United States, Rudolph was among the first in a wave of well-known Western architects who built iconic structures for the rapidly growing Asian region. Income from these projects was not always reliable, but it was enough to allow him to live well in Manhattan and to continue renovating his apartment; additionally he held out hope that these works would help revive his career.

The majority of the many projects Rudolph designed for Asian locales—from skyscrapers to villas, schools, churches, and an entire new town outside of Surabaya, Indonesia—were not built. However, he succeeded in completing four tall buildings in Singapore, Hong Kong, and Jakarta, finally fulfilling his dream of becoming a "skyscraper architect." Ambitious as ever in his seventh and eighth decades, Rudolph viewed each tower as an opportunity to explore urban relationships, challenge postmodernism, and improve on the standard rectangular form of the tall building. To give his towers a regional quality, he drew on Southeast Asia's historic forms, such as the pagoda, anticipating how other Asian skyscrapers, such as Cesar Pelli's minaret-inspired Petronas Towers in Kuala Lumpur (Malaysia, 1992–98), would soon evoke regionally significant forms. Rudolph compromised with his clients, tending to their wishes more than he ever had before, and this may have led to better buildings, at least in the case of the Jakarta tower.

Though it was not recognized at the time, aspects of these late works anticipated the green or sustainable movement of the early twenty-first century. Rudolph's towers had open-air accessible terraces, providing natural ventilation nearly unheard of in the climate-controlled high-rises of the United States, and their cooling, protective overhangs saved energy. With exposed frameworks and highly figured facades, Rudolph's buildings achieved new levels of expression that heralded the extravagant and singular buildings of the turn of the twenty-first century. His final challenges to the status quo in architecture, Rudolph's Asian towers served as an appropriate conclusion to his search for expression.

Rudolph's last days were spent elaborating on some of his unbuilt Asian projects, making them ever more dramatic and complex. He died on August 8, 1997, at age 78, in New York, with close friends, including several clients, in attendance. The cause of death was mesothelioma, a cancer perhaps contracted from exposure to asbestos in the Brooklyn Navy Yards during World War II.[1]

Prototype

The prototype for Rudolph's Asian skyscrapers was his City Center (1979–83), a pair of similar but not identical, prismatic office towers of thirty-two and thirty-seven stories in Fort Worth, Texas. Employing a reflective glass curtain wall that at one time he would have disdained showed a willingness on Rudolph's part, made mandatory by the need for work, to accede to clients' wishes and accept the conventions of contemporary construction.

The commercial office towers were in a low-rise, historic district called Sundance Square that the brothers Sid and Ed Bass preserved and redeveloped in an attempt to revive downtown Fort Worth (figure 9.1). Consisting for the most part of office space, Sundance Square exemplified how the privately funded redevelopment schemes of the 1980s differed from the publicly funded ones of the postwar era, where the centerpieces had often been public buildings. Rudolph's relationship with the Basses was well established. The residence for Sid and Anne Bass (Fort Worth, 1970-72) was among the most important of his later residential projects. Ed Bass, who had studied architecture at Yale in the late 1960s, was also familiar with Rudolph's work.

The towers were speculative; that is, they were built for lease by numerous tenants (and for the Basses' offices), not as single-tenant structures or corporate headquarters, which were commonly considered more prestigious. Rudolph served as the design consultant; the Dallas firm 3D International Architects was the architect of record, executing working drawings, supervising construction of the towers, and designing the parking garage between the two structures.

City Center resembled other notable Texas towers of the 1970s, such as Pennzoil Place in Houston (1973–75) by Philip Johnson and John Burgee. Built by the developer Gerald Hines, Johnson's complex consisted of a pair of reflective glass-clad towers. The two buildings had trapezoidal plans and distinctive sloped roofs. They were acclaimed for breaking out of the box still typical of most corporate architecture at that time. With Pennzoil Place, Hines established a model for high-end real estate development, showing how to enlist well-known architects to build profitable commercial structures; the Basses studied it carefully.[2]

For City Center Rudolph initially wanted to join his two towers with a "fine space," an urban plaza like those that had been regular features of his earlier projects (figure 9.2). This concept was not implemented, but Rudolph memorialized the idea by incising the pattern of a square at the intersection between the two obliquely aligned towers. A multistory atrium lobby in the western tower, raised one story above street level, became the primary public area for the complex.[3] Popularized by developer and architect John Portman, enclosed atrium lobbies became characteristic of 1970s and 1980s office towers. The urban projects of those years turned their backs on the cities around them with atriums and other devices, including the raised bridges known as skyways in cities such as Minneapolis, which protected inhabitants from harsh weather and perceived urban disorder alike. Though he liked open-air permeable spaces such as terraces, porticos, and balconies, Rudolph admired the Minneapolis Skyway system and Portman's sealed atriums for their grandeur, spatial complexity, and

> 9.1 Rudolph, City Center (Fort Worth, Texas, 1979-83).

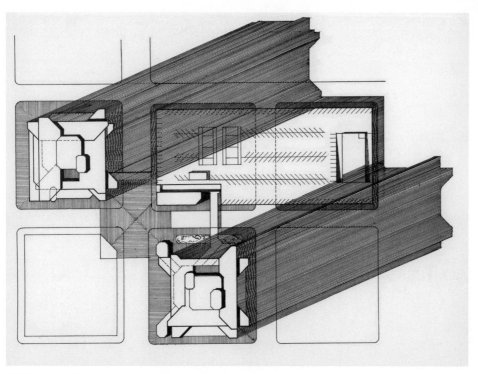

9.2 Site plan, City Center.

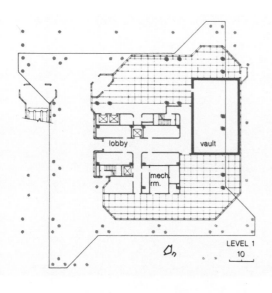

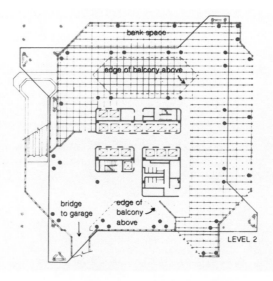

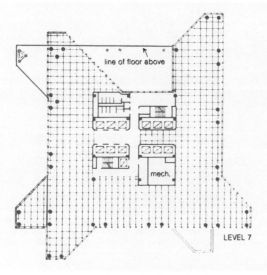

9.3 Plans, West Tower, City Center.

inward-looking orientation, which probably reminded him of his own megastructures. The desire for both open and enclosed spaces created interesting tensions in Rudolph's late works.[4] In Fort Worth, he linked the two towers to each other and to the parking garage via skyways and tunnels. He balanced this "totally enclosed environment," as extolled by publicity for the complex, with a series of open, columned spaces at the buildings' bases.[5]

The realities of building commercial office space caused Rudolph to adopt elements and materials for City Center that he previously would have disdained. He wanted to clad the towers in the local buff-colored brick, but Sid Bass believed that reflective glass would be more likely to attract tenants.[6] Rudolph liked employing reflective materials for interiors, but he had long decried the reflective curtain wall, warning about its alienating qualities already in the 1950s. By the late 1970s, however, Rudolph had little choice but to accept the curtain wall. Concrete was identified with brutalism and had fallen out of favor along with modernism; concrete construction was also more costly than steel and glass. Rudolph managed to incorporate innovative features that distinguished City Center from its contemporaries, including a special solar-reflective glass cladding that worked in concert with a computer-controlled system for "optimum energy efficiency."[7]

Although he was not working in concrete, Rudolph still tried to give his Fort Worth towers the plastic, sculptural qualities he favored by forming pinwheel-shaped plans with what he called trapezoidal "ears" pointing in different directions at each corner (figure 9.3). To enhance the building's plasticity he elaborated on the ears at the skyline level, giving each edifice a distinctive turreted silhouette.

Rudolph exposed the towers' structural columns at the base level, something that he did in all of the tall buildings of his later years, grouping them in twos and threes in order to reduce their scale and relate to smaller structures nearby (figure 9.4). He explained in an interview, "With towers this tall, the columns would have to get rather large at the base. Instead of bringing gravity loads to ground through single columns, it seemed to me that a certain lightness could be achieved if we split the gravity load into a tripod, tied together at several points along its height. At upper, typical floors, where the columns are behind glass (and tied in with floor framing), the inboard columns would be omitted, and outboard columns would continue on up in clustered pairs."[8] To make the frame sturdier and prevent swaying, P. V. Banavalkar of CBM Engineers joined the columns with triangular trusses.[9] The City Center towers, and their manifestation of Rudolph's ongoing concerns, established a vocabulary that reappeared in nearly all his Asian skyscrapers: exposed frameworks with grouped columns, substantial bases, and facades with extruded floors.

Rudolph believed passersby would identify with the columns in terms of scale, and even read them anthropomorphically, in a way that would elucidate his thinking about humanizing the city. He said of the City Center, "Urbanistically, the towers resemble human beings or robots. They walk proudly among the three-to-six-story high buildings as giants, for they cannot and should not disguise their size." Explaining his towers as alternatives to the architecture of the postmodernists, whom he scornfully called the "Paint Modernists," he added, "My intention was to relate to the three-story-high buildings by scale, not by materials, or paint, or 'motifs.'"[10] Ironically, Rudolph appeared to be returning to the structural rationalism of his Florida days at the precise moment when his "symbols of structure" might have been seen as similar to the one-dimensional "motifs" of postmodernism.

The skyline turrets of the City Center, which refuted the flat roofs of the modernist skyscraper, were another element that could have been interpreted favorably by the postmodernists. Rudolph, however, had said buildings should relate to the sky long before the postmodernists adorned their skyscrapers with pediments.[11] And he left no doubt that he was determined to march away from postmodernism, no matter how out of step this was with the times. In a 1986 interview he said, "I realize I'm out of sync, you see, with practically everything, but that is okay: I regard everybody else as being out of sync, not me."[12]

Although the monumentality and grand civic urbanism of the 1960s were further casualties of postmodern thinking, Rudolph still believed they were among the most significant qualities of architecture. For him, the raised outdoor platforms beneath each of the Fort Worth towers were public spaces, like the loggias of historic Italian public buildings. As built, however, the bases, with their enclosed skyways and escalators, had little of the openness of traditional public spaces, or much of a relationship to the city streets.

Despite his attempts to give the buildings expressive qualities, the completed towers in Fort Worth were more awkward than compelling. The relationship between the huge new towers and the restored low-rise buildings around them was weaker than the nuanced associations between old and new achieved by Rudolph in the past. The architect himself was dissatisfied with the towers, thinking that their silhouettes were not "strong enough" and that the towers should have been more powerfully plastic.[13] A local critic, however, thought that the City Center overwhelmed its surroundings. He said the ominously futuristic-looking towers loomed over downtown Fort Worth like the "Star Wars" movie villain, Darth Vader.[14]

The City Center was not financially successful either. The Basses found few tenants because of the Texas economic recession of 1982. Rudolph had succeeded early in his career in part because he had come of age in the 1950s and 1960s, an era of unprecedented growth in America, but beginning in the 1970s, cycles of economic booms and busts dogged him and his projects. Nor did the towers resuscitate Rudolph's practice or help his career in Texas. Although he built a handful of other projects in the state, he never established himself in Texas as Johnson and many of his contemporaries did with great success in the 1970s and 1980s.[15]

In fact by 1983, when the Fort Worth towers were completed, Rudolph's career in America was at its nadir. His expressionism was considered old fashioned and had never appealed to the corporations who sponsored the most prestigious commissions of the 1980s. His New York patrons, principally the Edersheims and a few other families, supplied him with a small but steady stream of work ranging

> 9.4 Base level, City Center.

9.5 Rudolph, Modulightor (New York, 1989).

from home renovations to an apartment building. A few institutional clients with whom he had long-standing relationships, such as the Burroughs Wellcome Corporation and the University of Massachusetts, Dartmouth, asked him to expand what he had already built for them, but the City Center was Rudolph's last notable large-scale project in the United States. Fortunately he found new clients in Asia who had virtually no interest in the traditionally inspired forms of postmodernism, then at its high point in the United States. These new clients limited his freedom as a designer more than he was used to, and the fast-paced economic climate of Asia proved challenging, but it was an exile that ultimately became a refuge for Rudolph.

Asian Years

Rudolph's first Asian commission was in Singapore, which became the base for his activities in the region. A local firm, Pan-Lon Engineering and Construction, with which he had developed an unrealized scheme for a hotel in Jerusalem (project, 1972), recommended him to real estate developer Kwee Liong Tek, who wanted to build a hotel. Anticipating the celebrity-driven architecture of the 1980s, Kwee hired Western architects to bring prestige to his projects. The hotel commission went to John Portman, but not long after, Kwee gave Rudolph a project for an apartment house. Soon other Singapore developers followed Kwee's lead, hiring Rudolph for a variety of projects.[16]

Rudolph established long-lasting, close relationships with these clients and their families; he designed for them a handful of little-known white villas that were simpler versions of the Bass Residence in Texas. Rudolph's Asian clients enjoyed working with him. Several, including Kwee, had studied architecture and engineering abroad during the 1950s and 1960s and remembered Rudolph's renown in the United States and Europe.

The city of Singapore was a receptive if carefully controlled environment for architecture. Westerners frequently characterized the city-state as authoritarian because of its limited democracy and many laws governing daily life. Rudolph was apparently untroubled by these limitations; likewise, many other Western architects, such as John Portman, Richard Meier, I. M. Pei, and Rem Koolhaas, considered Singapore a congenial place to build. Rudolph found the city-state's close monitoring of what could be built more disturbing than its limits on civil liberties. There were other challenges as well. In the 1980s and 1990s, Singapore and other Southeast Asian countries were particularly subject to the booms and busts of global economics; frequent upheavals affected the city's economy and caused Rudolph's projects to be cancelled or delayed for years. For the most part, however, Rudolph enjoyed working in Southeast Asia because of the clients who allowed him to design tall buildings, always his greatest ambition.

The Asian projects brought Rudolph some prosperity in the 1980s, although the income was subject to the vagaries of the economy in the Far East. His personal pleasures had not changed: travel, a new Porsche, and regular attendance at musical and theatrical performances. He used the earnings to continue to improve his Beekman Place residence and also to buy, in 1989, a small townhouse at 246 East

58th Street to house Modulightor, the lighting firm he founded with Ernst Wagner. He gave it a new steel-framed facade and added a duplex rental apartment similar to his Beekman Place penthouse. Rudolph also anticipated vertical expansion, almost as if it were a miniature version of one of his Asian skyscrapers (figure 9.5). Rents from the townhouses on Beekman Place and 58th Street paid the buildings' mortgages and, along with a pension from Yale, supplemented Rudolph's income.

Returning to the peripatetic ways of his early days in practice, Rudolph traveled to Singapore five or six times a year in the mid-1980s, often staying for several weeks. He also regularly traveled to Hong Kong, Jakarta, Kuala Lampur, and Bangkok, though few projects in these areas were completed. In Asia, Rudolph generally served as a design consultant who worked closely with a local firm chosen by the developer. Rudolph prepared conceptual designs and presentation drawings in his New York office and refined them in Asia; the local firm prepared working drawings and supervised construction. Rudolph often arrived in Singapore with only his drawing tools, a model in a brown paper bag, and an extra white shirt (figure 9.6). He had become even more ascetic as he aged. He looked much as he had always looked, sporting his trademark crew cut, but

9.6 Rudolph (c. 1984).

he had added heavy horn-rimmed glasses, similar to those worn by Le Corbusier.

Rudolph's energies were undiminished. Working drawings and details were sent back and forth by express mail and, starting in the early 1990s, by fax. Less given to showmanship than in his glory days, Rudolph focused entirely on working in the most economical way possible when in Asia, presenting plans to his clients one day, revising them overnight, and delivering improved schemes the next morning. Rudolph's clients and fellow architects in Asia found his directness, commitment to design and work, personal integrity, and modesty compatible with their own ethics and culture. Rudolph had changed. To his Asian circle he seemed humble, a word not once associated with him in his prime.

Working in this fashion suited Rudolph well; he had never been adept at managing a large office or supervising construction. By the early 1980s, his New York staff had dwindled to fewer than ten. Some office stalwarts departed, such as Donald Luckenbill in 1982, but others remained for many years, such as Ronald Chin, who was office manager for most of the 1980s. Low-paid, recent architecture school graduates refreshed the office ranks regularly. Rudolph left his longtime office at 57th Street in 1990, moving first to the living room of his Beekman Place penthouse, then to the Modulightor townhouse, and in the mid-1990s, when he was in ill health, back to the penthouse.[17]

Rudolph found a small office organized like an atelier around himself to be ideal. It was a return to how he had run his Florida office after he had split with Ralph Twitchell. He designed at least twenty-six projects for Asia during his last two decades, but only about seven, including the villas, were built, and a few never even made it onto his office's project list.

Overall, Rudolph derived satisfaction from his Asian projects. He told several of the young architects who assisted him in Asia that he preferred working as a design consultant to managing a large staff of his own.[18] Though often still brusque, Rudolph had to an extent mellowed. He mentored many of the young architects from the Asian firms he was working with; the young designers found his explanations of his design process and critiques of their work inspiring. Rudolph repeatedly told Wagner that his Asian buildings would restore his reputation late in life, just as Frank Lloyd Wright had revived his career when he was in his seventies.[19]

The Colonnade

Rudolph's first completed building in Asia was an apartment building called the Colonnade (1980–86) on Grange Road in Singapore, built in association with the Singapore architectural firm Archiplan Team. The tower consisted of twenty-six stories of luxury rental apartments topped by a penthouse for the building's owner, Kwee Liong Tek, the man responsible for introducing Rudolph to Singapore in 1979.

Rudolph saw his Asian buildings as opportunities to realize aspects of earlier, unbuilt projects (figure 9.7). With the Colonnade, he at last succeeded in building something resembling his Trailer Tower project of 1954 for Sarasota.

9.7 Rudolph, the Colonnade, Singapore (1980–86).

9.8 Construction, the Colonnade.

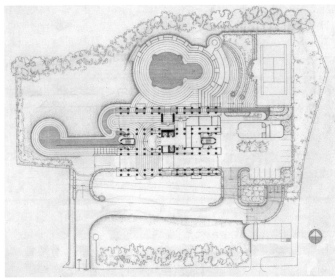

9.9 Site and ground floor plan, the Colonnade.

Assemblies that looked like rectangular, prefabricated units, which recalled his twentieth-century bricks, were inserted into a framework of exposed concrete columns. Rudolph said that the stacked units made the Colonnade a "vertical village," a new concept of his that informed many of the Asian towers. Living and working were integrated, as they would be in a traditional village. Rudolph's work on megastructures also informed the concept, especially the Graphic Arts Center (New York, 1967). The Colonnade's stacked units created an impression of wondrous multiplicity, an aesthetic quality of the unbuilt New York project as well.[20] Additionally, the plasticity of the Colonnade recalled Rudolph's Crawford Manor (New Haven, 1962–66), and the overall pattern formed by the rectangular units is likely another of his attempts to construct decoration.

As was true of many of Rudolph's social inventions, achieving the vertical village proved elusive. The Colonnade was not prefabricated, nor was it a building where occupants worked and lived. Rather it was a residential structure built of conventional brick and concrete and erected in the manner typical of Singapore. White paint protected the brick walls from the elements and gave the building a cohesive appearance. Paint also masked the individual bricks, making the building look as if it had been constructed of prefabricated units (figure 9.8).

Suggestions that this approach was not true to the structural rationalism that Rudolph appeared to be reembracing with his exposed frameworks left him unmoved. His thinking about architectural expression and structure remained as complex as ever. In a 1986 interview he said, "The idea of what you express and what you don't express is a tantalizing thing. I think it probably comes as close to getting at the art of architecture as any single thing. . . . The literal showing of the structure isn't necessarily better."[21] Rudolph's long-time friend Mildred Schmertz, an editor at *Architectural Record*, wrote in an article about the Colonnade that in Asia he was "determined to continue expanding upon the ideas that interest him most." Thus he would "approximate the formal concepts of a new structural concept even if the requisite technology is not yet feasible."[22]

The warm weather of Southeast Asia, which reminded Rudolph of Florida, also provoked a return to past concerns; regionalism and climate, which had defined his Florida houses to a large degree, were again at the forefront. Located just 85 miles north of the equator, Singapore receives tropical heat and rains year-round. In one of the few talks Rudolph gave in Asia, a 1982 lecture in Singapore, he said, "Regionalism, so lacking today, and yet so important for understanding ourselves is possibly made most clear in high rise domestic architecture, where outside space, with its shadows, recesses, and very human character, lends a humanness so difficult to achieve in other kinds of buildings."[23]

The subject of regionalism enjoyed renewed interest in the 1980s with emergence of the theory of "critical regionalism." Rudolph, however, had little interest in this ideology. For him, regionalism remained chiefly an investigation of climate, though in certain projects he engaged with traditional regional forms, as he had in his Florida houses.[24] Consideration of climate and temperature allowed him to

225

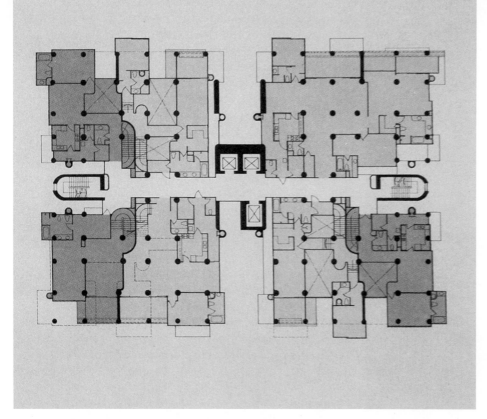

9.10 Typical floor plan, the Colonnade.

open up his towers to the outdoors in novel ways. Unlike tall buildings in the United States, Singapore, or indeed nearly anywhere, the Colonnade was cooled in part by wide hallways that were open at the ends.

The Colonnade was further distinguished from the typical luxury apartment houses of Singapore by an air of tropical fantasy. Such exoticism appealed to the Colonnade's tenants, primarily Western businesspeople on short stints in Singapore. The site of a demolished colonial villa, the grounds of the tower included a lushly planted garden. Rows of columns in the open-air lobby, source of the building's name, recalled classical colonnades or the majestic hypostyle halls of ancient Egyptian temples (figure 9.9).[25] An outdoor reception desk, fountains, terraces, tropical foliage, and a swimming pool in a shape resembling an enormous turtle made it seem like an opulent resort in Bali rather than an urban high-rise.

Above the lobby, the residential floors were divided into quadrants by open corridors and passages (figure 9.10). The four to eight exceptionally spacious apartments on each floor were geared toward American and European standards, with all the latest conveniences, including air-conditioning. Many of the ingeniously planned units had double-height living rooms spanned by bridges and stairways, recalling the interior complexity of Rudolph's own Manhattan penthouse (1977–97) (figure 9.11). The four different types of one- and two-bedroom apartments fit together within the larger structure in intricate interlocking ways that recalled another of the building's predecessors, Le Corbusier's Unité d'Habitation (Marseilles, 1946–52). Kwee Liong Tek's duplex penthouse floated atop this geyser of continuously refreshed rental income. The size of a large villa, the penthouse was complete with swimming pool.

Sought after because of its proximity to high-end shopping on Orchard Road, the Colonnade was the city's premier rental building when it was completed in 1986. For Rudolph, it was the fulfillment, in terms of form if not of method, of the type of prefabricated tower he had wanted to build for over thirty years. Yet the Colonnade was admired and not emulated—the fate of so many of Rudolph's buildings. The open-air lobby and corridors engaged with the outdoors and lessened cooling costs, but also admitted undesirable humidity. Saving energy was not a priority in the mid-1980s, and in general open-air corridors were considered more suitable to public housing than to elegant residential buildings.

The Concourse

The Concourse (1979–94), Rudolph's second completed project in Singapore, was a commercial office, retail, and residential complex; its prolonged gestation was due to economic crises in the region. Intended to serve the same population of Westerners as the Colonnade, it came closer to the vertical village concept: residents could work in a thirty-eight story, eight-sided office tower and live in an adjoining five-story wing containing a shopping mall, parking garage, and luxury furnished and staffed apartments.

The Concourse was built by a long-time admirer of Rudolph's, K. P. Cheong, known as "the Chairman." Part of a Singapore real estate dynasty, Cheong was excited to commission a building from a hero of his youth. He had studied civil engineering and architecture in Australia in the 1960s, when Rudolph had been at the height of his fame. Once again serving as a design consultant, Rudolph worked closely with Cheong and with Joseph Cheang and Ashvin Kumar from Architects 61, the local architecture firm. Singapore's Urban Redevelopment Authority envisioned the Concourse as one of several large buildings that would transform a main avenue, Beach Road, into an office

9.11 Apartment interior, the Colonnade.

and shopping district called the Golden Mile. Rudolph wanted his tower to be the Golden Mile's primary landmark, the first notable structure seen by visitors arriving from the airport.

In Rudolph's initial scheme (1979–82), the polygonal tower was a marked departure from the rectangular towers typical of office development in Singapore and elsewhere (figure 9.12). A mixed-use high-rise with apartments and offices, it realized Rudolph's notion of a vertical village. It was significant that the architect employed concrete for this scheme, his preferred material for achieving plasticity, rather than reflective glass, which he had used reluctantly for Fort Worth's City Center. Rudolph raised the tower on exposed columns and broke it down into multistory groupings, each articulated with different sun breakers and balconies; in this way, his solution recalled the variations on the *brise soleil* of Le Corbusier's tall buildings.[26] The partially enclosed spiral-shaped plaza atop the low-rise wing had Rudolph's characteristic radiating lines incised into the pavement.

By invoking forms he had favored in the past, Rudolph caused some of his American colleagues to conclude that there was little new in his Asian work. When Rudolph presented the Concourse at a conference on the current state of architecture at the University of Virginia in 1983, Jacquelin Robertson, one of Rudolph's former Yale students, asked if the building was not the same one Rudolph had been designing for years. Rudolph's building was considered out of step with the others presented, most of which exemplified postmodernism, then at its most popular. Johnson offered praise, but not unqualified approval. Pointing out Rudolph's isolation from his American colleagues, he said, "I don't know any other architect who is so off by himself and so successful." It was among the last important conferences in which Rudolph participated. Most of his subsequent Asian projects would be dismissed or ignored in the United States.[27]

Rudolph's drawing of the first scheme for the Concourse was, however, one of his most masterful of this period. Less work in the 1980s meant more time available for Rudolph and his New York staff to devote immeasurable hours to making ever more complicated presentation drawings with laboriously fine-tuned hatching and line work. Beginning in the early 1970s or possibly earlier, Rudolph turned to colored pencils to convey the expressive qualities and atmospheric effects of his spaces, often employing a bold red for structural elements. The complexity and novel viewpoints employed in the drawings of the Asian projects made them even more compelling than some of Rudolph's finest presentation drawings of the 1960s.[28]

Rudolph had plenty of time to draw because a recession delayed construction of the Concourse for a decade (figure 9.13). Completed in 1994, the thirty-eight-story tower was aluminum and glass instead of concrete; still in place was the low wing housing a shopping mall and short-term rental apartments (figure 9.14). Supported by twelve columns and roughly octagonal in shape, the tower exhibited a distinctive profile, with each floor flaring outward.

The inverted canted floors of Rudolph's building were an attempt to give it a regional quality, in this case by referring to a traditional Asian form: Rudolph likened the contours

9.12 Rudolph, first scheme, the Concourse (Singapore, 1979–82).

9.13 The Concourse (Singapore, 1994).

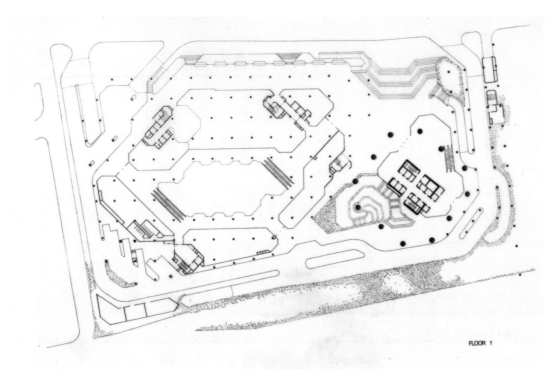

9.14 Ground floor plan, the Concourse.

of the tower to an upside-down pagoda. Some of the other landmark Asian skyscrapers of the 1990s also invoked traditional forms to suggest regional identity, including the minaret-shaped Petronas Towers by Cesar Pelli in Kuala Lumpur (Malaysia, 1992–98) or the pagoda-like Taipei 101 by C. Y. Lee (Taipei, Taiwan, 1998–2004).[29] But since there were no pagodas in Singapore, Rudolph's inversion of the form might have been another of his mannerisms, like the reversed fluting of his "fluted" concrete blocks. Rudolph may actually have been looking beyond Asia to Wright, who had modeled some of his towers on the pagoda, such as the Johnson Wax Research Tower (Racine, Wisconsin, 1944–51).[30] Rudolph denied consciously invoking Wright's tall buildings, but the resemblances are unmistakable.[31]

The Concourse tower was innovative in its organization. Rudolph divided the structure into sections of four floors each that could be rented to tenants as large-scale, multilevel suites. Each had its own three-level atrium that served as a lobby and communal space. Terraces, unusual for the upper levels of a tall office building, provided atriums and many offices with access to the outside. The atypical configuration of commercial office space anticipated Norman Foster's Commerzbank Tower (Frankfurt, Germany, 1994–97) with its lushly planted interior atriums, and the open-air terraces prefigured those of Ken Yeang's award-winning "tropical skyscraper" in Malaysia, the Menara Mesiniaga (Subang Jaya, Selangor, Malaysia, 1990–92), lauded for its use of natural ventilation. These parallels suggested that Rudolph continued to have some influence, especially on those who had admired his work when they were young.

Rudolph incorporated shading devices to cool his buildings. The flaring floors created a distinctive outline but also shaded the levels beneath. The downward-sloping windows deflected the sun's rays. Rudolph clad the tower and its adjoining lower wing in white, prefabricated aluminum panels. The light metal contrasted with the dark glass and deflected heat as well. Terraces planted with hanging vines absorbed heat and also emitted oxygen. These aspects of the design addressed sustainability concerns well before the rest of the profession did; nevertheless, they attracted little attention when the building was completed.

The Concourse was most memorable aesthetically. The banks of windows of the lower wing formed an impressive rippling facade, which Rudolph thought echoed the waves of the Pacific Ocean, visible in the distance (figure 9.15). In fact, he compared the entire structure to a wave or a reef: "The building seems to move in and out, back and forth, thereby suggesting a living organism by the sea."[32] Although Rudolph had attempted to create a regional quality by invoking the pagoda form, and to foster a welcoming character by referring to natural forms, the Concourse had a cool, anonymous corporate aura. Representing the choices of the Chairman more than Rudolph's own preferences, the tower's immense, granite-paved lobby and smooth glass and aluminum surfaces had a slickness about them appropriate for its largely transient, cosmopolitan tenants.

Despite the great investment made in its design, the Concourse was not financially successful. Cheong saw the economic potential of Rudolph's vertical village and hoped that Westerners working in the tower would live and shop in the complex, but this symbiotic relationship never developed. Nor did the Golden Mile become the high-end district anticipated by Singapore's planners. The Concourse remained isolated at the edge of Singapore's business district, a destination for few shoppers or pedestrians. In 2009, only fifteen years after completion of the complex, the low-rise mall of shops and apartments was demolished to make way for two condominium towers, each over twenty stories tall, leaving the tower freestanding and forlorn. The economic forces that had produced the Concourse quickly dismembered it as well.

231

9.15 Mall and apartment wing, the Concourse.

Bond Centre

As he had in the United States, Rudolph often designed
multiple projects for a single client or a group of related
clients. Relatives of Kwee Liong Tek, who had built the
Colonnade, were part of a consortium that enlisted Rudolph
to design the Bond Centre in Hong Kong (1984–88) (figure 9.16).[33] The two nearly identical octagonal glass towers resembled the City Center towers in Fort Worth but
were bulkier and slightly taller. They were located close to
the harbor front in the dense downtown business district
known as Central. The towers received more international
attention than Rudolph's other Southeast Asian projects in
part because of their proximity to two important contemporaneous structures, I. M. Pei's Bank of China (1982–90) and
Norman Foster's Hong Kong–Shanghai Bank Corporation
headquarters (HSBC) (1979–86).

For the Bond Centre, Rudolph worked as a design consultant with the established Hong Kong firm of Wong &
Ouyang. The American architect formed a close friendship
and professional relationship with Nora Leung, a young
associate from the firm, who assisted Rudolph with details
and finishes. He maintained greater control over these
aspects of the design than in his Singapore projects, even
choosing the granite facing for the elevator's call buttons.
Leung's book about the Bond Centre illuminates all of
Rudolph's Asian projects.[34]

The Bond Centre was designed and built within the
economically and politically troubled atmosphere of Hong
Kong, which was preparing for transfer to Chinese rule in a
decade. In part because of Hong Kong's uncertainty about
its future, the Bond Centre passed through the hands of
several different owners while under construction. In 1982,
the original developers and their architects conceived of it
as two conventional rectangular towers, identical except
for their height. In 1983, soon after the foundations were
poured, a financial panic caused by anxiety about the transfer forced the developers to sell the project at a loss of one
billion Hong Kong dollars, a record for its time. The Kwee

family and their partners bought it and appointed Rudolph
architect by 1984.

Then, halfway through construction, the Kwee family sold
the majority of their interest in the project to Alan Bond,
an Australian financier who named the project after himself. He, in turn, lost control of it soon after its completion
in 1988, leading to its eventual acquisition and renaming
by Lippo, an Indonesian bank. Rudolph found these rapid
transferrals of ownership surprising and "disconcerting."[35]
He hoped that his buildings would be stable, long-lasting
monuments, but his clients in Asia saw them as commodi-
ties to be traded, altered, and if need be, demolished.

In any case, Rudolph found Hong Kong and the Bond
Centre's site magnificent. The city's urban complexity,
especially its miles-long network of raised pedestrian
walkways, fascinated Rudolph. The elevated paths, above
streets and through buildings, probably recalled for him the
multiple levels of circulation that he had envisioned for his
City Corridor (New York, project, 1967–72).[36] Yet Rudolph
believed that Hong Kong needed greater urban order and
that the Bond Centre could reorganize and stabilize the city
around it. Whether Hong Kong needed fixing was question-
able. Rudolph's analysis was based on his own observations
rather than on any prolonged study of its people, economics, or ways, making it again a largely scenographic or aesthetic approach to urbanism.

The overall urban topography of Hong Kong was a
vital component in Rudolph's vision for the Bond Centre,
as it had been in New Haven, Boston, and New York. He
believed that his towers, Pei's nearby Bank of China, and
Foster's HSBC building would form a "triangle of foreground buildings," a stable urban figure amid the dense
ranks of anonymous skyscrapers in the chaotic Central
district. Establishing this relationship would put his speculative office building on par with Pei's and Foster's more
prestigious corporate headquarters. Unfortunately, the
correspondence existed only in Rudolph's imagination.
Despite the close proximity of the buildings, Pei, Foster,
and Rudolph never met to discuss their projects. Even so,
Rudolph acknowledged each architect whenever he arrived

9.16 Rudolph, Bond Centre (Hong Kong, 1984–88).

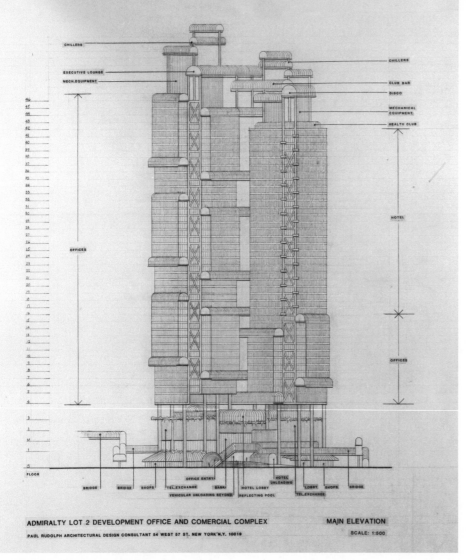

ADMIRALTY LOT 2 DEVELOPMENT OFFICE AND COMERCIAL COMPLEX   MAIN ELEVATION

PAUL RUDOLPH ARCHITECTURAL DESIGN CONSULTANT 54 WEST 57 ST. NEW YORK 'N.Y. 10019   SCALE: 1:500

9.17 Rudolph, first scheme, Bond Centre (c. 1984).

at the Bond Centre site with playful military salutes toward their buildings.[37]

Rudolph particularly admired Foster's HSBC. He wrote a detailed, seventeen-page study of the building, appraising its exposed framework and the accessibility to the city of its open base.[38] It is not clear why Rudolph wrote this evaluation, or what he intended to do with it; perhaps because of his habitual reserve he never showed it to Foster. It does indicate Rudolph's awareness of the industrially inspired "high-tech" architecture of the late 1970s of Foster and another of Rudolph's former Yale students, Richard Rogers. While Rudolph had been considered a pioneer in high-tech interior design, he was not usually associated with architecture given that name. Nevertheless, the first scheme for the Bond Centre had a distinctly high-tech quality to it that suggests Rudolph was attempting to keep up with this emergent tendency (figure 9.17). The external bracing resembled that of Foster's HSBC, while the vaulted bridges linking the towers recalled the vaults of Rogers's high-tech landmark, the Lloyd's Building (London, 1979–84). Rudolph's final scheme for the Bond Centre was quite different. The massing changed, the external bracing disappeared, and the bridges were eliminated because one of the investors thought they too closely resembled those linking together his Indonesian factories.[39]

Even though it had changed ownership several times, the Bond Centre was completed in 1988, just four years after Rudolph was engaged and far more quickly than any of Rudolph's Singapore projects. In their final form, the 46- and 48-floor towers appeared more crystalline than high tech. The eight different surfaces of each tower were clad with reflective glass and faceted with multistory raised panels that furnished more corner offices than in most standard rectangular buildings. The panels protruded from the building facades like immense ornamental reliefs forming an interlocking pattern, another example of Rudolph's construction of decoration and a nod to the expressive and varied portions of the Forth Worth City Center's facades. Single-story "sky floors" extended from the corners of the panels. They were another device Rudolph used to signal relative scale; in this case, they were inspired by the balconies Hong Kong residents often enclosed to enlarge their living spaces.[40] He believed the sky floors helped the observer understand the immense scale of the building because the one-story height of each sky floor was a scale to which most people could easily relate.[41]

As in Fort Worth, Rudolph accepted the reflective glass curtain wall as an unavoidable characteristic of contemporary construction. He was determined to exploit it to the best of his abilities despite his previous opposition to

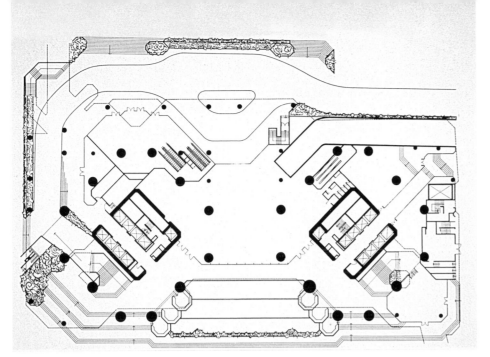

9.18 Lobby plan, Bond Centre.

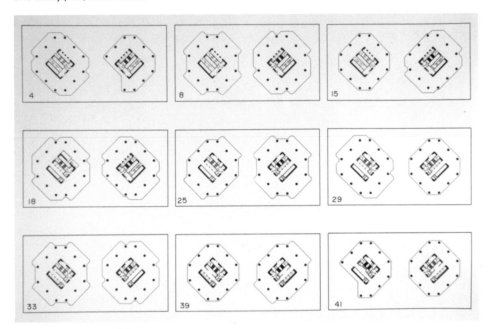

9.20 Tower plans, Bond Centre.

it. After all, it did offer the type of shiny, reflective surface he often appreciated. Describing the Bond Centre towers in 1988, Rudolph wrote, "The aesthetic intent is to . . . give the building 'presence' when seen from a great distance, from the middle distance, and from close at hand. At the same time, it is intended that the building inhabit the sky, and become dematerialized by reflecting the ever changing light."[42] Even with the glass and the efforts in the direction of dematerialization, Rudolph's towers seemed heavy. He massed or shaped them, especially the sky floors, in a way that recalled the plastic masonry construction he had always preferred; in other words, the Bond Centre towers looked like masonry buildings rendered in glass.

Rudolph was able to use masonry in a limited way at the Bond Centre. He stabilized the towers within the swirling eddies of Hong Kong traffic by placing them on top of a massive podium of stepped terraces sheathed with red granite, a favored local building material. The podium base

had to be large in order to straddle the existing Admiralty mass transit stop. The podium contained a shared lobby for both towers, raised several levels above the street (figure 9.18). Rudolph explained in unpublished notes that the open terraces, sheltered by the overhanging towers, were intended to "contribute to the public life of Hong Kong"; the architect had essayed something similar in his Fort Worth buildings.[43] Outdoor staircases and bridges joined the podium to the raised pedestrian walkways of the Central district (figure 9.19).

The towers were masterful demonstrations of Rudolph's adroitness at manipulating geometry and structural elements to suggest movement, an ability that became ever more pronounced in his later years. Rudolph rotated every octagonal floor plan 45 degrees so that no two were completely in alignment. To enhance the towers' sculptural

> 9.19 Base, Bond Centre.

235

qualities, he configured the edges of each concrete floor pad differently, achieving in a relatively economical way an astonishing fifty-eight different floor plans between the two buildings. Such diversity was unheard of in most towers, especially speculative ones (as was the Bond Centre), where floor plans tended to be identical (figure 9.20).

Hong Kong's press and citizenry admired the Bond Centre, but as was often the case, Rudolph's intentions were difficult for the average observer to discern. Hong Kong residents did not see the articulated pattern of panels and sky floors as elements that helped them understand the scale of each tower, but as giant koala bears climbing trees, traditional Chinese frieze patterns, stalks of bamboo, or large-scale depictions of the letter S. Believers in geomancy and feng shui appreciated the Bond Centre's jewel-like, crystalline qualities, seeing the towers as lucky.[44]

American architectural journals paid attention to the Bond Centre—more than they had to many of Rudolph's late buildings, probably because of interest in Hong Kong's political situation—and most press accounts were favorable. Proximity to the already well-known headquarters buildings by Foster and Pei gave the towers a context that Westerners could understand. Yet the Bond Centre was ultimately more disquieting than compelling and not as successful as its neighbors. Rudolph's complex seemed earthbound in relation to Pei's soaring Bank of China. The base of the Bond Centre raised it high above the streets and cut it off from the city around it in contrast to the lively, accessible public space at the base of Foster's HSBC building. The urban triangle Rudolph had pictured between his towers and the two others was indiscernible amid the dense and growing skyscrapers of the district; in fact, these soon overwhelmed the Bond Centre. Though Rudolph chose the interior finishes, the lobbies and corridors were anodyne compared to his previous works. Rudolph's endeavor to make the Bond Centre into an iconic landmark for the city could not overcome the conventions of the commercial building type.

Wisma Dharmala Tower

Rudolph's work on Wisma Dharmala Tower in Jakarta, Indonesia (1983–88) (later renamed Intiland tower), was almost simultaneous with his work on the Bond Centre. With its distinctive flared eaves and exposed structural system, it was the most successful realization of regionalism in Rudolph's late career: the building evoked Indonesia's tradition of post and beam buildings as well as the overall feeling of the place. By comparison, Rudolph's exploration of the local in Singapore and Hong Kong was limited.

Jakarta was different from orderly, rich Singapore or fast-paced Hong Kong. The capital of a vast developing country, the megalopolis was inhabited in 1980 by 6.5 million people, many of whom were living in rudimentary conditions. Village life was tangible in Jakarta, so envisioning a tall building as a vertical village was more plausible, if in the end no more feasible. The authorities exercised little control over the project, a situation far different from highly regulated Singapore, and Rudolph could work closely with the client and workmen to develop solutions on the site.

The project was initiated in the early 1980s when the Wisma Dharmala Group, a real estate and trading enterprise, decided to build a new headquarters in Jakarta. Like Rudolph's Singapore clients, the firm wanted to hire a famous, foreign architect. A small conglomerate by Western standards, Wisma Dharmala would occupy only the penthouse stories of the building; association with a prestigious designer would appeal to tenants renting the remaining floors.

Wisma's board of directors turned to Johannes Gunawan, an Indonesian architect who was experienced at implementing foreign architects' designs in Jakarta, to find an architect and oversee design and construction. Gunawan had long admired Rudolph's Florida buildings; he was also aware of Rudolph's new work in Southeast Asia. In 1982 he recommended the American architect to Wisma's board; Rudolph was the design consultant while Gunawan was the architect of record in Indonesia. Indeed, Gunawan acted as the de facto client for the project in ways that resulted in the Wisma Dharmala Tower being Rudolph's best in Asia.

Gunawan introduced him to the architectural community and the vernaculars of Indonesia. As a result, Rudolph engaged with local architects far more in Indonesia than in Singapore or Hong Kong. Gunawan organized several events for the Indonesian architectural community that celebrated Rudolph and his architecture, including a 1984 exhibition at an arts center in Jakarta, sponsored by Wisma Dharmala, of Rudolph's twenty-five study models and drawings for the conglomerate's tower. They were displayed along with his other new Asian works and his most important projects of the past. Well attended, the exhibition and opening discussion reinvigorated debate among the country's architects about the relationship between modernism and Indonesia's vernacular, a theme of longstanding interest.[45]

Rudolph himself found inspiration in the country's traditional architecture soon after arriving in Indonesia in 1983. He visited an open-air museum park on the outskirts of Jakarta that had a collection of traditional houses from the country's many different islands.[46] He also lectured at the Institute of Technology Bandung; on the journey there with Gunawan, Rudolph noted village streets lined with post and beam houses dominated by gabled roofs with pronounced overhangs. The large overhanging roof, in countless variations, was the common denominator for Indonesian architecture throughout the enormous archipelago.

In fact, the traditional roof had inspired attempts throughout the twentieth century to create for Indonesia a modern architecture based on vernacular precedents.[47] Dutch colonial exemplars at the Institute of Technology Bandung included Henri Maclaine-Pont's majestic, traditionally inspired academic buildings of the 1920s, which featured flared eaves and broad, overhanging shingled roofs (figure 9.21). Frederick Silaban, the leading Indonesian modernist of the 1950s and 1960s, also singled out the overhanging roof as the salient element of the nation's vernacular and the defining element of a new Indonesian modernism.[48]

Rudolph was not interested in using regional forms to foster identity or nationalism, as Indonesian architects were, but he found the roofs of the country's vernacular fascinating neverthless. In 1988 he explained, "Indonesian architecture covers some 13,000 islands, many cultures and a wide variety of architectural solutions to the problems of the climate. The unifying element in this rich diversity is the roof, which in Indonesian hands has produced some of the world's most beautiful buildings. The Dharmala Office Building takes the 'roof' and adapts it to a high rise, air-conditioned office building and its supporting functions. Most importantly, the building is designed to give a sense of 'place,' of being appropriate to Jakarta. It is the antithesis to the anonymous air-conditioned 'box' constructed all around the world."[49]

Gunawan helped Rudolph understand how to adapt his building to the demanding tropical climate (figure 9.22). The Indonesian architect specified orienting the tower in relation to the sun and planning every detail to offset the extremes of heat and rain typical of Jakarta.[50] Cantilevered overhangs cooled the building naturally, sheltered its windows from direct sunlight, and cast the expressive, shifting shadows Rudolph was partial to. The deep overhangs heightened the building's sculptural qualities and made its window glazing practically invisible: it appeared to be a tall building without glass. Rudolph had developed projecting overhangs and articulated structural systems in his other Asian towers, but here they also called to mind the Indonesian post and beam vernacular, giving the Jakarta building a more pronounced regional quality than the other buildings.

The Wisma Dharmala project also offered Rudolph a welcome opportunity to return to concrete. With the help of Seng Lip Lee, an engineering professor from the National University Singapore, Rudolph developed a high-strength concrete that made the Wisma Dharmala building one of the most technologically innovative Indonesian structures of its time.[51] A framework of paired concrete columns, like that of the City Center in Fort Worth, supported the building; the columns were joined together and braced by stiffeners with a distinctive corbel-like profile that became a decorative

leitmotif for the entire project. In a tropical climate, concrete must be painted or clad in some way; Rudolph surfaced the columns and walls of Wisma Dharmala with rectangular white tiles, five by twenty-two centimeters, of a type often used for new buildings in Indonesia. The tile-covered walls resembled the fluted-concrete-block surfaces of Rudolph's Crawford Manor and other buildings of the 1960s. The tiles also reflected sunlight, lent some texture to the building's surface, and were washable.

When completed in 1988, the Wisma Dharmala Tower was markedly different from the rectangular glass office towers rising in Jakarta at the time. The cantilevered projecting floors gave the twenty-six-story tower the most memorable and dramatic appearance of any of Rudolph's Asian towers. While the flared profiles of each floor recalled traditional Indonesian roofs, the tower's overall form and triangulated geometry again recalled Frank Lloyd Wright's tall buildings, particularly his Price Tower (Bartlesville, Oklahoma, 1952–56).

Wisma Dharmala was located at a prestigious address on Jakarta's primary commercial avenue, the rapidly growing Jenderal Sudirman. The narrow strip of new office buildings and hotels along the Jenderal Sudirman was oriented toward the boulevard, with little relationship to the existing city or nearby low-rise neighborhoods of traditional houses. In contrast, and as he had earlier, Rudolph conceived the Wisma Dharmala Tower as a sculptural entity to be seen in the round from multiple viewpoints. Its projecting overhangs reached out to both new and old Jakarta. The building's entrance faced the new Jakarta of glass and steel commercial structures along the boulevard; its rear featured a low wing containing a cafeteria and additional services that looked out to the traditional residential compounds of Indonesia, aligning the tower with the vernacular buildings and villages that had been part of its inspiration.

Though the Wisma Dharmala Tower did not fulfill the multifunction criteria of the vertical village, Rudolph said

9.21 Henri Maclaine-Pont, Institute of Technology (Bandung, Indonesia, 1919–25).

9.22 Rudolph, Wisma Dharmala Tower (Jakarta, Indonesia, 1983–88).

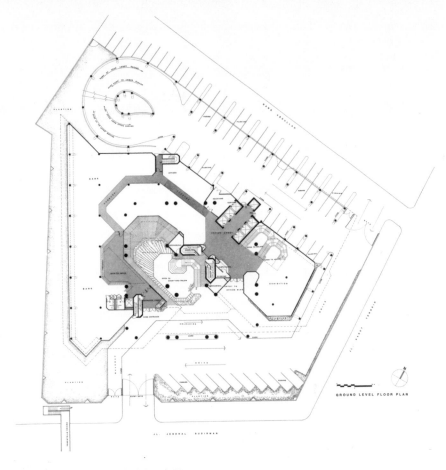

9.23 Ground floor plan, Wisma Dharmala Tower.

that the base and courtyard were meant to be "like a village, with all the ease of access and variety that villages always possess."[52] The base contained a parking garage, atrium lobby, and twelve-story, roofed open-air courtyard surrounded by shops, a small exhibition space, and a restaurant (figure 9.23). The courtyard was one of the most remarkable spaces of Rudolph's late career (figure 9.24). Sheltered by the tower and planted with trees and shrubs that grew over the years, it was a paradisiacal, vine-covered outdoor room overlooked by balconies, twisting staircases, and multilevel terraces and cooled by small canals, carp-filled ponds, and waterfalls (figure 9.25). The balconies, terraces, and inclined surfaces of the projecting eaves funneled cool, surprisingly strong breezes into and through the courtyard. The great space descended from the umbrella-covered courtyard of Rudolph's U.S. Embassy in Jordan (Amman, Jordan, project, 1954–58) and recalled some of his other most significant interiors, such as the multilevel common rooms of Humanities I at SMTI (Dartmouth, Massachusetts, 1963–65).

The internal organization of the Wisma Dharmala building owed something to the Concourse. The conglomerate's corporate offices occupied the top six floors. The remainder of the tower consisted of a series of stacked, independent three-story office suites; elevators and services with special areas to accommodate Muslim washing practices were offset. Each discrete "garden office," as they were called by Rudolph, had its own multistory interior lobby and terraces. Like those in the Concourse, the garden offices were conceptually similar to the "sky courts" that would be found in some of the first tall, green buildings of the 1990s.

Wisma Dharmala suggested a way for Indonesia to modernize while maintaining its identity (though Rudolph denied that he was interested in such issues), and several of its first tenants, such as the national airline, identified strongly with Indonesia. The building stimulated discussion in the Indonesian architectural community. Gunawan reported that the building's protective overhangs and naturally cooled spaces achieved long-term energy savings; as before, these qualities garnered little notice in Western architectural journals in the late 1980s because oil and gas were still relatively inexpensive.[53] Its lasting value may be as a demonstration of how relatively simple means such as overhangs and ventilation can make a more energy-efficient skyscraper.

Despite the care that went into its planning and the pride with which it is still maintained, Wisma Dharmala is nearly overwhelmed by Jakarta's problems in the early twenty-first century. Washing the white tile surfaces is labor intensive. While the building has a striking presence, it does not engage with the surrounding city as directly as Rudolph would have liked. Perched above street level on a podium containing parking, the tower is walled off from the adjoining residential area due to concerns about crime and terrorism. New, taller buildings have blocked distant views of Wisma Dharmala, and the pedestrian approach to the building is difficult because of the noise and traffic along the multi-lane Jenderal Sudirman. Nevertheless, the tower was Rudolph's best building in Asia for various reasons: its striking appearance; its engagement with Indonesia and its culture; and its anticipation of the sustainable skyscraper, particularly in a tropical climate. Unlike some of Rudolph's

241

other Asian clients, Wisma Dharmala seemed committed to the tower over the long term. The corporation renamed itself Intiland in the late 1990s and changed the name of their Jakarta tower to reflect this.

Overall, however, neither Wisma Dharmala nor Rudolph's other Asian buildings captured the attention or admiration of his Western colleagues. Articles about them by long-time friends such as Mildred Schmertz and the scholar Robert Bruegmann, Nora Leung's book about the Bond Centre, and efforts by other supporters were unable to return Rudolph to the forefront of architecture during his final years. He exhibited his Asian projects at museums in Chicago and New York in the late 1980s and early 1990s.[54] Though many in the architectural community still had strong doubts about Rudolph's work, these shows demonstrated that he had become an "old master" in the pantheon of modernism.

Although he had few new projects and was ill, Rudolph continued to work doggedly during his last two years. He made a final journey to Asia in the spring of 1996 to see clients and make progress on a few projects that were nearing completion, namely the Eu House in Singapore (1994–97) and an office building in Surabaya, Indonesia, for Intiland (1994–97). He worked on details for them daily, even as his condition worsened, and they were finished posthumously. When he passed away in the summer of 1997, obituaries in the architectural and national media celebrated his remarkable body of work and acknowledged his larger importance. The critic Michael Sorkin wrote in *Architectural Record* that

"Paul Rudolph was the greatest American architect of his generation, the most unself-conscious, the most direct." His vicissitudes were seen as key for understanding architecture's postwar trajectory and the broader sweep of history. The *New York Times* architecture critic Herbert Muschamp wrote that Rudolph's "loss of prestige came to represent the collapse of the liberal consensus culture under assault from left and right." Misgivings were voiced about how he had been treated during his last decades by colleagues and critics.[55] It was clear from these comments that Rudolph was a significant figure for modern architecture who was due for a more balanced critical appraisal.

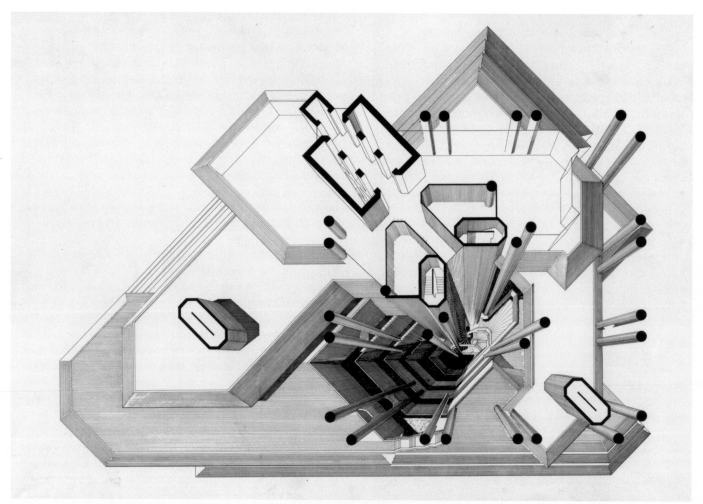

9.24 Typical floor plan in perspective with courtyard at center, Wisma Dharmala Tower.

9.25 Covered courtyard, Wisma Dharmala Tower.

Conclusion
Reevaluating Rudolph

Although many critics saw him as eclectic and self-indulgent, and Rudolph was himself proudly defiant in his later years about being "out of sync" with the times, in retrospect his architecture perfectly embodied the concerns of his era: a Florida vacation house symbolized the liberating joys of the postwar era in its swooping form, a monumental concrete civic structure expressed the grand aspirations of the liberal consensus, and an Asian skyscraper reflected the shaky finances of the newly globalized economy with a torsioned frame. Rudolph's focus on subjects such as decoration and symbolism anticipated many of the preoccupations of postmodernism, and his interest in natural ways of ventilating and cooling buildings predicted the twenty-first century's concern with sustainability.

The trajectory of Rudolph's career and his changing reputation illuminate not only shifts in architecture but the larger vagaries of fame. By the standards of the twenty-first century, the level of expression achieved by Rudolph is almost typical, rather than extraordinary. It is taken for granted that an architect puts his imprint on a project. Completed in 1997, the year Rudolph died, Frank Gehry's extravagantly expressive Guggenheim Bilbao (Bilbao, Spain, 1993–97) ushered in a new era of spectacular, singular buildings. Had he lived longer, Rudolph might have found new clients in China or Dubai who would have encouraged him to take his search for expression in even bolder directions. In the late 1990s, popular and critical opinion rediscovered Rudolph as it enthusiastically reembraced postwar modernism. Rudolph's primary and enduring themes patently warrant the twenty-first century's growing appreciation of his work.

Monumentality

Rudolph was one of the foremost developers of the expressive, concrete monumentality known as brutalism that became the primary language for modernist public buildings in the 1960s. Rudolph engaged with the program for the new monumentality formulated by Sigfried Giedion, Josep Lluís Sert, and Fernand Leger in the 1940s and reworked its points in his own fashion and as inflected by the humanism of Vincent Scully and A. Whitney Griswold at Yale. Rudolph found justification for his views about a monumentality based on his subjective viewpoint in Geoffrey Scott's *Architecture of Humanism*, a celebration of aesthetics, creativity, and the architect as artist, hero, and genius. Rudolph approached monumentality differently from others of his era because he focused on the human being rather than on the collective, thus reflecting the value Americans placed on individuality. His monumentality stimulated empathic reactions chiefly through spatial and representational means; its ethos had much in common with that of abstract expressionist painting.

The scale, roughened concrete surfaces, and complicated spatial sequences of Rudolph's buildings disquieted many users over the years; visitors today will probably see that Rudolph's buildings share many similarities to buildings that in the postwar era were considered more human or humane than his, such as those by Louis Kahn. Although Rudolph's monumentality was considered a failure by the late 1960s, that evaluation says more about his times than it does about his buildings. The many crises that beset the Yale Art & Architecture Building and the incomplete and poorly maintained state of the Boston Government Service Center and other works suggest that what may actually have failed was the will of the society that built such edifices. The brooding, opaque structures of postwar brutalism are considered unattractive, but aversion to them also stems from their association with government. The discrediting of government since the early 1970s by both the politically left and right has made it difficult to conceive of or appreciate civic architecture, much less monumentality.

Urbanism

Integrally related to Rudolph's monumentality was his urbanism. His attitude to the city was notable for an awareness of the existing context, as was demonstrated by the Yale A & A Building's nuanced relationship to its surroundings. Drawing on the forms of traditional Italian cities, Camillo Sitte's thinking about artistic city planning, and postwar concepts such as Sert's city core, Rudolph sought to formulate an emotionally resonant, intuitive urbanism with impressive, compelling, scenographic qualities. His approach contrasted with the urbanism typical of immediate postwar planning, which was objective in tone and often based on research in the social sciences. He rejected the freestanding superblock-amid-greenery model popularized by Le Corbusier in favor of the denser urbanism of historic cities. Rudolph acknowledged traditional buildings and traditional urban forms at a time when modernism had difficulty engaging with architecture that preceded it. He anticipated the contextual approach to urbanism associated with postmodernism, but disdained its literalism. He was involved with some of the most important urban redevelopment projects of the 1960s, but took exception to their approaches. Projects such as his Boston Government Service Center and New York Graphic Arts Center critiqued the master planning strategies of the day.

Rudolph's urbanism has both strong and weak points. Projects often considered unwieldy, even unmanageable, in scale, such as the Boston Government Service Center, engaged with the city in specific and interesting, if largely aesthetic, ways. Rudolph proportioned his buildings in relation to passing pedestrians; structures that were large in scope reflected the increasing scale of the twentieth century. Experimental projects, for example Rudolph's City Corridor, express a romantic, if overwrought, appreciation for the city rather than the authoritarian tendencies they were criticized for at the time. On the other hand, he paid little attention to the social life of cities, which Jane Jacobs said should be the primary consideration for urban planning. Despite hopes to improve and humanize the city, attempts by Rudolph and his contemporaries to create public spaces often inadvertently exacerbated isolation and alienation, the very things that they were intended to overcome. As is true of his expression and monumentality, reappraisal of Rudolph's approach to urbanism will doubtless prove productive.

Symbolism and Decoration

Rudolph's experiments with symbolism and decoration were closely intertwined and met with varying degrees of success. In pursuing them, Rudolph upheld the aesthetic and the creative, subjects that troubled modernism in the 1940s and early 1950s. Reflecting the thinking of Matthew Nowicki and more distantly Eugène Viollet-le-Duc, Rudolph's investigations of "symbols of structure" in the mid- and late 1950s advanced symbolism in architecture to a more complicated representational level. Concepts put forth in his unbuilt schemes for the Jewett Arts Center at Wellesley, which integrated symbols, structures, and services to form a weave or mesh with decorative qualities, were realized in his Boston Blue Cross and Blue Shield Building. As proved problematic for abstract expressionism, which employed a similar archetypal symbolism, the meaning of Rudolph's symbols, such as his pinwheels and gateways, was often inchoate to the broader public and sometimes to those in architecture as well.

Rudolph's thinking about symbolism and structure related to his approach to decoration, a subject virtually prohibited by modernism, which is one of the most intriguing and least understood aspects of his work. It is especially complex because it involved yet other subjects, like new materials and prefabrication. As is evident in his undergraduate thesis from the Alabama Polytechnic Institute, Rudolph had long been preoccupied with using new materials to make decoration. His diverse experiments ranged from his handful of decorative murals to sunscreens, bush-hammered, corrugated concrete surfaces, fluted concrete blocks, and brightly colored carpeted floors. His mural projects manifested a relationship between decoration and representation of the male figure and sexuality, along with other related themes, such as heroism and struggle. Though homosexuality was not something that Rudolph consciously wanted to express through his work, signs of it are evident and relevant, especially in relation to the architecture of some of the other leading homosexual architects of the period, such as Philip Johnson and Charles Moore.

Rudolph's experiments with symbolism and decoration had a deeper relationship to architectural discourse than has been recognized. His engagement with concepts such as the construction of decoration in relationship to Augustus Pugin's decoration of construction demonstrates where his buildings may be sited within the longer continuum of architecture and its problems. Of all his contemporaries, he was probably the most engaged with postwar modernism's agenda of forging an expressive architecture as an alternative to functionalism and the International Style. In his attempts to create buildings that were forceful and cohesive with strong plastic qualities, Rudolph blurred the line between structure, symbols, and decoration. His buildings became expressive forms resembling large-scale decorations or sculpture, a tendency of postwar American architecture particularly evident in his Crawford Manor in New Haven and Eero Saarinen's TWA Terminal, among others. Rudolph's experiments with expression, symbolism, and decoration at Crawford Manor, and the manner in which they were assessed in Venturi, Scott Brown, and Izenour's *Learning from Las Vegas,* were taken up again in the 1990s, as for example in the patterned surfaces created by Herzog & de Meuron.

Legacies

Rudolph and his work are of interest for more than his engagement with monumentality, urbanism, symbolism, and decoration. His teaching, his methods of practice, his carefully crafted delineations of his buildings, and his development of his own image as a bold maverick were all ways in which he upheld individuality and self-expression. These contributions to the architecture culture of Rudolph's day were as important as his buildings and have informed it ever since.

He left no identifiable Rudolph School behind him, yet evidence of his thinking is apparent in the work of his students. His tolerance and encouragement of different types of architecture likely enabled his students to practice it in diverse, even opposing, ways. The external structure and brightly painted ducts of the Centre Pompidou (Paris, 1971–77), by Rudolph's student Richard Rogers in collaboration with Renzo Piano, may be a conceptual echo of the symbolic structural system of Rudolph's Blue Cross and Blue Shield Building. Norman Foster has consistently represented his projects with the perspective section, a favorite of Rudolph's. Though Robert A. M. Stern, a traditionalist in his own work, had misgivings about Rudolph's legacy and architecture in the early 1970s, once he became dean of the Yale School of Architecture in 1999, he reinvigorated the school by emphasizing manifold, innovative approaches to design, recalling Rudolph's similar emphasis on diversity at Yale years before.

Rudolph's management of his firm is an interesting case study in itself. He never expanded his atelier-like office into a large corporate one managed by partners, as was typical of his most ambitious contemporaries. Although this has appeared to have been a fatal misstep for him, in fact it may have been advantageous. Rudolph suggested a different, more flexible model for architectural practice in which an architect who had a distinctive style might move from firm to firm in the role of a consultant. Keeping one foot in teaching and one in practice, as Rudolph did in the 1950s and early 1960s, has become typical for many of the most innovative architects of the late twentieth and early twenty-first centuries. Rudolph was impressively prolific, completing over one hundred fifty buildings and designing an almost equal number of unbuilt ones over five decades of practice. If productivity is a standard for success, then Rudolph was a bigger success than many of his contemporaries.

Rudolph's distinctive method of rendering and use of forms such as the perspective section were widely emulated in the 1960s and for some years after, suggesting the importance of representation for architecture in the postwar period. It was the image that he fashioned of himself as the crew-cut maverick of modernism that was one of his most important creations. As with so much about Rudolph, it was a double-edged sword: the public perception would link him to the Establishment in the minds of those who opposed it. Rudolph's heroic image and fame also anticipated the rise of the star architects of the 1980s and after, and is an aspect of his career that continues to intrigue.

Twenty-First-Century Recognition

Rudolph's buildings are increasingly appreciated in the early twenty-first century for their dramatic aesthetic and spatial qualities, the very things for which they were once reviled.[1] The revival of his reputation began with the rediscovery of his Florida houses in the early 1990s by architects and interior designers; other major architects and designers of the era, such as Saarinen and Charles and Ray Eames, were likewise subject to reappraisal at that time. The American architectural establishment that fostered and then spurned Rudolph has reembraced him, and the popular and architectural press of the U.S. Northeast has followed suit. Regular references to Rudolph appear in the *New York Times*, *New York Magazine*, architectural journals, and popular home design magazines. The architect himself is remembered, somewhat romantically, as a tragic figure, a martyr to the modernist cause.

Rudolph's monumental buildings fascinate a new generation. Although many observers still find the concrete monumentality of the 1960s ugly or overbearing, young architects envy the bold architectural achievements of the 1950s and 1960s—in part because few large-scale civic structures are being built, with the exception of museums, in the early twenty-first century (partly as a result of the long fallout from the collapse of the liberal consensus), and in part because remarkable expressive forms prevail in architecture once more. A 2009 exhibition in Boston by a group of young architects extolled the city's 1960s concrete buildings, including Rudolph's Government Service Center, and proposed calling them "heroic" rather than brutalist.[2] A website devoted to brutalism celebrates Rudolph's buildings and similar ones by his contemporaries from around the world.[3]

The academy, too, has rediscovered Rudolph. Architectural historians refer to Rudolph and his work with increasing frequency as they attempt to explain postwar modernism, and they study the preservation of modernist buildings, a problem that has arisen as the buildings of the 1950s and 1960s age.[4] Architecture schools have used projects by Rudolph as the basis for studio assignments, such as a 2011 studio at Harvard's GSD that proposed an addition to the Boston Government Service Center. Projects such as City Corridor appeal again at a time when building big has become rare for twenty-first-century America, except for convention centers, stadiums, big box chain stores, or Las Vegas developments. Students at the Cooper Union Institute in New York reconstructed the

10.1 Chris Mottalini photographed Rudolph's Micheels House (Westport, Connecticut, 1972) shortly before its 2007 demolition.

Conclusion

246

10.2 Rudolph Hall, formerly the Yale A & A Building, was restored and expanded with a new wing by Charles Gwathmey in 2009.

enormous model of City Corridor in 2010, a demonstration of renewed wonder at Rudolph's boldness.[5]

Modernist Preservation

Despite the reappraisal of Rudolph's architecture, his buildings have suffered, especially during the real estate boom of the early twenty-first century. Several early houses in Florida aged badly and were demolished. New buyers uninterested in Rudolph or modernism demolished others. Yet a few have been restored. Lost in an early 1960s hurricane, the Hiss House's umbrella was rebuilt in 2010.

Rudolph's threatened buildings became rallying points for the nascent modernist preservation movement in the 1990s and 2000s. In 2002, Ernst Wagner established the Paul Rudolph Foundation to commemorate Rudolph and serve as a watchdog to protect his legacy. The Rudolph Foundation and Docomomo, the international group devoted to preserving important modernist works, fought to save structures such as the Cerrito House in Watch Hill, Rhode Island (1956), Micheels House in Westport, Connecticut (1972), and Riverview High School in Sarasota, Florida (1957–58)—unsuccessful efforts all. The destruction of these buildings seemed to symbolize the discarding of postwar modernism itself, inspiring the photographer Chris Mottalini to photograph the last days of these doomed works (figure 10.1).[6] Other Rudolph buildings were spared by the recession that began in

2008: the Blue Cross and Blue Shield Building in Boston was almost replaced by a tower the size of the Empire State Building. The Orange County Government Center (Goshen, New York, 1963–71) also narrowly escaped demolition.[7] In some quarters, Rudolph's buildings are still decried for their functional drawbacks, but their potential is being reassessed. Innovative developers renovated Rudolph's Endo Labs on Long Island (Garden City, New York, 1960-64), understanding that its turrets, corrugated concrete walls, and baroque-inspired staircases could attract creative tenants.[8]

The Yale Art & Architecture Building provides an especially significant success story. The changing fortunes of the structure serve as an index to understanding Rudolph's changing reputation. The A & A was renovated, at a cost of $126 million, between 2007 and 2008. Rudolph's former students and supporters led the effort to restore the building, complete with orange carpeting. Stern spearheaded the campaign for preservation; Sid Bass contributed the majority of funds for restoration; and Charles Gwathmey carried out the renovation and designed an addition to its north side for the art history department and the art and architecture library, expanding the building as Rudolph had anticipated (figure 10.2).

Gwathmey corrected problems that dated from its completion. He installed air-conditioning and removed all traces of the ill-conceived, post-fire renovations, such as the partitions that blocked sight lines within the building.

Conclusion   248

Most importantly, the university provided other accommodations for the studio art and other departments, leaving the original building completely to the school of architecture and alleviating the overcrowding that had been one of its greatest drawbacks. The building was renovated with practicality in mind: many of its original qualities were preserved or re-created, but not every single aspect. A replica of the Minerva statue was reinstated in the drafting room, while a code governing how students can alter their desk areas preserves the openness of the space. The building will not be preserved like a relic. Rudolph Hall—the name was requested by Sid Bass—will be allowed to change over time. And it will provoke new generations of students, whether they admire the building or not, to think about the complexity of architecture, forever fulfilling Rudolph's stated intentions.

Buildings and Projects
by Paul Rudolph

Project = unbuilt

Paul Rudolph in Collaboration with Ralph Twitchell

1941	Ralph Twitchell House, Siesta Key, Florida
1946	Alexander Harkavy House, Siesta Key, Florida
1946	Miller Boat House, Casey Key, Florida, project
1946–47	Denman House, Siesta Key, Florida
1947	Goar House, Sarasota, Florida, project
1947	Shute House, Siesta Key, Florida, project
1947	Guest House for Roberta Healy Finney, Siesta Key, Florida, project
1947–48	Miller House, Casey Key, Florida
1947–48	Russell House, Sarasota, Florida
1947–48	Steinmetz Studio, Sarasota, Florida
1947–48	Recreation Center, St. Petersburg, Florida, project
1947–51	Lucienne Twitchell House, Martha's Vineyard, Massachusetts
1948	Siegrist House, Venice, Florida
1948	Revere Quality House, Siesta Key, Florida
1948	Revere Development, Siesta Key, Florida, project
1948	Lamolithic Houses, Siesta Key, Florida
1948–49	Deeds House, Siesta Key, Florida
1948–50	Healy "Cocoon" Guest House, Siesta Key, Florida
1949–50	Burnette House, Sarasota, Florida
1949	Miller Guest House, Casey Key, Florida
1949–51	Bennett House, Bradenton, Florida
1950	Beach Pavilion, site unknown, project
1950–51	Kerr House, Melbourne Beach, Florida
1950–51	Cheatham Swimming Pool, Lakeland, Florida
1950–51	Watson House, Gainesville, Florida
1950–51	Leavengood House, St. Petersburg, Florida
1951	Knott House, Yankeetown, Florida, project
1951	Walker House, Sanibel Island, Florida, project
1951	Coward House, Siesta Key, Florida
1951	Wheelan Cottages, Siesta Key, Florida
1951–52	Haskins House, Sarasota, Florida
1951–52	Maehlman Guest House, Naples, Florida
1951–53	Rubin House, Pensacola, Florida

Paul Rudolph, Architect

Note: Associated architects have not been listed.

1940	T. P. Atkinson House, Auburn, Alabama
1952	SAE Fraternity House, Miami, Florida, project
1952	Good Design, installation designed by Rudolph for exhibition curated by Edgar Kaufmann, Jr., Merchandise Mart, Chicago, Illinois, and Museum of Modern Art, New York
1952–53	Hook House, Siesta Key, Florida
1952–53	Sanderling Beach Club, Siesta Key, Florida
1952–53	Floating Islands, Leesburg, Florida, project
1952–53	Hayward Apartments, Siesta Key, Florida, project

1952–53	Walker Guest House, Sanibel Island, Florida
1953	Davidson House, Bradenton, Florida
1953	Stroud and Boyd Development, Sarasota, Florida, project
1953	Bourne House, St. Petersburg, Florida, project
1953–54	Davis House, Sarasota, Florida
1953–54	Wilson House, Sarasota, Florida
1953–54	Burgess House, Burgess Island, Florida, project
1953–55	Cohen House, Siesta Key, Florida
1954	Alex Miller House, Sarasota, Florida, project
1954	Hiss "Umbrella" House, Sarasota, Florida
1954	Family of Man, installation designed by Rudolph for exhibition curated by Edward Steichen, Museum of Modern Art, New York
1954–55	Tastee-Freez, Sarasota, Florida
1954–58	United States Embassy, Amman, Jordan, project
1955	Experimental School for Plywood Association, project
1955	Grand Rapids Homestyle Center House, Grand Rapids, Michigan, project
1955–56	Taylor House, Venice, Florida, project
1955–56	Sarasota-Bradenton Airport, Florida, project
1955–58	Jewett Arts Center, Wellesley College, Wellesley, Massachusetts
1955–58	Stinnett House, Sarasota, Florida
1955–58	Biggs House, Delray Beach, Florida
1956	Fletcher House, Venice, Florida
1956	Applebee House, Auburn, Alabama
1956	Yanofsky House, Newton, Massachusetts
1956	Woman's Home Companion House, Warson Woods, Missouri
1956	Donut Stand, Tampa, Florida, project
1956	Public Beach Development, Siesta Key, Florida, project
1956	Bramlett Company Building, Miami, Florida, project
1956	St. Boniface Episcopal Church, Siesta Key, Florida, project
1956–57	Burkhardt House, Casey Key, Florida
1957	Martin House, Athens, Alabama
1957–58	Harkavy House, Lido Shores, Florida
1957–58	Riverview High School, Sarasota, Florida
1957–59	Greeley Memorial Forestry Laboratory, Yale University, New Haven, Connecticut
1957–60	Blue Cross and Blue Shield Building, Boston, Massachusetts
1958	Master Plan for Tuskegee Institute, Tuskegee, Alabama, project
1958	Liggett House, Tampa, Florida
1958	McCandlish House, Cambridge, Massachusetts
1958–60	Sarasota Senior High School, Sarasota, Florida
1958–60	First New Haven National Bank, New Haven, Connecticut, project
1958–60	Church Street Redevelopment, New Haven, Connecticut, project

11.1 Rudolph at Sanderling Beach Club (Siesta Key, Florida, 1952–53).

1958–61	Kappa Sigma Fraternity House, Auburn University, Auburn, Alabama
1958–63	Temple Street Parking Garage, New Haven, Connecticut
1958–63	Yale University Art & Architecture Building (now Rudolph Hall), New Haven, Connecticut
1959	Addition to Payne-Whitney Gymnasium, Yale University, Connecticut, project
1959	Fullham House, Newtown, Pennsylvania
1959–60	May Memorial Unitarian Church, Syracuse, New York, project
1959–61	Milam House, Ponte Vedra, Florida
1960	Experimental Theater for Ford Foundation, project
1960	Friedberg Residence, Baltimore, Maryland
1960	Portland Cement Company Theme Center for 1964 New York World's Fair, Flushing, New York
1960	Daisley House, Ocean Ridge, Florida
1960	Pi Kappa Phi Fraternity House, University of Florida, Gainesville, Florida, project
1960	Lake Region Yacht Club, Winter Haven, Florida
1960	O'Brien's Motor Inn, Waverly, New York, project
1960–61	Married Student Housing, Yale University, New Haven, Connecticut
1960–64	Endo Laboratories, Garden City, Long Island, New York
1960–69	Interdenominational Chapel, Tuskegee Institute, Tuskegee, Alabama
1961	Boston City Hall Competition, project
1961	Silvas House, Greenwich, Connecticut
1961	Wallace House, Athens, Alabama
1961	Addition to Juvenile Detention Home, Bridgeport, Connecticut
1961	Paul Rudolph House and Office, 31 High Street, New Haven, Connecticut
1961	Additions to office and cafeteria for CIBA Pharmaceutical Company, Summit, New Jersey, project
1961	Manager's Office for Parking Authority, City of New Haven, Connecticut, project
1962	Bostwick House, Palm Beach, Florida, project
1962	Master Plan and Library for Guilford Free Library Association, Guilford, Connecticut, project
1962	Hotchkiss School, Master Plan, two dormitories, auditorium building, and classroom building, Lakeville, Connecticut, project
1962–66	IBM Research and Manufacturing Facilities, East Fishkill, New York
1962–66	Crawford Manor Housing for the Elderly, New Haven, Connecticut
1962–67	Christian Science Student Center, University of Illinois, Urbana, Illinois
1962–71	Mental Health Building (now Lindemann Mental Health Center), Boston Government Service Center, Boston, Massachusetts, design consultant for Desmond and Lord, Boston
1962–71	Health, Education and Welfare Tower, Boston Government Service Center, Boston, Massachusetts, design consultant for Desmond and Lord, Boston, project
1962–71	Boston Government Service Center, coordinating architect, Boston, Massachusetts
1963	Master Plan for Southeastern Massachusetts Technological Institute, Dartmouth, Massachusetts
1963–65	Humanities I, Southeastern Massachusetts Technological Institute, Dartmouth, Massachusetts
1963–66	Charles A. Dana Creative Arts Center, Colgate University, Hamilton, New York
1963–66	Apartment Building for Beneficent House, Weybosset Hill Housing, Providence, Rhode Island
1963–71	Orange County Government Center, Goshen, New York
1964	Syracuse City Hall, Syracuse, New York, project
1965	International Bazaar for the International Area of Interama, Miami, Florida, project
1965	Callahan House, Birmingham, Alabama, project
1965	Competition entry for Franklin Delano Roosevelt Memorial, Washington, D.C., project
1964–65	Paul Rudolph Office, New York
1964–69	John W. Chorley Elementary School, Middletown, New York
1965	House for Mr. Stanley Kinney, Hamilton, New York, project
1965	New Art Building for the Manoa Campus of the University of Hawaii, Honolulu, Hawaii, project
1965–75	Master Plan and buildings for East Pakistan Agricultural University, Mymensingh, Bangladesh
1966	Master Plan and buildings for Stafford Harbor, Virginia, project
1966	Monteith College Center for Wayne State University, Detroit, Michigan, project
1966	High School, New Canaan, Connecticut, project
1966	Master Plan and Three Office Buildings for Brookhollow Corporation, Dallas
1966	John Jay Park for Department of Parks, New York, project
1966	Master Plan, Northwest #1 Urban Renewal Area, Washington, D.C., project
1966	Caspi Penthouse, New York, project
1966	Addition to Beth El Synagogue, New London, Connecticut
1966–67	Alexander Hirsch House, New York
1966–71	Sid W. Richardson Physical Sciences Building, Texas Christian University, Forth Worth, Texas
1967	Married Student Housing, Charlottesville, Virginia, project
1967	Graphic Arts Center, New York, project
1967	Parcells House, Grosse Pointe, Michigan
1967	Brown House, New York
1967	Dental Office for Dr. Nathan Shore, New York

11.2 Rudolph, Tastee-Freez Ice Cream Stand (Sarasota, Florida, 1954–55).

1967	Three Parks and Playgrounds for Department of Parks, New York, project
1967	Mrs. Henry J. Kaiser Apartment, New York
1967	Davidson Houses, two apartment houses for New York City Housing Authority, Bronx, New York
1967	Fox Hill Development, apartments, school, commercial center, Staten Island, New York
1967–72	City Corridor and Lower Manhattan Expressway (LOMEX), New York, project
1967–74	Tracey Towers, Bronx, New York
1967–77	Paul Rudolph Apartment, 23 Beekman Place, New York
1968	Stadium, Dammam, Saudi Arabia, project
1968	Magnolia Homes Housing, Vicksburg, Mississippi, project
1968	Fort Lincoln Housing, Washington, D.C., project
1968	Green House, Cherry Ridge, Pennsylvania
1968	Study of the uses of extruded cement asbestos for United States Plywood, New York, project
1968	First and Second Church, Boston, Massachusetts
1968–71	Oriental Masonic Gardens, New Haven, Connecticut
1968–72	Student Union for Southeastern Massachusetts Technical Institute, Dartmouth, Massachusetts
1968–81	New Haven Government Center, New Haven, Connecticut, project
1969	Raich House, Quogue, New York, project
1969	Lewis House, Boston, Massachusetts, project
1969	Pistell House, Lyford Cay, Nassau, Bahamas, project
1969	Cowles Apartment, New York
1969	Hospital Trust Tower, Providence, Rhode Island, project
1969–70	Deane House, Great Neck, New York
1969–71	Natural Science Building, State University of New York, Purchase, New York
1969–72	Burroughs Wellcome Corporate Headquarters and related research facilities, Research Triangle Park, North Carolina
1969–74	Earl W. Brydges Library, Niagara Falls, New York
1969–77	Buffalo Waterfront and Shoreline Apartments, Buffalo, New York
1970	Ten Apartment Towers, Kew Gardens, New York, 1970, project
1970	Rockford Civic Center, Rockford, Illinois, project
1970	Shuey House, Bloomfield Hills, Michigan, project
1970	Davidson House, Bloomfield Hills, Michigan, project
1970	Suffolk Office Park, Hauppauge, Long Island, New York, project
1970	Edersheim Apartment, New York
1970–72	Bass House, Fort Worth, Texas
1970—72	Five Units of Public Housing, New York State Urban Redevelopment Corporation, New York, project
1971	Urban Complex for Fakhri Brothers, Beirut, Lebanon, project
1971	Dweck House, Deal, New Jersey
1971	Elman Apartment, New York
1971	Daiei House Building, Nagoya, Japan

1972	Micheels House, Westport, Connecticut
1972	Pillsbury House, Cannes, France, project
1972	Rogers House, Houston, project
1972	Office Building, Madrid, Spain, project
1972	Edersheim Office, Drexel, Burnham & Company, New York
1972	Staten Island Community College, Staten Island, New York, project
1973	East Northport Jewish Center, East Northport, New York, project
1973	Dormitory, Davidson College, Davidson, North Carolina, project
1973	3500 Dwelling Units, Miami, Florida, project
1973	Staller House, Lloyd Harbor, New York
1973	Modular Housing Exhibition, [no site], project
1973	East Northport Jewish Center Synagogue and Master Plan, project
1973–74	Joanna Steichen Apartment, New York
1974	Renovations to Aston Magna, Elman House, Great Barrington, Massachusetts
1974	Apartment Hotel, Jerusalem, Israel, project
1974	Morgan Annex Housing, New York, project
1974	Morgan House, Aspen, Colorado, project
1974	Renovation of Pitts Theological Library, Candler School of Theology, Emory University, Atlanta
1975	Strutin Apartment, New Rochelle, New York
1975	Houston House, Westerly, Rhode Island
1975–81	William R. Cannon Chapel, Emory University, Atlanta
1976	Addition to Burroughs Wellcome Corporation Headquarters, Research Triangle Park, North Carolina
1976–78	Bernhard House, addition, Greenwich, Connecticut
1977	Fein House, addition, Sands Point, New York
1977–97	Paul Rudolph Penthouse, 23 Beekman Place, New York
1978	Benjamin Apartment, New York
1978	Carrillo Apartment, New York, project
1978	Hedaya House, Deal, New Jersey
1978	Young House, Livingston Manor, New York, project
1978	Siegel House remodeling, Westhampton Beach, New York, project
1978	Zucker Townhouse remodeling, New York
1978	Harrington Cancer Care Center, Amarillo, Texas
1978	Master Plan and New Campus Entrance for Tuskegee University, Tuskegee, Alabama, project
1979	Marina Center, Singapore, project
1979	Palmer Road, residential and shopping complex, Singapore, project
1979	74-Unit Apartment Building, Singapore, project
1979–83	City Center, Fort Worth, Texas
1979–94	The Concourse, Singapore, project
1980	Ten Condominiums for Hong Fok Investment, Hong Kong, project
1980	Kwee House, Singapore, project

11.3 Rudolph, Endo Laboratories (Garden City, Long Island, New York, 1960–64).

> 11.4 Rudolph, Milam House (Ponte Vedra, Florida, 1959–61).

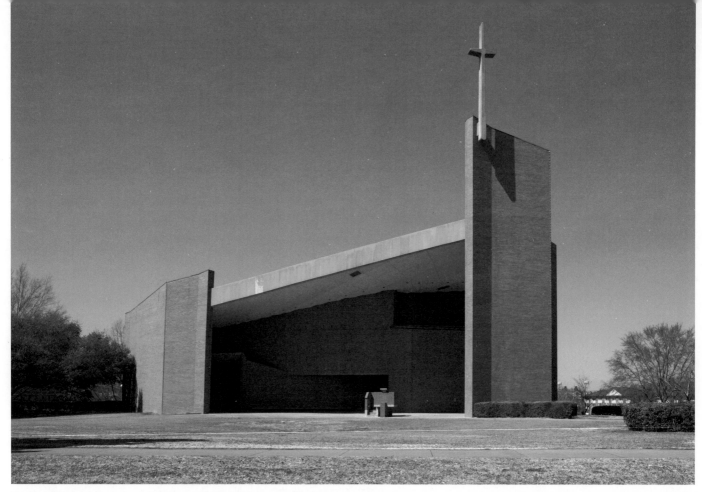

11.5 Rudolph, Interdenominational Chapel, Tuskegee University (Tuskegee, Alabama, 1960–69).

1980	Corporate Headquarters for Electronic Data Systems Corporation, Dallas, project
1980	Marsh Offices, Amarillo, Texas
1980	Channel 7 Television Station, Amarillo, Texas
1980–86	The Colonnade, Singapore
1981	Coffee Memorial Blood Bank, Amarillo, Texas, project
1981	Oxley Rise Condominium Housing, Singapore, project
1981	Sherman House, renovations and addition, Wilton, Connecticut
1981	Office Shopping Complex for Hong Fok, Singapore, project
1981	Cambridge Research and Development Group, office renovations, Westport, Connecticut, project
1982	Burroughs Wellcome Headquarters, south building expansion, Research Triangle Park, North Carolina
1982	Master Plan for Burroughs Wellcome Headquarters, Research Triangle Park, North Carolina, project
1982	Edersheim House alterations, Marmaroneck, New York
1982	Beverly Park Estates House, Beverly Hills, California, project
1982	General Daniel "Chappie" James Center for Aerospace Science and Health Education, Tuskegee University, Tuskegee, Alabama, project
1982	Floersheim-Strauss Apartment renovations, New York
1983	Rogers House renovations, Palm Beach, Florida, project
1983	Tobias House remodeling, Remsenburg, New York
1983–88	Wisma Dharmala Tower (now Intiland), Jakarta, Indonesia
1984	Glazer House, Los Angeles
1984	Pavarini House, Greenwich, Connecticut, project

1984	Tuttle House, Rock Hall, Maryland
1984–88	Bond Centre (now Lippo Centre), Hong Kong
1985	Licht House renovations, Hewlett Harbor, New York
1985	Macy's Department Store, Danbury, Connecticut, project
1985	Macy's Department Store, Birmingham, Alabama
1985	Hotel and Condominiums, Fisher Island, Miami, Florida, project
1985–89	Norman Dion Science and Engineering Building, Southeastern Massachusetts University, Dartmouth, Massachusetts
1986	Cheng Wai Keung, House, Singapore, project
1986	Murphy House, Greenwich, Connecticut, project
1986	Blue Cross and Blue Shield Building addition, Boston, Massachusetts, project
1986	Treistman House renovations and additions, Englewood, New Jersey
1987	Institution Hill Housing, Singapore, project
1988	Dreams and Details, Installation for exhibition of major works by Rudolph at Steelcase Design Partnership, New York
1989	Office and showroom, for Modulightor, New York
1989	"The Future," apartment building, New York
1989	United States Courthouse and Federal Municipal Office Building, New York, project
1989	Edersheim Guest House, Mamaroneck, New York
1989	Mark Edersheim Office, Drexel Burnham Lambert, New York
1989	Sino Land Company Tower, Hong Kong, project

11.6 Rudolph, Burroughs Wellcome Corporate Headquarters (Research Triangle Park, North Carolina, 1969–72).

1990	Cikini Office Building, Dharmala Group, Jakarta, Indonesia, project
1990	Gatot Subroto, Office Condominium, Jakarta, Indonesia, project
1990	Hotel and Office Building for Dharmala Group, Surabaya, Indonesia, project
1990	East Coast Surabaya, new town for 250,000 people, Dharmala Group, project
1990	International Building, Singapore, Hong Fok, project
1990	Medical Building, Pontiac Land Company, Singapore, project
1990	Harrington Cancer Care Center, Phase II, Amarillo, Texas, project
1990	Wee Ee Chao House, Singapore
1990	Waduk Melati, urban development project, Jakarta, Indonesia, project
1991	Edersheim House, addition, Marmaroneck, New York
1991	Fox-Firestone House, Sherman, Connecticut, project
1991	Brookhollow Office Towers, renovations, Dallas, project
1991	Contogouris House, New York, project
1993	Chapel for Maris Stella University, Singapore, project
1994	Formanek House, Memphis, Tennessee
1994	Engel House, addition, Harrison, New York
1994	Mark Edersheim Office, Smith Barney, New York
1994	Wee Duplex, Hong Kong, project
1994–97	Eu House, Singapore
1994–97	Wisma Dharmala Office Building (now Intiland), Surabaya, Indonesia
1995	Zucker House, Easthampton, Long Island, New York, project

11.7 Rudolph, Sino Land Company Tower (Hong Kong, project, 1989).

Notes

Abbreviations: Works from the Paul Rudolph Archive at the Library of Congress are preceded by the prefix PMR. Works from Manuscripts and Archives at Yale University are preceded by the prefix YMA.

Introduction: Rudolph's Search for Expression

1. "Bright New Arrival," *Time* 75 (February 1, 1960): 60.

2. Four especially relevant examples of this body of scholarship are Eric Mumford, *The CIAM Discourse on Urbanism, 1928–1960* (Cambridge: MIT Press, 2000); Sarah Goldhagen, *Louis Kahn's Situated Modernism* (New Haven: Yale University Press, 2001); Eeva-Liisa Pelkonen and Donald Albrecht, *Eero Saarinen: Shaping the Future* (New Haven: Yale University Press, 2006); and Alice T. Friedman, *American Glamour and the Evolution of Modern Architecture* (New Haven: Yale University Press, 2010).

3. Walter McQuade describes Rudolph's "personal search" in "The Exploded Landscape," *Perspecta* 7 (1961): 83; Vincent Scully, *American Architecture and Urbanism* (New York: Henry Holt, 1969, revised edition 1988), 202.

4. The best known discussion of the "genius hero" architect is in Andrew Saint, *The Image of the Architect* (New Haven: Yale University Press, 1983), 1–18.

5. Gerhard Kallmann, "The 'Action' Architecture of a New Generation," *Architectural Forum* 111 (October 1959): 134.

6. Neutra's attempts to work like a psychoanalyst have been discussed in Sylvia Lavin, *Form Follows Libido: Architecture and Richard Neutra in Psychoanalytic Culture* (Cambridge: MIT Press, 2004); Mark Jarzombek describes the impact of psychology on related disciplines and explores empathy in *The Psychologizing of Modernity: Art, Architecture and History* (Cambridge: Cambridge University Press, 2000).

7. Geoffrey Scott's popular book *The Architecture of Humanism: A Study in the History of Taste* (1914) was reprinted many times; page references herein are to the 1999 reprint by W. W. Norton, with a new introduction by Paul Barolsky.

8. Philip Johnson, lecture for Vincent Scully's modern architecture survey class, May 9, 1958, "Retreat from the International Style to the Present Scene," in *Philip Johnson Writings,* foreword by Vincent Scully, introduction by Peter Eisenman, commentary by Robert A. M. Stern (New York: Oxford University Press, 1979), 84–97.

9. Neil Levine discusses problems of structure and representation from the eighteenth through the twentieth century in *Modern Architecture: Representation and Reality* (New Haven: Yale University Press, 2009).

10. Robert A. M. Stern, *New Directions in Modern Architecture* (New York: George Braziller, 1969), 36.

11. Russell Bourne, "Yale's Paul Rudolph," *Architectural Forum* 108 (April 1958): 129.

12. The historical origins of the term "closeted" are unclear, but the term is best known from Eve Kosofsky Sedgwick's *Epistemology of the Closet* (Berkeley: University of California Press, 1990). More recent queer theory could open up new approaches to Rudolph's work .

13. Rudolph is not mentioned in Kenneth Frampton, *Modern Architecture: A Critical History* (London: Thames and Hudson, 1989, 3rd edition 1992). Two textbooks discuss Rudolph briefly but with reservations: William J. R. Curtis, *Modern Architecture since 1900* (London: Phaidon, 1982, 3rd edition 1996), 560; Leland Roth, *American Architecture: A History* (Boulder, Colo.: Westview Press, 2001), 446–47.

14. Timothy M. Rohan, "Architecture in the Age of Alienation: The Academic Buildings of Paul Rudolph" (PhD diss., Harvard University, 2001); dissertation committee: Neil Levine, Yve-Alain Bois, Sarah Williams Goldhagen.

15. My estimates of the numbers of Rudolph's built works and unbuilt projects are conservative. They are based on his own project lists and lists compiled at the Library of Congress. However, the number of works by Rudolph will probably rise in the future as more information emerges about projects in the Rudolph Archive at the Library of Congress that are fragmentary and whose sites and dates are difficult to determine.

One. Origins

1. Robin Middleton, "Disintegration," *Architectural Design* 37 (May 1967): 204.

2. Rudolph's mother tells anecdotes about his childhood in Andrew Sparks, "His Architecture May Change Tomorrow's Cities," *Atlanta Journal and Constitution Magazine* (March 31, 1968), 23–31; author's interview with Rudolph's sister Marie Murphy, January 5, 2003.

3. Sparks, "His Architecture May Change Tomorrow's Cities," 24; Murphy interview.

4. Jeanne M. Davern, "A Conversation with Paul Rudolph," *Architectural Record* 170 (March 1982): 92.

5. Author's interview with Frances Garth Wallace, January 7, 2003, who studied with Rudolph in Ida O'Keeffe's class.

6. "Paul," *Crow's Nest* (May 2, 1936), 2.

7. Ibid.; Wallace interview.

8. Rudolph dismisses his API education in Paul Rudolph, *The Architecture of Paul Rudolph*, with an introduction by Sibyl Moholy-Nagy, captions by Gerhard Schwab, and comments by Paul Rudolph (New York: Praeger, 1970), 90. He speaks favorably of Beaux-Arts urbanism in Paul Rudolph, "The Six Determinants of Architectural Form," *Architectural Record* 120 (October 1956): 183.

9. Burkhardt knew the architectural vernacular because he supervised the Historic American Buildings Survey (HABS) for Alabama, which was completed just as Rudolph enrolled at API. See Robert Gamble, *The Alabama Catalog: A Guide to the Early Architecture of the State* (Tuscaloosa: University of Alabama Press, 1987), 177–87.

10. Rudolph describes visiting the Rosenbaum House in "Excerpts from a Conversation," *Perspecta* 22 (1986): 103–4.

11. Henry-Russell Hitchcock and Philip Johnson, *The International Style: Architecture since 1922* (New York: Museum of Modern Art, first published 1932; 1995 edition), 43.

12. Hitchcock and Johnson, *International Style*, 81–89.

13. Paul Rudolph, *Glass in Architecture and Decoration*. Undergraduate thesis, Alabama Polytechnic Institute, 1940, Special Collections, Auburn University, unpaginated.

14. One popular manifestation of expressionism in American art during the 1920s and 1930s was Lynd Ward's woodcut novels with grandiose themes, including *Gods' Man* (1929) and *Vertigo* (1937). See the reprints of both edited by Art Spiegelman (New York: Library of America, 2010).

15. To better understand the strains homosexual men of Rudolph's generation experienced, see Robert J. Gober, *Homosexuality in Postwar America: Resistance and the Crisis of Masculinity* (Durham, N.C.: Duke University Press, 1997).

16. Rudolph explains why he chose Harvard in Stephanie Williams, "Class of '44," *World Architecture* 19 (September 1992): 30.

17. William Rupp, Rudolph's employee when he relocated to Sarasota, says that Rudolph was left "literally speechless for a year" by the daily tasks of working in the Birmingham office; "Paul Rudolph (PMR): A Brief Biography," in "Paul Rudolph: The Florida Years," an unpublished paper written for Professor Paul Norton at the University of Massachusetts, Amherst, 1978, unpaginated.

18. Letter from Rudolph to Twitchell's secretary, Lu Andrews, November 17, 1941; courtesy of John Howey.

19. "Wins Scholarship," *Nashville Tennessean* (May 11, 1941), B-9. The article appeared in a Tennessee newspaper because Rudolph's father had left Athens College to become president of Pulaski College, Pulaski, Tennessee, another Methodist institution, around 1940.

20. Correspondence in Rudolph's file at Harvard's GSD indicates that he had a $500 scholarship. His transcript shows that he fulfilled the degree with four studio problems taken at the GSD in fall 1941 and early 1942, and fall 1946 and early 1947. Harvard fall semesters began in September and ended in February. Paul Rudolph File, Graduate School of Design, Registrar's Office, Harvard University.

21. Author's interview with Philip Johnson, March 10, 1998; author's interview with Victor Lundy, October 11, 2006. Admission to Gropius's studio was competitive; see Jill Pearlman, *Inventing American Modernism: Joseph Hudnut, Walter Gropius, and the Bauhaus Legacy at Harvard* (Charlottesville: University of Virginia Press, 2007), 108. For a history of the GSD, see Anthony Alofsin, *The Struggle for Modernism: Architecture, Landscape Architecture, and City Planning at Harvard* (New York: W. W. Norton, 2002).

22. Rudolph remarks about the importance for him of Giedion's book in William Marlin, "Paul Rudolph: Drawings," *Architectural Forum* 138 (June 1973): 50. Rudolph talks about Gropius and the "new space concept" in Paul Rudolph, "3 New Directions: Paul Rudolph, Philip Johnson, Buckminster Fuller," *Perspecta* 1 (1952): 21.

23. Gilbert Herbert, *The Dream of the Factory-Made House: Walter Gropius and Konrad Wachsmann* (Cambridge: MIT Press, 1984), 243–99.

24. Rudolph discusses what influenced him at the GSD, including Wachsmann, in Rudolph, "3 New Directions."

25. James Lamantia (GSD, class of 1949) knew Rudolph and remembered that Wright was almost never discussed at the GSD; author's interview with Lamantia, May 27, 2009. Alofsin (*Struggle for Modernism,* 176) notes that Wright was "off limits to students as a model."

26. Rudolph, "3 New Directions," 21.

27. Rudolph explains the evolution of his drawing methods in Paul Rudolph, "From Conception to Sketch to Rendering to Building," *Paul Rudolph: Architectural Drawings,* edited by Yukio Futagawa (New York: Architectural Book Publishing Company, 1972), 11–12.

28. Charles Kaiser, *The Gay Metropolis, 1940-1996* (New York: Houghton Mifflin, 1997); Alan Bérubé, *Coming Out Under Fire: The History of Gay Men and Women in World War Two* (New York: Free Press, 1990).

29. Author's interview with Peter Blake, October 15, 1997.

30. Kurt W. Forster, "Hey, Sailor: A Brief Memoir of the Long Life and Short Fame of Paul Rudolph," *ANY* 21 (1997): 13.

31. A long-time friend of Rudolph's, Peter Blake was a journalist and curator at MoMA in the 1940s. He discussed MoMA and the significance of its homosexual circles, which included Philip Johnson, Arthur Drexler, and Rudolph, with the author in an interview, October 15, 1997. He elaborates on this subject in his book *No Place Like Utopia* (New York: W. W. Norton, 1993), 132–35.

32. Eugene R. Gaddis, *Magician of the Modern: Chick Austin and the Transformation of the Arts in America* (New York: Alfred Knopf, 2000). Austin brought Hitchcock, McAndrew, and other northeastern academics to the Ringling Museum for a three-week seminar about modern architecture in April 1948 (Gaddis, 392).

33. For Rudolph's work in Florida, see Joseph King and Christopher Domin, *Paul Rudolph: The Florida Houses* (New York: Princeton Architectural Press, 2002).

34. "Round-Robin Critique," *Progressive Architecture* 31 (August 1950): 66.

35. "Round-Robin Critique," 69.

36. Alofsin (*Struggle for Modernism,* 196) notes that Hudnut, dean of GSD, opposed "accelerated programs" for veterans, but an exception seems to have been made for Rudolph.

37. Rudolph, "Excerpts from a Conversation," 102.

38. Author's interview with Rudolph's contemporary at the GSD James Lamantia (class of 1949), May 27, 2009. Rudolph was not a fellow at the American Academy; he was probably staying there temporarily.

39. Author's interview with Rudolph, November 29, 1996.

40. Special issue edited by Paul Rudolph and with a catalogue of works by Gropius's students, "Walter Gropius et Son Ecole / Walter Gropius: The Spread of a New Idea," *L'Architecture d'aujourd'hui* 20 (February 1950). Rudolph's contribution to the catalogue was his and Twitchell's Revere Quality House (Siesta Key, 1948), 100–101. Inspired by the architecture of Mies van der Rohe, the residence demonstrated Rudolph's move away from Gropius's functionalism.

41. Sigfried Giedion, *Walter Gropius, Work and Teamwork* (New York: Reinhold, 1954).

42. Rudolph, Preface, *L'Architecture d'aujourd'hui* 20: 4.

43. Alofsin (*Struggle for Modernism,* 222–27) discusses the GSD students' skepticism about functionalism.

44. Pearlman, *Inventing American Modernism,* 39, 197.

45. Kay Fisker, "The Moral of Functionalism," *Magazine of Art* 43 (February 1950): 66.

46. Eric Mumford, *Defining Urban Design: CIAM Architects and the Formation of a Discipline, 1937–1969* (New Haven: Yale University Press, 2009), 109–10.

47. For an article discussing the advantages of Cocoon, using Rudolph's Healy House as an example, see Guy G. Rothenstein, "Sprayed-on Vinyl-Plastic Sheeting," *Progressive Architecture* 33 (July 1952): 99–102.

48. Rudolph published detailed drawings of the Healy House in "Sagging Ceiling on Siesta Key," *Interiors* 110 (January 1951): 94–101.

49. Rudolph, *Architecture of Paul Rudolph,* 34.

50. John Howey, *The Sarasota School* (Cambridge: MIT Press, 1995), 51.

51. For the "Primitive Hut" see Abbé Laugier's 1755 *An Essay on Architecture,* translated and with an introduction by Wolfgang and Anni Herrmann (Los Angeles: Hennessey and Ingalls, 1977). On the importance of structural rationalism, see Neil Levine, *Modern Architecture: Representation and Reality* (New Haven: Yale University Press, 2009), 46–74; see also Kenneth Frampton, *Studies in Tectonic Culture: The Poetics of Construction in Nineteenth and Twentieth Century Architecture* (Cambridge: MIT Press, 1995). The structure of the Healy House, especially its diagonally aligned external bracing, suggested that Rudolph had some familiarity with Viollet-le-Duc's concepts from *Entretiens sur l'architecture* (*Discourses on Architecture*), his illustrated collection of lectures completed in 1872.

52. Peter Collins, *Changing Ideals in Modern Architecture, 1750–1950* (Montreal: McGill-Queen's University Press, 1965), 217.

53. Rudolph's drawing of the flaming hearth in the Healy House appears in his "Sagging Ceiling on Siesta Key," 97-98.

54. Michael Leja, *Reframing Abstract Expressionism: Subjectivity and Painting in the 1940s* (New Haven: Yale University Press, 1993).

55. For Stoller's remarks about Rudolph and these houses, see William Saunders, *Modern Architecture: Photographs by Ezra Stoller*, with commentary to the plates by Ezra Stoller (New York: Abrams, 1990; reprinted 1999), 207–8. For more about Rudolph and Stoller's working relationship, see Erica Stoller and Nina Rappaport, *Ezra Stoller, Photographer* (New Haven: Yale University Press, 2012).

56. King and Domin, *Florida Houses,* 38–39.

57. For this observation about the final breakup with Twitchell, see Rupp, "Paul Rudolph (PMR): A Brief Biography," in "The Florida Years." In another section of this unpaginated manuscript, "Notes on Works without Plates," Rupp remembers that Rudolph says he designed the Twitchell Residence (1941) by himself. Rupp believes that Twitchell did little of the design work for the firm; see the section "A Few Words on Personalities: Ralph Twitchell." Many of Rudolph's former employees have repeated to me Rudolph's claims that he was entirely responsible for the firm's designs, for example Gene Leedy in an interview with the author, November 10, 2004.

58. Howey, *Sarasota School,* 69.

59. Hans Busso von Busse, "Hans Busso von Busse on Paul Rudolph," in *Architects on Architects,* edited by Susan Gray (New York: McGraw-Hill, 2002), 198.

60. Author's interview with Bert Brosmith, August 14, 2002.

61. Rupp mentions Rudolph's Riley in the section "A Small Florida Office," in "The Florida Years."

62. Rudolph, "3 New Directions," 21. The two other directions were accounts by Philip Johnson and Buckminster Fuller of their own work.

63. Ibid.

64. Form was so frequently a topic in discussions of architecture that *Time,* the weekly news magazine, sponsored a traveling exhibition, organized by Cranston Jones and the American Federation of the Arts, about the work of important American architects titled *The Form Givers at Mid-Century.* Rudolph was not included (catalogue by Cranston Jones, published New York: Time-Life Books, 1959).

65. Eliel Saarinen, *Search for Form* (New York: Reinhold, 1948); Louis Kahn, "Order Is" (1955), reprinted in *Louis I. Kahn: Writings, Lectures, Interviews*, edited and with an introduction by Alessandra Latour (New York: Rizzoli, 1991), 58-59; Susanne K. Langer, *Feeling and Form: A Theory of Art* (New York: Charles Scribner's Sons, 1953).

66. See also Cammie McAtee's forthcoming dissertation on form, *Form and Formalism in American Architecture in the 1950s and '60s* (Harvard University, supervised by Neil Levine).

67. Vincent Scully, "Archetype and Order in Recent American Architecture," *Art in America* 42 (December 1954): 250-61.

68. King and Domin, *Florida Houses,* 125.

69. The term "Sarasota School" was probably coined by Philip H. Hiss, its most important patron, in Hiss, "Whatever Happened to Sarasota?" *Architectural Forum* 126 (June 1967): 64-65. Howey's *The Sarasota School*, gave it wider currency.

70. According to Rudolph's first employee, Bert Brosmith, Le Corbusier's vaulted projects inspired the Hook House. Author's interview with Brosmith, August 14, 2002.

71. Rudolph, *Architecture of Paul Rudolph*, 36.

72. Rudolph explained how the Hook House roof was the culmination of a series of efforts to build a lightweight, inexpensive roof. "Rudolph and the Roof: How to Make a Revolution on a Small Budget," *House & Home* 3 (June 1953): 140-45.

73. Author's interview with Gene Leedy, November 10, 2004.

74. Colin Rowe, "Neo-'Classicism' and Modern Architecture 1," written 1956-57, first published in *Oppositions* 1 (September 1973), reprinted in Rowe, *The Mathematics of the Ideal Villa and Other Essays* (Cambridge: MIT Press, 1976), 120-38.

75. Paul Rudolph, "Enigmas of Architecture," *A + U* 80 (July 1977): 317.

76. John Knox Shear, "Walker Guest House, Sanibel Island, Florida, 1953, Paul Rudolph," *Architectural Record* 121 (February 1957): 204.

77. See King and Domin, *Florida Houses,* 115; author's interview with Dr. Walter Walker, January 30, 1998.

78. Rudolph, "Enigmas of Architecture," 317. Rudolph first described the Walker Guest House and its shutters in a talk for the Gulf States Regional Meeting of the American Institute of Architects in September 1953. He published the entire talk as an article in Paul Rudolph, "Regionalism in Architecture," *Perspecta* 4 (1957): 12-19.

79. Rupp quotes Rudolph in Howey, *Sarasota School,* 65.

80. Alice Friedman, *Women and the Making of the Modern House: A Social and Architectural History* (New York: Abrams, 1998). For a detailed account of Farnsworth's discomfort with her glass house, see 126-59.

81. Paul Rudolph, "A Sunday Afternoon," *Philip Johnson Festschrift, ANY* 90 (July 1996): 44-45.

82. Rudolph, "Regionalism in Architecture," 17.

83. For human subjectivity's importance for abstract expressionism, see Leja, *Reframing Abstract Expressionism.*

84. Rudolph, "Regionalism in Architecture," 16. Rudolph also referred to caves and goldfish bowls in "3 New Directions" (22).

85. Skidmore, Owings & Merrill's glass-walled Manufacturers Hanover Bank (New York, 1954) was often described as a goldfish bowl at the time; see "Putting Bankers in a Gold-Fish Bowl," *Business Week* (31 July 1954): 31. For this usage, see also Robert A. M. Stern, Thomas Mellins, and David Fishman, *New York 1960: Architecture and Urbanism between the Second World War and the Bicentennial* (New York: Monacelli Press, 1997), 373.

Two. Challenging the International Style

1. "Awards at Sao Paulo Biennial," *Architectural Review* 115 (1954): 413-14.

2. "AIA Convention," *Architectural Forum* 101 (July 1954): 116-19.

3. For Rudolph's collaboration with Saarinen, see Eeva-Liisa Pelkonen and Donald Albrecht, *Eero Saarinen: Shaping the Future* (New Haven: Yale University Press, 2006), 177; with Sert, see Eric Mumford, *Defining Urban Design: CIAM Architects and the Formation of a Discipline, 1937-69* (New Haven: Yale University Press, 2009), 115; with Walker, see Jane C. Loeffler, *The Architecture of Diplomacy: Building America's Embassies* (New York: Princeton Architectural Press, 1998), 154-57.

4. Excerpts from the panel were published as "The Changing Philosophy of Architecture," *Architectural Record* 116 (August 1954): 180-83. Rudolph's speech was published in full as "The Changing Philosophy of Architecture," *Architectural Forum* 101 (July 1954): 120-21.

5. Rudolph, "Changing Philosophy of Architecture," 120-21.

6. All of the members of the AIA panel "The Changing Philosophy of Architecture" were involved in the program as advisors or architects. Walker was an advisor from 1954 to 1956; Saarinen built the London Chancellery (1955-60); Sert designed the Baghdad Embassy (1955); Wurster had just returned from Hong Kong, where he was building a consulate for the program (1954).

7. For an account of the FBO's genesis and activities, see Loeffler, *Architecture of Diplomacy.*

8. For a contemporary discussion about romantic modernism and nomenclature for the style, see Jules Langser, "Neo-Classicism? Ornamented Modern? The Quest for Ornament in American Architecture," *Zodiac* 4 (1959): 70-81. Robin Boyd discussed how problematic its popular appeal was in *The Puzzle of Architecture* (London: Cambridge University Press, 1965), 1-3.

9. Loeffler, *Architecture of Diplomacy,* 152. In 1954-55, Rudolph taught at MIT, where Belluschi was dean of architecture. Rudolph wrote an appreciation of Belluschi after his death in 1994: Paul Rudolph, "Pietro Belluschi, August 18, 1899-February 14, 1994," unpublished, PMR 3067-2.

10. According to Rudolph's site plan, the new embassy was to be on the boulevard Al-Kulliyya Al-Eilmiyya Al-Islamiyya in Amman. Author's interview with Bert Brosmith, August 14, 2002; Brosmith supervised most of Rudolph's projects in his Sarasota office during the 1950s, including the embassy.

11. R. W. Hamilton, *Khirbat al Mafjar: An Arabian Mansion in the Jordan Valley*, with a contribution by Oleg Grabar (Oxford: Clarendon Press, 1959). My thanks to Walter Denny for bringing the mansion to my attention.

12. Paul Rudolph, "3 New Directions: Paul Rudolph, Philip Johnson, Buckminster Fuller," *Perspecta* 1 (1952): 21; Brosmith interview.

13. Brosmith interview. For the embassy project, Rudolph collaborated with the landscape architects Sasaki & Novak in Boston, the established structural engineering firm of Seelye, Stevenson & Knecht in New York, and Ebaugh & Gothe, structural engineers from Gainesville, Florida. They were probably chosen for their convenience to Rudolph's offices.

14. Rudolph's contemporaries, including Philip Johnson and Josep Lluís Sert, designed projects that emulated Le Corbusier's umbrella roof for the High Court. Johnson described the Chandigarh projects in "Correct and Magnificent Play," *Art News* 52 (September 1953): 16–17, 52–53, reprinted in *Philip Johnson Writings,* foreword by Vincent Scully, introduction by Peter Eisenman, commentary by Robert A. M. Stern (New York: Oxford University Press, 1979), 200–205.

15. The Arab tent as a model for Rudolph's embassy in Amman is mentioned in "The United States Embassy for Jordan," *Architectural Record* (February 1957): 162–65, and in "Ambassade des Etats-Unis en Jordane," *L'Architecture d'aujourd'hui* 28 (September 1957): 90–91. Rudolph refers to Le Corbusier's High Court as an "Arab tent" in "To Enrich Our Architecture," *Journal of Architectural Education* 13 (Spring 1958): 9. Rudolph had also thought about sheltering a building beneath a tent in a project with Twitchell for a beach pavilion of 1950; see Joseph King and Christopher Domin, *Paul Rudolph: The Florida Houses* (New York: Princeton Architectural Press, 2002), 219.

16. Rudolph, letter to Peter Blake, September 14, 1954, uncatalogued, Peter Blake Papers, Avery Archive, Columbia University; author's interview with Blake, October 15, 1997; Blake, letter to the author, May 16, 1998. Rudolph's correspondence with Blake seems to have informed an article by Blake, "The New Generation of Architects: Paul Rudolph," *Casabella Continuita* 204 (February–March 1955): 65.

17. Brosmith interview.

18. Isabelle Hyman, *Marcel Breuer, Architect: The Career and the Buildings* (New York: Harry N. Abrams, 2001), 156–57. Breuer's bush-hammered concrete was also often described as "corrugated."

19. Brosmith interview. These techniques are also described in "The United States Embassy for Jordan," 162–65, and in "Ambassade des Etats-Unis en Jordane," 90–91.

20. For an overview of the monumentality dilemma for modernism, see George R. Collins and Christiane C. Collins, "Monumentality: A Critical Matter in Modern Architecture," *Harvard Architecture Review* 4 (1984): 15–35.

21. Rudolph, "The Six Determinants of Architectural Form," *Architectural Record* 120 (October 1956): 183, 186. Rudolph listed six factors but did not discuss each equally, obviously seeing some as more important than others. They were environment and site, functional aspects (about which he had little to say), region, materials, psychological demands, and spirit of the times.

22. Rudolph, letter to Blake, September 14, 1954.

23. Loeffler, *Architecture of Diplomacy*, 154–57.

24. Loeffler, *Architecture of Diplomacy*, 157; Brosmith (author's interview), however, is convinced that ground was about to be broken. The U.S. Embassy in Amman of 1988–92 was by Perry, Dean, Rogers & Partners.

25. James Marston Fitch, "Wellesley's Alternative to Collegiate Gothic," *Architectural Forum* 111 (July 1959): 88.

26. For a history of the Wellesley campus and the design of the Jewett Center, see Peter Fergusson, James F. O'Gorman, and John Rhodes, *The Landscape and Architecture of Wellesley College* (Wellesley, Mass.: Wellesley College, 2000). Rhodes (201–27) provides an in-depth analysis of the building in regard to the college's particular concerns and how Rudolph was selected for the commission.

27. Information about how Rudolph split work with Anderson, Beckwith, and Haible comes from the author's interview with William Morgan (July 21, 2010), who was working in Rudolph's office, and "a professional practice report" about the Jewett Arts Center he coproduced with four other students at the Harvard Graduate School of Design in 1957 that described its development in detail. Though Rudolph met with Anderson, Beckwith, and Haible regularly, it is unclear what they contributed to the project. Nelson Chin, Byron Ireland, Roland Kluver, William Morgan, and Michael Zimmer, *The Mary Cooper Jewett Arts Center* (1957), unpaginated. GSD Special Collections, Harvard University.

28. Morgan (author's interview) said Serge Chermayeff had the office next door. Fumihiko Maki remembered meeting Rudolph in Cambridge at this time and regularly having breakfast with him (author's correspondence with Maki, October 27, 2011).

29. Author's interview with Morgan.

30. Mumford, *Defining Urban Design*, 122–25.

31. Vincent Scully, "Archetype and Order in Recent American Architecture," *Art in America* 42 (December 1954): 260–61.

32. Eugène-Emmanuel Viollet-le-Duc, "Lecture XV: General Observations on the Internal and External Ornamentation of Buildings," in *Discourses on Architecture*, vol. 2, translated by Benjamin Bucknell (1872; 1889; New York: Grove Press, 1959), 198–99. Rudolph owned the 1959 edition, according to an uncatalogued list of his books at the Library of Congress.

33. Rudolph, "The Changing Philosophy of Architecture," 121. For the Japanese House, see Arthur Drexler, *The Architecture of Japan*, "Supplement: Japanese Exhibition House" (New York: Museum of Modern Art, 1955), 262–79.

34. Matthew Nowicki, "Origins and Trends in Modern Architecture," *Magazine of Art* 44 (November 1951): 273–79.

35. Fergusson, O'Gorman, and Rhodes, *Landscape and Architecture of Wellesley College*, 224–25.

36. In a note dated June 14, 1958, to Wellesley president Margaret Clapp, faculty member and building committee member Agnes Abbot suggests that Rudolph cover the art wing with screens like those of Edward Durell Stone's Manhattan townhouse (1956), similar to those of his New Delhi Embassy; see file marked A89-37 1/3, uncatalogued records of the Art Department, Jewett Arts Center, January–June 1958.

37. "Fitting the Future into the Past," *Architectural Forum* 105 (December 1956): 102.

38. Rudolph, "The Changing Philosophy of Architecture," 120.

39. Ibid.

40. Gerhard Kallmann, "The 'Action' Architecture of a New Generation," *Architectural Forum* 111 (October 1959): 134.

41. This final portion of the chapter is based on my article "Challenging the Curtain Wall: Paul Rudolph's Blue Cross and Blue Shield Building," *Journal of the Society of Architectural Historians* 66 (March 2007): 84–109.

42. For a history of the curtain wall and its origins, see David Yeomans, "The Origins of the Modern Curtain Wall," *Bulletin, Association for Preservation Technology* 32 (2001): 13–18.

43. Lewis Mumford, "Skin Treatment and New Wrinkles," *New Yorker* 30 (October 23, 1954), reprinted in Lewis Mumford, *From the Ground Up* (New York: Harcourt, Brace, Jovanovich, 1956) 96; Vincent Scully, *Modern Architecture: The Architecture of Democracy* (New York: George Braziller, 1961), 34.

44. "The Monotonous Curtain Wall," *Architectural Forum* 111 (October 1959): 143.

45. For an in-depth analysis of the Blue Cross and Blue Shield organization's needs and motives and the overall building campaign, see Robert Loverud, Leon Setti, and John Shenefield, "The Blue Cross and Blue Shield Building: A Case Study in Architectural Practice," an unpublished report submitted to Professor Walter E. Bogner, Harvard University, Graduate School of Design, undated, though Harvard's catalogue lists it as "1960?"

46. Critics noted the traditional appearance of Skidmore, Owings & Merrill's John Hancock Building (1958–59) in San Francisco. See Allan Temko, "San Francisco's Newest Tower," *Architectural Forum* 112 (April 1960): 124–31.

47. Reyner Banham, "Neoliberty: The Italian Retreat from Modern Architecture," *Architectural Review* 125 (April 1959): 230–35.

48. Ernesto Rogers, "Preexisting Conditions and Issues of Contemporary Building Practice," *Casabella Continuità* 204 (February–March 1955): 36.

49. Gerhard Kallmann, "Modern Tower in Old Milan," *Architectural Forum* 108 (February 1958): 109.

50. Rudolph, "The Changing Philosophy of Architecture," 120.

51. William J. McGuiness, "Exterior Ducts Follow Leaf Ribs," *Progressive Architecture* 41 (April 1960): 11–12, 13, 15.

52. John Damico, an architect who worked in Rudolph's office at the time, helped explain this system in an interview with the author, March 14, 2003.

53. Rudolph, "The Changing Philosophy of Architecture," 120.

54. Rudolph talks about the need to enrich modernism with ornament and decoration in his article "To Enrich Our Architecture," *Journal of Architectural Education* 13 (Spring 1958): 7–12.

55. For Contract Interior's work on the BC-BS Building, see "Quietly Contemporary: New Look on Boston's Federal Street," *Interiors* 4 (April 1962): 118–19.

56. Paul Rudolph, "A Sunday Afternoon," *Philip Johnson Festschrift*, ANY 90 (July 1996): 44–45.

Three. Humanism, Yale, and New Haven

1. William Grindereng says the Tastee-Freez was one of the first studio problems Rudolph gave at Yale in 1956. See Bruce Barnes, "Interview with William Grindereng: Longtime Architectural Associate of Architect Paul Rudolph" (June 28, 2006), 1, available at the website "Paul Rudolph and His Architecture," University of Massachusetts, Dartmouth, http://prudolph.lib.umassd.edu/home

2. For a detailed history of the Yale Department of Architecture from 1950 through Rudolph's tenure, see Robert A. M. Stern, "Yale, 1950–1965," *Oppositions* 4 (October 1974): 35–62.

3. Johnson seems to have felt no ill will toward Rudolph for winning the appointment of chairman of Yale's architecture department and became a regular visitor to it during Rudolph's tenure. Kahn would have greater difficulties at Yale after Rudolph's appointment. Stern asserts that Kahn left Yale at the end of spring semester 1959 because of pedagogical differences with Rudolph (Stern, "Yale, 1950–1965," 46–47). Kahn had other issues with Rudolph, however; he was disconcerted by the renovations of the loft-like spaces of his Yale University Art Gallery into a series of enclosed rooms carried out by Rudolph at the request of gallery director Andrew Ritchie in 1957; see Patricia Cummings Loud, *The Art Museums of Louis I. Kahn* (Durham, N.C.: Duke University Press, 1989), 90–92.

4. Richard Pommer, "The Art and Architecture Building at Yale, Once Again," *Burlington Magazine,* 114 (December 1972): 853–61. Pommer (854) suggests that Saarinen advocated Rudolph's selection as chairman.

5. Godfrey Hodgson coined the term "liberal consensus" in *America in Our Time* (New York: Doubleday, 1976); other scholars have since expanded on the concept.

6. On Griswold's liberalism, see Geoffrey Kabaservice, *The Guardians: Kingman Brewster, His Circle, and the Rise of the Liberal Establishment* (New York: Henry Holt, 2004), 154–55. President John F. Kennedy was the Yale commencement speaker in June 1962.

7. A. Whitney Griswold, "Higher Education for the Artist and His Audience," *Art in America* 46 (Fall 1958): 50–51.

8. For an account of Griswold's patronage of architecture at Yale, published shortly after his death, see Walter McQuade, "Building Years of a Yale Man," *Architectural Forum* 118 (June 1963): 88–93. Griswold explained the policy that informed the Yale commissions in his dedication of Morse and Stiles Colleges at Yale in 1962, reprinted in Don Metz and Yugi Noga, *New Architecture in New Haven* (Cambridge: MIT Press, 1966), unpaginated.

9. For the prevalence of humanism in postwar North American architecture schools including Yale, see *Architecture School: Three Centuries of Educating Architects in North America*, edited by Joan Ockman, with Rebecca Williamson, research editor (Cambridge: MIT Press with Association of Collegiate Schools of Architecture, Washington, D.C., 2012), 135–40.

10. For an overview of Scully's thinking, see Neil Levine, "Vincent Scully: A Biographical Sketch," in Vincent Scully, *Modern Architecture and Other Essays* (Princeton: Princeton University Press, 2003), 12–33. For the impact of Camus on Scully, see Stern, 50. See also Geoffrey Scott,

The Architecture of Humanism: A Study in the History of Taste (1914; reprinted, with a new introduction by Paul Barolsky, New York: W. W. Norton, 1999).

11. Johnson said Scott was his bible in a letter to Dr. Jürgen Joedicke, December 6, 1961; reprinted in *Philip Johnson Writings,* foreword by Vincent Scully, introduction by Peter Eisenman, commentary by Robert A. M. Stern (New York: Oxford University Press, 1979), 125.

12. Scott, *Architecture of Humanism,* 177. Scully quotes this passage from Scott in his "Modern Architecture: Toward a Redefinition of Style," *Perspecta* 4 (1957), 4–10. Neil Levine discusses the article's importance in Scully, *Modern Architecture and Other Essays,* 84. The essay became the book Vincent Scully, *Modern Architecture: The Architecture of Democracy* (New York: George Braziller, 1961).

13. Scully, "Modern Architecture: Toward a Redefinition of Style."

14. Helene Sroat has admirably framed the Yale A & A Building in the context of postwar humanism in Helene K. Sroat, "The Humanism of Brutalist Architecture: The Yale Art and Architecture Building and Postwar Constructions of Aesthetic Experience in American Universities and Architecture" (PhD diss., University of Chicago, 2003).

15. Paul Rudolph, "Architecture: The Unending Search," *Yale Alumni Magazine* 21 (May 1958), reprinted in Paul Rudolph, *Writings on Architecture: Paul Rudolph,* edited by Nina Rappaport, foreword by Robert A. M. Stern (New Haven: Yale School of Architecture, 2008), 39–42, quote on 39.

16. Ibid., 41.

17. Ibid., 42.

18. Meeks describes his congenial working relationship with Rudolph in a letter to Vincent Scully in Athens, March 19, 1958. YMA, Carroll L. V. Meeks Papers, 1930–1966. MS 706.

19. William de Cossy (Yale class of 1957), visiting critic 1959 to 1963 and Rudolph office employee 1957 to 1959. De Cossy remembers Rudolph being exacting in his running of the department. Author's interview with de Cossy, June 22, 2007, and de Cossy's unpublished notes about dinners at Mory's with Rudolph, February 1997.

20. Author's interview with Vincent Scully, April 12, 1999.

21. Paul Rudolph, "Excerpts from a Conversation," *Perspecta* 22 (1986): 105.

22. Norman Foster, foreword to Tony Monk, *The Art and Architecture of Paul Rudolph* (Chichester, West Sussex: Wiley-Academy, 1999), 4; author's interview with Foster, January 21, 2002.

23. Author's interview with de Cossy.

24. Author's interview with Robert A. M. Stern, October 24, 2011.

25. The Department of Architecture produced annual reports called "resumes" listing staff and curricular changes, visiting critics, jury members, and lecturers. I have drawn on resumes from Rudolph's years at Yale, 1955–65. Specific dates were not listed for lectures or visiting critics. See YMA, "School of Architecture, Yale University: Reminiscences and Documentation of Architecture Students Collected by Robert A. M. Stern," Box 4, Folder 104. Stern collected the resumes in the early 1970s for his article "Yale, 1950–1965."

26. Kurt W. Forster, "Hey, Sailor: A Brief Memoir of the Long Life and Short Fame of Paul Rudolph," *ANY* 21 (1997): 13.

27. Author's interview with Ellis Ansel Perlswig, October 29, 2009. Perlswig remembered the homosexual "witch hunts" in academia of the 1950s and 1960s, discussed as well in Martin Duberman, *Cures: A Gay Man's Odyssey* (New York: Penguin, 1991), 41–62.

28. David De Long, *Bruce Goff: Toward Absolute Architecture* (New York: Architectural History Foundation and MIT Press, 1988), 135–36. Moore's homosexuality was a factor that contributed to his dismissal from Princeton's architecture faculty; see Jorge Otero-Pailos, "LSDesign: Charles W. Moore and the Delirious Interior," *Architecture's Historical Turn: Phenomenology and the Rise of Post-Modernism* (Minneapolis: University of Minnesota Press, 2010), 108.

29. Stern interview.

30. Foster, foreword to *The Art and Architecture of Paul Rudolph,* 4; author's interview with Foster, January 21, 2002.

31. Author's interview with Robert Engman, July 31, 2012.

32. Ada Louise Huxtable, "Historical Survey," *Progressive Architecture* 41 (October 1960): 144. *Architectural Forum* 117 (September 1962) was also devoted to innovations in concrete.

33. Author's interview with William Grindereng, October 25, 2002.

34. Philip Johnson, lecture for Vincent Scully's modern architecture survey class, May 9, 1958, "Retreat from the International Style to the Present Scene," in *Philip Johnson Writings,* 85.

35. "Concrete Orchard: Yale's Architectural Renaissance Is Furthered by a Laboratory for Forestry Research by Paul Rudolph," *Architectural Forum* 111 (October 1959): 138–41.

36. Those in Rudolph's circle at the Museum of Modern Art took a strong interest in art nouveau in the late 1950s. There were two exhibitions devoted to the style at MoMA: Henry-Russell Hitchcock's exhibition (December 18, 1957–February 23, 1958) and catalogue for *Gaudi* (New York: Museum of Modern Art, 1957), followed by Peter Selz and Mildred Constantine's exhibition (June 8–September 6, 1960) and catalogue for *Art Nouveau: Art and Design at the Turn of the Century* (New York: Museum of Modern Art, 1959).

37. Thomas H. Creighton, "The New Sensualism," *Progressive Architecture* 40 (September 1959): 141–47, and "The New Sensualism II," *Progressive Architecture,* 40 (November 1959): 180–87.

38. Rudolph quoted in Elizabeth Mills Brown, *New Haven: A Guide to Architecture and Urban Design* (New Haven: Yale University Press, 1976), 171. Brown quotes Rudolph at length in what is the fullest description of the Greeley building in his words, but her source is not noted, and I have been unable to find it.

39. Walter McQuade, "Rudolph's Roman Road," *Architectural Forum* 118 (February 1963): 104–8.

40. Ibid., 108.

41. Numerous articles documented the rise of Lee's Model City, such as Joe Alex Morris, "He Is Saving a 'Dead City,'" *Saturday Evening Post* (April 19, 1958), 31, 115–16, 118. For a critical overview, see Douglas Rae, *City: Urbanism and Its End* (New Haven: Yale University Press, 2003).

42. "New Haven Is Becoming a Model City—Architecturally," *New Haven Register* (January 6, 1963), 13.

43. Rudolph was also a consultant for Church Street Redevelopment. His suggested improvements for the mall (1958–60) were never used,

and his planned adjacent First New Haven National Bank (1958–60) remained unbuilt. For more about Rudolph's projects in New Haven, see Timothy M. Rohan, *Model City: Buildings and Projects by Paul Rudolph for Yale and New Haven* (pamphlet for exhibition at Yale School of Architecture, November 3, 2008–February 6, 2009).

44. "Paul Rudolph Designs a Place to Park in Downtown New Haven," *Architectural Record* 133 (February 1963): 146.

45. For a detailed discussion of Lee's New Haven redevelopment projects and Church Street, see Rae, *City*, 312–60. For numbers of those displaced by Church Street Redevelopment, see Rae, *City*, 339.

46. For a contemporary description of the design and construction of the Temple Street Parking Garage, see Samuel R. Blair, "The Temple Street Parking Garage, New Haven, Connecticut" (unpublished thesis, Department of Architecture, Harvard University, 1962), unpaginated, available in the GSD Special Collections. Walter D. Ramberg prepared drawings for the Temple Street Parking Garage and discussed them with the author (August 6, 2012). Rudolph's student and employee John Damico shared with the author memories about working on the garage (October 4, 2012).

47. "Four Current Projects by Paul Rudolph," *Architectural Record* 129 (March 1961): 152. It is worth noting that Rudolph might have had Mies's Concrete Office Building (project, Berlin, 1923) in mind as a model.

48. Rudolph, *Architecture of Paul Rudolph*, 114. No images of this concept have come to light.

49. For Kahn's plans for Philadelphia, see Peter Reed, "Philadelphia Urban Design," in David B. Brownlee and David G. De Long, *Louis Kahn: In the Realm of Architecture* (New York: Rizzoli and the Museum of Contemporary Art, Los Angeles, 1991), 409–18.

50. "Paul Rudolph Designs a Place to Park in Downtown New Haven," 146.

51. Ramberg interview. For Rudolph supervising construction of formwork, see Blair, "The Temple Street Parking Garage," subheading #6.

52. McQuade, "Rudolph's Roman Road," 108.

53. Rudolph briefly described Chandigarh in Paul Rudolph, "The Contribution of Le Corbusier," *Architectural Forum* 114 (April 1961): 99. Rudolph remarked on the roughness of Chandigarh in "Paul Rudolph Designs a Place to Park in Downtown New Haven," 148.

54. McQuade, "Rudolph's Roman Road," 108.

55. "Paul Rudolph Designs a Place to Park in Downtown New Haven," 148.

56. For Pugin's remarks about the construction of decoration and the decoration of construction, see A. W. N. Pugin, *The True Principles of Pointed or Christian Architecture: Set Forth in Two Lectures Delivered at St. Marie's, Oscott* (1841; reprint of 1853 edition, Oxford St. Barnabas Press, 1969), 1. Rudolph owned a crumbling, undated, nineteenth-century copy published by W. Hughes, King's Head Court, Gough Square, London. See uncatalogued Rudolph Book List from Rudolph Archive, Library of Congress. For a discussion of the significance of Pugin's point, see Neil Levine, *Modern Architecture: Representation and Reality* (New Haven: Yale University Press, 2009), 122–28.

57. Vincent Scully, "Louis Sullivan's Architectural Ornament: A Brief Note Concerning Humanist Design in the Age of Force," *Perspecta* 5 (1959): 73–80.

58. McQuade, "Rudolph's Roman Road," 108.

59. Robert Venturi, Denise Scott Brown, and Steven Izenour later explained postwar modernism's tendency to make architecture into sculptural forms or decoration in *Learning from Las Vegas* (Cambridge: MIT Press, first published 1972; 1977 edition) when they discussed (87–103) Rudolph's highly plastic Crawford Manor (New Haven, 1962–66).

60. Blair ("The Temple Street Parking Garage," subheading #6) reports that Rudolph was going to make a profit on the garage; author's interview with Damico.

61. Victor Gruen, *The Heart of Our Cities: The Urban Crisis: Diagnosis and Cure* (New York: Simon and Schuster, 1964), 153–54.

62. Ramberg interview.

63. James Stirling, "'The Functional Tradition' and Expression," *Perspecta* 6 (1960): 88–97.

64. Alison and Peter Smithson, "The New Brutalism," *Architectural Design* (April 1957): 113.

65. Reyner Banham, "The New Brutalism," *Architectural Review* 118 (December 1955): 354–61.

66. Philip Johnson, "School at Hunstanton, Norfolk, Alison and Peter Smithson," *Architectural Review* 116 (September 1954): 148–52.

67. Author's correspondence with M. J. Long, a Rudolph student, August 25, 2011.

68. Brian Appleyard, *Richard Rogers: A Biography* (London: Faber and Faber, 1986), 96.

69. Marshall Burchard, "New Urban Pattern: Married Students Apartments at Yale," *Architectural Forum* 116 (March 1962): 99–100.

70. Reyner Banham, *The New Brutalism: Ethic or Aesthetic?* (London: Architectural Press, 1966). Banham included discussion of Rudolph's Yale Married Student Housing (130, 164–65) and expressed his regrets (135) that brutalism had become associated with Rudolph and other American architects.

71. Russell Bourne, "Yale's Paul Rudolph," *Architectural Forum* 108 (April 1958): 128. Determining how much Rudolph earned yearly is nearly impossible from his few remaining office records and those available from Yale.

72. No archival materials remain about 31 High Street. For drawings and photos, see "Paul Rudolph: Projected Extension of the Architect's Office, October 1961/The Architect's Apartment," *Perspecta* 9/10 (1965): 249–64. The *Perspecta* article dates Rudolph's extension to October 1961, but renovations may have begun earlier since former staff members remember working in the office in 1958 (Ramberg interview). New Haven land records indicate that Rudolph had a mortgage for the building by February 1958.

73. Ramberg interview.

74. Barnes, "Interview with William Grindereng," 10–11.

75. Ibid., 3.

76. Author's interview with Der Scutt, March 21, 2006.

77. Author's interviews with Rudolph's friends Carl Black (July 23, 2010) and Michael Black (July 24, 2010).

78. "Paul Rudolph, Changing the Look of American Architecture," *Vogue* 141 (January 15, 1963): 84–91, 106.

Four. The Yale Art & Architecture Building

1. Ada Louise Huxtable, "Winner at Yale: The New Art and Architecture Building Lives Up to Great Expectations, " *New York Times* (November 10, 1963), X19.

2. Reyner Banham, "Convenient Benches and Handy Hooks: Functional Considerations in the Criticism of the Art of Architecture," in Marcus Whiffen, editor, *The History, Theory and Criticism of Architecture, Papers from the 1964 AIA-ACSA Teacher Seminar* (Cambridge: MIT Press, 1965), 102.

3. Most of the minutes and motions from the Yale Buildings and Grounds Committee and the Yale Corporation are administrative in nature, providing little insight into the design process. Richard Pommer documents them in the first and definitive scholarly article about the A & A: Richard Pommer, "The Art and Architecture Building at Yale, Once Again," *Burlington Magazine* 114 (December 1972): 853–61. Pommer added the qualifier "once again" because journalists had written so much about the building by 1972 that he thought readers believed they knew everything about it already.

4. See interviews with Rudolph cited throughout this chapter. The best description by Rudolph is in his article "Yale Art and Architecture Building," *Architectural Design* 34 (April 1964): 161.

5. Pommer, "Art and Architecture Building Once Again," 853–57.

6. Rudolph, "Enigmas of Architecture," *A + U* 80 (July 1977): 318.

7. Michael J. Crosbie, "Paul Rudolph on Yale's A & A," *Architecture* 77 (November 1988): 101.

8. Growing uneasiness about Rudolph's perceived eclecticism is evident in an article about his Blue Cross and Blue Shield Building, "Inside Out Office Building," *Architectural Record* 128 (December 1960): 112. Paul Heyer summarizes criticism of Rudolph in Heyer, *Architects on Architecture: New Directions in America* (New York: Walker and Company, 1966), 295–307.

9. Banham's "Ballet School" remarks are excerpted in an article about Saarinen's U.S. Embassy in London, "Controversial Building in London," *Architectural Forum* 114 (March 1961): 84.

10. Mark Girouard, *Big Jim: The Life and Work of James Stirling* (London: Chatto and Windus, 1998), 120.

11. Peter Collins mentioned Rudolph briefly but favorably in his attempt to recategorize modern architecture in his *Changing Ideals in Modern Architecture, 1750–1950* (Montreal: McGill-Queen's University Press, 1965), 287–88. On Collins's shared affinity for concrete, see Peter Collins, *Concrete: The Vision of a New Architecture: A Study of Auguste Perret and His Precursors* (New York: Horizon Press, 1959).

12. Peter Collins, "After Frank Lloyd Wright," *Manchester Guardian* (November 10, 1960), reprinted with some changes as "Whither Paul Rudolph?" *Progressive Architecture* 42 (August 1961): 130–33, quotes on 130, 131.

13. Henry A. Millon, "Rudolph at the Cross-Roads," *Architectural Design* 30 (December 1960): 497–500.

14. Paul Rudolph, "For Perspecta," *Perspecta* 7 (1961): 51.

15. The student editors of *Perspecta* 7 asked several historians, journalists, and architects, including Peter Collins (who did not mention Rudolph in his essay), to critique the recent work of Rudolph, Johnson, Saarinen, Johansen, and Kahn in order to assess the state of architecture. Fears that modernism might collapse are apparent in Thomas L. Creighton, "The Sixties: A P/A Symposium on the State of Architecture," *Progressive Architecture* 42 (March 1961): 122–33.

16. Walter McQuade, "The Exploded Landscape," *Perspecta* 7 (1961), 83.

17. This number is cited in the catalogue of the exhibition organized by students at the Yale School of Architecture, October 31–November 19, 1988, *Paul Rudolph: Drawings for the Art and Architecture Building at Yale, 1959–1963,* edited by Gilbert Schafer and Robert Young (New Haven: Yale School of Architecture, 1988).

18. There has been speculation over the years that Rudolph wanted to create a multistory atrium at the center of the A & A Building, but no sketches for such a configuration have been found. See, for instance, Alexander Tzonis, Liane Lefaivre, and Richard Diamond, *Architecture in North America Since 1960* (Boston: Little Brown, 1995), 63–64.

19. Rudolph explains how the A & A Building could be expanded northward in Rudolph, "Yale Art and Architecture Building," 161.

20. Rudolph's student Allan Greenberg recalled that Rudolph drew a map of the university core, pinpointing vantage points from which features that tied the campus together, like gateways, could be observed, and recommended admiring the courtyards at different times of the day. Allan Greenberg, *The Architecture of Democracy: American Architecture and the Legacy of Revolution* (New York: Rizzoli, 2006), 18.

21. Rudolph mentions Cullen in "The Changing Philosophy of Architecture," *Architectural Forum* 101 (July 1954): 120. For Cullen's ideas, see Gordon Cullen, *Townscape* (London: Architectural Press, 1961). For criticism of Cullen's approach, see Reyner Banham, "The Revenge of the Picturesque, 1945–1965," in *Concerning Architecture,* edited by John Summerson (London: Penguin Press, 1968), 265.

22. Kevin Lynch, *The Image of the City* (Cambridge: MIT Press, 1960); Jane Jacobs, *The Death and Life of Great American Cities* (New York: Random House, 1961); Christian Norberg-Schulz, *Intentions in Architecture* (Cambridge: MIT Press, 1965).

23. Paul Rudolph, "Architecture: The Unending Search," *Yale Alumni Magazine* 21 (May 1958), reprinted in Paul Rudolph, *Writings on Architecture,* edited by Nina Rappaport, foreword by Robert A. M. Stern (New Haven: Yale School of Architecture, 2008), 39–42.

24. Philip Johnson, "Whence and Whither: The Processional Element in Architecture," *Perspecta* 9/10 (1965): 167–68.

25. Rudolph, "Yale Art and Architecture Building," 161.

26. Ibid.

27. Author's interview with James McNeeley (Yale class of 1960), March 11, 2009. The term "corrugated concrete" was not unique to Rudolph's work, having been used also with reference to Marcel Breuer's concrete surfaces. Rudolph's corrugated concrete was also described as textile-like. One account said it was "ribbed and fuzzy looking, like a collegiate Shetland sweater" ("A & A, Yale School of Art and Architecture," *Progressive Architecture* 45 [February 1964]: 111).

28. William H. Jordy, "The Encompassing Environment of Free-Form Architecture: Frank Lloyd Wright's Guggenheim Museum," in *American Buildings and Their Architects,* vol. 5, *The Impact of European Modernism in the Mid-Twentieth Century* (New York: Oxford University

Press, 1972). Jordy (342) points out how these architects were inspired by seashells and provides a footnote with several publications from 1960 that attest to this.

29. Paul Rudolph, "From Conception to Sketch to Rendering to Building," in *Paul Rudolph: Architectural Drawings*, edited by Yukio Futagawa (New York: Rizzoli, 1972), 7.

30. My thanks to Robert A. M. Stern for pointing this out to me and providing a translation from Tange Kenzo and Fujimori Terunobu, *Tange Kenzo = Kenzo Tange* (Tokyo: Shinkenchikusha, 2002; in Japanese), 184–85.

31. "Yale Plans to Add Two Buildings," *New York Times* (June 18, 1960), 25.

32. In his detailed analysis of the A & A Building's development, Pommer notes how it changed after Rudolph returned from Japan and India in the spring of 1960. Pommer did not know about Rudolph's visit to Tange's building (Pommer, "Art and Architecture Building Once Again," 859). As noted in chapter 3, Rudolph briefly described Chandigarh in Paul Rudolph, "The Contribution of Le Corbusier" *Architectural Forum* 114 (April 1961): 99.

33. Rudolph, "To Enrich Our Architecture," *Journal of Architectural Education* 3 (Spring 1958): 11.

34. Engman made a series of sculptures similar to *Column*. Author's interview with Robert Engman, July 31, 2012.

35. Rudolph explains his fascination with Engman's *Column* in an interview with C. Ray Smith, YMA, "Smith (C. Ray) Manuscript and Research Files on the Yale Art and Architecture Building by Paul Rudolph," MS 1948, Box 1, Folder 10, Paul Rudolph interview transcript, March 15, 1978, 10.

36. Vincent Scully, "Louis Sullivan's Architectural Ornament: A Brief Note Concerning Humanist Design in the Age of Force," *Perspecta* 5 (1959): 73–80.

37. For the competition for the Roosevelt Memorial (1960–61), see Thomas H. Creighton, *The Architecture of Monuments: The Franklin Delano Roosevelt Memorial Competition* (New York: Reinhold, 1962).

38. The Yale colloquium was called "Monumentality in Art, Architecture, Graphic Design and City Planning" and was held April 25–27, 1963 (Yale University Press Release, #322, YMA, RU 690, Box 41, Series 1, Folder 669, Photos of Events & Activities School of Architecture, 1952–68).

39. For Paul Rudolph's unpaginated speech "Monumentality Versus Humanism in Architecture," see PMR 3025-2 (F size).

40. For the debates about the FDR memorial, see Isabelle Hyman, "Marcel Breuer and the Franklin Delano Roosevelt Memorial," *Journal of the Society of Architectural Historians* 54 (December 1995): 446–58. Rudolph himself entered a second competition for the memorial in 1965, which Marcel Breuer won.

41. In notes for his speech "Monumentality Versus Humanism in Architecture," Rudolph alludes to the 1948 symposium on monumentality reported on in the article "In Search of a New Monumentality: A Symposium," *Architectural Review* 104 (September 1948): 117–28.

42. Sibyl Moholy-Nagy, "The Measure," *Architectural Forum* 120 (February 1964): 78.

43. "A & A, Yale School of Art and Architecture," 113.

44. Probably the most frequently reproduced drawing by Rudolph, especially after the building was completed in 1963, the perspective section of the A & A first appeared in print soon after the December 1962 groundbreaking: "Yale's New Art and Architecture Building," *Architectural Record* 131 (January 1962): 16–17. The original I refer to is in the YMA.

45. For the de Kooning curtain, *Labyrinth* (1946), see Sally Yard, *Willem De Kooning* (New York: Rizzoli, 1997), 30–31.

46. Author's interview with Carl Black, graduate student in French and friend of Rudolph's, July 25, 2010. Based on research he conducted about color for the A & A, Black founded a paint company that made custom colors, Liberty on the Hudson, Athens, NY.

47. Black (author's interview) has said that Rudolph found Albers's concepts difficult to apply to architecture. Albers's most famous work on color was published the year the A & A was completed: Josef Albers, *Interaction of Color* (New Haven: Yale University Press, 1963).

48. Black interview. Black and Bagnall's choice of red and yellow for the A & A Building recalls ideas prevalent in popular manuals about color from the time, such as Faber Birren's *Color, Form and Space* (New York: Reinhold, 1961); see especially chapters 3 and 4 concerning architecture and pages 172–73 for the significance of red.

49. For Carroll Meeks's notes about choosing art for the A & A, see "List of Original Objects of Art, Art and Architecture Building," undated, YMA, Carroll L. V. Meeks Papers, Group 706, Box 4.

50. "A & A, Yale School of Art and Architecture," 113.

51. Ibid., 115.

52. Paul Rudolph, "The Six Determinants of Architectural Form," *Architectural Record* 120 (October 1956): 183.

53. Vincent Scully, "Art and Architecture Building, Yale University," *Architectural Review* 135 (May 1964): 326.

54. Rudolph quoted in Jonathan Barnett, "A School for the Arts at Yale," *Architectural Record* 135 (February 1964): 118. It was a common misconception that Gropius had removed the casts from the GSD's home in Robinson Hall at Harvard; in fact, it was Dean Joseph Hudnut who had done so; see Jill Pearlman, *Inventing American Modernism: Joseph Hudnut, Walter Gropius, and the Bauhaus Legacy at Harvard* (Charlottesville: University of Virginia Press, 2007), 54–55.

55. Rudolph quoted in "A & A, Yale School of Art and Architecture," 115.

56. Scully, "Louis Sullivan's Architectural Ornament," 73–80.

57. Philip Johnson, "Is Sullivan the Father of Functionalism?" *Art News* 55 (December 1956): 44.

58. Meeks, "List of Original Objects of Art, Art and Architecture Building," 1.

59. Rudolph quoted in Barnett, "A School for the Arts at Yale," 116.

60. An article by Irving Sandler outlines the history of the art department based on interviews with alumni. Josef Albers's resistance to abstract expressionism is discussed, though curiously he had hired Willem de Kooning to teach at Yale in the early 1950s. Sandler, "The School of Art at Yale: 1950–1970: The Collective Reminiscences of Twenty Distinguished Alumni," *Art Journal* 42 (Spring 1982): 14–21.

61. Nikolaus Pevsner, "Address Given at the Inauguration of the New Art and Architecture Building at Yale University, November 9, 1963," *Journal of the Society of Architectural Historians* 26 (1967): 4–7.

62. M. J. Long observed Rudolph's expression closely during Pevsner's speech (author's correspondence with Long, August 25, 2011). Her observations are repeated in Mark Girouard, *Big Jim: The Life and Work of James Stirling* (London: Chatto and Windus, 1998), 126.

63. Jon Owen, "Architecture Students Warned of Imitation," *New Haven Register* (November 10, 1963), 1, 16.

64. Ada Louise Huxtable, "Winner at Yale: The New Art and Architecture Building Lives Up to Great Expectations," *New York Times* (November 10, 1963), X19.

65. Moholy-Nagy, "The Measure," 79.

66. Scully, "Art and Architecture Building, Yale University," 332.

67. Vincent Scully, "A Note on the Work of Paul Rudolph," in *The Work of Paul Rudolph,* exhibition catalogue for Yale University Art Gallery, November 9, 1963–January 6, 1964, unpaginated.

68. Black interview.

Five. Scenographic Urbanism

1. This estimate is based on Rudolph's project list in Paul Rudolph, *The Architecture of Paul Rudolph*, with an introduction by Sibyl Moholy-Nagy, captions by Gerhard Schwab, and comments by Paul Rudolph (New York: Praeger, 1970), 237–39.

2. For an overview of redevelopment policies and finances from the period that discusses the involvement of I. M. Pei and other significant architects, see Charles Abrams, *The City Is the Frontier* (New York: Harper and Row, 1965), 159. There are new and more focused studies about postwar urban redevelopment, such as Samuel Zipp, *Manhattan Projects: The Rise and Fall of Urban Renewal in Cold War New York* (New York: Oxford University Press, 2010).

3. For the New Frontier, see Irving Bernstein, *Promises Kept: John F. Kennedy's New Frontier* (New York: Oxford University Press, 1991); for the Great Society, Bernstein, *Guns or Butter: The Presidency of Lyndon Johnson* (New York: Oxford University Press, 1996).

4. Thomas H. O'Connor, *Building a New Boston: Politics and Urban Renewal, 1950-1970* (Boston: Northeastern University Press, 1993).

5. Rudolph himself entered the competition for the Boston City Hall at the behest of the firm of Desmond and Lord, but only fragments of his entry remain in the Rudolph Archive at the Library of Congress; see PMR-0098. For an account of the development of the Government Center master plan and Rudolph's BGSC, see Charles G. Hilgenhurst, "Evolution of Boston's Government Center," *Architectural Design* 41 (January 1970): 11–22.

6. Sitte's book was little known in the United States until it was translated into English and published here in 1945 with a preface by Ralph Walker: Camillo Sitte, *The Art of Building Cities: City Building According to Artistic Fundamentals* (New York: Reinhold, 1945), translated by Charles S. Stewart, with an introductory note by Eliel Saarinen and introduction by Ralph Walker. Walker may have introduced Rudolph to the book in the mid-1950s, if he did not know it already. Interest in Sitte's book grew during the 1950s and 1960s along with interest in urbanism, resulting in a new English translation in 1965 with a more accurate title. All references in this chapter are from Camillo Sitte, *City Planning According to Artistic Principles,*

translation of the 1889 Austrian edition by George R. Collins and Christiane Crasemann Collins (New York: Random House, 1965). The Collinses discuss Sitte's thinking and its impact in George R. Collins and Christiane Crasemann Collins, *Camillo Sitte: The Birth of Modern City Planning* (New York: Rizzoli, 1986).

7. Sitte, *City Planning According to Artistic Principles,* 45.

8. Sitte, *City Planning According to Artistic Principles,* 122.

9. For Sitte, Sert, and Le Corbusier, see Francesco Passanti, "The Aesthetic Dimension in Le Corbusier's Urban Planning," in *Josep Lluís Sert, The Architect of Urban Design, 1953-1969*, edited by Eric Mumford and Hashim Sarkis with Neyran Turan (New Haven: Yale University Press and Harvard Graduate School of Design, 2008), 25-37. For Sitte and Saarinen, see Alan J. Plattus, "Campus Plans, Context and Community," in *Eero Saarinen: Shaping the Future*, edited by Eeva-Liisa Pelkonen and Donald Albrecht (New Haven: Yale University Press, 2006), 312.

10. Paul Rudolph, "A View of Washington As a Capital—or What Is Civic Design?" *Architectural Forum* 118 (January 1963): 64-70.

11. Rudolph's Mental Health Building at the BGSC is today known as the Erich Lindemann Mental Health Center for the psychiatrist who pioneered studies of grief.

12. Author's interview with Grattan Gill, who worked for Desmond and Lord in the early 1960s, August 18, 1999.

13. Author's interview with William Grindereng, October 25, 2002.

14. Rudolph, *Architecture of Paul Rudolph*, 94.

15. Hilgenhurst, "Evolution of Boston's Government Center," 14-15; Gill interview.

16. Author's interview with James McNeeley, March 11, 2009.

17. William Grindereng spent considerable time in Boston as well as in New Haven and executed many of the BGSC drawings. See Bruce Barnes, "Interview with William Grindereng: Longtime Architectural Associate of Architect Paul Rudolph" (June 28, 2006), 9-10, available at the website "Paul Rudolph and His Architecture," University of Massachusetts, Dartmouth, http://prudolph.lib.umassd.edu/home

18. Ibid.

19. Rudolph describes his Boston complex as a bowl in Rudolph, "Enigmas of Architecture," *A + U* 80 (July 1977), 319.

20. For Lynch's "high spine," see Robert S. Sturgis, "Urban Planning: Changing Concepts," *Architectural Education and Boston: 1960-1989*, edited by Margaret Henderson Floyd (Boston: Boston Architectural Center, 1989), 113-14.

21. Rudolph was interested in Jacoby's rendering methods. Author's interview with Der Scutt, March 21, 2006.

22. Rudolph's BGSC and its courtyard are compared through photographs to the Piazza del Campo, Siena, and Piazza San Marco, Venice, in "Another Major Project for Boston," *Progressive Architecture* 45 (February 1964): 62-65.

23. Sitte, *City Planning According to Artistic Principles,* 6.

24. Ralph Alswang was known for experimenting with the "living screen," where live stage action was combined with motion pictures. The Ford Foundation funded Rudolph and Alswang's experiment as part of a project pairing architects and theater professionals to design new theaters. Collaborating with the Ford Foundation, the American

Federation of the Arts published the results in *The Ideal Theater: Eight Concepts* (New York: American Federation of the Arts, 1962). For Rudolph and Alswang's contribution, see 13–26.

25. Sitte, *City Planning According to Artistic Principles,* 109.

26. Sigfried Giedion, *Space, Time and Architecture* (Cambridge: Harvard University Press, 1941), 41–61.

27. For an account of the deinstitutionalization of the mentally ill in the 1960s and the Community Mental Health Act, see Gerald N. Grob, *From Asylum to Community: Mental Health Policy in Modern America* (Princeton, N.J.: Princeton University Press, 1991), 222–27.

28. Author's interview with Michele Anzaldi, Lindemann Center site director, October 27, 2011. Philip Nobel tells some anecdotes about the BGSC in Nobel, "The Architecture of Madness: Buildings Can Drive You Crazy, But Can They Restore Mental Health?" *Metropolis* 19 (October 1999): 128–31, 161.

29. Walter J. Cass describes the genesis of SMTI in "A History of the Southeastern Massachusetts Technological Institute in Cultural Perspective" (PhD diss., Boston University School of Education, 1967), 3–25.

30. For commuter colleges, see Paul Venable Turner, *Campus: An American Planning Tradition* (New York: Architectural History Foundation and MIT Press, 1984; paperback edition 1987), 286–91. For a contemporary source about campus planning, see Richard P. Dober, *Campus Planning* (New York: Reinhold, 1964). For an overview of issues for campuses and strategies for planning them in the postwar United States, see Stefan Muthesius, *The Postwar University: Utopianist Campus and College* (New Haven: Published for the Paul Mellon Centre for Studies in British Art by Yale University Press, 2000), 11–58.

31. "Architects Show Model Giving Plans for SMTI," *New Bedford Standard Times* (November 4, 1963), 1.

32. Gill interview.

33. Postcard from Rudolph in Venice to Richard Thissen of Desmond and Lord in Boston, August 1964. Grattan Gill personal papers.

34. Oscar Newman, "The New Campus," *Architectural Forum* 124 (May 1966): 47, 49.

35. A similar example of this "forced perspective" that would have appealed to Rudolph was Scamozzi's famous urban stage set the Teatro all'antica in Sabbioneta, Italy (1588–90), where a raked stage and a set that diminished in height as it receded created, within a relatively cramped space, the illusion of a street of palazzos stretching infinitely into the distance.

36. Sitte, *City Planning According to Artistic Principles,* 28.

37. Giedion, *Space, Time and Architecture,* 41.

38. "Campus Architecture," *Architectural Record* 157 (January 1975): 129.

39. Muthesius (*Postwar University,* 187–94) discusses the phenomenon of the "single structure campus" particularly popular in Canada and exemplified by John Andrews' Scarborough College, Ontario (1963–66), and Arthur Erickson's Simon Fraser University, Vancouver, British Columbia (1963–65).

40. Rudolph, *Architecture of Paul Rudolph,* 152.

41. Rudolph, "Enigmas of Architecture," 320.

42. Author's interview with Bruce Barnes, University of Massachusetts, Dartmouth, librarian and alumnus, April 13, 2005.

43. Paul Rudolph, "To Enrich Our Architecture," *Journal of Architectural Education* 3 (Spring 1958): 11.

44. Rita Reif, "Designers Take a Shine to Silvery Look," *New York Times* (February 10, 1967), 41. Reif mentions Rudolph's silvery curtains at SMTI.

45. Ada Louise Huxtable, "How Success Spoiled SMTI," *New York Times* (February 12, 1967), 17, 19.

46. Gill interview. Rudolph talks about how he was fired and rehired at SMTI in an interview with Lasse B. Antonsen, "Sub Rosa: Interview with Paul Rudolph," January 12, 1996, available at the website "Paul Rudolph and His Architecture," University of Massachusetts, Dartmouth. http://prudolph.lib.umassd.edu/home. Grindereng also talks about Rudolph at SMTI and the architect's dismissal in his interview with Barnes (June 28, 2006), 14, available at the same website.

Six. Prefabrication and the Megastructure

1. Gilbert Herbert, *The Dream of the Factory-Made House: Walter Gropius and Konrad Wachsmann* (Cambridge: MIT Press, 1984).

2. For the Wilson House, see "Paper Prefab Is Strong, Well-Insulated and Cheap," *House and Home* 7 (January 1955): 144–47.

3. John Howey, *The Sarasota School of Architecture* (Cambridge: MIT Press, 1995), 137, 197.

4. Paul Rudolph, "Proposed Trailer Tower," *Perspecta* 11 (1967): 191. The project is not dated in *Perspecta,* but the sketch is reproduced and dated 1954 in Paul Rudolph, *The Architecture of Paul Rudolph,* with an introduction by Sibyl Moholy-Nagy, captions by Gerhard Schwab, and comments by Paul Rudolph (New York: Praeger, 1970), 196.

5. Author's interview with Bill Bedford, August 28, 2008.

6. William H. Jordy, "Seagram Assessed," *Architectural Review* 124 (December 1958): 374–82. For a comparison between Rudolph's striations and classical fluting, see "Paul Rudolph Designs a Place to Park in Downtown New Haven," *Architectural Record* 133 (February 1963): 148.

7. Colin Rowe is listed as a juror in 1963 in "Yale Department of Architecture, Annual Report, 1962–1963," YMA, "School of Architecture, Yale University: Reminiscences and Documentation of Architecture Students Collected by Robert A. M. Stern," Box 4, Folder 104. Rowe drew parallels between Andrea Palladio's work, mannerism, and modernism that may have encouraged Rudolph's formal inventiveness in two well-known articles: "The Mathematics of the Ideal Villa," *Architectural Review* 101 (March 1947): 101–4, and "Mannerism and Modern Architecture," *Architectural Review* 107 (May 1950): 289–99 (both republished in Rowe, *The Mathematics of the Ideal Villa and Other Essays* [Cambridge: MIT Press, 1976]).

8. Robert Venturi, *Complexity and Contradiction in Architecture,* with an introduction by Vincent Scully (New York: Museum of Modern Art, 1966); Rudolph is quoted (1977 edition, 16) about Mies van der Rohe. Venturi and Denise Scott Brown talk about their interest in mannerism in an interview with Dean Sakamoto, July 24, 2009, published in the catalogue *What We Learned: The Yale Las Vegas Studio and the Work of Venturi, Scott Brown and Associates,* Yale School of Architecture

Gallery, October 29, 2009–February 5, 2010 (New Haven: Yale School of Architecture, 2009), unpaginated, see under "Mannerism."

9. Rudolph met Robert Venturi when both worked with Eero Saarinen in his Detroit office in 1954, according to Kevin Roche, who also worked there at the time; author's interview with Roche, November 23, 2010. For Venturi's time as a visiting critic at Yale who assisted Rudolph in the spring of 1963, see David B. Brownlee, David G. De Long, and Kathryn B. Hiesinger, *Out of the Ordinary: Robert Venturi, Denise Scott Brown and Associates* (New Haven: Philadelphia Museum of Art in association with Yale University Press, 2001), 247.

10. Philip Johnson, "Whence and Whither: The Processional Element in Architecture," *Perspecta* 9/10 (1965): 167.

11. Rudolph quoted in Robert A. M. Stern, "Secrets of Paul Rudolph: His First Twenty-Five Years," *Kokusai-Kentiku* 32 (April 1965), reprinted in Robert A. M. Stern, *Architecture on the Edge of Postmodernism: Collected Essays, 1964-88*, edited by Cynthia Davidson (New Haven: Yale University Press, 2009), 14.

12. "Crawford Manor Apartments," *Progressive Architecture* 48 (May 1967): 125.

13. Rudolph calls the balconies "Romeo and Juliet," ibid., 127.

14. Paul Rudolph, "A Note to the Architects of Japan" *Kokusai-Kentiku* 32 (April 1965): 20.

15. Henry A. Millon, "Rudolph at the Cross-Roads," *Architectural Design* 30 (December 1960): 497.

16. Kurt W. Forster, "Hey, Sailor: A Brief Memoir of the Long Life and Short Fame of Paul Rudolph," *ANY* 21 (1997): 13.

17. "Paul Rudolph's Elaborated Spaces: Six New Projects," *Architectural Record* 139 (April 1966): 145.

18. Allan D. Wallis, *Wheel Estate: The Rise and Decline of Mobile Homes* (New York: Oxford University Press, 1991). For "Trailer Estates," Bradenton, Florida, see 167-68.

19. Rudolph discusses the twentieth-century brick in "The Essence of Architecture Is Space," *House & Garden* 136 (November 1969): 32.

20. Wallis, *Wheel Estate*, 16-29.

21. These failed previous projects were Magnolia Mobile Home Units, Vicksburg, Mississippi (1968); Married Student Housing in Charlottesville, Virginia (1967); and Fort Lincoln Housing (Washington, D.C., 1968). The projects were derailed because of the stigmas associated with the mobile home.

22. Elizabeth K. Thompson, "Apartments: Paul Rudolph's 20th Century Brick Used in Cluster Apartments," *Architectural Record* 148 (September 1970): 143.

23. The Gardens was named after a local African-American fraternal organization, the Oriental Masons, that had little involvement with the complex's design.

24. "Romney Expands Effort to Build Housing for Poor," *New York Times* (May 9, 1969), 1; Francis J. Whalen, "Lee Invites Romney to See Housing Plan," *New Haven Register* (July 2, 1969), 1. For a history of Operation Breakthrough, see Wallis, *Wheel Estate*, 208-11.

25. Rita Reif, "Thanks to Prefabs, out of the Slums and into Their Own Co-Ops," *New York Times* (February 11, 1972), 18.

26. "Twentieth-Century Bricks," *Architectural Forum* 136 (June 1972): 48-51.

27. Thompson, "Apartments," 143.

28. Rudolph interview by John W. Cook and Heinrich Klotz, "Paul Rudolph," in *Conversations with Architects* (New York: Praeger Publishers, 1973), 109.

29. Fumihiko Maki, *Investigations in Collective Form* (Saint Louis: School of Architecture, Washington University, 1964), 8.

30. For an account of the Graphic Arts Center's origins and history, see Robert A. M. Stern, Thomas Mellins, and David Fishman, *New York, 1960: Architecture and Urbanism between the Second World War and the Bicentennial* (New York: Monacelli Press, 1995), 718.

31. Wallace, McHarg, Roberts, and Todd; Whittlesey, Conklin and Rossant; and Alan M. Voorhees & Associates, *The Lower Manhattan Plan* (New York: New York City Planning Commission, 1966). For a summary see Stern, Mellins, and Fishman, *New York 1960*, 210-11.

32. Ian Ball, "Storey with an Unhappy Ending," *London Daily Telegraph* (December 13, 1968), 29-34.

33. Rudolph never mentions Burke, but Paul Goldberger suggested that City Corridor evoked Burke's sublime in a brief description of the model of the project reconstructed by Cooper Union students in 2010 and exhibited at the school in association with The Drawing Center; see Paul Goldberger, "Paul Rudolph's Manhattan Megastructure," *New Yorker* blog post (November 8, 2010), http://www.newyorker.com/online/blogs/comment/2010/11/paul-rudolphs-manhattan-megastructure.html#slide_ss_0=1

34. Many descriptions of Rudolph's project erroneously referred to it as LOMEX, but that is the name of Moses's proposed highway. Rudolph called his proposed urban complex that would cover the highway "City Corridor."

35. For LOMEX, see Stern, Mellins, and Fishman, *New York 1960*, 259-63. For Jacobs's opposition to LOMEX, see Anthony Flint, *Wrestling with Moses: How Jane Jacobs Took on New York's Master Builder and Transformed the American City* (New York: Random House, 2009), 137-78.

36. Rudolph's colleague, friend, and Harvard classmate, architect Ulrich Franzen, proposed the grant and contributed his own hypothetical project for the Upper East Side to the study. The results were published in Ulrich Franzen and Paul Rudolph, *Evolving City,* with text by Peter Wolf (New York: American Federation of the Arts, 1974). As part of the study, a film titled *City Corridor* was made by Francis Thompson and was eventually deposited in the Department of Film at the Museum of Modern Art, New York. The author viewed the film at MoMA in 2004, but subsequent attempts to find it there have been unsuccessful.

37. David Gissen, "Exhaust and Territorialisation at the Washington Bridge Apartments, 1963-1973," *Journal of Architecture* 12:4 (2007): 449-61.

38. Stern, Mellins, and Fishman, *New York 1960*, 930-31.

39. Franzen and Rudolph, *Evolving City*, 61.

40. Ibid., 53.

41. Ibid., 59.

42. Ibid., 83.

43. Tange employed the A-frame for his Boston Harbor project (1959) as well. Reyner Banham discusses the popularity of the A-frame for

megastructures; see Banham, *Megastructure: Urban Futures of the Recent Past* (London: Thames and Hudson, 1976), 16.

44. Banham, *Megastructure*, 11. Rudolph's perspective section of the low-rise portion of City Corridor in Soho appeared on the dust jacket of Banham's *Megastructure*.

45. Raymond Grinroz and David Lewis, "Urban Design: Contact Sport or Ivory Tower?" *Architectural Record* 157 (February 1975): 45, 47.

46. Gail Collins, "A 'Vision' of the Future Now an Eyesore," *New York Times* (April 29, 1979), 1, 7.

Seven. Reversal of Fortune

1. Author's interview with Ellis Ansel Perlswig, October 29, 2009; author's interview with Robert A. M. Stern, October 24, 2011.

2. On Brewster's presidency of Yale, see Geoffrey Kabaservice, *The Guardians: Kingman Brewster, His Circle, and the Rise of the Liberal Establishment* (New York: Henry Holt, 2004), 375–418.

3. The inscribed copy of this book is at the Paul Rudolph Foundation, New York.

4. For Chermayeff's impact on Yale, see Robert A. M. Stern, "Yale 1950–1965," *Oppositions* 4 (1974): 53–54; for students who built houses in Vermont, see 54–55. Also a student and admirer of Rudolph's, Alexander Tzonis worked with Chermayeff as well and provides an interesting perspective on both men in Tzonis, "Recollections of Paul Rudolph," in Tony Monk, *The Art and Architecture of Paul Rudolph* (Chichester, West Sussex: Wiley-Academy, 1999), 22–24.

5. Richard W. Hayes, with foreword by Robert A. M. Stern, *The Yale Building Project: The First Forty Years* (New Haven: Yale School of Architecture, 2007); author's interview with James Volney Righter, who was a student at Yale from 1966 to 1970 and taught at the school in 1969, June 24, 2011.

6. Andrew P. Garvin, "Moore Starts Hammering," *Yale Daily News* (September 23, 1965): 1, 16.

7. Righter interview.

8. C. Ray Smith, *Supermannerism: New Attitudes in Post-Modern Architecture* (New York: E. P. Dutton, 1977). Smith (108–11) describes changes to the A & A Building under Moore and "Project Argus," an experimental structure built in the middle of the exhibition room in 1968.

9. C. Ray Smith interview with Rudolph. YMA, "Smith (C. Ray) Manuscript and Research Files on the Yale Art and Architecture Building by Paul Rudolph," MS 1948 Box 1, Folder 10-3/15/78-interview between Rudolph and Smith, titled "draft 2/27/78," 4–5.

10. Timothy Bates, "Artists Rap A & A Building," *Yale Daily News* (May 4, 1967), 1; "Art and Architecture Petition" and studio art faculty member Deane Keller's letter to the editor, "The Worst Place," *Yale Daily News* (May 9, 1967), 2.

11. David Jacobs, "The Rudolph Style: Unpredictable," *New York Times Magazine* (March 26, 1967), 46–47, 49, 52, 57.

12. Ellen Perry Berkeley, "Yale: A Building As a Teacher," *Architectural Forum* 127 (July–August 1967): 47–53.

13. Author's interview with Ellen Perry Berkeley, March 20, 2012.

14. Favelas were discussed in architectural circles during the mid- and late 1960s. The British architect John F. C. Turner's thinking about how favelas could be an alternative model for modernism was popular in some American architecture schools; see John F. C. Turner, "The Squatter Settlement: An Architecture that Works," *Architectural Design* 38 (1968): 355–60.

15. Berkeley, "Building as a Teacher," 47, 52.

16. Berkeley, "Building as a Teacher," 53.

17. Author's interviews with Peter Blake, October 15, 1997, and correspondence May 16, 1998. Blake generously shared several painful letters between Rudolph and himself from 1967 regarding Berkeley's article in *Architectural Forum*; correspondence between Blake and Rudolph, September 1967, Peter Blake Papers, Avery Archive, Columbia University.

18. Sibyl Moholy-Nagy, "A & A Dialogue," *Architectural Forum* 127 (September 1967): 12.

19. William H. Chafe, *The Unfinished Journey: America since World War II* (New York: Oxford University Press, 2007), 364.

20. Kabaservice, *Guardians*, 375–418.

21. See Joseph Lelyveld, "After Fire, Yale Smolders," *New York Times* (June 27, 1969), 39.

22. "Yale Building Burns," *New Haven Register* (June 15, 1969), 1. A good summary of the events appears in "Forum," *Architectural Forum* 131 (July–August 1969): 41–42.

23. "No Arson Is Found at Yale in Inquiry on Art School Fire," *New York Times* (July 29, 1969), 39. C. Ray Smith interviewed New Haven fire marshal Thomas Lyden, who was adamant that it was cans of combustible rubber cement that caused the fire. YMA, "Smith (C. Ray) Manuscript and Research Files on the Yale Art and Architecture Building by Paul Rudolph," MS 1948, Box 1, Folder 10, Fire Marshall Leyden interview transcript, October 11, 1979, 21–22.

24. De Cossy carried out the A & A renovations while working for Douglas Orr Associates. Author's interview with William de Cossy, March 31, 2007.

25. Christopher Smart and Gabriella Stern, "University Balances Budget for the First Time in a Decade," *Yale Daily News* (May 8, 1980), 1. This article refers to the policy of deferred maintenance followed for most of the 1970s as a budgetary measure at Yale.

26. Nine months after the fire, *Time* wrote that the reason for the delay in the A & A's renovation was that "students and teachers feel that the building did not work." "Art: Too Much Form, Too Little Function?" *Time* 95 (March 16, 1970): 58.

27. *New York Times* critics chronicled the A & A's prolonged decline and the various ups and downs in how students regarded it during the 1970s. See Ada Louise Huxtable, "The Building You Love to Hate," *New York Times* (December 12, 1971), D29; Paul Goldberger, "Yale Art Building: A Decade of Crises," *New York Times* (April 30, 1974), 1, 48. Paul Goldberger, "Yale Students Lend a Hand to an Abused Building," *New York Times* (November 20, 1988), 39.

28. Rudolph says he disliked talking about the A & A Building and these events, in an interview given in 1988, when the A & A was twenty-five years old. Michael J. Crosbie, "Paul Rudolph on Yale's A & A: His First

Interview on His Most Famous Work," *Architecture* 77 (November 1988): 101.

29. For Rudolph's acquaintance and working relationship with Venturi at Yale, see chapter 6, note 9.

30. Robert Venturi, Denise Scott Brown, and Steven Izenour, *Learning from Las Vegas* (Cambridge: MIT Press, first published 1972; 1977 edition), 163.

31. Paul Rudolph, "Sibyl Moholy-Nagy," *Architectural Forum* 134 (June 1971): 29.

32. Author's interview with Venturi and Scott Brown, May 23, 2009. Venturi described writing a letter of apology to Rudolph years after the publication of *Learning from Las Vegas*. I have not seen Venturi's letter to Rudolph, though it may yet surface in either the Rudolph or the Venturi archive. Venturi also mentions the letter in an interview with Vladimir Paperny, originally published in *Russian Architectural Digest* (undated), that can be found online at www.paperny.com

33. See Godfrey Hodgson's discussion of the Establishment in Hodgson, *America in Our Time* (Garden City, N.Y.: Doubleday, 1976), 111–33. More recently, James T. Patterson provides context for it in the postwar period in his *Grand Expectations: The United States, 1945–1974* (New York: Oxford University Press, 1996), 84, 98–104.

34. Ada Louise Huxtable, "Creations of 3 Top Architects Shown," *New York Times* (September 30, 1970), 38.

35. Rudolph interviewed by John W. Cook and Heinrich Klotz, "Paul Rudolph," in *Conversations with Architects* (New York: Praeger Publishers, 1973), 92.

36. Paul D. Kramer, "Summary of an Interview with Paul Rudolph, New York," *Werk* (April 1973), 457.

37. Paul Rudolph, *The Architecture of Paul Rudolph*, with an introduction by Sibyl Moholy-Nagy, captions by Gerhard Schwab, and comments by Paul Rudolph (New York: Praeger, 1970). Paul Rudolph, *Paul Rudolph: Architectural Drawings*, edited by Yukio Futagawa (New York: Architectural Book Publishing Company, 1972). A third book about Rudolph's work was part of the Library of Contemporary Architecture series: Rupert Spade, *Paul Rudolph* (New York: Simon and Schuster, 1971).

38. G. C. Thelen, Jr., "Nixon Seen Switching Plans for Cities," *Boston Evening Globe* (February 6, 1970), 1.

39. Franz Schulze, *Philip Johnson: Life and Work* (New York: Knopf, 1994), 306–9.

Eight. Turning Inward

1. Author's correspondence with Alexander Tzonis, December 3, 2011.
2. Author's interview with Ellis Ansel Perlswig, October 29, 2009.
3. Paul Rudolph quoted in Paul Heyer, *Architects on Architecture: New Directions in America* (New York: Walker and Company, 1966) 303.
4. C. Ray Smith, "Rudolph's Dare-Devil Office Destroyed," *Progressive Architecture* 50 (April 1969): 98. Smith discusses Rudolph's office, supergraphics, and the new interiors of the period in C. Ray Smith, *Supermannerism: New Attitudes in Post-Modern Architecture* (New York: E. P. Dutton, 1977).
5. Smith, "Rudolph's Dare-Devil Office Destroyed," 98.
6. John Pearce, Yale class of 1965, who worked for Rudolph from 1965 to 1967, remembered falling between the desks. Author's interview with Pearce, June 28, 2011.
7. Smith, "Rudolph's Dare-Devil Office Destroyed," 98.
8. Perlswig interview.
9. Pearce interview.
10. Emilio Ambasz discusses the significance of the Duchampian ready-made in the interiors of the late 1960s and 1970s in Joan Kron and Suzanne Slesin, with foreword by Emilio Ambasz, *High-Tech: The Industrial Style and Source Book for the Home* (New York: Clarkson N. Potter, 1978), ix–xi.
11. Rudolph quoted in "Designers: Floating Platforms," *Progressive Architecture* 49 (October 1967): 198.
12. Alice Friedman explains the Glass House and Brick House in terms of homosexual closeting, with the Brick House as a place for eroticism, in Alice Friedman, *Women and the Making of the Modern House: A Social and Architectural History* (New York: Abrams, 1998), 147–54.
13. Perlswig interview; Paul Rudolph, "A Sunday Afternoon," *Philip Johnson Festschrift*, ANY 90 (July 1996): 44–45. Rudolph describes being present at the Glass House the day Frank Lloyd Wright visited it in 1956, on his way to the opening of the New York Coliseum.
14. Perlswig interview. Joel Goldsmith was a twenty-five-year-old architecture student who dated Rudolph for about six months in 1975. He recognized the homoerotic quality of Rudolph's Roman torso and other sculpture he collected. Author's interview with Goldsmith, October 20, 2009.
15. Rudolph's mirrored bedroom could be interpreted in light of Jacques Lacan's mirror stage and also Eve Kosofsky Sedgwick's concept of closeting. Jacques Lacan, "Mirror Stage As Formative of the I, As Revealed in Psychoanalytic Experiences," in *Ecrits: A Selection*, translated by Bruce Fink in collaboration with Heloise Finkand Russell Grigg (New York: W. W. Norton, 2002), 3–9; Eve Kosofsky Sedgwick, *Epistemology of the Closet* (Berkeley: University of California Press, 1990).
16. Barbara Plumb, "Paul's Pacesetter," *New York Times Magazine* (July 23, 1967), 188.
17. Author's interview with Robert A. M. Stern, October 24, 2011. Stern remembers that Samuel Ratensky, an administrator for the New York City office of Housing and Urban Development who was involved with Rudolph's Tracey Towers project for the city, was incredulous when the photo of the mural appeared in the *New York Times Magazine*.
18. Perlswig interview. I have been unable to find any newspaper accounts about the male model suing Rudolph.
19. Ellen Perry Berkeley, "Yale: A Building As a Teacher," *Architectural Forum* 127 (July–August 1967), 47–53.
20. Author's interview with Lewis Turner, May 20, 2004.
21. Paul Rudolph, *The Architecture of Paul Rudolph*, with an introduction by Sibyl Moholy-Nagy, captions by Gerhard Schwab, and comments by Paul Rudolph (New York: Praeger, 1970), 90.
22. Turner interview. Stoller's photo of the living room was published in "Total Townhouse," *House and Garden* 136 (November 1969): 122–27.
23. Eveline Schlumberger, "L'Inepuisable collection Campana," *Connaissance des Arts*, 143 (February 1964): 46. The article is about

a large collection of objects from diverse periods that formed the basis of several European museum collections; Domenico's cassone is one of the illustrated examples. For Rudolph's copy of the article, see PMR 13 CN 2011:214. Rudolph often looked at journals late at night in the Yale A & A library, as one of his students remembered: see Shin'ichi Okada, "Learning from Paul Rudolph," in Tony Monk, *The Art and Architecture of Paul Rudolph* (Chichester, West Sussex: Wiley-Academy, 1999), 21.

24. Turner interview.

25. For apartments by Rudolph, Gwathmey, Stern, and other architects from this experimental period for interiors, see Robert A. M. Stern, Thomas Mellins, and David Fishman, *New York, 1960: Architecture and Urbanism between the Second World War and the Bicentennial* (New York: Monacelli Press, 1995), 535–57.

26. "Color, Curves, Carpet in a Great Apartment," *House and Garden* 143 (March 1973): 85.

27. The silvery look had become fashionable a few years before the Edersheim apartment was built, as noted in Rita Reif, "Designers Take a Shine to Silvery Look," *New York Times* (February 10, 1967), 41.

28. Rudolph's light fixtures were part of a late 1960s wave of experimentation in lighting. Examples of his fixtures can be seen in Jean W. Progner, "The Kinetic Electric Environment," *Progressive Architecture,* 49 (October 1968), 198–206.

29. See Ambasz, *High-Tech,* 128–29; author's interview with Joan Kron, June 7, 2010.

30. Author's interview with Rudolph's friend Carl Black, July 23, 2010.

31. Sid Bass knew that Rudolph had been fired from a Manhattan project because of a dispute over the hanging of a painting. Author's interview with Sid Bass, November 21, 2011.

32. Anne Bass quoted in Mildred F. Schmertz, "Texas Tour de Force," *House and Garden* 163 (December 1991): 164–73, quote on 165; author's interview with Anne Bass, March 7, 2010.

33. Sid Bass interview.

34. Paul Rudolph, "Notes Concerning the Bass House, Fort Worth, Texas, from an Architectural Point of View," dated June 3, 1991, PMR 3056–1 "Bass House." Rudolph prepared these extensive notes to assist Mildred F. Schmertz when she was writing her account of the house, "Texas Tour de Force."

35. Also known as the "New York Five," the "Whites" were a group whose work was exhibited and discussed at the 1969 Conference for the Study of the Environment (CASE) as explained in Arthur Drexler, *Five Architects: Eisenman, Graves, Gwathmey, Hejduk, Meier* (New York: Wittenborn, 1972).

36. Paul Rudolph, "Frank Lloyd Wright Kaufmann House, 'Fallingwater,' Bear Run, Pennsylania, 1936," *Global Architecture* 2 (1970), unpaginated.

37. Rudolph, "Notes Concerning the Bass House," 5.

38. Anne Bass interview; Sid Bass interview. Plans of the Bass House have not been included out of respect for the owners' privacy.

39. Author's interview with Robert Rotner, December 11, 2010.

40. Stern interview.

41. Author's interview with Peter Eisenman, November 16, 2011.

42. Introduction by Peter Eisenman to Paul Rudolph "Alumni Day Speech: Yale School of Architecture, February 1958," *Oppositions* 4 (1974): 141. Originally Paul Rudolph, "Architecture: The Unending Search," *Yale Alumni Magazine*, 21 (May 1958). It is reprinted in Paul Rudolph, *Writings on Architecture*, edited by Nina Rappaport, foreword by Robert A. M. Stern (New Haven: Yale School of Architecture, 2008), 39.

43. Eisenman interview.

44. Robert A. M. Stern, *New Directions in Modern Architecture* (New York: Braziller, 1969; revised edition 1977), 36.

45. Robert A. M. Stern, "Yale, 1950–1965," *Oppositions* 4 (October 1974): 46.

46. Stern interview.

47. Franz Schulze, *Philip Johnson: Life and Work* (New York: Knopf, 1994), 305–17.

48. Carl Black, Jr., "Vision of Human Space; Boston State Service Center," *Architectural Record* 154 (July 1973): 105–16. Carl Black, Jr., "Interdenominational Chapel, Tuskegee Institute, Tuskegee, Alabama, 1960–1969; Boston Government Service Center, Boston, Massachusetts, 1962–1971," *Global Architecture* 20 (1973): 2–43.

49. C. Ray Smith began a book during the mid-1970s about the Yale A & A but never published it. He left behind a manuscript and notes deposited at Yale's library: YMA, "Smith (C. Ray) Manuscript and Research Files on the Yale Art and Architecture Building by Paul Rudolph, MS 1948." During the 1970s, Rudolph also asked Stanford Anderson, professor of history and architecture at MIT, to write a book about his work (author's conversation with Anderson, September 19, 2008). Files in the Rudolph Archive at the Library of Congress show that Rudolph collected numerous articles and kept notes for a book.

50. Rudolph, "Enigmas of Architecture," *A + U*, 80 (July 1977): 317.

51. "A Spectacular Apartment by Paul Rudolph," *House and Garden* 148 (October 1976): 120.

52. Rudolph, "Paul Rudolph Apartment," *GA Houses* 5 (1978): 106.

53. Rotner interview.

54. For a helpful summary of the facts about 23 Beekman Place, see a report for the New York City Landmarks Preservation Commission that resulted in the building being designated a city landmark in 2010. Matthew Postal, "Paul Rudolph Penthouse & Apartments," (November 16, 2010), http://www.nyc.gov/html/lpc/downloads/pdf/reports/2390.pdf

55. Ernst Wagner, "Speech by Ernst Wagner at the Paul Rudolph House to Visiting Groups," Fall 1999, Paul Rudolph Foundation, New York; author's interview with Wagner, January 3, 2010.

56. Joseph Giovannini, "If There's a Heaven, It Should Expect Changes," *New York Times* (August 14, 1997), C1, C10.

57. Michael Sorkin, "The Light House: Paul Rudolph's Triplex Aerie Suspended over the Manhattan Skyline," *House & Garden* 160 (January 1988): 168.

58. Rotner interview.

59. Sorkin, "Light House," 168.

60. Sorkin, "Light House," 89.

61. Michael Sorkin, "The Invisible Man," *Village Voice* (March 1986), reprinted in Sorkin, *Exquisite Corpse* (London: Verso, 1991), 155–59; author's interview with Sorkin, March 9, 2012.

62. Michael Sorkin, "Achievements Awards Presentations on Barnes, Johnson, Pei and Rudolph, Plus Their Discussion," *GSD News, Harvard University Graduate School of Design* (Summer 1993), 44–47.

63. Accompanying the exhibition was a catalogue, *Paul Rudolph: Drawings for the Art and Architecture Building at Yale, 1959–1963,* edited by Gilbert Schafer and Robert Young (New Haven: Yale School of Architecture, 1988). The exhibition, October 31–November 19, 1988, was organized by students at the Yale School of Architecture.

Nine. Asian Finale

1. Herbert Muschamp, "Paul Rudolph Is Dead at 78; Modernist Architect of the 60's," *New York Times* (August 9, 1997), 50.

2. Author's interview with Sid Bass, November 21, 2011.

3. Mildred F. Schmertz, "From Object to Space: An Interview with Paul Rudolph," *Architectural Record* 173 (June 1985): 156.

4. Rudolph's mother, Eurie Stone Rudolph, talks about how he liked the atrium interior of Portman's Regency Hyatt House hotel in Atlanta (1967), in Andrew Sparks, "His Architecture May Change Tomorrow's Cities," *Atlanta Journal and Constitution Magazine* (March 31, 1968), 31. Rudolph points to Minneapolis's Skyways as a model for urbanism in notes for a lecture, "After Mies, the Megastructure," May 25, 1977, PMR 3035-1.

5. See PMR 3039-2, promotional material for Bass Brothers Enterprises.

6. Sid Bass interview.

7. See PMR 3039-2, promotional material for Bass Brothers Enterprises.

8. "Clustered Columns Play Hide-and-Seek," *Architectural Record* 170 (July 1982): 124.

9. Author's interview with P. V. Banavalkar, August 13, 2012.

10. Schmertz, "From Object to Space," 160, 156. Rudolph collected Japanese robots, painted their parts different colors, and displayed them in groups in his Beekman Place penthouse.

11. Paul Rudolph, "The Six Determinants of Architectural Form," *Architectural Record* 120 (October 1956): 187.

12. Robert Bruegmann, "Interview with Paul Rudolph," February 28, 1986, Chicago Architects Oral History Project, The Art Institute of Chicago, 1–2. http://digital-libraries.saic.edu/cdm/ref/collection/caohp/id/9861

13. Schmertz, "From Object to Space," 156.

14. David Dillon, "Darth Vader at the O.K. Corral: A Set of Downtown Towers Creates an Identity Crisis for Fort Worth," *Architecture: The AIA Journal* 72 (November 1983): 66–67.

15. Mark Gunderson, "Rudolph and Texas," *Texas Architect* 48 (May–June 1998): 50–52.

16. Bruegmann, "Interview with Paul Rudolph," 1–2.

17. Author's interview with Ron Chin, who worked for Rudolph from the early 1980s through the mid-1990s, January 11, 2011.

18. Interview with Nora Leung, Hong Kong, April 8, 2009. She worked with Rudolph on the Bond Centre, Hong Kong; interview with Joseph Cheang and Ashvin Kumar of Architects 61, Singapore, who worked with Rudolph on the Concourse, Singapore, April 13, 2009.

19. Ernst Wagner, "Speech by Ernst Wagner at the Paul Rudolph House to Visiting Groups," Fall 1999, Paul Rudolph Foundation, New York.

20. Bruegmann, "Interview with Paul Rudolph," 26. Rudolph elaborates on his views about the history of the skyscraper and how mixed-use tall buildings could become village-like in his lecture "The Vertical Village," in "Proceedings of International Conference on Tall Buildings", Singapore, October 22–26, 1984, unpublished. PMR 3120-3.

21. Breugmann, "Interview with Paul Rudolph," 12–13.

22. Mildred F. Schmertz, "Colonnade Condominiums, Singapore," *Architectural Record* 177 (January 1989): 80.

23. Rudolph, "The Vertical Village," 22.

24. Rudolph dismisses regionalism as identity; Bruegmann interview with Rudolph, 55–56. Kenneth Frampton outlined how "critical regionalism" could resist globalizing forces in "Towards a Critical Regionalism: Six Points for an Architecture of Resistance," in Hal Foster, editor, *The Anti-Aesthetic: Essays on Post Modern Culture* (Port Townsend, Wash.: Bay Press, 1983), 16–30.

25. Rudolph was interested in the large scale of the columns of the ancient Egyptian temples at Luxor; they were a model for the Colonnade, as also for his Bond Centre, Hong Kong. Nora Leung, *Experiencing Bond Centre* (Hong Kong: Studio Publications, 1990), 66.

26. Author's interview with Joseph Cheang and Ashvin Kumar, of Architects 61. April 13, 2009. They said the Obus E project for Algiers (1939) was an inspiration for the Concourse.

27. *The Charlottesville Tapes: Transcript of the Conference at the University of Virginia School of Architecture, Charlottesville Virginia, November 12 and 13, 1982,* edited by Jacquelin Robertson and Stephen Corellia (New York: Rizzoli, 1985), 87, 88.

28. Rudolph exhibited his drawings in New York art galleries; see Joseph Giovannini, "Architecture: Drawings by Rudolph on View," *New York Times* (February 24, 1986), 16.

29. Paul Rudolph, "The Concourse-Singapore-notes regarding architectural design," undated, unpaginated. PMR 3013-3.

30. M. F. Hearn, "A Japanese Inspiration for Frank Lloyd Wright's Rigid-Core High-Rise Structures," *Journal of the Society of Architectural Historians* 50 (March 1991): 68–71.

31. Bruegmann, "Interview with Paul Rudolph," 31–32.

32. Rudolph, "The Concourse-Singapore."

33. The project was first called "Admiralty Lot 2," before Alan Bond became involved, and the complex was eventually renamed "Lippo Centre" after Bond's departure.

34. Author's interview with Nora Leung, April 8, 2009; Leung, *Experiencing Bond Centre*, 49.

35. Stephen Rogers uses the Bond Centre as an example of Hong Kong's changing economic and political fortunes in "Black Cloud Hangs Over Property Sector," *South China Morning Post* (January 18, 1988), 1. In Zoheir Hasanbhai, "Bond Centre Focus," *Asian Architect and Contractor* (October 1987), Rudolph talks about being "disconcerted" by the changes in ownership (40).

36. Paul Rudolph, "Notes on Bond Centre," April 1987, unpaginated. PMR 3088-1. This file contains several differently titled and dated sets of notes by Rudolph about Bond Centre.

37. Leung interview.

38. Paul Rudolph, "The Hong Kong and Shanghai Corporations Headquarters," undated manuscript, copy in the collection of Ronald Chin.

39. Leung, *Experiencing Bond Centre*, 31.

40. Leung interview.

41. Leung, *Experiencing Bond Centre*, 34.

42. Paul Rudolph, "Notes Regarding the Architectural Design of the Bond Centre, Hong Kong," January 18, 1988. PMR 3088-1.

43. Ibid.

44. Juanita Cheung and Andrew Yeoh, *Hong Kong: A Guide to Recent Architecture* (London: Ellipsis, 1998), 144.

45. The exhibition was entitled *Paul Rudolph, Architectural Projects, 1946–1984* and was held at the Taman Ismail Marzuki Arts Centre, Jakarta, Indonesia, organized and sponsored by Ikatan Arsitektar Indonesia and PT Wisma Dharmala Sakti, May 5–10, 1984. There was no catalogue, but see PMR 3098-1 for an advertisement.

46. Rudolph discusses visiting what was probably the Tamal Mini Indonesia Indah Park in Bruegmann, "Interview with Paul Rudolph," 52–53.

47. Inwan Sudradjat, *A Study of Indonesian Architectural History* (PhD diss., University of Sydney, 1991).

48. Shin Muramatsu and David Sagita, *Silaban's House* (Bogor, Indonesia: Modern Asian Architecture Network with School of Architecture, Tarumanagara University), 46.

49. Paul Rudolph, "Dharmala Sakti Office Building, Jakarta," *Mimar* 30 (1988): 18. Rudolph describes at length how vernacular elements informed his design, in Bruegmann, "Interview with Paul Rudolph," 52–56.

50. Author's interview with Johannes Gunawan, April 20, 2009. Others have noted the green qualities of Rudolph's projecting overhangs and terraces for the Wisma Dharmala building; see Zenin Adrian, "Green, the Underappeciated Design Approach," *Jakarta Post* (August 26, 2007), 10.

51. Gunawan interview.

52. Mildred F. Schmertz, "Resolutely Modernist: Three Projects in Southeast Asia," *Architectural Record* 177 (January 1989): 82.

53. Gunawan interview.

54. Four exhibitions in the 1980s and 1990s presented Rudolph's Asian projects. *Paul Rudolph: Four Recent Projects in Southeast Asia*, Chicago, May 6–28, 1987 (catalogue by Robert Bruegmann, published Chicago: Graham Foundation and the Art Institute of Chicago, 1987); *Dreams and Details*, New York, January 11–February 17, 1989 (catalogue by Robert Bruegmann and Mildred F. Schmertz, published New York: Steelcase Design Partnership, 1989); *Paul Rudolph: Explorations in Modern Architecture, 1976–1993*, New York, November 17, 1993– February 12, 1994 (catalogue by Donald Albrecht, published New York: National Institute for Architectural Education, 1993); *From Concept to Building: A Project in Singapore*, New York, November 22, 1993–May 1, 1994, Smithsonian, Cooper-Hewitt, National Design Museum.

55. Michael Sorkin, "Paul Rudolph: A Personal Appreciation," *Architectural Record* 185 (September 1997): 40; Muschamp, "Paul Rudolph Is Dead," 50.

Conclusion: Reevaluating Rudolph

1. See Paul Goldberger's discussion of the reassessment of the A & A Building in Goldberger, *Why Architecture Matters* (New Haven: Yale University Press, 2009), 177–82.

2. Robert Campbell, "The Beauty of Concrete: Young Architects Say There's Much to Love about City's 'Heroic' Building," *Boston Globe* (January 3, 2010), 1.

3. The young designer Michael Abramson runs a website called "Fuck Yeah Brutalism" and guest-edited an issue of the journal *CLOG* devoted to brutalism in 2013. See Fuckyeahbrutalism@tumblr.com

4. The conference "Concrete City: Brutalism and Preservation" at Rutgers University, New Brunswick, N.J., February 17, 2012, reviewed new scholarship, chiefly about British brutalism, with some references to Rudolph's work, and considered preservation efforts.

5. Organized with the Drawing Center, the exhibition *Paul Rudolph: Lower Manhattan Expressway* at the Cooper Union (October 1– November 14, 2010), exhibiting the reconstructed model, was curated by Ed Rawlings and Jim Walrod (catalogue by Steven Kilian, Ed Rawlings, and Jim Walrod, published New York: Drawing Center, 2010).

6. Chris Mottalini, *After You Left, They Took It Apart (Demolished Paul Rudolph Homes)* (Chicago: Columbia College Press, 2013).

7. David Hay, "Modern Antiquity: The Paul Rudolph Housing Crisis," *New York Magazine* (November 23, 2008), http://nymag.com/ arts/architecture/features/52410; Robin Pogebin, "Orange County Votes to Save Modernist Building," *New York Times* (February 11, 2013), http://artsbeat.blogs.nytimes.com/2013/02/11/ orange-county-votes-to-save-modernist-building/?ref=arts

8. Dawn Wotapka, "Beauty of an Ugly Duckling," *Wall Street Journal* (August 24, 2011), http://online.wsj.com.

Bibliography

Works by Rudolph in Chronological Order

The Architecture of Paul Rudolph, with an introduction by Sibyl Moholy-Nagy, captions by Gerhard Schwab, comments by Paul Rudolph (New York: Praeger, 1970).

Paul Rudolph: Architectural Drawings, edited by Yukio Futagawa (New York: Architectural Book Publishing Company, 1972).

Rudolph and Ulrich Franzen, *The Evolving City*, with text by Peter Wolf (New York: American Federation of the Arts, 1974).

Writings on Architecture, edited by Nina Rappaport, foreword by Robert A. M. Stern (New Haven: Yale School of Architecture, 2008).

Works about Rudolph in Chronological Order

John Howey, *The Sarasota School* (Cambridge: MIT Press, 1995).

Tony Monk, *The Art and Architecture of Paul Rudolph* (Chichester, West Sussex: Wiley-Academy, 1999).

Joseph King and Christopher Domin, *Paul Rudolph: The Florida Houses* (New York: Princeton Architectural Press, 2002).

Roberto De Alba, *Paul Rudolph: The Late Work* (New York: Princeton Architectural Press, 2003).

Special Issues of Journals Devoted to Rudolph

"Paul Rudolph," *Kokusai-Kentiku* 32 (April 1965).

"Chronological List of Works by Paul Rudolph," *Architecture and Urbanism (A + U)* 49 (January 1975).

"100 by Paul Rudolph," *Architecture and Urbanism (A + U)* 80 (July 1977).

Bibliographies

Smith, Charles R., *Paul Rudolph and Louis Kahn: A Bibliography* (Metuchen, N.J.: Scarecrow Press, 1987).

Bruce Barnes, *Paul Rudolph and His Architecture,* website and regularly updated bibliography, University of Massachusetts, Dartmouth. http://prudolph.lib.umassd.edu/biblio

Films

"Spaces, The Architecture of Paul Rudolph," Eisenhardt Productions, directed and produced by Robert Eisenhardt, narrated by Cliff Robertson, 1982.

"Rudolph and Renewal," Yale School of Architecture, 2008. Directed and produced by Stephen Taylor and Elihu Rubin. Created for the exhibition *Model City: Buildings and Projects by Paul Rudolph for Yale and New Haven*, November 3, 2008–February 6, 2009.

Index